After Hype

From artificial intelligence (AI) to quantum computing, every new technology is surrounded by 'hype' – but what exactly is hype, and how does it work? This is the first book to take hype seriously, showing how it is made, managed, and mobilised across today's innovation landscapes. Far from being just empty talk, hype has become a structured practice and even a business in its own right. The authors uncover the machinery that drives markets, guides innovation, and shapes whole promissory economies. They also initiate 'Hype Studies' – a new way of understanding how innovation unfolds in the digital age and beyond. *After Hype* not only establishes hype as a serious object of study but also reveals it to be one of the most powerful yet overlooked forces shaping and influencing our technological future(s). This title is also available as Open Access on Cambridge Core.

NEIL POLLOCK is Professor of Innovation and Social Informatics at the University of Edinburgh and a Fellow of the Academy of Social Sciences. He is an award-winning researcher of digital innovation and has authored several influential books on technology and markets, including *How Industry Analysts Shape the Digital Future* (Oxford University Press, 2016).

ROBIN WILLIAMS is Professor of Social Research on Technology at the University of Edinburgh. A pioneer in the social shaping of technology, he has led interdisciplinary research in Science and Technology Studies for over forty years; founded the Institute for the Study of Science, Technology and Innovation; and chairs the UK Association for Science, Technology and Innovation Studies.

After Hype

The Business of Taming the Digital Economy

NEIL POLLOCK
University of Edinburgh

ROBIN WILLIAMS
University of Edinburgh

Shaftesbury Road, Cambridge CB2 8EA, United Kingdom

One Liberty Plaza, 20th Floor, New York, NY 10006, USA

477 Williamstown Road, Port Melbourne, VIC 3207, Australia

314–321, 3rd Floor, Plot 3, Splendor Forum, Jasola District Centre,
New Delhi – 110025, India

Cambridge University Press is part of Cambridge University Press & Assessment,
a department of the University of Cambridge.

We share the University's mission to contribute to society through the pursuit of
education, learning and research at the highest international levels of excellence.

www.cambridge.org
Information on this title: www.cambridge.org/9781009644068

DOI: 10.1017/9781009644013

First published 2026

A catalogue record for this publication is available from the British Library

A Cataloging-in-Publication data record for this book is available from the Library of
Congress

ISBN 978-1-009-64406-8 Hardback
ISBN 978-1-009-64404-4 Paperback

For Luca – thank you for inspiring and sustaining my fascination with the 'animal spirits' of the digital economy.
Neil Pollock

For Ben and Leon – for their love and support and sceptical wisdom.
Robin Williams

Contents

Figures

Tables

Boxes

Acknowledgements

We didn't set out to write a book about hype. What began as a modest attempt to write a short paper on the Hype Cycle Chart grew into something more ambitious. We imagined a relatively quick piece on the chart – perhaps a year of work at most. But the deeper we delved, the more we realised how little we understood about the phenomenon of hype itself. Nor did we find much academic guidance to help us. The further we explored, the more expansive – and elusive – the topic became.

Several years later, this book is the result of that initial enquiry. In many ways, it is the book we wished had existed when we first set out to understand the Hype Cycle Chart. It is also a book about how a deceptively simple chart opened up a much larger set of questions – about markets, futures, evaluation, and the machinery that organises what John Maynard Keynes famously called the 'animal spirits' of the economy. Hype, we came to see, was not simply a by-product of innovation but a structuring force – one that shapes how technology futures are imagined, contested, and acted upon.

To our knowledge, this is the first book devoted entirely to the phenomenon of hype. While scholars have examined adjacent concepts – such as bubbles, speculation, expectations, and promissory discourse – hype itself has rarely been the direct focus of sustained analysis. And yet it plays a critical role in the innovation economy: directing attention, mobilising capital, and coordinating belief. Writing a book about something so pervasive yet under-theorised has been far from easy. But we have been fortunate to draw on the support, encouragement, and generosity of a wide community of institutions, colleagues, and friends.

We are especially indebted to the Economic and Social Research Council (ESRC), whose funding, through the Ranking the Rankers (ES/M007626/1) and The Second Most Important Pitch (ES/R010447/1) projects, made the empirical work in this book possible.

Neil Pollock carried out the majority of the fieldwork, with assistance and accompaniment at various stages from several valued collaborators. Duncan Chapple undertook some of the fieldwork reported in Chapter 4, Suwen Chen conducted several of the interviews described in Chapter 5, and Najmeh Hafezieh participated in many of the interviews that inform Chapter 6.

Throughout the long course of researching and writing, we were sustained by the insights, criticisms, and encouragement of many colleagues and friends. Our sincere thanks go to Michael Barrett, Suwen Chen, Yusun Cheng, Alex Christian, Jean Clarke, Franck Cochoy, Elizabeth Davidson, Luciana D'Adderio, Vassilis Galanos, Marian Gatzweiler, Susie Geiger, Vern Glaser, Nina Granqvist, Matthew Grimes, Najmeh Hafezieh, Richard Harrison, Sampsa Hyysalo, Pierre Joly, Christian Koch, Kornelia Konrad, Martin Kornberger, Donald MacKenzie, Paul Martin, Katy Mason, Liz McFall, Gemma Milne, Eric Monteiro, Teea Palo, Michael Power, Paolo Quattrone, Susan Scott, Richard Tutton, and Harro van Lente, whose feedback, encouragement, and good humour helped bring this project to completion.

We would especially like to thank Harro van Lente, Kornelia Konrad, Vassilis Galanos, Alex Christian, and Aaron Pagel, who provided helpful comments on an early draft of the book.

We are also grateful to Najmeh Hafezieh and Marian Gatzweiler (co-authors of Chapter 6) for permission to use our joint work here.

We owe a debt of gratitude to the many industry analysts and analyst relations professionals who generously shared their time, insights, and engaged in discussions throughout our research projects. We are grateful to Duncan Chapple, who not only introduced us to many of the experts whose voices appear in these pages but also sharpened our thinking through his thoughtful suggestions and reflections. We also owe a special debt of gratitude to Chris Holscher, Robin Schaffer, and Ludovic Leforestier, who facilitated our research in numerous different ways. Our thanks also go to Jackie Fenn, who graciously shared her recollections of the creation of the Hype Cycle Chart on two occasions – an origin story that helped shape the framing of this book.

We are grateful to Grace Ochieng for her editorial support during the final stages of the book, and to Cambridge University Press' Carrie

Parkinson and Valerie Appleby for their enthusiastic response to our initial hype-book proposal.

Finally, some parts of this book draw on fieldwork that has been previously published elsewhere. Chapter 4 is based on Chapple et al. (2022); Chapter 5 on Pollock et al. (2023); Chapter 7 on Pollock et al. (2022); and Chapter 8 on Pollock et al. (2021). We are grateful to the copyright holders for their permission to reuse this material here.

1 | Introduction

We Live in a World of Hype

In 2014, serial entrepreneur Steve Polsky launched Juvo, a fintech with a bold vision: to transform the lives of the world's 'underbanked' by providing them with digital financial identities. By leveraging mobile phone top-up data and machine learning, Juvo positioned itself as a company that could combine technological innovation with social impact. 'We can help hundreds of millions of people move up a path to a whole set of financial services', Polsky declared, 'starting with everyday interactions around your prepaid mobile phone'. Juvo's vision wasn't just social – it was economic: by giving people digital financial identities, the company projected it could unlock $250 billion in global GDP.[1]

In today's digital economy, few forces are as ubiquitous or as contested as *hype*. While it permeates all industries to some extent, it is most often associated with the digital economy. This space is steeped in what has been called 'hyper-hype' (Jordan, 2020). We argue that hype has become increasingly central to how technological innovation is organised, coordinated, and acted upon – particularly in the digital economy.

Yet, despite – or perhaps because of – its pervasiveness, our relationship with hype remains deeply ambivalent: we simultaneously rely on and criticise it, treat it as essential yet view it with suspicion. This contradiction raises a fundamental question: What exactly is hype, and how does it work?

At first glance, these questions appear straightforward. Hype is typically defined as a surge in attention, excitement, and expectations – often surrounding emerging technologies – mobilised through promissory narratives (van Lente, 2012). But in practice, the meaning and role of hype span a broad spectrum of interpretations. Some see hype as a

---

[1] This account draws on publicly available interviews, articles, and podcast discussions with Steve Polsky (Feldman, 2016; Oxford Economics, 2019; Mavadiya, 2020; Polsky, 2020a, 2020b).

kind of background 'noise' or distraction to be 'weeded out' (Jordan, 2020). Others regard it as a harmless or benign means to garner attention (Roberson, 2020). Still others view hype as a necessary (van Lente, 2012) or desirable (Potts, 2017) aspect of innovation. It has even been depicted as a driving force for the economy (Beckert, 2016, 2021).

Consider the example of Juvo, a start-up that claims to 'disrupt' traditional banking models. While the venture itself may be unfamiliar to readers, its story is not. This is a classic hype narrative: bold, future-oriented, and richly promissory. However, as the book will demonstrate, in the contemporary digital economy, hype depends not only on bold storytelling but also on how such narratives are structured, circulated, and sustained.

Juvo's story also illustrates a key challenge. The venture entered a crowded market filled with start-ups touting similarly disruptive claims. To gain traction, it needed more than a compelling narrative – it required recognition from the market's evaluative gatekeepers, particularly the industry analysts who shape perceptions by ranking, comparing, and categorising emerging ventures. The 'analyst briefing' is central to this process.

Juvo began briefing analysts but faced a familiar challenge: its narrative didn't fit neatly into existing market categories. Was it credit scoring? Fintech infrastructure? Mobile analytics? Its offering risked being overlooked precisely because it was too novel, too difficult to classify.

The breakthrough came when Juvo hired analyst relations experts – specialists in shaping how ventures present themselves to industry analysts. Working together, they reframed Juvo's story under a new category label: Financial Identity as a Service (FiDaaS). This was not just merely cosmetic rebranding – it was a strategic act of market making.

The turnaround was telling. By offering analysts a coherent and compelling narrative, the reframing enabled them to endorse FiDaaS as a credible emerging category. The subsequent industry analyst support led to amplified media attention – for instance, a Forbes article on FiDaaS quickly followed and helped convert promissory narratives into concrete market momentum. As visibility grew, major financial players – including Mastercard – began contributing to the construction of the FiDaaS market itself.

Juvo's story illuminates a crucial shift in the role of hype. No longer just background noise or exaggeration, hype is now deliberately cultivated, selectively mobilised, and embedded within innovation practices and market infrastructures. When strategically managed and aligned with evaluative infrastructures, hype does more than capture attention – it can actively create new markets. This reconfiguration has given rise to a new business – the business of hype – where specialist firms and consultants trade in promissory narratives. We call this transformation a move from 'wild hype' to 'tamed hype': from unruly, unaccountable claims to orchestrated and professionalised forms of promissory practice in the digital economy.

However, this does not mean that hype has been fully domesticated or unproblematically folded into the digital economy. On the contrary, it remains a deeply controversial issue. While it may be a pervasive aspect of start-up culture, critics argue that its influence is often distorting rather than productive. It has been suggested that hype contributes little to genuine informational value (Jordan, 2020) and that it misallocates scarce resources and attention, diverting them from more grounded, potentially transformative solutions to social and economic challenges (Funk, 2019). Others go further still, warning that hype can be 'dangerous', leading to 'poor decisions, misplaced hope, and distorted priorities' (Nightingale & Martin, 2004, p. 568).

Some envision a world *without* hype as one marked by more informed, cautious, and deliberate choices (e.g. Intemann, 2022). Try the simple experiment of imagining such a scenario – a landscape where emerging technologies arrive without fanfare, expectations are muted, and visions of the future no longer mobilise investment, shape agendas, or inspire collective effort. Would understanding and assessing emerging technologies or industries be more or less straightforward? Does hype confound decision-making, or does it provide relevant knowledge?

Now, consider what would be missing in such a world. Without promissory narratives to orient attention and coordinate action, would technologies gain traction at all? Some suggest that reducing hype could lead to challenges in generating interest and attention for innovation (Roberson, 2020). Others have reinterpreted hype as a generative mechanism within innovation systems – a 'productive good for innovation' (Potts, 2017, p. 1).

Indeed, it has been posited that many foundational innovations would *not* have been created without hype. The dotcom boom, while often remembered for its excesses, has been cited by some as having catalysed investment in digital infrastructures and emerging platforms that laid the groundwork for future technological progress (Quinn & Turner, 2023). On this reading, hype – however overblown – may have enabled developments that a more cautious climate would have stifled.

However, viewing hype through these polarised lenses – as either a dangerous distraction or an essential engine of innovation – risks over-simplifying a much more complex reality. This book argues that these seemingly opposing viewpoints are not mutually exclusive but represent different facets of a multidimensional and evolving phenomenon.

This ambivalence is not incidental – it is constitutive of how hype works. Hype simultaneously enables and distorts, mobilises and mis-leads. We argue that this tension is not a flaw to be corrected *but a condition to be understood*. This dual character of hype – both pro-ductive and problematic – demands a symmetrical approach that neither celebrates nor condemns but traces how actors navigate and live with this tension, finding ways to act amid uncertainty.

Moreover, by framing hype in simplistic binary terms – as either an inflated promise or outright deception – scholars have missed its evolving character. This book argues that far from being a static or uniform force, hype has undergone a significant transformation in the digital economy, particularly since the dotcom era, through the emergence of a growing constellation of actors who actively manage, evaluate, and strategically channel expectations. We will call these figures 'hype's new actors'. Their emergence signals a shift in how hype itself is produced, orchestrated, and embedded within the digital economy. To understand their emergence, we briefly turn to the rise and collapse of the late-1990s Internet market.

1.1 Internet Boom and Bust

The Internet boom – and subsequent crash – marked a watershed moment in our understanding of hype (Woolgar, 2002). Periods like this have been interpreted as the installation phase of a new techno-economic paradigm, characterised by surges of investment, bold claims, and the disruption of existing rules as economies reorganise around emerging technologies (Freeman & Perez, 1988). It was a time of intense excitement, with entrepreneurs entering the market armed with a 'distinctive vision of the future' and striving to be the 'first movers' who would 'revolutionise how people experienced all types of media' (Garud et al., 2021, p. 12). Yet these ambitious visions posed considerable challenges for investors and adopters alike. How could stakeholders evaluate such imagined ventures – the so-called dotcoms – in entirely uncharted territory? The Internet's novelty meant there were few established evaluative frameworks for assessing busi-ness viability, and the breakneck pace of innovation was said to render traditional metrics obsolete. As a result, stakeholders struggled to distinguish between 'fundamentals' and the surrounding hype (Garud et al., 2021).

This confusion had serious consequences. Exaggerated claims led to heavy investments in dotcoms with questionable business models. In the aftermath, the mass of unverified and overblown claims was dismissed as 'noise' and 'dangerous' – offering a cautionary tale about hype's destructive potential (Cellan-Jones, 2001).

But the story does not end there. Contrary to what one might expect, the bursting of the Internet bubble did not diminish the role of hype in technological innovation. Instead, it has re-emerged as a central concern in current discussions surrounding the digital economy (see Box 1.1; Minkkinen et al., 2023; Narayanan & Kapoor, 2025). However, the nature of this contemporary hype differs in important ways from its dotcom-era predecessor – a transformation that has largely escaped both academic and popular attention.

Box 1.1 Why focus on the digital economy?

We use the term 'digital economy' to refer to the constellation of markets, practices, and infrastructures structured around the development and deployment of digital technologies – especially software, data platforms, and artificial intelligence (AI) systems. While its boundaries are inherently blurry, our emphasis is on enterprise technologies and the innovation ecosystems that support them (Chiasson & Davidson, 2005). The hype dynamics discussed in this book can certainly be observed across a wide range of sectors. Yet digital innovation is of particular interest in the context of hype, partly because digital technologies – especially AI, platforms, and software systems – affect nearly all firms and industries, functioning as general-purpose technologies. It is also because digital tools increasingly act as 'organisational technologies' (Pollock & Williams, 2008): artefacts that not only support but actively reshape strategy, structure, and process. These features make digital innovation especially susceptible to the structured forms of hype management we analyse.[2]

---

[2] Hype has a lineage that long predates the dotcom boom and a reach that extends well beyond the digital economy. In this book, we focus on one especially revealing sector while at the same time opening the way for comparative research across other domains. We return to this theme in Chapter 10, where we situate our study within a broader landscape of hype.

Our research – spanning the dotcom boom of the 1990s (Cornford & Pollock, 2003), the rise of enterprise technologies (Pollock & Williams, 2008), the development of digital infrastructures (Monteiro *et al.*, 2014), the emergence of 'promissory organisations' (Pollock & Williams, 2010), and new forms of market expertise (Pollock & Williams, 2016), through to the recent fieldwork presented in this book – reveals not only the enduring presence of hype but also its evolution into new, more structured forms, with distinct characteristics and far-reaching implications. This evolution raises critical questions for our understanding of the digital economy: What direction is this transformation taking? How does contemporary hype differ from its historical forms? And what implications does this shift hold for innovation, investment, and technological development?

Despite hype's growing relevance, these questions remain largely unexplored. For all its visibility, hype continues to occupy an ambiguous place in scholarly work. While frequently invoked – and often disparaged – it is rarely the focus of sustained academic or empirical investigation. There is widespread acknowledgement of its existence, and numerous calls to 'move beyond the hype' (see, for instance, Dwivedi et al., 2022), but few studies take hype seriously as a phenomenon in its own right. Some have defined hype as a form of value judgement (Powers, 2012; Bourne, 2024), but far fewer have examined its creation and circulation as a professional practice that requires skill, coordination, and expertise. Moreover, when the characteristics of hype are discussed, this is often done without a significant empirical base.

This book argues for a more systematic exploration of how hype influences and moulds the digital economy. The ensuing pages examine hype and its shifting dynamics, aiming to contribute to an enhanced understanding of its trajectory in the digital economy. However, to do this, we must first move beyond the dominant view of hype as merely misleading or deceptive claims.

1.2 Beyond Hype as Misleading Claims

The concept of hype has deep historical roots, originating in classical rhetoric as 'persuasive speech' or 'hyperbole' (Claridge, 2010). By the early twentieth century, its meaning in American English had shifted to signify 'cheating' or 'deceiving' (OED). The term was also associated with minor criminal activities, such as 'talking rackets' and 'confidence tricks', which relied on the skilful use of speech to confuse or mislead victims (Wadhwani & Lubinski, 2025, p. 5). Over time, this negative connotation evolved into the modern sense of 'false publicity' or 'excessive publicity' (OED). In contemporary technoscience, hype is often defined as communication that inappropriately exaggerates potential outcomes (Intemann, 2022, p. 280). Some accounts add nuance, distinguishing between 'honest hype' – an unavoidable consequence of discussing technoscientific advancements – and 'politicised hype', which deliberately sensationalises claims to attract attention (Nerlich, 2013).

Contemporary discourse on hype is often framed in strongly critical terms. It is frequently characterised as a collection of 'false claims' (Bender & Hanna, 2025), 'fundamentally dishonest' (Vinsel & Russell, 2020), or 'near-lies' (Min, 2024), in which promoters are seen as over-ambitious or outright fraudulent in mobilising expectations (Funk, 2024; Narayan & Kapoor, 2025). For example, Vinsel and Russell (2020, p. 11) draw a sharp contrast between 'actual innovation', which they define as tangible and measurable, and what they call 'innovation-speak' – dismissed as a mere 'sales pitch about a future that doesn't yet exist'. Such claims are said to generate the 'fog of hype', clouding our ability to evaluate technological claims (Jordan, 2020). The consequences can be severe: 'exaggerated' or 'excessive' publicity can damage both the innovation process and the reputation of the technology and its developers (Ruef & Markard, 2010, p. 319). Others warn that failed promises can 'tarnish reputations and erode trust', leading to 'disastrous consequences' not just for individual innovators but 'entire innovation fields' (Brown, 2003, pp. 6–9).

In response, there are growing calls to confront the 'moral' dimensions of hype (Garud et al., 2023; Hampel & Dalpiaz, 2025). These calls are underscored by allegations of 'fraud' in the recent Theranos case (Cheney-Lippold, 2024), in which entrepreneur Elizabeth Holmes was deemed to have crossed the line between 'hype' and 'lies' (Cheney-Lippold, 2025, p. 4173). This has prompted demands for greater accountability, not just from entrepreneurs but also from the broader array of players – including journalists, consultants, and even social scientists (Funk, 2019; Zankl & Grimes, 2024).

However, this book proposes a shift in perspective. Rather than echoing the pejorative treatment of hype typical in popular discourse and certain academic writing, we challenge the notion that hype is merely a distortion that can be corrected through more accurate assessments (Intemann, 2022). Such views often stem from an overly rationalistic, technical worldview (e.g. Min, 2024). We also resist the moral positioning that equates hype with lies or fraud, as this perspective leads to calls for eliminating rather than understanding how hype has become a required ingredient for the functioning of the future-oriented economy.

If hype is so harmful, why does it persist – and even flourish? This paradox remains largely unexplored in the academic literature. While social scientists have often disparaged hype, few have examined how it has become a routine, expected, and even strategic part of innovation work. Enthusiasm for hype shows no sign of waning (Bourne, 2024). As we demonstrate in this book, its social role and institutional embedding are undergoing significant change. Although still frequently framed in negative terms, hype is no longer universally dismissed as misleading or excessive; in some circles, it is viewed in a very different light.

Consider again the case of Juvo. For entrepreneurs like Steve Polsky, crafting a promissory narrative is not merely expected – it could be problematic not to present the venture as disruptive. Resource providers often 'expect and even encourage entrepreneurs to engage in hype as a legitimation strategy' (Wadhwani & Lubinski, 2025, p. 3). Experienced entrepreneurs recognise and exploit this dynamic (Rady et al., 2025). As one of our informants put it, 'if you're not hyping, you don't know the game'.

In light of this, we argue for a conceptual reorientation. Rather than treating hype as rhetorical noise or moral failure, we suggest that it be analysed as a socially embedded and evolving practice. It is no longer sufficient to 'call out' hype or critique its excesses (e.g. Bender & Hanna, 2025). As Tihanyi et al. (2022, p. 718) observe, 'despite the prevalence of hype in society, it remains an understudied concept'.

We propose that it is time to take hype seriously, not as something to be debunked but as a social phenomenon that demands empirical and theoretical attention. In this book, we call for the foundation of *Hype Studies*: a research agenda that moves beyond identifying and critiquing hype to analysing how it is produced, sustained, and institutionalised – and how its modes of operation and meanings shift over time.

1.3 Is Entrepreneurial Capitalism Possible without Hype?

Contrary to perspectives that treat hype as a dangerous distortion to be avoided, other bodies of scholarship argue that it is not only inevitable but essential to a flourishing innovation economy. The Sociology of Expectations, for instance, contends that innovation does not merely survive hype – it depends on it (van Lente, 2012). From this vantage point, promoting new technologies without hype would be, if not impossible, then considerably more difficult.

Consider Juvo's experience in the crowded digital financial services market. Here, hype served not merely as promotional noise but as a vital mechanism for gaining visibility and credibility. Hype becomes 'necessary to get a hearing' (Borup et al., 2006, p. 290). Its function extends beyond attracting attention, acting as a resource to legitimise emerging technologies and justify their support (van Lente, 2012). Crucially, its power lies in its collective momentum: the more actors who engage with and reinforce a narrative – such as Juvo's reframing of its offering as FiDaaS – the more credible and durable that narrative becomes. When this collective traction is achieved, hype can generate a 'protected space' in which future-oriented promises are not only more easily made but also more readily accepted (van Lente & Rip, 1998, p. 41).

Organisation and Management Theory (OMT) and Cultural Entrepreneurship research have extended this insight into the realm of venture creation. In the digital economy, where start-ups like Juvo must compete for limited attention and capital, hype functions as a cultural resource. It can be a means through which 'innovators and entrepreneurs might encourage greater early stakeholder support and resources' (Logue & Grimes, 2022, p. 7). Entrepreneurs often position themselves within 'hot markets' to attract attention, legitimacy, and funding they might otherwise not secure (Pontikes & Barnett, 2017). In this sense, hype generates not only anticipation but also actor mobilisation, building momentum and triggering the flow of investors, collaborators, and other stakeholders into a space (Valliere & Peterson, 2004).

Beyond individual ventures, hype is increasingly recognised as a structural driver of economic dynamism. In *Imagined Futures*, economic sociologist Jens Beckert (2016, p. 12) argues that capitalism *depends* on the 'evocative overload of fictional expectations'. This conception highlights hype's twofold affective force: it produces both excitement and fear. It creates temporal pressure that drives market actors to act under conditions of uncertainty. This aligns with Zaloom's (2009) description of hype as an 'affective lightning rod', and her broader thesis that the contemporary economy operates through a productive tension between calculation and affect. Building on this, Geiger and Gross (2017, p. 449) show how hype generates states of 'feverish anticipation and expectations' that precipitate strategic decisions – often ahead of clear evidence (see also Bourne, 2024).

1.4 Hype's Operationalisation

After Hype addresses a critical gap in our understanding of contemporary capitalism. While scholars have established hype's integral role in capitalist dynamics (Beckert, 2016; Bourne, 2024), the crucial question of its *operationalisation* remains underexplored.

Traditional accounts often portray hype as a diffuse and intangible aspect of the 'contemporary Western start-up culture' (Wadhwani & Lubinski, 2025, p. 11), spontaneously emerging from innovation communities (Goldfarb & Kirsch, 2019) and as an 'unbounded resource' (Logue & Grimes, 2022) that everyone can access. Yet such treatments often obscure the specific mechanisms through which hype is generated, circulated, and institutionalised. We argue instead for a more focused analytic approach – one that treats hype not as part of the broader cultural milieu (Powers, 2012) but as the outcome of deliberate practices carried out by identifiable actors, using concrete tools and techniques.

By *operationalisation*, we refer to the tangible material practices and artefacts involved in hype's production, evaluation, distribution, and consumption. As these practices and artefacts become increasingly complex, hype is no longer the terrain of naive speculation but the domain of skilled practitioners equipped with specialised knowledge. Konrad and Alvial-Palavicino (2017) differentiate between those responsible for *creating innovations* and those *generating hype around innovations*, highlighting the varying degrees of involvement in the operationalisation of hype among different actors. Geiger and Gross (2017, p. 451) similarly call for greater attention to the 'roles and responsibilities of specific promissory actors' in the generation, evaluation, and circulation of hype.

After Hype contributes to this emerging agenda by analysing four key dimensions of hype's operationalisation:

Producing: The generation of hype is rarely spontaneous. It involves deliberate strategies tailored to different audiences and phases of venture development. In Juvo's case, hype was not simply generated through enthusiasm but carefully refined into a more calculated, evidence-based narrative. This involved aligning interests, redefining categories, and targeting key stakeholders. We argue that hype production is a dynamic and responsive practice. Building on Konrad and Alvial-Palavicino (2017), we examine how hype generation strategies evolve over time. We ask: What drives these shifts? How are new audiences identified and mobilised? And who coordinates these transitions?

Consuming: Hype must not only be created but also received, interpreted, and acted upon. Much of the literature presents market actors as paralysed by hype, suggesting it inhibits decision-making (Grodal & Granqvist, 2014), leaving them at a 'loss for direction' (Wenzel et al., 2020, p. 1442). And yet, despite the noise and uncertainty, actors *do* act. Technologies are adopted, investments are made, and new markets take shape. This tension raises a surprising and underexplored question: If hype is disorienting, how do actors nonetheless move forward? What tools or frameworks allow them to navigate inflated promises? How are decisions made amid ambiguity, speculation, and overstatement? These questions remain largely unanswered.

Upscaling: Hype often scales beyond individual ventures to shape entire markets and industries. Local narratives can be elevated into new market categories, such as Juvo's coining of the 'FIDaaS' label, or mapped onto industry 'hype cycles' that embed them within a recognised arc of rising, peaking, and falling expectations. Yet we still know little about how such venture-level narratives make this leap – becoming categories in their own right and, in the process, shaping sector-wide market making. This process is far from automatic. As Garud et al. (2025) note, these macroscale dynamics are coordinated – not spontaneous – requiring infrastructure, expertise, and legitimacy. Understanding how local hype narratives scale up is key to understanding their systemic effects.

Evaluating: Perhaps the most underexplored dimension of hype is its evaluation. Hype is often treated as unfolding in an unregulated or unstructured space, where scrutiny is limited and claims go unchecked (Joly, 2010). But this is no longer the case. One of our central claims in *After Hype* is that a new class of market expert – what we call 'hype's new actors' – has emerged. These gatekeepers and experts play a growing role in legitimising or dismissing hyped expectations, and their influence is central to how hype is tamed, institutionalised, and made actionable within the digital economy.

1.5 Hype's New Actors

Comparing the development of start-up ventures like Juvo today with the development of dotcoms from just a couple of decades ago (Garud et al., 2019), we have been struck by the number of market gatekeepers and experts that now steer hype. One of the lesser-discussed issues following the bursting of the Internet bubble has been the emergence and rapid growth of a small but powerful class of actors – the *industry analyst* – who, in some crucial respects, have colonised (Suddaby & Greenwood, 2001) the hype phenomenon. Just as important, their emergence was quickly followed by a second group – *analyst relations* (AR) experts – created by technology vendors to navigate and shape analysts' growing influence.

1.5.1 Industry Analysts

Today, industry analysts are among the most influential gatekeepers in the digital economy. Alongside the media (Vasterman, 2005; Byrne & Giuliani, 2025; Magalhães & Smit, 2025), governments (Christian et al., 2025), research funders (Konrad & Alvial-Palavicino, 2017), investors (Spivack et al., 2025), entrepreneurial support organisations (Bergman & McMullen, 2022), and others, analysts play a central role in shaping how hyped expectations are created, evaluated, and disseminated (see Box 1.2). As we will demonstrate, their work undergirds much of the operation of hyped expectations within the digital economy. Analyst firms have established expertise in identifying, framing, visualising, and actively amplifying hype.

Box 1.2 The emergence of industry analysts

The emergence of the industry analyst profession is a relatively recent phenomenon. Virtually absent during the dotcom boom, the field has since expanded rapidly. From a small group of North American specialists, it has grown to encompass more than 1,000 firms globally, with the 'Big Three' – Gartner, Forrester, and IDC – accounting for over half of the $10 billion market (Pollock & Williams, 2016). These firms earn the bulk of their revenue by helping technology buyers understand the capabilities and positioning of ventures.

Industry analysts are an 'evaluative audience' (Slavich & Castellucci, 2016) who has emerged to produce knowledge and assessment on difficult-to-evaluate factors such as venture viability and potential. Although there has been little direct research on industry analysts (but see Pollock & Williams, 2016), their role and methods are similar to analogous groups such as investment analysts and securities analysts (Benner & Beunza, 2025).

Industry analysts can be considered 'frame-makers', a term used to describe how they organise and make sense of new market phenomena (Beunza & Garud, 2007; Giorgi & Weber, 2015). They provide 'detailed analyses and offer assessments of what is happening in the present and project future developments' (Mützel, 2022, p. 74), often positioning themselves as impartial guides – the 'Which? Magazine' of the digital economy (Aldridge, 1994).

1.5.2 Analyst Relations

The growing influence of industry analysts has given rise to a second key actor group in the digital economy: the AR expert (see Box 1.3). In response to the growing influence of analysts in shaping market perceptions, many vendors now invest substantial resources in managing these relationships, including hiring dedicated AR experts. Although often overlooked in accounts of how hype is operationalised, AR experts play a central role. Their expertise lies in refining and reworking promissory narratives to align with the evaluative frameworks used by analysts. Both start-ups and established vendors often struggle to communicate the distinctiveness and potential of their innovations to these influential gatekeepers (Schindler et al., 2024).

Box 1.3 The emergence of analyst relations (AR) experts

Analyst relations (AR) is a specialised branch of the wider public relations (PR) field. Within the marketing and communications departments of larger technology vendors, dedicated staff and teams were created to manage relationships with industry analysts (Ikeler, 2007). The AR category includes both in-house professionals and external advisers who guide vendors on which analysts to engage with and how to build visibility and influence in the technology market. By the early 2000s – led in particular by IBM – many major vendors had already begun employing specialist expertise to track, and where possible respond to, the growing number of industry analyst rankings. Today, substantial numbers of these so-called AR pros work within vendors. Even smaller digital vendors without access to the budgets of the larger players make use of this expertise through hiring specialist consultancy from the various AR agencies that have sprung up (Pollock et al., 2018). Entire departments now exist to respond to and influence industry analysts, underscoring that hype management has evolved into a formal service function – one where managing promissory narratives is as critical to strategy as delivering technology. Their presence is now commonplace across the spectrum of ventures, from the technology giants like Amazon and Google to early-stage start-ups. It is estimated that around 10,000 such professionals are employed worldwide in full- or part-time roles (Duncan Chapple, personal communication, 9 August 2025).

AR specialists bridge this gap by coaching marketing and technical teams on how to craft and deliver compelling briefings. As we saw with Juvo, AR experts help ventures present their narratives. They know how to make a venture's story salient to catch the analyst's eye.

Together, industry analysts and AR experts exemplify the emergence of professional groups for managing hype. We argue that one of the most significant impacts of their work has been the creation of *managed channels* within the otherwise wild and turbulent sea of hype. To capture this shift, we introduce a key conceptual distinction between 'hype in the wild' and 'tamed hype'.

1.6 From Hype in the Wild to Tamed Hype

Much of the existing literature has focused on what we term 'hype in the wild' – the unbounded and largely unregulated narratives generated by charismatic entrepreneurs such as Elon Musk, Peter Thiel, and Sergey Brin. These individuals are often portrayed as 'promise entrepreneurs' (Joly & Le Renard, 2021) and 'masterful storytellers' (Goldfarb & Kirsch, 2019), able to shape public discourse through the sheer force of their visionary rhetoric. Their narratives typically circulate through diffuse and loosely connected discourse coalitions (Hajer, 1995), gaining traction not through formal validation but through affective appeal and performative momentum, such as statements that shape outcomes simply by being uttered and widely adopted. It is argued that 'more broadly [their narratives] are believed, the more likely they are to produce the envisioned result' (Goldfarb & Kirsch, 2019, p. 61).

The received view is that these kinds of promissory narratives operate largely unchecked. In emerging technology fields, bold claims often circulate without systematic scrutiny or consequence. These actors are rarely held accountable for their claims – even when those promises remain unfulfilled. This is due to the perceived absence of formal oversight and the weakness of evaluative mechanisms in nascent innovation domains (Brown, 2003; Joly, 2010; Grodal & Granqvist, 2014). In short, hype is seen as largely ungoverned, allowing speculation to flourish with minimal institutional constraint.

While hype in the wild remains an influential force, we argue that it is only one manifestation of the more diverse and evolving hype phenomenon. This book challenges the tendency – common in both academic and popular accounts – to treat hype as a singular, undifferentiated force. In particular, we critique how much of the existing scholarship applies the same analytical frameworks indiscriminately across disparate cases: from the exuberance of the Internet boom and bust (Garud *et al.*, 2021), to the high-profile narratives of promise entrepreneurs like Elon Musk (Goldfarb & Kirsch, 2019), to the more structured and strategically mediated claims of ventures such as Juvo.

This flattened or homogenised view of hype risks overlooking crucial distinctions: differences in the types of innovation at stake, their likelihood of success, and the varying degrees of technical feasibility, organisational maturity, and business model coherence they involve. By failing to account for these variations, prevailing analyses obscure the complex – and increasingly institutionalised – ways in which hype operates across different contexts within the digital economy. Instead, we argue that the digital economy is characterised not by a singular 'hype economy' or unified 'promissory culture' (Bourne, 2024) but by multiple, distinct forms of hype. As Konrad and Alvial-Palavicino (2017, p. 17) note, there may not be 'one common hype dynamic'; different forms of hype emerge from specific governance arrangements, institutional structures, and expectations.

To reflect this plurality, we propose the concept of 'tamed hype' – which we define as the process by which unstructured, exaggerated, or uncertain promissory narratives about emerging technologies are shaped into more credible, navigable, and actionable forms. This taming, we will show, represents a significant but underexplored facet of the digital economy. The trajectory of Juvo illustrates this dynamic: what began as an open-ended, future-oriented narrative was progressively refined and rearticulated through sustained engagement with industry analysts and AR professionals.

This book traces how such taming unfolds across the digital economy. We will show that it occurs through the involvement of specialised actors, tools, and practices. While Juvo is only one case, it exemplifies key mechanisms by which promissory claims are translated into more strategically positioned and credible narratives – a pattern explored further in the chapters that follow.

All technology ventures in the digital economy – from small start-ups to established giants – are shaped, in one way or another, by these experts. Their interactions with industry analysts and analyst relations teams constitute some of the most critical relationships they can cultivate. Yet, despite their importance, these relationships remain among the least examined and least understood in terms of their influence on hype and the broader digital economy.

We argue that the growing alignment between hyped expectations and hype's new actors marks a shift in how promissory narratives are produced and sustained. Where such narratives once arose and spread more spontaneously, they are now forged through highly structured interactions between vendors, industry analysts, and AR professionals. These interactions matter: they influence how ventures craft their stories and, in doing so, reshape the structure and dynamics of the digital economy.

By 'After Hype', we do not mean the end of hype. Instead, we refer to its transformation. What comes 'after' is not its disappearance but the reconfiguration of hype – from unregulated, wild forms to more managed and professionalised practices. This title signals a conceptual shift: away from hype as spontaneous and disorderly, towards forms that are increasingly coordinated through institutional actors, evaluative infrastructures, and promissory products.

We do not claim that hype is now fully domesticated or controlled. Indeed, attempts to tame hype can generate second-order forms of speculation. As vendors, analysts, AR experts, etc., try to manage or navigate hype, their very actions can produce new anticipatory momentum. Thus, taming is best viewed not as containment but as a recursive and strategic effort to organise expectations in the face of uncertainty.

Turning to our subtitle, *The Business of Taming the Digital Economy*, the book explores how hype's new actors actively manage and modulate expectations. We argue that hype is no longer an incidental element of technology culture; it has become a business domain in its own right. For instance, industry analysts have cultivated a broad and influential client base (Pollock & Williams, 2016). Their research and opinion are closely followed by enterprises worldwide, many of which contract with analyst firms to guide strategic decisions and manage innovation risk (Dennington & Leforestier, 2014). Organisations now treat hype management as a strategic investment – through subscriptions, consulting fees, and related services – highlighting that hype must be studied as a business practice as well as a cultural phenomenon. Industry analysts and AR professionals have become key players in the innovation ecosystem, monetising the management of expectations. This book approaches hype as a business: a network of firms, services, and mechanisms dedicated to producing and taming promissory narratives.

If hype has evolved into a more structured and managed process, the next question is how it is moderated, channelled, and brought under control. The notion of 'taming' captures this shift. The OED highlights that 'taming' encompasses multiple, intertwined dimensions. Guided by its etymology and drawing on a broad and interdisciplinary body of scholarship, we identify four interrelated facets of taming hype:[3]

Reclaiming (Hype) from the Wild: Analysts work to curb and temper excessive promissory claims. When ventures like Juvo brief industry analysts and 'sell their vision', these claims are subject to scrutiny – analysts routinely challenge narratives, demanding evidence and substantiation. As the case of Juvo suggests – and as we explore in greater detail in the pages to come – critical feedback can lead to a recalibration of hype, encouraging ventures to moderate speculative elements and align more closely with analyst expectations.

Making (Hype) Tractable or Navigable: Analysts not only constrain hype – they amplify it. They often valorise the localised hyped expectations of individual ventures, elevating them into more coherent narratives or broader meta-level phenomena (van Lente & Rip, 1998; Palavicino, 2016). In Juvo's case, the market category *Financial Identity as a Service* (FiDaaS) emerged through this narrative structuring.

Domesticating (the Evaluator): As analysts' influence has grown, technology vendors have responded by developing specialist AR expertise. AR professionals help craft sophisticated promissory narratives that align with analysts' evaluative criteria, anticipating both current and future scrutiny. In this way, gatekeepers are no longer simply external threats but strategic actors to be engaged and influenced.

Cultivating and Improving (Hype): Taming also involves equipping market actors – particularly organisational decision-makers – with tools to navigate

---

[3] A key influence on our concept of taming is Hacking's (1990) historical account of statistical models as efforts to stabilise domains of volatility and uncertainty. This concern with managing unpredictability also connects with recent work in the Sociology of Finance on 'noise', where scholars such as Preda (2019, 2020) show how apparent disruption can be channelled and made productive through interpretive and organisational work. Our thinking is further shaped by Latour's (2012) notion of 'purification': the disentangling and stabilising of heterogeneous elements to render them tractable and actionable. Taken together, these strands frame taming as a set of practices for ordering complexity, managing uncertainty, and enabling intervention.

and respond to hype. Industry analysts play a key role in this process by helping to interpret what constitutes hype, identifying where and when it emerges, and advising clients on how to engage with it. We will explore this final process in greater detail in the next section.

1.7 Navigating Hype

A central aim of *After Hype* is to unravel how decision-makers navigate an environment saturated with competing promissory claims. While recent scholarship suggests that hype generates uncertainty and may encourage a 'wait and see' approach (Endenich et al., 2022), the reality is more complex. In periods of radical innovation, hype can indeed provoke caution – but it also creates pressure to act swiftly. The urgency of technological disruption compels stakeholders to make decisions before a clear consensus or robust evidence has emerged (Kumaraswamy et al., 2018). This creates a tension: decision-makers must act decisively while navigating an uncertain, exaggerated, and often contradictory stream of claims.

This paradox raises a crucial question: How do stakeholders decide in a landscape characterised by multiple, competing, hyped and exaggerated claims? Our answer lies in analysing how market gatekeepers have transformed the sea of hype by introducing a series of 'promissory products' (Pollock & Williams, 2010, 2016). By the 2020s, analyst firms had developed a sophisticated array of evaluation tools – rankings, trend analysis tools, categories, and appellations – for assessing whether ventures live up to their hype. Yet, the origins, evolution, and influence of these products have not been adequately researched.

After Hype's novelty is to throw light on the construction of these promissory products. Our sustained close access to this community allowed us to explore the development and evolution of these products, as well as how, for instance, industry analysts decide to create a new ranking, plot a Hype Cycle Chart, craft and launch a category, and identify a 'Cool Vendor', among other things. Thus, we describe in rich detail how these products are created and developed based on unique fieldwork access.

The primary consumers of these products are organisational managers, predominantly those responsible for technology adoption. Managers, confronted by a flood of potentially disruptive narratives like Juvo's, often struggle to comprehend the dynamic innovation landscape and discern which opportunities are most promising (Webster & Gardner, 2019). Compounding this challenge is the pressure to act before solid evidence emerges – when the performance and prospects of innovations remain uncertain and it is challenging to distinguish grounded evidence from promissory claims or speculative hype (Kumaraswamy et al., 2018).

The prevailing scholarly view holds that separating hype from 'fundamentals' is only possible in hindsight. As Master and Resnik (2013, p. 324) note, '[i]t may be difficult to determine whether publicity/ promotion constitutes hype, because one may not know whether it is excessive until the field ... being publicised delivers (or fails to deliver) on its promised goals'. Similarly, van Lente (2012) argues that hype can only be evaluated *retrospectively* – typically when attention has shifted elsewhere and few are interested in revisiting earlier claims.

This creates a dilemma for technology adopters who want to understand what hype is, where and when it emerges, and how to respond. The received view asserts that this information is not available in real time (e.g. Brown, 2003). While hindsight may eventually reveal the true extent of the hype, this retrospective clarity arrives too late to guide decision-making when it matters most.

After Hype challenges the notion that this dilemma is irresolvable. While the circularity between hype and fundamentals cannot be eliminated *in principle*, we show that it is navigated *in practice*. The claim that there is no way to distinguish between hype and fundamentals fails to account for the emergence of actors who aim to exercise precisely this kind of discretion. We examine how hype's new actors attempt to equip clients with relevant knowledge at the moment of choice.

The actors described in this book offer guidance to their clients during periods of uncertainty. The crucial challenge for these analysts is to provide advice that supports timely action. Managers must make decisions under conditions where no definitive evidence of an innovation's value exists. While analysts cannot determine the accuracy of a vendor's claims in advance, they can assess a claim's credibility and its potential to be realised (Beckert, 2021). In doing so, they help clients discern which narratives are less likely to materialise and adjust their strategies accordingly.

Thus, our book argues that hype's new actors are reshaping *how* organisational managers consume and interpret hype. Once dismissed as peripheral 'noise', hype is increasingly central to managerial judgement. Through the design and dissemination of promissory products, analysts have reframed hype as a legitimate object of strategic concern – something to be tracked, evaluated, and acted upon. In doing so, they have introduced new tools for reflection where few previously existed. This shift signals a broader transformation in the digital economy: hype, once regarded as an uncontrollable by-product of innovation, is now being actively structured, curated, and governed.

1.8 Defining Hype

While we offered a preliminary definition of hype earlier – as a surge in attention, excitement, and expectations – we suggest that this captures what hype *looks* like, but not how it *works*. To understand it more fully, we must examine how hype is constructed, operationalised, and channelled through tools, practices, and infrastructures. These mechanisms are especially salient in contexts marked by radical innovation – where timelines are long, outcomes are unclear, and the promised futures are difficult to evaluate.

Hype tends to cluster around radical rather than incremental innovations, reflecting the heightened uncertainty and novelty intrinsic to transformative technologies (Beckert, 2016). Such uncertainty typically renders promissory statements difficult – if not impossible – to verify in the present, as their validation depends on future evidence that may not yet exist. As we will argue in later chapters, this temporal gap is not merely a hurdle for innovators and evaluators; it is the very space in which hype flourishes – enabling bold visions that can mobilise resources and commitment, while also amplifying the risks of overreach, misjudgement, and eventual disillusionment.

This dual potential has often been overlooked in traditional scholarship, which tends to cast hype in a predominantly negative light, as 'near-lies' (Min, 2024) or 'fundamentally dishonest' (Vinsel & Russell, 2020). Such characterisations, while capturing a common critique, are reductive and analytically limiting.

Hype often runs ahead of evidence, and while the resulting uncertainty surrounding promissory claims renders them unverifiable, it does not necessarily make them misleading. The lack of verifiability can stem from the absence of evidence needed to substantiate claims, rather than from any intent to deceive (Konrad, 2006). From this perspective, inflated expectations do not merely distort – they *bridge present aspirations and future possibilities*, allowing actors to mobilise resources, attention, and commitment in the face of uncertainty.

Bringing these insights together, we define hype as *strategic practices that mobilise attention, excitement, and expectations through promissory narratives that remain unverified due to inherent uncertainty and the absence of settled evidence.* This definition moves beyond the simplistic binary of truth versus deception, foregrounding instead the dynamic processes through which claims are produced, assessed, and legitimised in the context of shifting and unknowable futures.

We examine how each element of this definition unfolds in practice in the next chapter and throughout the book. In particular, we advocate for a *symmetrical sociology of hype* – that is, an approach which does not predefine hype as either true or false but instead examines how it produces effects in practice. This perspective resists moralising accounts that cast hype as inherently deceptive or naively optimistic. Rather, we treat hype as a situated practice, enacted through specific strategies and generating effects that are uneven, contingent, and open to empirical enquiry. Hype can both accelerate technological innovation and divert investment into ultimately sterile avenues; its overall impact, therefore, remains an open empirical question – one that demands systematic investigation rather than prior assumption.

1.9 Studying Hype

Our proposed taming perspective is as much a methodological orientation as it is an empirical and analytical one. In *After Hype*, we argue that to study hype, the fieldworker must trace the circuit of production, evaluation, distribution, and consumption of hyped expectations – following them through to the actions they enable or provoke. This requires examining how hype is generated and assessed through the contested and competitive circulation of ideas across heterogeneous communities of actors.

Yet hype presents a peculiar methodological paradox: the more successful it is, the harder it becomes to study. In principle, hype should be visible – indeed, its purpose is to attract attention! The better it is crafted, the more prominent it becomes. However, visibility does not guarantee traceability. The more hype circulates, morphs, and moves across settings, the more difficult it is to pin it down empirically.

As Ram and colleagues (2024, p. 364) observe, hyped expectations are 'difficult to study directly'. How might one undertake an ethnography of hype, therefore, when the phenomenon is so diffuse and fluid?

Traditional ethnographic approaches, often grounded in specific locations or bounded organisational settings (Marcus, 1995), struggle to account for hype's boundary-crossing. While the origin of a promissory narrative – say, from a start-up like Juvo – might be identifiable, tracking its evolution, audience reactions, and eventual uptake or rejection is far more elusive. How might one 'follow the actors' (Latour, 1987) when those actors involved in producing and shaping hype are scattered across organisations, sectors, and discourse arenas (Hajer, 1995)?

Our solution to this challenge emerges from our concept of tamed hype. The problem of studying hype – its pervasive, unbounded, and amorphous character – is significantly reduced when we shift our focus to the actors who actively channel and shape it. Rather than treating hype as a spontaneous outgrowth of innovation communities (Goldfarb & Kirsch, 2019) or as a diffuse element of the cultural imagination (Powers, 2012), we examine how it is domesticated, mediated, and rendered actionable by hype's new actors.

After Hype is grounded in over a decade of qualitative and ethnographic fieldwork, offering a rare view of how ventures, industry analysts, and AR experts co-produce hyped expectations within an evolving and increasingly complex promissory arena. Much of this activity occurs behind closed doors, yet we were able to negotiate access to previously understudied – but highly consequential – sites of engagement. Our research did not merely document hype – it inhabited the spaces where hype is created, translated, and performed. (A detailed account of our research methods is provided in Appendix: Research Design and Methods.)

Our entry point was the Institute for Industry Analyst Relations (IIAR), a membership body established to support the growing community of AR experts. From there, we gained access to a central arena where narratives are negotiated and evaluated: *the analyst briefing.* In these structured, high-stakes encounters, venture stories are not only presented but also tested, reshaped, and often fundamentally transformed. They offered us a unique vantage point on the mechanics of promissory narrative construction, revealing how hype is not simply projected outward but also actively domesticated (see Box 1.4).

Box 1.4 Why study analyst briefings?

We refer to analyst briefings as the 'Second Most Important Pitch', after investor briefings. Ventures actively seek these meetings to gain analyst endorsement and market visibility. As the Juvo case illustrates, briefings are not just routine updates – they are sites where narratives are created, modified, and refined.

What makes these briefings analytically rich is not only the exchange between ventures and analysts but also the wider promissory arena they assemble. They convene analysts, vendors, and analyst relations professionals in a shared evaluative space where hyped expectations are collectively shaped. These are not one-off events. To maintain visibility, ventures must return frequently – multiple times each year – creating an extended temporal arc that allows us to observe narrative evolution over time.

Our fieldwork included observation of pre-briefing preparation sessions, where teams crafted and rehearsed their messages, and post-briefing debriefs, where performances were assessed and revised. These cycles of iteration revealed how hype is not just projected but continuously managed.

Analysts, for their part, are not passive recipients of venture narratives. They interrogate claims, particularly from new or unfamiliar vendors. As one analyst told us, the goal is not to 'promote a vendor' but to 'find the best and most appropriate one', noting that 'you have to worry about whether it's viable or whether they're telling me the truth' (A4, interview). Briefings are thus crucial sites where hype's credibility is tested, and promissory narratives are scrutinised before being recirculated in broader markets.

To assess whether a venture is telling 'the truth', analysts may conduct what Knorr Cetina (2010, p. 189) calls 'proxy-ethnographies'. This approach involves drawing not only on formal information but also on insights gathered through direct contacts, site visits, and the search for 'customer use cases' that demonstrate a venture's ability to deliver on its promises (Smith, 2009).

1.10 Plan of the Book

This book is organised into five interconnected parts that together build the conceptual, empirical, and theoretical case for rethinking hype – not as a marginal by-product of innovation but as a central, professionalised, and increasingly institutionalised force shaping the digital economy.

Part I, *Reframing Hype*, lays the conceptual groundwork. It charts the shift from the early, loosely regulated hype of the dotcom bubble to today's more strategically managed and institutionalised variants. Here we introduce hype as an overlooked but increasingly crucial dynamic of innovation economies and make the case for treating it as a research topic in its own right.

Chapter 2, *What Is Hype?*, reviews how hype has been theorised across disciplines, clarifying its relationship to other related forms of technological expectations. It advances the argument that hype is a distinct object of enquiry requiring its own conceptual vocabulary and introduces seven tenets to guide future research.

Chapter 3, *Decision-Making about Unpredictable Technology Futures*, traces how hype is moving from the periphery to the centre of organisational attention, generating uncertainty that compels decision-makers to rely on specialised tools and experts to interpret, respond to, and even strategically capitalise on hype.

Part II, *The Gatekeepers of Hype,* begins the empirical analysis by focusing on industry analysts and AR professionals – key figures who operationalise hype. Drawing on unprecedented access to analyst briefings, we show how start-up narratives are scrutinised, repaired, and made credible.

Chapter 4, *The Second Most Important Pitch,* introduces the analyst briefing as a key site in the taming of hype. The chapter demonstrates how industry analysts probe and problematise start-up narratives and how entrepreneurs – accustomed to investor pitches – struggle to adjust to the evaluative criteria of analysts. The central insight is that entrepreneurs must refine and repair their narratives to align with analysts' frameworks.

Chapter 5, *Cool Vendors*, focuses on how analysts search for the next disruptive start-up, which they then label as *Cool Vendor, Hot Vendor, Market Disruptor*, etc. These designations act as a funnelling mechanism, amplifying ventures that align with analysts' expectations and sidelining those that do not – illustrating a new model of how hype legitimises.

Part III, *The Promissory Products That Make Hype Actionable*, turns from the world of start-ups to the broader tools through which hype is formalised and mediated. It introduces some of the promissory products – trend analysis frameworks and categories – developed by analysts to make hype actionable for market actors.

Chapter 6, *Navigating the Hype Cycle,* examines the Gartner Hype Cycle Chart as a key instrument for visualising and taming hype. It shows how analysts blend affective and calculative elements in the construction of the tool – shaping market attention, investment behaviour, and timing of market entry in the process.

Chapter 7, *Categorising the Sea of Hype*, focuses on how analysts attempt to order and structure the unruly sea of hype for technology adopters through launching categories. The chapter examines the puzzle of why some categories are introduced only to be withdrawn shortly thereafter.

Part IV, *Competing for Ranking and Recognition*, shifts the understanding of hype from mere exaggerated claims to a professionalised, credible narrative-building process tailored to manage and influence rankings.

Chapter 8, *Managing the Metrics*, examines how rankings have evolved from evaluative tools into contested arenas where vendors compete as much on their ability to craft persuasive promissory narratives as on their technical merits.

Part V, *What Comes after Hype?*, considers how hype is evolving – becoming institutionalised, professionalised, and integrated into the very fabric of the digital economy. It reflects on the long-term implications of tamed hype for innovation, organisation, and capitalism.

Chapter 9, *Managed Channels in the Wild Sea of Hype*, traces the shift in the digital economy from spontaneous, unregulated 'hype in the wild' to structured, strategically 'tamed hype'. It shows how analysts deploy formal mechanisms to evaluate, organise, and legitimise expectations, introducing the concept of a *managed spiral of promissory products* to capture this evolving infrastructure.

Chapter 10, *Towards Hype Studies*, proposes a new interdisciplinary research agenda to study the changing role of hype in the digital economy. It positions *Hype Studies* as a new research programme concerned with how technological futures are imagined, legitimised, and contested.

The chapters can be read sequentially, following our argument from the emergence of hype 'in the wild' to its institutionalisation through taming practices. They can also be approached selectively. The empirical chapters (4 to 8) stand as self-contained studies: some

address hype directly, while others examine adjacent phenomena –
entrepreneurial storytelling, market categorisation, and rankings – that
illuminate the wider promissory arenas in which hype takes shape.
This variation reflects both the iterative character of our research and
the value of engaging neighbouring literatures to develop a richer
conceptual vocabulary for understanding hype's institutionalisation
in the digital economy.

Reframing Hype

This first part lays the groundwork for the book's argument that hype is a significant and evolving phenomenon deserving sustained academic attention. Interest in its effects is growing – particularly in how actors engage with technologies surrounded by heightened expectations (Logue & Grimes, 2022; Garud et al., 2023; Ometto et al., 2023) – yet the topic remains relatively underexplored (Bourne, 2024). We still lack clarity on what scholars mean by hype and what it offers as an analytical lens distinct from related concepts. Existing discussions are scattered across diverse fields – Media Studies, Philosophy, Science and Technology Studies (STS), Organisation and Management Theory (OMT), Economics, Sociology, and Market Studies – each with different assumptions and definitions. This disciplinary fragmentation hinders cross-field understanding, even as the breadth of work suggests hype's potential as a valuable research concept. We also identify a need to study *hype's new actors* – the expert groups that have emerged to produce, circulate, and manage responses to hype.

The following two chapters address these gaps. *Chapter 2, What Is Hype?*, reviews and consolidates existing scholarship, proposing a more nuanced understanding that goes beyond simplistic notions of exaggeration or deception. We emphasise hype's dynamic, structured, and strategic role in promissory arenas and introduce *Seven Tenets* to guide future research and contribute to the emerging field of Hype Studies.

Chapter 3, Decision-Making about Unpredictable Technology Futures, examines how hype has moved from the periphery to the centre of organisational strategy. In markets where emerging technologies can redefine entire sectors, organisations must now actively engage with hype to remain competitive. This chapter explores how technology adopters, investors, and other market participants navigate its risks and opportunities under conditions of incomplete knowledge. The chapter also introduces the *business of hype* – a growing set of promissory products that help organisations evaluate and act on hyped claims, marking the professionalisation of hype management in contemporary innovation landscapes.

2 | *What Is Hype?*

This chapter develops the conceptual foundation for Hype Studies by reviewing how hype is treated across different fields and proposing seven core tenets for its analysis. It clarifies how hype overlaps with, but is distinct from, concepts such as speculative bubbles, fashions, organising visions, and promises. Despite its prevalence, hype remains inconsistently defined and theoretically underdeveloped. To address this, we synthesise insights from Science and Technology Studies (STS), especially the Sociology of Expectations; Organisation and Management Theory (OMT); Information Systems (IS); Economics; Economic Sociology; and Cultural Entrepreneurship. Each of the seven tenets addresses a key dimension of hype, offering a framework to better understand how it operates and why it matters. This set of tenets is not intended to be exhaustive – especially when considering areas beyond the digital economy – and some are illustrated more fully than others. Nonetheless, they introduce and foreground the central themes developed in the chapters that follow, and we hope they provide a helpful foundation for the approach to hype advanced in this book.

2.1 Tenet One: Who Creates Hype – Beyond Promise Entrepreneurs to Collective Promissory Arenas

Brown (2003, p. 13) asks, 'Where do expectations of the future originate', and 'by what means do they come to take hold of our imaginations and actions?'. Building on that provocation, we ask whether hype is created by singular 'promise entrepreneurs' or emerges from broader 'promissory arenas' in which future claims circulate and gain force.

Much existing work emphasises charismatic narrators. Economic analyses of technological bubbles point to 'narrative accelerators' (Shiller, 2019; Goldfarb & Kirsch, 2019). Cultural Entrepreneurship research foregrounds entrepreneurial 'storytelling' and 'projective storytelling' as mechanisms for mobilising audiences and resources

(Lounsbury & Glynn, 2001; Garud et al., 2014b). STS scholars similarly identify the 'promise entrepreneur', who crafts promissory claims to galvanise action (Joly & Le Renard, 2021).

Yet such individualised accounts risk creating heroic, actor-centred narratives that retrospectively attribute innovation success to persuasive entrepreneurs while overlooking the institutional, relational, and infrastructural conditions that render their narratives actionable. They also invite survivor bias, leading to an overemphasis on successful innovation stories and an under-representation of those involving failed innovation (Geels & Smit, 2000).

We therefore foreground 'promissory arenas' – the collective platforms, networks, and communities through which future-oriented narratives circulate, compete, reinforce one another, and gain power (Bakker *et al.*, 2012). Individual storytellers matter, but they draw influence from broader infrastructures of promise-making that enrol multiple actors and interacting narratives.

The Sociology of Expectations provides a helpful lens for analysing these promissory arenas. Van Lente's (1993) classic work introduced 'promise-requirement cycles' in technological development: an initial generic promise mobilises interest; users, funders, regulators, and other stakeholders translate that promise into more specific requirements; progress is subsequently assessed against emerging milestones; and promises are recalibrated – strengthened, qualified, or withdrawn – in light of results. Gaps between promise and performance may be tolerated; success builds credibility and mobilises additional support, while shortfalls prompt adjustments or raise doubts. Importantly, the cycle repeats: promises are updated, expectations reset, and resources mobilised or withdrawn depending on whether interim results 'live up' to prior claims.

Such longitudinal, cyclical work shows that hype must be continually sustained and negotiated throughout the innovation process. When bold claims remain unproven, actors engage in repair work – adjusting narratives, supplying evidence, or reframing trajectories to maintain credibility (Garud et al., 2014b; Hampel & Dalpiaz, 2025). In this sense, hype is not a one-off act of overstatement but an evolving dialogue between promise-makers and promise-takers that unfolds over time.

Subsequent scholarship extends analysis from local promise-requirement exchanges to the broader ecology of discursive and institutional formations that support and contest technological futures (Bakker *et al.*, 2011). These studies highlight 'arenas of expectations', field-level settings in which entrepreneurs, investors, corporations, regulators, media, analysts, and others contend over competing technological visions (Bakker *et al.*, 2011). Multiple arenas may coexist at different levels of aggregation (Bakker *et al.*, 2011).

Ruef and Markard (2010) identify three levels of expectations that operate across and within such arenas. First, *specific expectations* are often attached to particular innovations or projects and can be volatile. Second, more *general expectations* concern the trajectory of a broader technological field and tend to be more durable. Third, *higher-level societal imaginaries* articulate the technology's role in society and typically endure longest.

The promissory world is complex and loosely bounded, encompassing multiple expectational alignments of differing intensity, duration, and scale. As Joly (2010, p. 4) argues, this calls for attention to the 'diversity of arenas' and for mapping the 'topology of this space' of expectations in what he terms the 'economics of techno-scientific promises'. We build on this point to foreground how hype now underpins a market of its own – a coordinated set of actors and tools devoted to producing and exploiting promissory narratives. In our account, this diversity of arenas is no longer simply a descriptive feature of the promissory world but the basis of an organised economic field in which specialist actors occupy distinct niches, develop proprietary tools, and trade in the management of expectations. By tracing how these arenas interconnect and transact, we show how the business of hype operates as a structured market within the broader economy of expectations.

2.2 Tenet Two: Not All Technologies Generate Hype Equally

Hype is often seen as pervasive in today's digital economy, but do all technologies generate it to the same extent? Garud *et al.* (2018, p. 4) raise this question directly, asking whether 'all fields experience hype cycles' – prompting us to consider what varies when hype takes shape. Our analysis suggests that hype is far from uniform: both its prevalence and character are uneven. Some domains are intensely saturated with hype, while others remain relatively muted – or even appear 'hype-resistant' (Potts, 2017). We identify at least three dimensions along which hype varies: how it functions as a resource, how it operates as a structure, and who (and what) serve as its key catalysts.

2.2.1 Hype as a Resource

Hype confers legitimacy, direction, and coordination capacity in early innovation, yet it also creates obligations that can later backfire. Van Lente (2012) conceptualises hype as a resource that performs three critical functions in innovation processes. First, it provides *legitimacy*, helping to support emerging technologies and create 'protected spaces' where promissory narratives can circulate with fewer challenges (van Lente & Rip, 1998). Second, it offers *direction*, reducing uncertainty by suggesting plausible technological trajectories and guiding actors through moments of indeterminacy (Deuten & Rip, 2000). Third, it enables *coordination*, helping to align diverse stakeholders by defining roles, expectations, and responsibilities within innovation networks.

Yet this resource is not without risk. As van Lente *et al.* (2013) caution, hype can unravel when expectations are not met. Ruef and Markard (2010) expand on this, warning that declining hype can lead to disappointment, resource withdrawal, and a loss of momentum, as attention wanes and actors begin to exit the field. Similarly, Logue and Grimes (2022, p. 1055) characterise hype as a 'short-term resource but long-term risk', suggesting that while hype may initially attract interest and support, it can also generate a growing burden of accountability. Over time, the promises embedded in hype create a sense of obligation between ventures and their audiences – obligations that may prove challenging to satisfy and that can backfire when expectations are not met.

2.2.2 Hype as Structure

When many actors repeatedly draw on hype as a resource, their efforts can sediment into broader structures of expectation. Palavicino (2016, p. 26) distinguishes between individual 'hyping practices' and the emergence of 'meta-level' hype phenomena, such as categories. In practice, this means repeated promotional storytelling around a technology can crystallise into a shared narrative or category that transcends any promoter. The case of Juvo's FIDaaS category exemplifies this process, where what began as a strategic label for a single venture evolved into a recognisable market category. Rip and Voß (2009) characterise as an 'umbrella term' the categories that structure expectations and align actors.

This analytical aspect raises important questions about how hype evolves from individual performance to collective infrastructure. Van Lente and Rip (1998) offer a helpful lens, theorising how emergent hype categories can become 'macro actors' – entities that not only gain visibility but also shape the contours of a field, including its dominant narratives and key players. Logue and Grimes (2022, p. 1055) similarly stress the importance of 'collective expectations' and argue that individual acts of entrepreneurial hyping – however compelling – may fail unless embedded in a 'corresponding vision that is collectively espoused and increasing in attention'. They suggest that projective storytelling risks ringing hollow without this shared uptake, lacking the structural support necessary to mobilise wider belief and engagement.

2.2.3 Hype's Catalysts

Building on the insight above that multiple actors inhabit promissory arenas, we ask who amplifies or filters hype, and what events set hype in motion. Research in the Sociology of Expectations and further afield has differentiated between types of actors, noting that not everyone involved in innovation contributes to hype equally. For instance, Konrad and Alvial-Palavicino (2017) draw a line between 'innovation creators' and 'hype creators'. Scientists or developers ('innovation creators') may focus on making the technology and only engage in minimal 'expectation work' if necessary. In contrast, other actors – specialised journalists, consultants, and analysts ('hype creators') – devote much of their effort to shaping narratives about innovations, despite not being directly involved in building the innovations themselves.

Bakker and Budde (2012) offer a complementary typology, distinguishing between 'hype enactors' – such as innovators and entrepreneurs – and 'hype selectors' – including investors, adopters, and industry analysts. Hype enactors are those directly engaged in *developing* technologies or promoting specific futures, whereas hype selectors *evaluate* these futures, deciding whether to allocate resources, endorse claims, or adopt emerging solutions. Selectors' due diligence and critical distance are vital: their filtering function strongly conditions whether hype diffuses, stalls, or dissipates (Bakker & Budde, 2012).

Moreover, hype often coalesces around 'trigger events' – moments that amplify attention, mobilise interest, and shape early public perceptions (Kiefer, 2013). For example, Simakova and Coenen (2013) emphasise the role of 'conferences' in animating hype, which Garud and colleagues (2008) conceptualise as 'field-configuring events' – events that serve as pivotal interventions that help construct and legitimise technological futures by establishing early narratives and drawing diverse actors into alignment. Brown (2003) draws attention to the 'press release' in scientific contexts, framing it as a 'point of translation' through which technical research is transformed into accessible and often promissory public narratives. Similarly, Pontikes and Barnett (2017) examine 'vital events' such as major venture capital (VC) funding rounds, which generate visibility and credibility, helping to construct 'hot markets' around nascent technologies. As Konrad et al. (2016) noted, government investment initiatives also operate as trigger events, signalling institutional commitment to specific futures and lending weight to accompanying promotional claims.

2.2.4 Uneven Distribution of Hype

Returning to our guiding question, hype accompanies most innovations to some degree, but its intensity, reach, and duration vary widely. Most innovations are subject to some level of heightened expectation, driven by the inherent uncertainty surrounding their outcomes. However, hype's intensity, reach, and duration can vary considerably depending on the nature of the technology. In some cases, hype remains localised and short-lived; in others, it becomes widespread, sustained, and strategically cultivated over long periods.

Radical or disruptive innovations are especially prone to attracting significant public interest and media attention (Beckert, 2016; Byrne & Giuliani, 2025; Magalhães & Smit, 2025). These technologies typically involve ambitious long-term visions, requiring substantial investment and extended timelines before outcomes can be realised. Gaining support thus demands a particularly proactive process of mobilising expectations and sustaining belief across multiple stakeholders. As Beckert (2016) argues, the more uncertain the future path of an innovation, the greater the effort required to coordinate imaginations – and the more intense the surrounding hype tends to be (see also van Lente & Bakker, 2010).

By contrast, incremental innovations often receive lower (and more localised) levels of hype, even though they may deliver significant cumulative gains (Gardner et al., 2015). Why is this? Several factors help explain this disparity. Incremental developments usually emerge within established technological communities, where claims can be more easily evaluated and scrutinised through existing relationships and accountability mechanisms. Familiarity with vendors and prior evaluation criteria may thus reduce the space for exaggerated expectations.

Certain technologies draw more hype for other reasons. Some are more 'hype-able' than others (Potts, 2017). For example, in the 1980s, industrial robots dominated public and policy discourse, while other, arguably more impactful automation tools, such as programmable logic controllers, received far less attention (Fleck et al., 1990). The robot served as a striking, media-friendly figure, offering a simplified and intelligible representation of complex developments. In contrast, less visually or imaginatively compelling technologies, such as programmable logic controllers, despite their profound real-world effects, remained largely invisible in public and policy discussions.

This asymmetric distribution of hype has significant consequences. If hype is understood as a resource, visibility becomes a critical currency in the digital economy. While all technologies require attention to progress, only a select few succeed in attracting the concentrated expectations that unlock funding, legitimacy, and broader momentum (Faxon et al., 2024).

Crucially, the capacity to generate and circulate hype appears to be unevenly distributed (Byrne & Giuliani, 2025). As Brown (2003, p. 5) observes, hype reflects the 'asymmetries between people and groups in their access to information within the knowledge economy of expectations'. This leads to a spotlight effect, where highly hyped technologies overshadow other promising innovations (Potts, 2017). Technologies lacking access to influential sponsors or gatekeepers may struggle to gain visibility, regardless of their technical merits. As Bakker and Budde (2012) suggest, such innovations often falter due to insufficient attention and resource mobilisation. In some cases, this may even contribute to the emergence of 'innovation deserts' – fields that remain underdeveloped not because of a lack of potential but because of a lack of hype (Sharma & Meyer, 2019).[1]

---

[1] See, for instance, the Frontier Tech Hub's 'Nine Underhyped Frontier Technologies for International Development' report. www.frontiertechhub.org/underhyped-tech.

2.3 Tenet Three: Hype's Conceptual Boundaries – Overlaps with but Distinct from Similar Concepts

Research identifies various 'modes of constructing the future' (Konrad et al., 2016, p. 11), including speculative bubbles, fashions, promises, visions, and imaginaries. What is the relationship between hype and these other related future-based concepts? It is interesting to explore how various contributions with different disciplinary roots and concerns have converged on a specific area of expectations (with many explicitly considering hype). Notwithstanding this convergence, the multiple traditions have their own conceptual baggage and concerns. These concepts share commonalities with hype, but each operates through distinct mechanisms and emphasises different dynamics. In our view, hype is a defining (if variable) feature of emerging technology futures, surfacing in diverse forms under conditions of uncertainty. While related to these concepts, hype also has unique characteristics that warrant closer examination. Below, we consider six adjacent concepts – speculative bubbles, management fashions, organising visions, promise, sociotechnical visions, and imaginaries – to clarify where hype aligns with and diverges from each.

2.3.1 Speculative Bubbles

Speculative bubbles are a market phenomenon in which asset prices rise rapidly to levels far exceeding their intrinsic value, often fuelled by 'irrational exuberance' and 'herd behaviour' (Shiller, 2015; Goldfarb & Kirsch, 2019). Kindleberger and Aliber (2005, p. 25) define an asset pricing bubble as an 'upward price movement over an extended period of 15–40 months that then implodes', while Taleb (2010) highlights the role of collective overconfidence in sustaining these inflated valuations. Central to bubbles is Greater Fool Theory – how investors buy overvalued assets expecting to sell them to someone else at a higher price (Barlevy, 2015).

Hype and bubbles share common patterns of rapid escalation in attention and investment. Both are fuelled by optimism and anticipation, often amplifying expectations well beyond current realities. However, while speculative bubbles are typically followed by a sharp correction or dramatic collapse, hype does not necessarily follow the same trajectory. As Goodnight and Green (2010, p. 116) put it, bubbles are 'temporary departures from rational norms awaiting correction'. Floridi (2024, p. 127) notes that while hype cycles may resemble 'tech bubbles in the making', they do not always culminate in collapse. All bubbles involve hype, but not all hype produces bubbles. Hype may instead persist, evolve, or taper without implosion – especially when underlying promises begin to be realised. As Logue and Grimes (2022) observe, bubbles tend to implode when expectations are not met, whereas hype can stabilise and mature if evidence emerges that supports its claims.

2.3.2 Management Fashions

Management fashions are transitory waves of managerial ideas that diffuse and fade as attention shifts among knowledge consumers. OMT has long used the concept of management fashions to describe the fads and waves of popular ideas in the business world, such as Total Quality Management, Six Sigma, and Business Process Reengineering. Abrahamson and Fairchild (1999, p. 709) define management fashions as 'relatively transitory collective beliefs that certain management techniques are at the forefront of rational management progress'. Like hype, fashions generate bursts of enthusiasm, creating temporary spaces for exploration and experimentation before enthusiasm wanes and the field moves on (Rip, 2000).

Yet there are critical differences between fashions and hype, and we foreground one in particular: *carrying capacity*. Abrahamson and Fairchild (1999, p. 713) argue that management fashions have a 'finite carrying capacity', because 'knowledge consumers can only attend to a limited number of fashions simultaneously'. In other words, the management world can only sustain a handful of dominant fashions at any one time; the collapse of one would free up space for another to take its place.

Hype, by contrast, appears to operate on a very different scale and is not subject to the same dynamics. Industry analysts now track hundreds of concurrent 'hype cycles' in the digital economy (see Chapter 6), where management fashions once moved in relatively slow, sequential waves. Hype more closely resembles a 'sea of expectations' – to borrow van Lente's (2012) evocative phrase – with countless overlapping narratives simultaneously competing for attention. This proliferation suggests that hype has far greater carrying capacity:

it can sustain a crowded, turbulent ecosystem of expectations without requiring one narrative to collapse before another can rise.

2.3.3 Organising Visions

Organising visions are practitioner-anchored community ideas that make a digital innovation intelligible, useful, and actionable (Swanson & Ramiller, 1997). An organising vision provides a shared way for practitioners to name, explain, and justify an emerging technology: what it is, why it matters, and how it might be implemented. Swanson and Ramiller (1997, p. 460) define an organising vision as a 'focal community idea for the application of information technology in organisations'. By furnishing a common vocabulary and set of usage scenarios, organising visions helps align users, vendors, consultants, and other stakeholders around a technology's potential.

Organising visions have temporal 'careers' (Ramiller & Swanson, 2003). They often emerge in vague form, struggle for legitimacy, and – if they gain traction – diffuse, stabilise, and eventually fragment or decline as new visions take their place (Swanson et al., 2025). Classic examples include Enterprise Resource Planning (ERP) and Customer Relationship Management (CRM) (see Chapter 7).

Because organising visions must support implementation conversations, they usually require a threshold level of stability and clarity; practitioners need to be able to discuss scope, benefits, and integration choices to act (Swanson et al., 2025). Hype, by contrast, can thrive on ambiguity, allowing multiple audiences to project their hopes and interpretations onto an innovation well before a coherent community forms. Put differently, an organising vision acts as a sense-making device for a community; hype functions as an attention-making device that can precede community formation and, at times, help bring one into being.

2.3.4 Promise

In the Sociology of Expectations, a *promise* is a problem-oriented commitment that maps a pathway from an identified challenge to a prospective technological solution. Numerous terms – such as promise, expectations, visions, and imaginaries – have been used within the Sociology of Expectations with varying consistency and are often employed in overlapping ways. These differences in terminology can partly be attributed to the distinct initial problems they address, with each term carrying a heritage that has influenced subsequent discourse. The concept of promise, for example, forms the foundation of the Sociology of Expectations, yet it is frequently discussed alongside the notion of vision. For instance, Borup et al. (2006) often refer to 'expectations and visions' in tandem, reflecting their interconnected roles.

Promise is also used interchangeably with hype, yet each concept encapsulates distinct dynamics. Brown and Michael (2003, p. 3) describe promises as 'crucial to providing the dynamism and momentum upon which so many ventures in science and technology depend', highlighting their role in framing a pathway towards specific solutions. Similarly, Joly (2010, p. 5) observes that promises focus on addressing a clearly defined 'problem which has to be fixed', making them particularly compelling when the problem is urgent and widely recognised.

While hype and promise share a focus on mobilising attention and resources, they diverge in scope and emphasis. Research on promises examines how generic claims are translated into specific, achievable requirements and obligations over time. Promises are typically more structured and directed, anchoring innovation as a targeted response to particular stakeholders or societal challenges. In contrast, hype operates more diffusely, amplifying the urgency and visibility of promises while broadening their appeal. It thrives on creating excitement and attention across a competitive landscape, emphasising the potential of multiple innovations to dominate the field and securing resources for expected winners.

Promises are foundational elements in the innovation narrative, setting precise trajectories for development and offering a rationale for investment and support (Berkhout, 2006). Hype, however, magnifies the scope of these promises, leveraging the dynamics of attention and commitment to generate widespread anticipation. Where promises articulate targeted goals and solution pathways, hype acts as a force multiplier – extending reach, intensifying urgency, and inserting those promises into broader competitive contexts.

2.3.5 Sociotechnical Visions

Sociotechnical visions articulate value-laden images of preferred futures that link technological change to social orders, policy goals, and cultural commitments. The work on visions starts with the problem faced by technology application developers and later emerging technology R&D programmes in envisioning a future technology and the world it would operate in. Arguably, the starting point was the concept of 'script' arising from Akrich's (1992) early work on user representations. The vision concept was used to analyse the sociopolitical agendas informing particular design choices. A key challenge with novel technologies is that there are no actual users or markets in the early stages of radical innovation. Therefore, what mobilises support is visions of potential users and uses. Scholarship here aims to make explicit the (often tacit) sets of ideas that shape the development effort. Innovators are seen to mobilise visions and expectations, with visions thus having a normative role in motivating support (while temporarily ignoring counter-programmes and their dystopian vision) (Berkhout, 2006). So, envisioning is the work of bringing these representations into existence and mobilising support around particular representations and scripts.

Visions represent broad, collective images of the future that capture a community or society's shared expectations regarding the trajectory and benefits of scientific and technological advancements (Konrad et al., 2016). As Berkhout (2006, p. 300) notes, 'visions of the future tend to be 'moralised', in the sense of being encoded and decoded as either utopias or dystopias'. Thus, visions are deeply rooted in cultural values and societal goals, providing a framework for conceptualising and working towards a collective future that influences the direction of technological development by aligning research, policy, and social objectives. Similarly, as Konrad et al. (2016, p. 3) note, visions 'imply normative connotations, often being statements of desirable or preferable futures, while not necessarily including assessments of likelihood or plausibility'.

In contrast, while hype is more focused on capturing immediate attention and tends to be short-lived, visions are longer-term, stable, and woven into societal frameworks. Hype can support a vision by attracting attention and resources to bring about a particular future; however, a vision is not solely reliant on hype. Instead, they form part of a larger narrative about society's aspirations for its technological potential. While hype typically builds around specific visions, the latter, as Konrad et al. (2016, p. 3) point out, 'relay a fuller portrait of an alternative world that includes revised social orders, governance structures, and societal values'.

2.3.6 Sociotechnical Imaginaries

Sociotechnical imaginaries extend visions by embedding future technologies within institutionally stabilised, publicly performed narratives about desirable social orders. Imaginaries present a future technology and the world in which it is embedded, providing commentary on why particular collectively imagined societies are emerging and being upheld through institutions and public discourse. The notion of imaginary thus extends the account of the better world into which technology will be introduced and explicitly recognises the roles and practices involved. Though the term can be traced back to Gregory (2000) and Hyysalo (2006), Jasanoff has popularised it. Jasanoff and Kim (2015, p. 6) define sociotechnical imaginaries as 'collectively held, institutionally stabilised, and publicly performed visions of desirable futures, animated by shared understandings of forms of social life and social order attainable through, and supportive of, advances in science and technology'. Hype differs from an imaginary in that it does not ask you to judge the direction of innovation or choose a desirable or preferred future. Instead, it generates interest in innovation, bringing it to the attention of key players in the innovation landscape and facilitating the securing of investments.

2.3.7 Hype's Characteristics

Having compared hype with related concepts, we can now provisionally distil what makes it distinctive as a phenomenon of interest. We identify four core characteristics that differentiate hype and help explain its influence on technologies: (i) mobilisation and interessement, (ii) exaggeration and the 'Hiding Hand', (iii) uncertainty amplification, and (iv) shifting focus and demobilisation. Together, these dynamics illuminate how hype mobilises resources, amplifies excitement, directs (and redirects) attention, and shapes the innovation process.

2.3.7.1 Mobilisation and Interessement

Hype primarily functions to mobilise attention and resources, especially in contexts marked by uncertainty and unpredictable outcomes, such as the projections surrounding radical technologies. At its core, hype generates attention and the conditions for investment in radical or disruptive technologies. It concentrates attention and attracts resources in the face of high uncertainty, drawing diverse actors into provisional alignment – what Callon (1984) terms *interessement*.

The funding and interest that hype attracts can accelerate innovation. Brown (2003, p. 11) observes that the resources mobilised by hype are 'fundamental to producing the incentives and obligations necessary' for a new technological sector to grow. By priming audiences and committing resources before performance evidence exists, hype can speed technological development beyond what incremental, evidence-led investment would permit. Its generativity lies in its capacity to embed a technology in the collective imagination, reshaping expectations ahead of demonstrable proof.

Radical innovation requires that belief precede evidence. While some view this as hype producing 'misleading claims' – implying unproductive technologies or overreach (Vinsel & Russell, 2020; Min, 2024) – early unverifiability need not imply deception. There are many reasons why claims cannot be fully verified at the outset (Konrad, 2006):

Limited Evidence. A technology may be beneficial, but there has not yet been sufficient time or opportunity to collect and appraise performance data. Radical novelty can generate Knightian uncertainty (Knight, 1921; see Chapter 3).

Social Learning. Novel technologies are often immature and require iterative refinement – in the product/service and the surrounding socio-technical context – before productivity can be realised (Arrow, 1962; Sørensen, 1996).

Scaling Dependencies. Without a critical mass of users and complementary producers, cost-effectiveness, profitability, and sustainability remain indeterminate (Williams et al., 2005).

Given these constraints, some level of inflated expectation is necessary – and, some would argue, beneficial (Potts, 2017) – enabling promising technologies to move towards realisation. Therefore, the test of whether hype is productive relies not on whether it is true but on whether it is 'performative' – insofar as it allows a promising technology to come to fruition. By enabling investors, entrepreneurs, and collaborators to behave as though the proposed outcomes are real, hype helps bring those outcomes about. In short, hype is more than mere optimism – it propels investment, collaboration, and experimentation towards the hyped vision (see Tenet Five for how this process unfolds).

2.3.7.2 Exaggeration and the 'Hiding Hand'

How might we conceptualise the role of exaggeration in hype? On the face of it, overstated promises and inflated expectations seem problematic, setting the stage for inevitable disappointment. Yet in the history of innovation, exaggeration often appears to have a generative role. Rather than merely distorting, it can stimulate action and commitment that might not otherwise occur.

Hirschman's (1967) idea of the 'Hiding Hand' provides one way to make sense of this paradox. The idea suggests that actors often embark on ambitious projects with misplaced or 'blind' confidence without fully understanding the challenges. While this initial misjudgement might appear detrimental, Hirschman (1967) posits that the subsequent confrontation with unforeseen challenges triggers a resourceful and creative response, ultimately transforming potential failure into success. Ironically, as Hirschman sees it, misplaced confidence – believing a project will be more straightforward than it is – enables the courage to start it in the first place. As Hirschman (1967, p. 13) explains, the hiding hand's value lies in 'inducing risk-averters to commit themselves to risk-taking behaviour', thereby enabling an 'acceleration of economic growth'.

This principle is especially instructive in analysing hype. The 'exaggeration of benefits' (Hirschman, 1967, p. 26), a hallmark of hype, serves a similar purpose: warding off the 'missed opportunity' of inaction driven by uncertainty or scepticism. The utility of hype extends beyond generating initial enthusiasm; it also fosters resilience and adaptability when unexpected challenges arise. As Hirschman (1967, p. 15) describes, market actors who have committed significant resources and energy to a project become motivated to 'generate all the problem-solving energy of which they are capable'. In this way, hype, like the Hiding Hand, transforms adversity into a catalyst for innovation and progress. This interplay between optimism and adaptability is central to transforming hype into realised innovations. It aligns with the broader discussions in *After Hype*, where hype is framed not merely as a by-product of innovation cycles but as a strategic tool for navigating the complexities and uncertainties of technological futures (Mouritsen & Kreiner, 2016).

2.3.7.3 Uncertainty Amplification

Hype is closely associated with breakthrough or disruptive technologies. Radical claims strain established evaluative frameworks, opening contested arenas in which bold projections proliferate. Beckert (2016, p. 186) notes that 'while levels of uncertainty differ among innovations, growth dynamics and high profits tend to come from the most radical ones, which are generally also the ones with the highest levels of uncertainty'. Felt et al. (2007) similarly show that hype both draws on and magnifies uncertainty about the future.

Crucially, the most-hyped technologies are framed as radically disruptive, and their claims can destabilise – or even render obsolete –

established evaluative frameworks. McBride *et al.* (2024, p. 410) describe this as the ensuing 'battle for assessment contexts' as actors compete to define the metrics by which these technologies should be judged. When no settled measures exist, bold projections more easily 'get a hearing' (Borup *et al.*, 2006, p. 410). Each wave of radical announcements enlarges this vacuum, triggering new rounds of hype. This destabilisation is not a side effect; it is what allows hype to flourish. By undermining established evaluative infrastructures, disruptive technologies create profound Knightian uncertainty (Knight, 1921; see Chapter 3), where new claims can circulate freely, inviting a proliferation of related projections (see Figure 2.1).

Our book captures the moment when radically framed technologies prompted industry analysts to develop new evaluation tools. They initially lacked metrics that could accommodate two critical developments: (i) the rise of emerging technologies (Chapters 6 and 7) and (ii) the proliferation of disruptive start-ups (Chapters 4 and 5). Both shifts initially sat outside established evaluative frameworks, creating fertile ground for hype to take hold. Metrics designed for mature

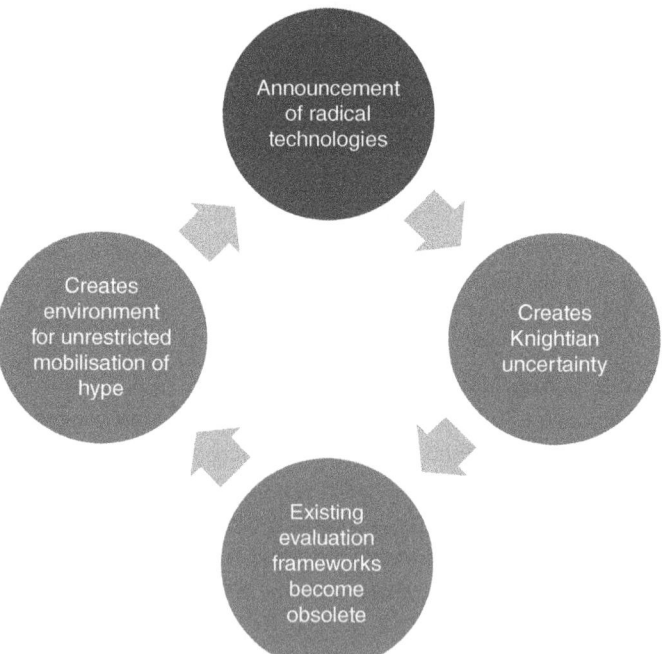

Figure 2.1 Battle for assessment contexts.

products – such as the Magic Quadrant – proved inadequate. We show how industry analysts – initially slow to recognise these developments – were eventually compelled to respond. They introduced instruments like the Hype Cycle Chart (HCC) and Cool Vendors, which foreground the prospective performance of emerging technologies and new ventures.

2.3.7.4 Shifting Focus and Demobilisation

Hype Rarely Stands Still. Unlike relatively stable expectations (imaginaries, visions, promises), hype is transient and shifting: it may surge rapidly to attract interest and investment, then fade, fragment, or migrate to the next opportunity. Because hype is transient, support can unwind, and attention can shift rapidly, disengaging actors from current projects and redirecting them towards the next opportunity. Its transient nature introduces phases of demobilisation: when expectations stall or disappoint, attention, investment, and organisational commitment can contract (Ruef & Markard, 2010). Importantly, hype not only generates new interest; it also reallocates attention, pulling resources away from ongoing developments. Stakeholders with weaker ties can switch allegiance quickly when a new, more hyped innovation appears (Bakker & Budde, 2012).

Promoting a new hyped technology often entails a strategic distancing from incumbent alternatives. Proponents typically have to 'fight against old technologies', and, as Joly (2010, p. 4) points out, that 'battle is not easily won'. Emphasising radical novelty helps recast existing solutions as outdated.

One way hype accelerates such shifts is by creating a sense of urgency. Innovation is often portrayed as a global race, with the implication that there is 'no time to lose' (Felt et al., 2007, p. 79). Hype pressures as well as excites. Fear of missing out (FOMO; Vinsel & Russell, 2020) implies that only early adopters – those bold enough to embrace the latest breakthrough – will emerge as winners. Under the grip of such promissory narratives, we may, Felt and colleagues caution, 'risk subordinating ourselves' to the imagined futures they project (2007, p. 79).

2.4 Tenet Four: Hype as an Actor Concept – Used and Managed Knowingly by Practitioners

Up to now, we have been examining hype from an *analytical* perspective – how we, as researchers, might conceptualise hype's origins, distribution, and distinct features. However, we want to shift the view to consider how market actors involved in innovation themselves understand and manage hype. We will argue that hype is not just an analyst's category; it is also an *actor's* category. While concepts such as imaginaries, promises, and visions function purely as analyst constructs, hype uniquely operates as both. The very word 'hype' is used by practitioners, investors, industry commentators, etc., as part of their everyday vocabulary. Put differently, hype functions as a 'folk concept' (Swedburgh, 2018) in innovation, meaning that it carries practical significance for those actors involved.

Recognising hype as an actor concept has important implications. It implies the existence of a lay theory of hype – one that may diverge from social-science accounts. Academic treatments often frame hype as noise or misleading exaggeration, yet our fieldwork indicates that market actors deploy a richer taxonomy of hype distinctions than scholars often credit (Swedberg, 2018). They sort 'good' from 'bad' hype and calibrate their language accordingly.

Take, for example, analyst relations (AR) experts – the professionals discussed in this book who coach technology ventures on how to pitch to industry analysts. They provide detailed guidance on crafting promissory narratives and explicitly caution against using specific 'hyped-up' terms that may undermine credibility. These include phrases like 'game changer', 'best in class', 'industry-leading', 'world-beating', and 'we have no competitors'. When overused, such language serves as a red flag to seasoned analysts, signalling either a lack of substance or naive over-enthusiasm.

This kind of practitioner insight forms part of what we mean by hype as an actor concept (see De Togni et al., 2024). To illustrate this, we compiled a list of commonly discouraged hype terms (see Box 2.1), drawn from AR advisory materials, showing that practitioners operate with their own informal heuristics for evaluating and deploying hype.

Why does it matter that market actors have a rich understanding of hype? For one, it suggests that academic analysis tends to produce a simplified, 'thin' account. Pollner (2002) warns of the dangers of 'conceptual deflation', where scholarly work fails to provide new insights or challenge taken-for-granted assumptions. The upshot is that we tell those we study what they already know (or even less than they know).

Box 2.1 List of hyped words to be avoided during analyst briefings*

'First'
'Game changer'
'Only'
'Superiority'
'Best in class'
'World class'
'The Leader' and related...'
'Industry leading'
'Market leading'
'We always beat [a market leader]'
'Top tier'
'We have no competitors' and related...'
'Our only competition is in-house development'
'Only indirect competitors are enterprise home-grown applications'
'We never see [a market leader]'
'We've open sourced our code'

*source: List compiled from an analyst relations (AR) website

---

One example is the growing number of academic studies suggesting that particular technologies have entered a 'hype cycle' (e.g. Geiger & Gross, 2017). Though such an observation may be helpful, scholarly discussion needs to do more than reproduce actor terms, which may simply confirm rather than challenge prevailing perceptions. One goal of this book is to develop a more nuanced empirical understanding of how hype is generated, assessed, and consumed, as well as its impact. If our existing analytical concepts are not significantly different (or perhaps even inferior) to those of the individuals we study, then we may need to develop new ones. In this book, we use the actor term but locate it within a more carefully considered framework.

While scholarship has not shown much interest in hype as an actor concept, some exceptions exist. A frequent starting point has been to emphasise the colloquial connotations of hype as overstatement. Thus, Palavicino (2016, p. 149) describes hype as a 'strategic act of exaggeration by innovation actors'. However, Wüstenhagen *et al.*

(2009, p. 123) note innovators' awareness of expectation dynamics and how they 'use them to their advantage, communicating (and sometimes overstating) the promise of the technology to garner these resources' (see also Minkkinen et al., 2023).

Birch's (2023) concept of 'reflexive expectations' goes further, highlighting actors' gameful generation of strategic narratives. He notes that actors are 'deliberately and consciously generating stories or acting reflexively concerning them as part of their investment expectations, decisions, and strategies' (Birch, 2023, p. 45). This means that at least some actors are *self-aware* about the game of hype – they know they are constructing narratives and do so with intent, adjusting their message as needed to keep investors interested.

One striking example of an actor concept is the Hype Cycle Chart (HCC), which Rip (2019) characterises as a 'folk theory'. Developed by the analyst firm Gartner, the HCC depicts the typical trajectory of hype associated with emerging technologies. While Rip critiques the model as being 'plainly wrong' in empirical terms, he also acknowledges its resonance, describing it as offering a 'plausible storyline about how things go' (2019, p. 361).

This discussion highlights a broader tension in scholarly debates around such tools. The assumption is that their value may not lie in empirical accuracy but in their social robustness and performative influence. As Rip puts it, the power of folk theories stems from their widespread circulation – 'their robustness derives from their being generally accepted, and thus part of a repertoire current in a group or in our culture more generally' (2019, p. 361). This insight invites us to take seriously how these devices operate, not just as representations but as instruments of coordination and influence.

Indeed, academic criticism of hype tools like the HCC can miss their practical significance. For instance, Borup and colleagues (2006, p. 292) have criticised the HCC for producing a 'highly linear understanding of a technology's path dependency and fails to account for the way artefacts or technologies actually change over time in a continual and practical process of reconfiguring and being reconfigured in use'. While these critiques are valid from an innovation scholar's standpoint, they overlook how such tools have become embedded in practice. Many decision-makers are aware that technologies may deviate from the HCC pattern (Chapter 6), but the key point is that it has become integral to the actor's toolkit, influencing market behaviour.

Therefore, studies of hype should incorporate how such folk theories of hype shape real-world actions (rather than only pointing out their flaws).

More scholarly attention could be dedicated to understanding hype as an actor concept. This is particularly important, given the emergence of hype's new actors and industry analyst tools like the HCC, which potentially encourage innovation communities to react differently to the uncertainties generated by the sea of competing claims. Embracing hype as an actor concept pushes us to ask new questions. For instance, how does introducing tools like the HCC change how technology adopters navigate hype? We suspect that with the institutionalisation of such hype tools, market actors no longer react to hype in the way they did before their introduction. For instance, as discussed in Chapter 6, the very act of saying a specific technology is in 'The Trough of Disillusionment now' (one of the HCC's stages) provides a narrative for timing investments that differs from the past.

This evolution suggests that the phenomenon of hype itself is changing. As actors become more reflexive – aware of recurring patterns and increasingly equipped with tools to manage them – hype waves may now inflate and deflate in ways that differ from the past. Hype is shifting from something that simply happens to actors to something they actively navigate and shape. This transformation invites a corresponding shift in scholarly approaches.

2.5 Tenet Five: Hype's Influence – From Performativity (Enacting Futures) to Reflexivity (Adapting Narratives)

One of the most contested questions in the study of hype concerns its ability not merely to describe possible futures but to help bring them into being. Does hype simply gesture towards a potential horizon, or can it actively contribute to realising that future (*performativity*) by mobilising belief, investment, and coordinated action? Or must it adapt as reality unfolds (*reflexivity*)?

Early work in the Sociology of Expectations and related fields focused on the *performativity* of expectations, suggesting that strong expectations can become self-fulfilling (Kriechbaum et al., 2021). Brown (2003, p. 5) argued that 'hype is constitutive', mobilising the 'future into the present'. Beckert (2013, p. 226, *our emphasis*) likewise suggested that 'imaginings of future states become *determinate*'. Garud *et al.* (2014a, p. 1183, *our emphasis*) observed that 'innovation is *driven* by entrepreneurs' imagination of the future'. More recently, Bareis and Katzenbach (2022, p. 876) pointed to the performativity of national artificial intelligence (AI) strategies. As they note, governments do not simply describe technological futures – they actively participate in 'coproducing the instalment of these futures' by backing visions with 'massive resources and investments', thereby 'locking in' particular 'trajectories'.

Together, these arguments support a performative view of hype: it does not just forecast; it can help enact what it proclaims by attracting resources and framing problems and solutions. This perspective offered a powerful rejoinder to dismissals of hype as mere exaggeration or noise. Traditional academic perspectives struggled with the fact that future outcomes are unknowable until hindsight reveals them – often too late to be useful (Master & Resnik, 2013). Performativity shifted the analytical focus: rather than asking whether early claims are 'true', it examined how they mobilise actors and resources in ways that can change what eventually becomes true.

However, the performativity thesis has not gone unchallenged. Critics note that it does not fully explain why some expectations become self-fulfilling while others are revised, deferred, or abandoned (Oomen *et al.*, 2022). In addition, the presumed performativity of hype often rests on episodic case studies that focus on the articulation of visions while implicitly assuming their eventual realisation. In doing so, researchers risk being drawn into the narrative frames of 'promise entrepreneurs', blurring the line between aspirational rhetoric and unfolding reality (e.g. Goldfarb & Kirsch, 2019, p. 61).

While the concept of performativity offers valuable insight, it requires more qualified application. The idea of *simple* performativity – where an a priori vision cleanly and fully shapes reality – is arguably no more plausible than imagining an engineer or manager could specify a successful innovation entirely in advance and then implement it exactly as planned (MacKenzie, 2009). When such direct performative effects do occur, they are often linked more to failure than to success (see MacKenzie, 2006, on counter-performativity). For example, branding a technology as 'overhyped' can dampen investment and support, potentially derailing a project that might otherwise have succeeded – though such negative feedback loops remain underexplored and merit further empirical study.

Crucially, context matters – and particularly the stage of innovation. In early-stage, exploratory science, hype can play a constitutive role in shaping the very emergence of a field. Stephens, Kind, and Lyall (2018) demonstrate how exaggerated future claims surrounding nanotechnology helped secure sustained R&D funding, attracting resources, attention, and talent over time.

Yet as innovations move towards commercialisation and broader diffusion, the role of hype often changes. In later-stage, market-facing contexts, hype is tempered by immediate feedback and heightened accountability. Narratives face closer scrutiny and must continually evolve to meet the shifting expectations of diverse, discerning audiences. Under these conditions, the kind of straightforward performativity sometimes seen in earlier stages becomes far less likely. Instead, hype takes on a more *transitional* (O'Connor, 2004) or *provisional* (Mützel, 2022) character – constantly reshaped as ventures pivot, iterate, and reposition themselves in response to ongoing evaluation.

To capture this adaptive narrative work, we draw on Birch's (2023) concept of *reflexive expectations*. While initial expectations often stem from compelling visions of radical innovation, they rarely remain static. As ventures transition from technoscientific promise to financial and commercial arenas, their narratives pivot to engage new evaluative audiences and criteria. These stories are continually revised as financing processes unfold and strategic roadmaps are recalibrated. As Birch (2023, p. 45) observes, entrepreneurs 'construct new stories or amend old ones to make valuation judgements and attract investment'.

In the Juvo case, for example, we observed how an initial focus on the product's disruptive technological potential gradually gave way to stories about market readiness, customer adoption, and value creation. These shifts did not occur in a straight line, nor were they under the sole control of the start-up founder. Instead, they were collaborative and iterative, involving analysts, AR specialists, investors, and other audiences who each contributed to reshaping the narrative.

Reframing hype's influence from performativity alone to a combination of performativity and reflexivity offers a more nuanced understanding of the complex, adaptive life of hyped expectations. Rather than a one-off performative act, hype – particularly in later stages – operates as a dynamic, negotiated, and recursive process in which claims are continually reworked in response to shifting evidence, audiences, and incentives. As Chapter 4 will show through its analysis of start-up storytelling, entrepreneurs must learn to adapt and recalibrate their narratives as they move from early-stage funding pitches to later-stage analyst briefings.

2.6 Tenet Six: When Hype Matters – Shifting Roles across the Innovation Lifecycle

The previous discussion highlights a critical gap in current scholarship where it fails to adequately engage with the different temporal settings of hyped expectations, particularly how hype operates across both early *and* later stages of innovation. While the Sociology of Expectations scholarship focused primarily on early-stage developments, our analysis reveals hype's crucial role *throughout* the innovation lifecycle, especially in processes of market making and market operation. This limitation is problematic because it tacitly underplays or ignores how hype continues into later phases, leaving us with a dearth of studies on how hype operates in market situations.

Prior research overwhelmingly positions hype as a 'front-end' phenomenon. Brown (2003, p. 11) places hype in the 'opening moments of resource and agenda building', emphasising how 'the whole language of novelty, newness and revolutionary potential is actually part and parcel of the hyperbolic discourse surrounding the early or opening moments of resource and agenda building'. Similarly, Wüstenhagen *et al.* (2009, p. 123) emphasise expectation dynamics in 'earliest stages of technology-driven innovation', while Palavicino (2016, p. 144) notes how hype 'brings actors together in early stages of technology development to take high-risk decisions under high uncertainty'. Taken together, these accounts suggest that once technologies solidify – products exist and markets form – hype recedes behind more concrete considerations.

This upstream bias has consequences. We know far more about hype before markets exist than about how it is translated, operationalised, and governed once market actors must buy, sell, compare, and adopt competing offerings (Gardner et al., 2015). Integrating upstream expectation work with downstream market decision-making remains rare (Rotolo et al., 2015). Hardly any scholarship has integrated this with the downstream world of market actors and organisational decision-makers, who decide whether to invest in particular firms or the decisions facing organisational users concerning the adoption of specific products. Despite its concerns about addressing futures, scholarship has failed to engage with these different temporal settings and how processes of creating, circulating, and consuming hype are differently modulated between early and later phases.

We extend hype analysis across the innovation lifecycle. Hype does not dissipate at market entry; it evolves – and can even intensify – as stakes, competition, and formal structures grow. Our research aims to bridge this gap by extending hype analysis to later phases, specifically the development of applications and their adoption by market actors, such as technology adopters. We contend that hype evolves its role throughout the innovation lifecycle rather than merely being a transient wave that dissipates after the introductory phase. For instance, by the time an innovation reaches the market, there are often more financial resources at stake, more competitors, and more formal structures in place – all of which shape the form of hype.

To help unpack this, we distinguish four overlapping stages that recur across many innovation journeys (Bergek et al., 2008): (1) exploratory science/field-forming (pre-market); (2) translational/venture-building (pre-commercial); (3) early market/market-making (initial customers, few vendors); and (4) established market/market operation (wider adoption, comparative evaluation). These stages provide a helpful framework for understanding how the role and management of hype shift over time. Hype plays different roles and is mediated by various actors and instruments at each stage of the process.

We find Konrad and Palavicino's (2016) study of graphene useful in this regard. While early hype helped spawn a research field and initial start-ups (stages 1 and 2), one might have expected that hype would die down once the initial excitement settled. However, their study shows that hype continued to shape the field over time (stage 3). A pivotal trigger came when the Nobel Prize was awarded for graphene research in 2010: the award reignited interest, attracted additional funding, conferred credibility, and fuelled renewed promises of applications.

Moreover, they note that the management of hype – and the actors involved in doing so – changed in these later phases. Konrad and Bohle (2019, p. 102) elaborate on how the graphene field witnessed an influx of policymakers and market actors engaging in 'practices of futuring', where there was the provision of 'market forecasts, carrying out foresight processes (e.g. Delphi studies), hype assessments, or developing dynamic models, scenarios or roadmaps'. These are hallmarks of stage 3 (early market) and stage 4 (established market), where more formalised instruments and governance structures begin to shape the trajectory of innovation. Konrad and colleagues argue that this moved graphene into a new phase with enhanced structure, governance, and planning. Yet despite these shifts, hype remained a driving force – now institutionalised through strategic roadmaps, government initiatives, and industry consortia.

In these later stages (3 and 4), hype also begins to perform boundary-setting and coordination functions. Logue and Grimes (2022, p. 7) point out that in later stages, actors leverage hype to formalise field boundaries and networks: actors 'take advantage of hype to configure boundaries around the field, create more efficient exchanges within the field, and situate their own ventures relationally within important networks'.

Our book will highlight how a key aspect of the digital economy is the prominent role of market gatekeepers, such as industry analysts, in these later stages. These actors typically enter when an emerging technology is on the verge of broader adoption – in the early market or established market phase (stages 3 and 4). They translate diffuse expectations into actionable decision inputs for buyers. Their focus is on the near future rather than the distant horizon. They introduce promissory products (like categories and rankings) that effectively operationalise hype, turning it into something that can be rated, ranked, and digested by decision-makers. By doing so, they bring a certain closure to the open-ended hype of earlier stages.

However, our book shows that these market gatekeepers are beginning to enter the process earlier, as the transition from stage 2 (venture-building) to stage 3 (early market) occurs, with technologies moving from translational efforts to initial commercialisation. Industry analysts, for instance, often produce their first reports on a technology when a handful of vendors begin to sell to customers, even if the technology is not yet mainstream (e.g. Cool Vendor appellations and HCCs).

Our contribution – and the focus of the empirical chapters that follow – is to demonstrate how hype is managed, particularly in stages 2, 3, and 4, when technologies transition from emergence to market consolidation. As technologies become more established, hype does not evaporate; it becomes embedded in promissory products that continue to shape expectations and flows of resources.

2.7 Tenet Seven: Living Up to the Hype – Emerging Accountability Mechanisms

A common presumption is that actors are rarely held accountable for the claims they make, creating a grace period in which bold assertions face little immediate scrutiny or sanction if they are not substantiated. This assumption rests on two key conditions: (i) the belief that there is little in the way of an evaluative infrastructure surrounding hyped claims; and (ii) the observation that proof often arrives only after attention, actors, and market conditions have shifted. In such circumstances, those who make grand claims may never be penalised; the accountability window can close before verdicts are rendered.

First, Joly (2010, p. 7) notes, 'there are few ways to assess [hype's] validity'; Grodal and Granqvist (2014, p. 141) similarly argue that without 'existing benchmarks for evaluation', this means that expectations 'become self-perpetuating and give rise to fads, hypes, and bubbles'. Second, Rip (2018) highlights the innovator's dilemma: they must hype their ideas enough to gain support, but the evidence to confirm or refute their claims will only emerge later, by which point audiences may have moved on (van Lente, 2012; Master & Resnik, 2013). By then, the evaluative context may have changed, and the original promissory conditions may no longer apply.

Indeed, according to Joly (2010), tools like the Gartner HCC have helped normalise deferred disappointment by building a 'Trough of disillusionment' into the expected trajectory. As he notes, '[o]ne of the effects of the cycle is to naturalise the disillusionment' – the 'Trough of disillusionment' is built into the tool as a natural, even necessary step in the innovation process (Joly, 2010, p. 13), thus further institutionalising the deferral of evaluation and deepening the accountability gap.

These perspectives rightly highlight the fluid and promissory nature of hype. However, a central argument of this book is that expectations are no longer as unaccountable as they once were. We contend that the landscape has shifted: hyped claims are increasingly subject to scrutiny and formal evaluation. In contrast to earlier eras where hype could run free (until a 'crash': see Garud et al., 2014b), today we see emerging mechanisms that hold promise-makers to account (albeit in new ways).

As innovation moves from speculative projections to more concrete phases of market implementation, new forms of accountability begin to crystallise. Yet we still know little about how these mechanisms function in practice. Beckert and Ergen (2021, p. 13) observe that the 'evaluative structures' surrounding hyped expectations represent a 'vast and understudied research field', highlighting the need for deeper empirical and conceptual enquiry.

Martin (2015) offers a useful framing for how accountability tightens over time, contrasting a 'regime of hope' with a 'regime of truth'. In the regime of hope, ventures like start-ups operate within a speculative space characterised by uncertainty and anticipation: they may have 'no products on the market', remain 'poorly integrated' into existing industry structures, and trade promissory assets that cannot yet be fully valued (Martin, 2015, p. 434). Here, hype functions as a key mechanism for attracting attention, credibility, and resources.

By contrast, the regime of truth marks a more mature stage of market engagement, where ventures have 'products on the market, significant sales and profits, a relatively large number of products in late-stage development', and are 'well-integrated' into the industry – what Martin calls 'the real economy' (2015, p. 437). At this point, the scope for speculation narrows, and demands for demonstrable results intensify (see also Hogarth, 2017).

Beckert's (2016) analysis also captures this shift, showing how early 'myths' about the future give way to demands for evidence and performance. Cultural Entrepreneurship scholars make a similar point: while exaggerated narratives may help attract initial interest and investment, they eventually entangle entrepreneurs in webs of accountability. Lounsbury and Glynn (2001), for instance, demonstrate that ventures founded on unverifiable or overly grandiose claims face reputational risks. Garud et al. (2014b) show how, during the dotcom crash, many firms were forced to revise their stories in light of missed milestones and shaken investor confidence.

In short, expectations remain pliable only up to a point. Logue and Grimes (2022) argue that ventures become bound by the stories they tell; to 'live up to the hype', they must ultimately deliver evidence. Early in this process, proxies in the form of 'social proof' – endorsements, awards, media coverage – can sustain credibility. But without the progressive accumulation of such markers, legitimacy erodes, and audiences begin to question not only the promise but the venture's capacity to perform.

While Logue and Grimes (2022) effectively illuminate the role of informal accountability mechanisms – such as social proof – in sustaining hype, we argue that more structured and formalised evaluation processes are playing an increasingly influential role in the digital economy. These include rankings, ratings, certifications, league tables, and other structured performance metrics that make technologies more comparable, auditable, and governable.

Among the most significant actors in this shift are industry analysts, who shape how hype is interpreted and made accountable. Unlike informal endorsements, which rely on reputation, charisma, or peer validation, analysts offer structured and ostensibly objective assessments that influence how technologies are understood, valued, and prioritised within markets. Taken together, this progression – from soft to institutionalised forms of accountability – is central to understanding how the digital economy governs its futures. Hype is not sustained by exuberant promissory narratives alone but also by the infrastructures that discipline, translate, and, at times, tame them.

Several important questions remain unresolved: How does the digital economy transition from a 'regime of hope' to a 'regime of truth'? Who mediates the shift from promissory claims to demonstrable outcomes? At what point do audiences begin to demand evidence beyond social proof? And how do evaluation tools influence both the timing and content of narrative pivots? These are questions we take up in the chapters that follow.

* * *

Together, these seven tenets provide a foundation for treating hype not as a peripheral phenomenon but as a dynamic, structured, and strategic resource shaping the digital economy. They also set the stage for a critical shift in focus: from understanding what hype is to examining how actors respond to it. In Chapter 3, we explore how organisations navigate the uncertainties generated by hype, sometimes treating it as a source of risk to be mitigated, and at other times as a resource to be cultivated.

3 | Decision-Making about Unpredictable Technology Futures

The previous chapters have begun to examine how hype is created, circulated, and increasingly institutionalised within the digital economy. We now shift our focus from producing hype to navigating, interpreting, and evaluating it. This chapter demonstrates that in an era of continual disruption, decision-makers are pressured to treat hype not as mere noise but as a strategic factor – one that demands deliberate evaluation, careful timing, and active management. We begin by illustrating the stakes through historical and contemporary examples, then examine the challenges posed by uncertainty in innovation, and conclude by showing how organisations are responding through emerging hype-evaluation practices. We trace the rise of hype's new experts – most notably industry analysts – tasked with helping organisations separate genuinely promising innovations from overblown claims.

This chapter, therefore, turns to the organisational decision-makers who must make sense of, and act within, an environment saturated with competing and exaggerated technological narratives. An unprecedented surge in digital innovations – particularly those billed as radical or disruptive – means that organisations face a dual challenge: spotting genuine opportunities while mitigating the risks of chasing inflated promises.

Consider a start-up like Juvo, which claims to disrupt traditional banking models. The instinctive reaction might be to dismiss such rhetoric outright. Yet, as argued here, decision-makers can no longer afford to ignore such claims. Hyped innovations have become a strategic variable with potentially life-or-death consequences for firms (Arnold et al., 2022).

A historical example illustrates how organisational responses to hype have evolved. One of the authors conducted research in the 1980s on the financial sector (Fincham et al., 1995), finding that banks at the time underestimated the disruptive potential of automated teller machines (ATMs). Professional bankers of that era dismissed predictions of significant industry change as speculative and unrealistic.

As their terminology reveals, they saw ATMs as mere extensions of the teller function – a means of improving efficiency rather than a transformative innovation. Yet within a decade, ATMs had not only proliferated but also paved the way for online banking – a transformation those bankers failed to foresee. This perspective reflected a wider mindset of the time, which treated computing technologies as incremental aids rather than as drivers of fundamental change. Indeed, ATMs – initially introduced simply as an 'automatic' teller – were not recognised as precursors to a major industry transformation (see Locatelli et al., 2021).

These historical missteps highlight the risks associated with discounting technological hype while underestimating the transformative potential of emerging innovations. Juvo's ambitious assertions may indeed be inflated, yet the possibility remains that they could catalyse significant disruption in the banking sector. This highlights a recurrent organisational dilemma: dismissing hype risks forgoing genuine opportunities for innovation while embracing it risks committing resources to ultimately insubstantial promises. Compounding this dilemma is a further contemporary challenge: organisations must increasingly navigate a *proliferation* of overlapping and competing promissory narratives – each pitched as a strategic opportunity or threat – without becoming paralysed or distracted.

3.1 The Timing of Innovation Responses

Today's landscape demands a fundamentally different approach to innovation. Kumaraswamy et al. (2018, p. 1026) observe that the twenty-first century is characterised by 'continual disruption in which technological innovations and new business model changes affect not just individual firms, but entire industries and ecosystems'. In this environment, understanding and responding to hype – in essence, managing the *timing* of innovation responses – has become a crucial issue.

Innovation has long been recognised as important for an organisation to survive in an increasingly competitive market; however, its role is now seen as far more strategic. In the past, innovation was viewed primarily as a way to sustain productivity and competitiveness (Godin, 2015). Today, however, it is increasingly seen as a strategic matter because of its potential to transform the industrial landscape and radically restructure the position of players within that landscape. Incumbent organisations may find themselves at risk of being displaced by challengers wielding radical new technologies (Freeman, 1994) or disruptive business models (Christensen, 1997), generating what Schumpeter (1942) characterised as 'gales of creative destruction'. Conversely, these developments open up opportunities for challengers like Juvo, which can ride these waves to achieve rapid growth, higher profits, and perhaps ultimately exclude rivals in winner-takes-all competitions (Palmié et al., 2020). The stakes are thus rising significantly.

This shift in focus to the strategic impact of innovation has coincided with a dramatic increase in the pace and dynamism of technological change. These trends further amplify the challenges that innovation poses to decision-makers. The field of Innovation Studies (Godin, 2015) emerged in the twentieth century, examining how major technological advances, such as steam power and electric motors, gradually worked their way through the economy, patterns reflected in generation-long Kondratiev waves (Perez, 2015). By contrast, the current era of digital innovation features vastly higher rates of development and uptake of new products.

Together with shorter product life cycles, this acceleration generates massive market turbulence (Perez, 2015). Large multidivisional firms with dedicated R&D departments – once the powerhouses of innovation in the nineteenth and twentieth centuries – have now been outpaced by a proliferation of smaller, newer players, particularly in digital innovation (Menz et al., 2021). There is, in consequence, a multiplication in the number of voices articulating claims about a rapidly growing array of novel solutions and the benefits these will bring (Yoo et al., 2012).

This accelerating flood of digital innovations – especially radical or disruptive ones – presents both opportunities and challenges for organisational managers and other market actors. The need to respond to potentially disruptive changes brings this dilemma to the forefront: How can managers navigate and evaluate these competing claims? As we will explore later, claims of novelty inherently – and often deliberately – generate uncertainty (Jalonen, 2012). It is in this context that the term 'hype' first emerged to highlight the risk (indeed, the likelihood) that vendor claims may be unrealistic. A vendor might behave opportunistically (Williamson, 1975), exaggerating potential benefits or underestimating the difficulties of achieving them.

Traditional business wisdom has emphasised the risks of failure associated with promising innovations, concluding that it is often best to delay adoption until the prospects are more clearly established (Khanagha et al., 2018). However, as hype's strategic significance grows, so does the need for structured approaches to evaluate and respond to it. In the following sections, we examine emerging frameworks for navigating the uncertainties inherent in hype-driven innovation.

3.2 Innovation Dilemma: The Used Apple Policy

Organisations face a profound tension in navigating technological innovation: the need to act early to seize opportunities versus the risk of committing to unproven solutions. This paradox – the *innovation dilemma* – requires balancing urgency with caution, particularly in today's rapidly evolving digital economy.

Theodore Levitt's (1965) classic paper in *Harvard Business Review* highlights the high costs, frequent failure and consequently deeply uncertain returns of new product developments. In a period in which the innovation literature focused on the maturation of product cycles of successful products, Levitt notes that 'most new products don't have any sort of classical life cycle curve at all'. Instead, 'from the very outset', they have 'an infinitely descending curve'. The 'product not only doesn't get off the ground; it goes quickly underground – six feet under' (Levitt, 1965, p. 82).

These costs and risks might be presumed to inhibit innovation altogether. However, Levitt goes on to propose a different strategy that 'badly burned' organisations have developed that he calls the 'used apple policy':

Instead of aspiring to be the first company to see and seize an opportunity, they systematically avoid being first. They let others take the first bite of the supposedly juicy apple that tantalises them. They let others do the pioneering. If the idea works, they quickly follow suit. ... [T]hey say 'We don't have to get the first bite of the apple. The second one is good enough', but they try to be alert enough to make sure it is only slightly used – that they at least get the second big bite, not the tenth skimpy one. (Levitt, 1965, p. 82)

Levitt's observation highlights the dilemma confronting organisational managers seeking to minimise risks and maximise benefits in uncertain technology markets. Innovation is highly uncertain. High costs and risks of failure can offset potentially high returns. These uncertainties vary substantially over the life cycle of an innovation. Uncertainties are highest in the early stages of development and adoption of a technology (Rosenberg, 2009). Levitt warns of the risks faced by early adopters, arguing that being first can be perilous. Rosenberg (1976) similarly wrote of 'anticipatory retardation' to describe situations where firms delay adoption due to expectations that improved versions of a technology are imminent. Thus, delaying adoption may be sensible. However, where technology creates strategic market transformation shifts rather than merely improving productivity, the difference between getting the first and last bite of the apple matters hugely (Geels & Smit, 2000).

Timing (concerning a technology's lifecycle) matters. It seems safer to delay investing in an unproven innovation. However, though uncertainty and the risk of expensive failures are highest at the early stages of a novel technology, so too are the potential benefits. Early adopters may secure a competitive advantage before this is eroded by the wide availability of equivalent functionality as the market matures (Ward, 1987). Entrepreneurs and investors may derive greatly enhanced profits from their temporary monopoly of exploitation of novel innovations (Schumpeter, 1942), which sweep through industries in a 'wave of creative destruction'. Today, attention focuses on the opportunity for disruptive innovators to displace existing incumbents and capture new market territory through new platform technologies and business models (Bower & Christensen, 1995).

Levitt's early contribution thus introduces some of the critical issues in our investigation into hype. The most significant opportunities for profit and growth arise in precisely the period when uncertainties are at their highest (Knight, 1921). Those wanting to share the benefits of early adoption and avoid being displaced by challengers like Juvo are called on to invest when reliable information to inform a decision is least available. This is the paradox at the heart of our enquiry. And it is growing more acute in the era of digital innovation, as the rate of new digital innovation increases, accompanied by shorter software development cycles and more rapid maturation and obsolescence (Nylén & Holmström, 2015). Platform innovations and other radical and disruptive innovations have gained huge salience with their promise to displace incumbents and deliver market share and profit to early investors and adopters (Gawer, 2011).

Adopters must invest in opportunities *before* verifiable evidence becomes available that the technologies will be productive (Spieth et al., 2021). This means the capability to gauge the plausibility of hype becomes critical. To avoid what Kumaraswamy et al. (2018) characterise as 'errors of commission', traditional business wisdom emphasises the risks of failure for promising innovations and concludes that it is often best to delay adoption until the prospects are more clearly established. However, the temporality of innovation responses has become a crucial factor.

Delaying a response until robust evidence emerges of the prospects of a promising technology may reduce the risk of costly investment in unsuccessful technology pathways. However, it creates new risks from delayed access to expected benefits, and more crucially, from missing out on new opportunities for first movers from radical and disruptive change and the elevated rewards they may bring for investors and adopters. In this scenario, catch-up strategies may be expensive and miss out on the most significant rewards – characterised by Kumaraswamy et al. (2018) as 'errors of omission'.

Timing is also vital because these complex digital and organisational innovations are not 'plug and play' solutions offering readily identifiable and achievable benefits (Pollock & Williams, 2008). Adopters may need to invest significant attention and money to assess novel, perhaps arcane, technological fields (Schot & Geels, 2008). They may also need to acquire the necessary expertise and intelligence to appraise and exploit/appropriate them.

Considerable work may be required to get a new offering operating effectively in its intended context, and over time, to optimise performance (Fleck, 1994). Organisational managers may also need to unlearn entrenched views of how technology may be utilised. Acquiring technologies and developing responses may be delayed by competition between organisational teams wedded to existing and novel approaches (Volberda et al., 2021).

To make timely decisions, decision-makers must, in the words of Kumaraswamy et al. (2018, p. 1030), 'cultivate the capacity to read weak signals about potentially disruptive innovations and explore options before it is too late'. But one effect of the 'continual disruption' (Kumaraswamy et al. 2018) described above is even greater uncertainty for those navigating the sea of hype.

3.3 Uncertainty and Innovation

Uncertainty is not just an incidental (if unwelcome) by-product of innovation. Innovation inherently generates uncertainty, disrupting traditional decision-making frameworks. However, this uncertainty is not merely a hurdle; it also drives economic dynamism, pushing organisations to develop new strategies for navigating risk and opportunity (Dorobat et al., 2025).

This paradox of innovation under uncertainty has long been recognised in economic thought. For instance, Knight's (1921) classic text argues that profit depends on imperfect knowledge and indeed that profit 'would not arise' under conditions of certainty (Knight, 1921, p. 198). Knight differentiates between risk, which involves calculable probabilities (such as market volatility), and uncertainty, where the combinatorial complexity of economic life and countless unknown factors make probabilities incalculable within business decision timeframes. His account marks a sharp departure from neo-classical models of markets composed of rational actors with perfect information. He proposes that imperfect knowledge and asymmetrical access to information are crucial for profit and even play a generative role in the economy. In short, because the future cannot be calculated in advance, decision-makers must rely on judgement and storytelling – which is exactly the space where *hype* operates.

Keynes (1936) focused on decision-making under uncertainty and introduced the concept of 'animal spirits' to describe the instincts, sentiments, and spontaneous urges that shape economic behaviour when rational calculation reaches its limits. For Keynes, in conditions where outcomes cannot be known by 'quantitative probabilities', investment decisions are not made purely through 'mathematical expectation' but are instead driven by confidence, mood, and social cues (Keynes, 1936, cited in Dow & Dow, 2012). In other words, he shows how exaggerated optimism or pessimism can drive decisions when evidence is lacking. As Keynes sees it, these animal spirits, which include emotions like confidence, optimism, pessimism, and fear, are not irrational; rather, they are necessary responses to radical uncertainty – 'of a spontaneous urge to action rather than inaction' (1936, p. 161) – arising in the absence of stable expectations. Keynes' perspective further challenges the image of the rational economic actor, underscoring how markets are propelled not just by information and analysis but by shifting waves of confidence and belief (Akerlof & Shiller, 2010).

Schumpeter (1947, p. 151) further develops this point, arguing that innovation is the primary driver of growth in capitalist societies. His evolutionary economic account revolves around the entrepreneur/innovator, willing to take a risk, and in return secure enhanced rent from monopoly exploitation of radical innovations by 'the doing of new things or the doing of things that are already being done in a new way'. For Schumpeter (1912, p. 163), innovation involves recombination: 'innovation combines components in a new way', with entrepreneurs using their 'more acute intelligence and a more active imagination' to envisage 'countless new combinations'.

In sum, these classic perspectives show that because the future cannot be calculated, judgement and persuasive narratives become crucial in innovation.

Building on these ideas, modern innovation economists note that radical innovations carry especially high uncertainty. Freeman (1974, p. 226) pointed out that radical innovations demand major shifts in skills and often bring in new players, thus entailing a 'very high degree of uncertainty'. Abernathy and Clark (1985) identified four innovation types based on whether an innovation conserves or disrupts existing competences and linkages. Particularly notable are architectural innovations (which disrupt competences and linkages) and revolutionary innovations (which disrupt competences but conserve linkages). This typology highlights that innovation is an inherently uncertain and combinatorial process, often requiring the creation of new knowledge and networks.

These were just the beginning of a growing body of work aimed at highlighting and classifying forms of innovation that diverge from existing technological and business models. A substantial body of literature has developed taxonomies to differentiate forms of innovation (Godin, 2015). Though little agreement exists about the relationship between these frameworks, they exhibit homologies (Edwards-Schachter, 2018). Many of these taxonomic efforts have focused on discontinuities in innovation (Breschi et al., 2000), which are variously conceived as a corollary to periods of stability. These accounts start with the observation that most innovation involves 'incremental' (Freeman, 1974) changes to existing technologies and processes in which the innovation 'trajectory' follows an established 'paradigm' (Dosi, 1982) or 'regime' (Nelson & Winter, 1982) patterned by broadly shared knowledge, design heuristics, standards, and regulations within a sector.

This emphasis on periods of stability also accentuates periodic shifts in technological paradigm (Constant, 1973; Dosi, 1982). The factors creating discontinuous forms of innovation have been labelled variously in successive accounts as *radical* (Freeman, 1974), *revolutionary* (Constant, 1973; Abernathy & Clark, 1985), *disruptive* (Christensen, 1997), or *emerging* (Ho & Lee, 2015; Rotolo et al., 2015). Though different authors use varying terms – radical, revolutionary, disruptive, emerging – these frameworks all point to the disruptive consequences of discontinuities in innovation (Constant, 1973; Dosi, 1982; Christensen, 1997; Rotolo et al., 2015). These paradigm shifts, variously conceived, all appear to involve changes both in the knowledge and understanding required and in relationships between actors (Abernathy & Clark, 1995), changes which pose deep uncertainties for the players involved.

This recurring emphasis on discontinuities in innovation raises questions about existing knowledge, suggesting that prior understandings may no longer be valid. Existing competences, routines, and evaluation criteria for technology design and business models are called into question (McBride et al., 2024). New understandings of the operation of a promising technology and its potential uses and users may need to be developed. The requirement for new kinds and combinations of knowledge may call for the inclusion of additional players and changes in the relationships between them (Breschi et al., 2000).

Uncertainty is not merely incidental but intrinsic to the claim of novelty that lies at the heart of innovation. Moreover, the claim to novelty by those vendors developing or promoting new innovations purposefully generates radical uncertainty. According to Joly (2010), this is intentional, as innovators must show how their ideas vastly differ from what came before to attract support and mobilise resources. This insight helps explain why hyped expectations around emerging technologies tend to unfold, as Joly (2010, p. 14) sees it, in predictable ways: the 'technology is presented as brand new' where 'it will create a new society'. However, by stressing this dramatic break from established methods, innovators and entrepreneurs inadvertently introduce profound uncertainties about these technologies as they declare existing evaluation criteria obsolete, and traditional metrics and assessment methods become less relevant in this context (see Tenet Three, which discusses how hype asserts the obsolescence of established evaluation criteria).

This generates a profound paradox for decision-makers. When innovation departs from known paradigms, traditional ways of understanding, and evaluating technologies – rooted in extrapolating from past performance – break down. How can organisations evaluate novel capabilities if old models no longer apply?

3.4 Evaluating Radical Futures

Given this paradox, the uncertainties surrounding radical innovation challenge traditional ideas of decision-making as a rational calculation among finite alternatives. Knight places at the core of his economic model what he called a 'theory of knowledge' (Knight, 1921, p. xii). He observed that the process of retrospectively classifying events with similar behaviours – the hallmark of 'mechanistic science' – cannot be applied to typical business decisions, which 'deal with situations which are far too unique, generally speaking, for any sort of statistical tabulation to have any value for guidance' (Knight, 1921, p. 231).

Knight's (1921, p. 209) theory of knowledge closely follows the traditional positivist model of science, describing it as a 'theory of exact knowledge, of rigorous demonstration'. Yet he shows that this model becomes unworkable in everyday economic life, where constant change undermines the stability required for such knowledge to function. As he notes, 'the properties of things and their relationships are constantly changing' (Knight, 1921, p. 207). As a result, profound uncertainty – what we now term Knightian uncertainty – arises. When there is 'real change' – for example, when considering emerging futures – 'it seems clear that reasoning is impossible' (Knight, 1921, p. 209). Put simply, Knight argues that the future cannot be known through statistical generalisation, as each business situation is irreducibly unique. Therefore, economic actors must make decisions in the absence of calculable probabilities, and it is this uncertainty that gives rise to the possibility of profit.

This insight casts doubt on the possibility of *knowing* technological futures in any definitive sense. Clardy (2022, p. 1) similarly argues that

studies of the future cannot produce 'knowledge' in the strict epistemo-
logical sense, because 'their actual truth values cannot be determined
until some later time'. Thus, claims about the future cannot be verified
or falsified in advance. Futures studies, therefore, grapple with a fundamental epistemic limitation.

Adam (2023, p. 280) echoes this position by arguing that the 'future
is not yet and as such cannot be considered factual'. Mirroring
Knight's (1921) critique of mechanistic science, Adam notes that 'in
the scientific mode of enquiry, the future per se is actually dis-
attended'. She writes that while it is 'possible to produce probability
calculations, predictions and models of the future, which are compat-
ible with scientific methods of enquiry', this 'way of knowing the future
is rooted in past and present actions or events, its results are inescap-
ably past-based simulations, masquerading as "knowledge" of a
future – at best imperfect' (Adam, 2023, p. 280). In other words,
scientific approaches project the future based on historical patterns,
but this projection is always provisional and incomplete.

Adam (2023, p. 280) further notes that the temporal orientation of
social science and economics is largely retrospective: 'The temporal
orientation of scientific investigation of this social world is focused
primarily on completed (past) acts or (present) reported anticipations'.
She writes (2023, p. 281) that when 'politicians, policymakers, economists and teachers, for example, want to know what lies ahead, they
rely on spatial and material knowledge of the past, from which they
extrapolate what might be'.

However, there are contrasting accounts that challenge the idea that
the past entirely constrains the future. Some scholars, on the one hand,
emphasise the future's open-ended indeterminacy. For instance, Selin
(2008, p. 1888) introduces the notion of the 'ontological indeterminacy of the future', suggesting that we are 'actively creating and re-
creating multiple futures'. Similarly, Köhler et al. (2019, p. 3) emphasise that the future is 'open-ended' and that it is 'impossible to predict
which [promising innovations] will prevail'. These perspectives highlight the radically contingent nature of the future but can risk presenting it as a vague or undifferentiated cloud of possibilities.

On the other hand, scholars argue that the future is not a blank slate.
For instance, Halford and Southerton (2023, p. 273) argue that the
future is 'not empty', open to 'any kind of hopes or possibilities' but is
'already here' – shaped by 'latent materialities' such as infrastructures,

investments, and institutional legacies. These pre-existing elements condition the shape of plausible futures. In their view, actors are not operating on a blank canvas but are constantly navigating futures already partly determined by historical and material constraints.

Rather than seeing the unknowability of the future as a dead end, other scholars (Tutton, 2017) focus on how future imaginaries function in the present. For example, while acknowledging that the facticity of future claims cannot be verified, Tutton (2017) argues that propositions about the future can still be studied in terms of their effects. Drawing on Bell and Mau (1971), he suggests that the future is real 'to the extent to which present alternatives or possibilities for the future are real', and that we can understand futures by analysing the 'images of the future' that guide present action (Tutton, 2017, p. 481). That is, imagined futures have a performative role and can be empirically examined as social facts. We can study how actors navigate and evaluate unpredictable technology futures as routine practice. In other words, despite the limits to knowing the future, actors and organisations are continually engaging in *future-oriented practices*. How does this play out in everyday business decision-making?

3.5 An Economy Obsessed with the Future

According to Joly (2010), there is an increasing orientation of market actors towards the future (see also Wenzel et al., 2025). If this is the case, how do market actors routinely assess and steer their way through the shifting terrain of plausible futures? Despite the uncertainties, actors routinely engage in practical, everyday activities to navigate and evaluate the future.

Halford and Southerton (2023, p. 274) argue that researchers must 'explicitly recognise [actors'] capacity to engage directly in future-making practice'. By *future-making practice*, they mean the 'doings and sayings of a diverse range of actants actively engaging in claiming what futures might and should be, and in materialising these claims' (Halford & Southerton, 2023, p. 274). In this view, organisations are not merely responding to a pre-given future but are actively shaping it through their expectations, plans, and investments.

Adam (2023) offers a complementary perspective, suggesting that much of daily life is conducted *with a view to the future*. As she puts it:

At the everyday level, life is conducted projectively: imagined, anticipated, expected, planned, designed and actioned within the open and fluid horizon of both past and future. People move in this temporal domain with great competence, encompassing the past and future simultaneously. Without giving much thought to the matter, they operate with equal confidence in the action domains of planning and future making, alternating their perspective between anticipated and enacted futures. (Adam, 2023, p. 280)

Bazzani (2023, p. 384) also explores this idea through the concept of 'practical consciousness', which enables actors to navigate the future without explicit deliberation. He describes it as the tacit knowledge that allows individuals to 'go on in the contexts of social life without being able to give them direct discursive expression' (Bazzani, 2023, p. 384). This form of engagement, he adds, often involves the deployment of 'routines', which are 'unreflective flows of activities in which habits do all the perceiving, recalling, judging, conceiving and reasoning that is done'.

Thompson and Byrne (2022) highlight the importance of constructing plausible visions of the future. They suggest that market actors develop *practical knowledge* distinct from scientific knowledge – a distinction they argue warrants further exploration. As they 'cannot act solely by identifying optimal choices based on past statistical information', they 'create and use imagined futures to attend to questions of possibility rather than epistemology' (Thompson & Byrne 2022, p. 248). It is these 'imagined futures' that help orient present actions. As Thompson and Byrne (2022, p. 248) explain:

Entrepreneurs, managers and workers aim to create convincing future scenarios to help shape reality. These 'imagined futures' become active forces in the present moment by influencing how people make decisions, form relationships, and set their expectations.

These ideas closely align with Beckert's (2016, 2021) influential concept of *fictional expectations*. Beckert (2021, p. 2) notes that 'organisations respond to the question of how to handle the future ... by creating imaginaries of the future as "placeholders" ... allowing them to make sense of the future and to act "as if" the future would unfold in a specific way'.

Together, these perspectives suggest that while the future remains fundamentally unknowable, it is not ungovernable. Moreover, it also points to how organisations are not paralysed by uncertainty. Despite the epistemic challenges, modern organisations are far from passive – in fact, they are increasingly future-oriented in their day-to-day operations. How, then, do they go about envisioning and assessing the future? Market actors deploy a range of tools, imaginaries, and practices – explicit and tacit – to make the future actionable. The task is not to predict the future with certainty but to engage with it through strategic and situated forms of judgement (Wenzel et al., 2025).

Crucially, Beckert goes further by arguing that actors not only navigate uncertainty through imaginative projection but also develop criteria for distinguishing more plausible futures from less plausible ones. Although fictional expectations cannot be verified in advance, he argues, it is clear that they can be evaluated for plausibility: 'They can be deemed credible, but their actual accuracy cannot be known' (2021, p. 4). For Beckert (2021, p. 4), fictional expectations do not mean 'fanciful fantasies, but rather assessments of future developments that combine known facts with assumptions, informed judgements and emotions'. He goes on,

> To what extent can this assessment of the foundations of credibility of fictional texts be applied to the analysis of expectations under conditions of uncertainty in the economy? One important difference is that in economic decision-making, actors scrutinise expectations not just with regard to their inherent convincingness as narratives, but with regard to their practical credibility. (Beckert, 2013, p. 225)

However, he notes that their 'broken relationship to reality' (Beckert, 2013, p. 225), which is an inherent characteristic of economic predictions under uncertainty: 'In Economics, people evaluate predictions not just on how compelling their narrative is but also on their practical credibility. This is because the future reality simply *cannot* be known in the present' (Beckert, 2021, p. 4, *emphasis in original*).

Beckert's choice of the term 'fictional' is doubtless chosen for its rhetorical value in displacing entrenched ideas of economic decision-making based on rational calculation. By highlighting the narrative creativity underpinning economic projections, he draws attention to the performative and imaginative dimensions of markets. The fiction terminology is potentially unhelpful as it implies an openness about articulating fictional claims.

Beckert himself acknowledges the risk of the term 'fictional' being misunderstood. In a later paper, he warns that departing from a rational-planning perspective could send us 'down the rabbit hole' of treating all knowledge as fiction (Beckert, 2021, p. 6). A way to circumvent this, he argues (Beckert, 2021, p. 6), is to distinguish between 'types of situations'. This seems important for our analysis of hype. He writes:

When crucial aspects of the future cannot be known, planning can be seen as having largely a symbolic role, which consists in providing 'rationality badges', labels proclaiming that organisations and experts can control things that are, most likely, outside the range of their expertise... Assumptions are made that appear plausible but lack empirical anchoring and thus lead to 'mystical numbers'. . . . In other situations, however, more facts are known or the distribution of power puts limits on what will happen in the future. Under these conditions, strategic planning can indeed play a rational role. (Beckert, 2021, p. 6)

In other words, Beckert invites us to *differentiate* between fictional expectations based on the degree of empirical grounding that is possible. In early-stage innovation, projections often serve a symbolic role – what he calls 'rationality badges' – providing an appearance of rigour even when mainly based on assumptions. Such predictions may involve 'mystical numbers', suggesting spurious precision. However, as innovations mature, expectations should be held to higher standards of evidence and credibility. Beckert (2021) thus reminds us that claims about the future are subject to varying forms of accountability. As he (2016, p. 177) sees it, the early phase of innovation is 'particularly prone to myths', but the later stage claims less so, as they are subject to more accountability.

Logue and Grimes (2022) make a similar point. They suggest that hype performs different roles over time and is subject to shifting forms of accountability: 'Inasmuch as hype presents entrepreneurs with both a resource for motivating early engagement and also a relational liability for sustaining such engagement, it is essential that new ventures understand how to manage hype over time' (Logue & Grimes, 2022, p. 1078).

These insights are directly relevant to our analysis of hype. While often dismissed wholesale as misleading or deceptive (Vinsel & Russell, 2020), the work of scholars such as Beckert (2016, 2021) and Logue and Grimes (2022) offers a foundation for distinguishing between different forms and contexts. As our book argues, hyped expectations vary in their plausibility – some are grounded in technical feasibility and accumulated expertise, while others rest on hopeful speculation or tenuous assumptions.

3.5.1 Towards Evaluating Hype

Rather than dismissing hype outright or accepting it blindly, decision-makers are beginning to parse hype in terms of plausibility. This allows us to reframe the conversation: hype should neither be dismissed wholesale nor accepted at face value. Instead, it can be assessed for plausibility by examining its underlying assumptions, supporting evidence, and the contextual conditions that render certain futures more credible than others. Not all hype is equal – some promissory narratives have more substance than others, even if they cannot be fully verified in advance.

This line of argument finds further support in the growing literature on 'non-knowledge', which reinforces the need to treat claims about the future as situated, variable, and assessable rather than inherently flawed or deceptive. For instance, the argument resonates strongly with Adam's (2023, p. 280) observation that 'engagement with the future is a confrontation with imperfect knowledge, ignorance, even non-knowledge'.

Non-knowledge refers to the recognition that ignorance, uncertainty, and the unknowable are integral to decision-making (Japp, 2000; Croissant, 2014). Agnotology scholars examine the social distribution of ignorance (Schiebinger & Proctor, 2008) and argue that non-knowledge is not uniform but varies between contexts (Japp, 2000; Croissant, 2014). Japp (2000) calls for the explicit identification and description of non-knowledge and distinguishes between 'specific unknowns' and 'unspecific unknowns'. The former refers to risks that can be identified and potentially mitigated; the latter signals areas where outcomes are fundamentally unknowable. Each form has distinct implications for how actors assess risk and make decisions.

While hype should not be reduced to non-knowledge, as some suggest (e.g. Intemann, 2022), insights from this literature help to illuminate its dynamics. Hype claims often span a spectrum. Some concern *specific unknowns* – for example, whether a start-up like Juvo can deliver on its technical promises – which can be probed through due diligence or benchmarking. Others hinge on *unspecific unknowns* – for instance, whether a technological innovation will transform an entire sector – which are far harder to anticipate or control. Attending to this distinction highlights how organisations can, and increasingly do, develop strategies to parse and respond to different forms of uncertainty.

Specifically, our book shows how hype's new actors, particularly market gatekeepers such as industry analysts, are emerging to help organisations navigate this complexity. Rather than dismissing all hype as empty or equal, these gatekeepers work to assess which parts of hyped narratives are credible and actionable, and which remain highly speculative. As we demonstrate in the pages that follow, they dissect claims, scrutinise their elements, and judge which uncertainties can be strategically tolerated, and which demand more substantial evidence before resources are committed. Evaluating hype, in other words, is not a binary exercise of truth versus falsehood. It is a matter of assessing *degrees of plausibility* under varying conditions of uncertainty.

In sum, because organisations cannot rely on traditional methods to evaluate novel technologies, they are developing new strategies and even outsourcing this function. In fact, an entire business – the 'business of hype' – has emerged to help organisational and market actors navigate unpredictable technology futures.

3.6 The Business of Hype

In the digital economy, the task of navigating and evaluating hype has shifted from being an in-house, ad hoc activity to the basis of a specialist business – and a big one at that. Today, navigating hype is itself outsourced to specialist experts – industry analysts and analyst relations (AR) professionals – indicating that interpreting hype has become a commodified business function. Indeed, it could be argued that hype mobilisation and evaluation is now an industry in its own right – traded through consulting services and subscription-based research products. What was once an informal narrative practice – undertaken by firms to generate interest and secure resources – has evolved into a structured business populated by expert actors.

Economic sociologist Mützel (2022) describes this as a 'market of expectations', where gatekeepers actively create and trade in stories – expectations, projections, and imaginings – about the future. It bears emphasising that hype's new actors profit from the very excitement they help stage-manage. Analyst firms derive substantial revenues from selling (hype) evaluations and advice, while technology vendors pay AR professionals and agencies to boost their (hype) visibility. In other words, hype has become a monetised service. The fervour around future technologies is not just a cultural phenomenon but a commercial commodity – one that is packaged, traded, and strategically modulated by expert firms in the business of hype.

In our previous research, we identified how this *business of expectations* was not accidental or unstructured but orchestrated by *promissory organisations* (Pollock & Williams, 2010, 2016) – organisations whose core function is to craft, manage, and circulate future-oriented expectations. Among the most prominent examples of such organisations are industry analyst firms, though they are by no means the only ones (see Beckert, 2021). What we want to do here is examine more closely how these firms produce what we call 'promissory products'.

Drawing on Espeland and Stevens (2008), we define promissory products as mechanisms for rendering hype visible and actionable – by checking, visualising, commensurating, and quantifying it. They are tools that allow technology adopters and investors to make sense of competing claims without having to vet each one individually. Whereas in the dotcom era, a technology buyer might have had to personally assess the credibility of dozens of start-up claims (Garud *et al.*, 2014), today – confronted with potentially an order of magnitude more claims – they are more likely to rely on promissory products such as the Gartner Hype Cycle Chart (HCC), Magic Quadrant, or something similar. These tools serve to pre-filter the deluge of expectations, effectively outsourcing the initial sorting and prioritisation of hype to specialised experts.

We previously explored how industry analysts arose in response to fundamental uncertainties in the supply of off-the-shelf software systems in the market (Pollock & Williams, 2016). These uncertainties centred on a solution's fit with a technology adopter organisation's specific requirement and working methods, alongside questions about software providers' capabilities to deliver on promises. Since these factors could not be established through simple inspection or a comparative assessment of vendors within the technology field, industry analysts introduced tools, such as the Magic Quadrant ranking, to help organisational managers make procurement decisions (Pollock & Williams, 2016).

However, the needs of industry analysts' core clients – primarily technology adopters – have evolved significantly since the 2010s. Driven by dramatic changes in digital innovation as discussed above (Nambisan, 2017), today's adopters must look beyond mature products to emerging innovations that are not yet fully developed or tested. This shift has created two crucial requirements:

Future Scanning: A temporal shift from examining existing mature products to anticipating emerging offerings, requiring new forms of anticipatory engagement (MacNaghten, 2020).

Horizon Scanning: The need to look beyond existing peers and their supply chains for radical innovations emerging from adjacent or entirely different sectors. While incremental innovation typically emerges within existing technology supply chains, radical innovations require broader search capabilities and expertise to track an array of potential solutions effectively (Lundvall, 1985).

These developments have increased the difficulty of technology appraisal, particularly for managers in adopter organisations. Unlike venture capital (VC) investors, who can specialise in specific domains and make concentrated bets (Pflueger & Mouritsen, 2024), organisational technology adopters must maintain a broad perspective. They need to monitor a wide portfolio of developments, often without the resources or incentives to conduct in-depth investigations. As a result, many organisations outsource these anticipatory functions to industry analysts, consultants, and other types of futurists (Mangnus et al., 2021).

Industry analysts have responded strategically to these changing demands, evolving from guiding buyers through existing markets to helping clients navigate the uncertainties of emerging technologies. Their analysts employ a 'T-shaped' distribution of expertise, combining in-depth knowledge of specific domains with a broad understanding of developments across the digital economy (Pollock & Williams, 2016). This capacity underpins the development of new products, such as the HCC and Cool Vendor designation, that target proto-fields and embryonic markets.

Our book examines the origins and motivation of various promissory products and the epistemic system surrounding their production and maintenance. We will focus on four key types of promissory products:

Hype Tools: We define hype tools as evaluative frameworks that guide organisational actors when approaching hyped markets, influencing the timing of their actions and decision-making processes. The HCC is a prime example of such a tool, designed to measure and quantify hype. Providing a visual and conceptual language for where a technology stands in its hype trajectory, it is both descriptive and performative: it describes what is hyped, and the mere act of being on the chart lends that technology a certain status (and omitting others implicitly devalues them). As we will argue, such tools aim to *tame hype* by predicting its rise and fall, thereby helping actors decide *when* to invest or adopt. Chapter 6 will demonstrate that the HCC represents a particularly sophisticated tool as it attempts to systematically capture, map, and convey the shifting credibility surrounding promising technologies, picking up signals at pace and across a broad remit – the entire digital economy and beyond.

Creating HCCs requires a large-scale research effort, involving the tracking of over a thousand emerging technologies to identify signals of progress or setbacks. According to Jackie Fenn, the Gartner analyst who created the tool, 'there's this massive database of 1,000 to 1,500 technologies that get updated and tracked on those [HCCs]' (Fenn, interview). This is hype management on an industrial scale – a capacity that was not present just a few decades ago. The HCC has very few direct competitors due to its scale and the resource requirements; the costs of scanning the whole territory prevent other players from entering the field. According to Fenn, 'not many organisations have the resources to put in that effort as an annual activity' (Fenn, interview). Thus, the HCC has become a de facto *standard* in discussing technology trends, providing a reference that entire industries use to calibrate their expectations.

Categories: These are classificatory schemes created by industry analysts to organise emerging innovations into named categories that guide evaluation, comparison, and investment decisions (Kennedy, 2008; Durand & Thornton, 2018). Chapter 7 shows that industry analysts frequently spearhead the introduction of new categories in the digital economy. The analyst's challenge is to make sense of competing narratives from vendors. When hype coalesces around a cluster of technologies, analysts may formalise it into a new category – naming it, defining its scope, and identifying its leading vendors.

Our book uncovers the extensive behind-the-scenes work by analysts that shapes the category lifecycle. For instance, we show that hype can precipitate *premature* category formation. Analysts work under intense pressure to remain relevant to their clients. Their challenge is to interpret the flow of narratives from vendors and other actors, identify the most promising narratives, and translate them into category interventions that clients can comprehend and deploy. Thus, industry analysts continuously scan emerging developments, coin names for new fields, delineate boundaries, and spotlight exemplary vendors.

Categories are not passive reflections of market developments but strategic tools designed with clients in mind. While analysts create categories for their clients, the introduction of a category can have broader effects on the digital economy. It can trigger a 'gold rush' effect, drawing a diverse range of vendors, investors and others into the nascent category/market. Yet, as Chapter 7 reveals, these categories can be retracted just as quickly, effectively extinguishing the very market they had animated, demonstrating how analysts act not only as observers of markets but also as powerful shapers of their trajectory. Why do they act in this way, and with what consequences for the broader digital economy?

The interplay between hype and categorisation offers a fertile field of study. We will argue that 'category work' increasingly constitutes an important form of 'hype work'. Because analysts attempt to organise ambiguity and channel enthusiasm, categories operate as infrastructures that render hype durable and actionable. They give hype a tangible and actionable form, linking it to market strategies and investment decisions. Categories, then, do more than label; they channel enthusiasm, organise ambiguity, and shape markets.

Rankings: The proliferation of rankings – such as Gartner's Magic Quadrant, Forrester's Wave, IDC's MarketScape, and numerous niche ones – reflects a need to continually evaluate the performance and promise of vendors within established technology sectors. In the digital economy, these rankings have become highly influential because purchasing enterprise technology is complex and fraught with information asymmetries (Williamson, 1975). Rankings respond to this by offering a comparative assessment of vendors' ability to deliver on their promises, literally mapping 'completeness of vision' against 'ability to execute' that vision. The Magic Quadrant exemplifies how hype can be distilled into a marketable format: its four-quadrant chart translates a chaotic landscape of promissory claims into a structured snapshot that decision-makers can readily digest as authoritative market guidance.

Yet, paradoxically, the growing influence of these evaluations has reshaped promissory practices in the digital economy. In some ways, the existence of rankings has also generated more hype. Much of today's hype is no longer self-generated but triggered in response to the demands of these rankings.

Our fieldwork indicates vendors now engage with dozens of such evaluations, pursuing what one interviewee called 'landmark evaluations', meaning those that can significantly influence customer perceptions. To excel in these evaluations, vendors must craft compelling future narratives and provide credible evidence of tangible progress towards fulfilling those promises. Thus, continuous rankings impose an ongoing accountability on hype: the vendor cannot simply claim leadership; an evaluator must anoint them as a leader, and they will re-evaluate each year.

Appellations: These are market devices that qualify products by attaching them to a designation that conveys specific, institutionally backed characteristics (Karpik, 2010). In the digital economy, analyst firms perform this role by bestowing labels – such as 'Cool Vendor' – to spotlight up-and-coming ventures, signalling a change in what – and who – counts as worthy of attention in emerging markets. Established in the mid-2000s, Gartner defines a Cool Vendor as a small company that 'offers technologies or solutions that are innovative, impactful and intriguing'. In most cases, Cool Vendors are seen as offering a 'major disruptive capability or opportunity' (Gartner, 2017).

Our discussion of the creation of the Cool Vendor designation shows how analyst firms adapted their promissory products to keep pace with shifting dynamics in digital innovation. As noted earlier, we examine these appellations at a pivotal moment – their introduction – when industry analysts began broadening their evaluative focus beyond large, established vendors to include previously overlooked start-ups. By the early 2000s, a growing sense within Gartner – and among its clients – was that the firm had already missed several key transformative developments (Chapter 6). At the same time, the rise of 'digital disruption' as a strategic concern meant that clients were increasingly focused on emerging technologies and fast-moving challenger ventures, such as Juvo, that often lay outside the conventional frame of reference of analysts.

These pressures coalesced into a mandate for a new evaluative tool, one better suited to tracking novelty and disruption across a rapidly expanding innovation field. As we discuss in Chapter 4, assessing such start-ups poses particular challenges, since the evidence available for scrutiny often consists solely of promissory narratives.

Such labels serve as sanctioned hype, highlighting a select few start-ups and essentially endorsing them with an official stamp. For the chosen start-ups, it is a significant boost – being named a Cool Vendor can put a young venture on the map and attract customers or investors who would otherwise not have noticed them (Chapter 5). These labels also create a sense of curated hype, rather than a free-for-all where any start-up can claim to be disruptive. It is another filtering mechanism, turning the chaotic space of start-ups into a ranked field of attention.

3.6.1 Promissory Product Spiral

The growth of promissory products in the digital economy has been striking – and highly consequential. (Indeed, it was this proliferation that first drew our attention to the question of taming in the first place.) A notable example is the increasing emphasis on start-up evaluation. Once Gartner formalised this with its Cool Vendor appellation, rival analyst firms quickly followed, launching their own frameworks – from *Hot Vendors* to *Innovators* and *Market Disruptors* – each designed to capture and monetise the momentum of emerging technologies. This proliferation of labels makes clear that analyst firms are active market-makers whose business models depend on producing, packaging, and selling hype. The sheer expansion of promissory products underscores that hype is no longer incidental or episodic but has been deliberately institutionalised as a core innovation strategy in the digital economy.

To theorise this institutionalisation, we introduce the notion of *the promissory product spiral*, inspired by Robert Merton's 'financial innovation spiral' (MacKenzie, 2000; Beunza, 2019). Merton (1992) originally used the term to describe how leading financial organisations continuously innovate and commodify services, which competitors then replicate. In response, the original innovators develop new services to stay ahead, thus triggering an ongoing cycle of product development and commoditisation.

A similar dynamic is now at play in the digital economy. As one promissory product gains traction, competing analyst firms seek to imitate its format, while the original developers pivot to create the next evaluative tool. This spiral of innovation, imitation, and differentiation has driven a rapid expansion in the number and variety of promissory products. A key feature of the spiral is that it operates on multiple levels – both across products and within them.

At the cross-product level, the spiral is evident in how competing analyst firms replicate each other's innovations. When Gartner introduced the Magic Quadrant in the mid-1980s, competitors soon followed with equivalent rankings, such as Forrester's Wave and

IDC's Marketscape. This dynamic continues today, as new evaluation frameworks are frequently launched and rapidly imitated, sustaining a competitive cycle of innovation and standardisation.

Moreover, successful products often branch out within an analyst firm: The Magic Quadrant started as one or two reports, but now there are more than a *hundred* versions of this ranking covering every niche domain. Each major technology category has been subdivided into subcategories and sub-sub-categories as industries have grown. This *internal proliferation* means that as innovation fields expand, the evaluative infrastructure multiplies alongside them.

Another core feature of the promissory product spiral is 'reactivity' – a dimension not present in Merton's (1992) original discussion of the financial innovation spiral, but one we import here as particularly useful for understanding the dynamics of promissory products. Borrowing from Espeland and Sauder (2016), who studied how ranked actors respond to rankings, we see how promissory products provoke recursive interactions between vendors and analysts. Introduced after the dotcom crash as a way to tame unregulated vendor hype, these tools soon became strategically significant. Vendors responded by investing in AR expertise and crafting more targeted narratives to improve their standing. Analysts, in turn, refined their frameworks to incorporate these inputs, generating more granular and differentiated evaluative tools. This reactivity fuelled further proliferation: each vendor adaptation prompted analysts to develop new products, which in turn required vendors to expand their strategies. Reactivity is thus not peripheral but constitutive of the spiral, locking vendors and analysts into a recursive relationship that institutionalises the management of hype.

Together, these dynamics have profound implications for the organisation of hype in the digital economy. What was once a largely unstructured phenomenon – 'hype in the wild' – has become increasingly formalised, structured, and governed through evaluative infrastructures. Hype is no longer simply a product of bold claims – it is shaped and mediated through layered systems of feedback between vendors, analysts, and AR experts. Each new promissory product (a ranking, a hype tool, a Cool Vendor appellation) generates demand for interpretation and response – spurring vendors to invest in specialist expertise and, in turn, prompting analysts to develop yet more tools. This spiral is not just an intellectual evolution; it is a business growth cycle, expanding the business of hype with every turn. This evolving promissory arena demands sophisticated forms of engagement from all sides, as vendors must navigate an expanding array of promissory products, and adopters must interpret them within increasingly complex evaluative environments.

We will return to this spiral metaphor in Chapter 9, where we develop it further to show how it operates as a managed process of adaptation and entrainment.

PART II

The Gatekeepers of Hype

This first empirical section examines the contradictory impulses involved in managing hype. Across two chapters, it explores the dual role that industry analysts play in moderating hype. On one hand, analysts scrutinise exaggerated claims to curb unrealistic expectations; on the other, they amplify the claims they deem most promising. Chapter 4 – *The Second Most Important Pitch* – focuses on entrepreneurial storytelling (Lounsbury & Glynn, 2001, 2019). Entrepreneurship research adopts a 'strategic perspective on hype as a form of storytelling' (Wadhwani & Lubinski, 2025, p. 2). It demonstrates how entrepreneurs secure stakeholder support for their ventures through 'projective' narratives (Kalvapalle et al., 2024). O'Connor (2004, p. 120) encapsulates this idea: 'Before a company exists, it is a story about an imagined future.'

However, as start-ups transition from pitching to investors to engaging with industry analysts, we demonstrate that their narratives must evolve. Entrepreneurs, therefore, undergo a strategic reorientation – shifting from imaginative, aspirational pitches to grounded, detail-rich accounts that meet analysts' evidentiary expectations. Our findings show that analyst briefings can be emotionally charged encounters that expose start-ups to a steep learning curve. Many ventures struggle to satisfy analysts' stringent evaluation criteria; these gatekeepers routinely probe, problematise, and deconstruct founders' narratives. When a story appears overly imaginative or lacks operational detail, analysts demand substance, precise timelines, and credible implementation plans.

Chapter 5 – *Cool Vendors* – investigates how industry analysts identify and amplify the narratives of select disruptive start-ups by bestowing labels such as 'Cool Vendor', 'Innovator', or 'Market Disruptor'. These designations endorse ventures that challenge traditional assumptions and have the potential to transform market practices, thereby boosting their visibility and legitimacy. The chapter addresses a paradox: analysts are typically critical gatekeepers, yet they actively promote the very ventures they evaluate. Drawing on the French sociologist François Vatin (2013), we distinguish between evaluation (assessing value) and valorisation (creating value) to explain this behaviour. By amplifying credible narratives while curbing unsustainable ones, analysts operate in both capacities – gatekeeping and promoting. This dual role illustrates a new model of how hype functions as a legitimising mechanism.

4 | *The Second Most Important Pitch*

An entrepreneur starts a venture. It's a software firm. It has been relatively successful. It's a growing venture in the space and challenging the incumbents. The next crucial step is to win coverage from industry analysts. The entrepreneur approaches the industry analyst briefing like the investor pitch to 'sell the vision' of the venture. However, the briefing did not go as planned; the analysts seemed unconvinced by what they heard. The meeting becomes antagonistic. The entrepreneur starts with: 'Hey, how are you? I am glad I have the chance to talk to you', and quickly says, 'I do not understand why you do not see this'. According to an analyst relations (AR) expert who advises entrepreneurs on how to brief industry analysts, it typically 'takes less than 30 minutes' for these initial meetings to break down, and this is not a one-off but 'happens every single time'. This scenario illustrates how entrepreneurs encounter industry analysts who now serve as critical gatekeepers in the digital economy. These gatekeepers represent the new business of hype – professional evaluators who commodify the interpretation of emerging technologies for clients.[1]

Crafting an appealing story is crucial when creating a new venture (Zilber, 2007; Bartel & Garud, 2009; Wry et al., 2011; Garud & Giuliani, 2013). Stakeholders can be unfamiliar with ventures (Lounsbury & Glynn, 2001), especially technology ventures, where products are often complex and the opportunity difficult to grasp (Martens et al., 2007). The task for the entrepreneur is to construct a narrative that frames the venture to build understanding and mobilise support (Davidsson, 2015). Studies to date have provided rich insights into the storytelling that entrepreneurs carry out with initial audience groups, such as investors (Lounsbury & Glynn, 2019).

Less frequently considered is how these storytelling processes are extended to a later-stage audience (Lounsbury & Glynn, 2019). It is recognised that if the venture is to continue surviving and growing, it

---

[1] Adapted from an interview with an analyst relations (AR) expert.

will need the support of a range of stakeholders (Fisher *et al.*, 2016). Yet, the storytelling that builds comprehension in an early-audience group may be less compelling in enrolling a future audience. As our discussion above of the entrepreneur attempting to brief an industry analyst shows, there are potential obstacles inherent in attracting a new audience. The 'pitch' that worked well with the investor does not seem to work as well with this audience group. Nor does the entrepreneur appear to understand what this new stakeholder is looking for and how to go about the 'briefing' (Überbacher et al., 2015; O'Neil & Ucbasaran, 2016).

There is a clear gap in the existing literature regarding how entrepreneurs extend storytelling processes beyond an early-stage audience to a new, later-stage audience group (Überbacher, 2014; Fisher, 2020). Research has suggested that different audiences will have different expectations of narrative, and different ways of assessing them (Fisher et al., 2017). However, it is unclear how entrepreneurs go about meeting the demands of new audience groups. To explore this important phenomenon, we ask: How do entrepreneurs revise processes of storytelling to meet the expectations of a later-stage audience, and how does this audience group probe and challenge the storytelling processes put forward such that they require revision?

We examine this issue through qualitative, inductive research of the way entrepreneurs brief industry analysts. Industry analyst briefings have become a mandatory stepping stone for emerging ventures in the digital sector (Petkova et al., 2013). As discussed in Chapter 1, these analysts function as new gatekeepers in the hype ecosystem, shaping which ventures gain visibility. Based on this research, we develop a model of how entrepreneurial storytelling processes are extended to this new audience. Our analysis suggests that entrepreneurs struggle to move beyond the initial investor pitch and understand what is expected in industry analyst briefings. However, they can still repair the connection with this group by revising their narratives. We also demonstrate that, while entrepreneurs benefit from garnering a new audience's support, this audience group can subject storytelling to greater scrutiny and additional probing, which in turn influences how ventures evolve.

4.1 Entrepreneurial Storytelling

Early studies have laid the groundwork for a perspective that views stories as playing a vital role in processes that enable new ventures to develop and survive (Hjorth & Steyaert, 2004). As such, storytelling could be considered central to entrepreneurship (Lounsbury & Glynn, 2001, 2019; Bartel & Garud, 2009; Wry et al., 2011; Garud & Giuliani, 2013). Entrepreneurial storytelling has been defined as 'accounts that legitimate individual entrepreneurs to networks of investors, competitors, and visionaries, who make resource decisions and take strategic actions based upon what the stories mean to them' (Lounsbury & Glynn, 2001, p. 545). Storytelling endeavours to make the 'unfamiliar familiar' by conceptualising the new venture in a way that is more readily 'understandable and thus legitimate' (Lounsbury & Glynn, 2001, p. 549). This focus on future-oriented narrative echoes our analytical framework for hype (Chapter 2), where we described how entrepreneurs' promissory stories help create and organise emerging technology fields. Storytelling can include the spontaneous accounts that form part of 'everyday conversations' through to the more 'scripted narratives' familiar to formal business presentations (Martens et al., 2007, p. 1109).

Storytelling is seen as particularly relevant in the case of technology entrepreneurship (Martens et al., 2007), which, because it is often 'knowledge-intensive', is more difficult for stakeholders to understand (Doganova & Eyquem-Renault, 2009, p. 1567). Scholars acknowledge that future-oriented and more promissory narratives are particularly crucial, as they highlight the possibilities surrounding a technology (Zilber, 2007). As Gartner (2007) writes, to construct an entrepreneurial narrative is to generate 'hypotheses about how the future might look and act' (p. 614). Similarly, Chiles *et al.* (2007) explain how stories 'create opportunities through expectations of an imagined future' (p. 467). Through writing the story, the entrepreneur comes to 'imagine the opportunity for novel ventures' (Cornelissen & Clarke, 2010, p. 539). As we argued in Chapter 2, such future-oriented, promissory storytelling is a core mechanism of technology hype, performing and shaping expectations in nascent markets.

4.1.1 Adjusting Storytelling for Later-Stage Audiences

There are calls to broaden entrepreneurial storytelling research (Lounsbury & Glynn, 2019). So far, the literature has primarily focused on how narratives are developed to engage early-stage audience groups, such as investors (Überbacher, 2014). However, as ventures move beyond the initial birth and growth stages, it is recognised that they require the support of further resource providers (Navis & Glynn, 2011). Lounsbury and Glynn (2019) argue that it is essential to distinguish between the early stages, where entrepreneurs craft stories to build 'the legitimate distinctiveness of the new venture' (p. 18) and later stages, where storytelling can appeal to resource providers who endow them with broader 'assets' (p. 23). Similarly, Fischer et al. (2016) point to the importance of researching how a venture transitions through 'different stages of development' (p. 401) as the dynamics surrounding its interactions with audiences will change at each growth phase. Building on Chapter 3's discussion of how ventures navigate uncertainty, we see here that entrepreneurs must adapt their narrative logics to different stakeholder expectations.

Given the importance of enrolling further stakeholders, scholars have begun to enquire whether a story that interests one audience will appeal to others (Überbacher, 2014; Fischer et al., 2016, 2017). Implicit in early research was the assumption that stakeholders would have the same or similar expectations of the entrepreneurial story (Überbacher, 2014). More recently, however, it has been posited that, as audiences change, expectations will likely change as well. For instance, Fischer et al. (2017) point to how different audiences will likely apply other evaluative criteria, or 'logics', when assessing ventures (p. 68). Such logics are non-trivial as they will encourage audiences to emphasise different things when judging ventures. As a result, there have been calls for research to study the evaluation of ventures by other audience groups to shed further light on this crucial issue (Überbacher, 2014).

Alongside changing audience expectations, existing research identifies the importance of studying how entrepreneurs learn to satisfy new audiences when storytelling. Understanding how entrepreneurs revise their narratives is significant because, as Lounsbury and Glynn (2001) point out, storytelling must 'align with audience interests' (p. 550). As emphasised in Chapter 2's actor-centred view of hype, entrepreneurs must tailor their narratives to each audience's logic; if not, audience interest wanes. Alternatively, if a story fails to resonate with key audiences, it will decrease their 'interest and commitment' (Navis & Glynn, 2011, p. 490; see also Giorgi, 2017). Fischer et al. (2016) discuss the demise of a promising digital venture that became 'distracted and confused' (p. 395) by the different expectations of a later audience, which, they argue, ultimately led to its downfall.

Yet, despite its evident importance, we know little about *how* entrepreneurs carry out storytelling processes with a new audience. We cannot assume they will possess the necessary competencies to gain the attention of a new audience group. As Überbacher et al. (2015) write, it may be that they would have to learn and gain the 'requisite cultural awareness and skills' (p. 945). However, it is unclear how entrepreneurs learn to meet the expectations of new audiences. Understanding how cultural competences are developed remains 'empirically underexplored and conceptually under-theorised' (Überbacher et al., 2015, p. 945).

We also lack an understanding of how a later-stage audience responds to storytelling, which perhaps reflects the emphasis in the current literature on 'black-boxing' the interactions between entrepreneurs and audiences (Lounsbury et al., 2019). This gap reflects a broader need, identified in Chapter 1, to understand how new gatekeepers (beyond early investors) influence entrepreneurial narratives. Previous studies have focused on the entrepreneurs' role, characterising them as 'skilled cultural operatives, able to influence how their audience understands the promise of their new venture, (Lounsbury & Glynn, 2001, p. 559). As Gegenhuber and Naderer (2019) argue, however, this implicitly portrays the audience as 'passive recipients of the entrepreneurial story' (p. 154), which means we lack insights into the specific demands an audience might have of processes of storytelling (Gehman & Soubliere, 2017).

Although little explicit focus has been on how entrepreneurs extend storytelling processes to a later-stage audience, two studies describing 'revised' storytelling offer potential insights. O'Connor (2004, p. 120) presents the case of an internet start-up that ended up with a 'transitional story' after it was required to recraft its 'visionary' narrative to a more conventional 'marketplace' story. Garud et al. (2014b) recount how a group of internet entrepreneurs engaged in storytelling to enrol the support of funders, but these stakeholders raised questions about story 'plausibility' (p. 1485).

Crucially, both studies emphasise how stories can be 'challenged'. O'Connor (2004, p. 120) reveals how a new investor considered a venture's story to offer little more than an 'armchair perspective' and suggested an alternative. In Garud *et al.*'s (2014b) case, whilst seemingly there had been little initial evaluation of the storytelling process, it was when entrepreneurs missed critical milestones that stakeholders held them 'accountable', which required 'revised storytelling' (p. 1485). These examples of narrative revision echo the idea from Chapter 3 that entrepreneurs face dilemmas as producers of hype; they must learn when to pivot or tighten their pitch. Though there has been progress in the literature, it remains unclear how entrepreneurs revise storytelling processes to meet new audience expectations or how a further audience group might probe and challenge storytelling processes to the extent that they require revision. These topics merit further investigation.

4.1.2 A Note on Analyst Briefings

This chapter is based on a study at the analyst relations (AR) agency in North America we will call 'Sunshine'. We negotiated permission to conduct a four-week-long observation at Sunshine, which typically facilitated three or four briefings each week between entrepreneurs and industry analysts. We were able to observe ten such briefings. Also, we were given access to a further seven previously recorded briefings stored in an online repository. All briefings were conducted online, and each one lasted around 60 minutes. Participating ventures were between four and ten years old. While no longer in the early stages of formation, they were still very much constructing their stories through addressing such questions as 'who we are' and 'what we do' (Navis & Glynn, 2011, p. 479).

Alongside briefings, we could witness and participate in the various 'prep' sessions, which would go into a detailed discussion of how entrepreneurs could improve their story's telling. Moreover, when briefings finished, it was common practice for the entrepreneur and AR expert to stay on the line to perform a short 'debrief' of what could be changed or improved next time. These observations produced insights that we followed up in informal conversations and more formal interviews, which we describe below. For instance, one critical insight that emerged from observations was that entrepreneurs had little or no understanding of what industry analysts were looking for in these briefings, creating numerous challenges and problems.

Throughout the book, we refer to interviewees using the following codes: A1, A2, A3, etc. for analysts; AR1, AR2, AR3, etc. for AR professionals; and V1, V2, V3, etc. for venture representatives. Each chapter is designed to be read as a standalone study, so an identifier such as A1 in Chapter 4 does not necessarily refer to the same individual as A1 in Chapter 5.

4.2 Entrepreneur Presents an Initial Story

For entrepreneurs, industry analyst briefings are not an easy task. For instance, there is nowhere near the same level of guidance one can find for investor pitches (Clarke et al., 2019). Winning the attention of an industry analyst firm is a challenging and lengthy endeavour? Such firms are inundated with briefing requests from up-and-coming enterprises. For instance, Gartner reports that its analysts sit through 12,000 briefings yearly (Hare, 2020). Moreover, if the venture wants to maintain analyst interest, it must brief them every few months and then continue to engage regularly with them, year after year. Our empirical data demonstrate that briefings would start with entrepreneurs *selling their vision*, but interactions would quickly turn sour as they *found opposition* to their story.

4.2.1 Selling the Vision

During briefings, entrepreneurs would attempt to 'come out strong', capture the analyst's attention, and 'try to keep it' (V1, prep). During these moments, analysts often seemed distracted by other tasks, such as checking email (V1, prep). As a result, entrepreneurs would attempt to capture the analyst's attention by starting with projections of how their technology would be developed, for example, by discussing roadmaps, forecasts of the potential market size, and estimates of competition.

One venture, for instance, evangelised around its vision to revolutionise lending in developing countries: 'We're doing this to start establishing the creditworthiness of ... populations that are highly off ... the grid in terms of the traditional credit bureaux and data sources' (V12, briefing).

Another entrepreneur was excited to showcase his new image-recognition technology demo: 'We have a proof of concept, and we'll have to reinforce that we are showing a future at this point and road-map stuff, but actually, we have a demo that I first got to see last week which I have been excitedly showing people' (V1, prep). Products were always 'next generation' (V1, prep) or 'next frontier' (V2, prep) and deliberate analogies with high-profile digital giants were typical: 'Our product is Google on top of social media' (V1, prep).

Throughout briefings, there was an inevitable discussion of displacement and disruption. Characteristically, entrepreneurs were confident about how their products measured up against competitors. The following, though bullish, was not rare: 'We really feel like we are far ahead of where [large rival 1 and 2], or even [very large rival 3] are, and we know we are already displacing those vendors in many, many cases' (V4, briefing). On hearing how a venture that had only been in existence a few years was displacing much larger rivals, the AR expert working with this venture leaned over to our fieldworker and whispered, 'That is a big claim!' (V4, briefing).

Briefings, almost always, made mention of 'strategic partnerships'. Reference to a partnership would encourage the analysts to probe further: 'What's ... the name of the partner you're working with?' (V1, briefing). Entrepreneurs would then take the opportunity to expand. One venture, for instance, advertised its growing partnership with 'BigTech': 'We're doing a lot with [BigTech] on a *strategic* nature, to make sure that we are treated as their most strategic partner level ... that we have alignment within their R&D team as well as within the various product teams' (V4, briefing).

4.2.2 Finding Opposition from the Analyst

Our informants described how it was customary for entrepreneurs to start with 'passion' and to be 'aggressive when it's about telling the story' (AR3, interview), but these meetings could become antagonistic. Expecting briefings to be similar to investor pitches, entrepreneurs were enthusiastic and animated about what they were saying. An AR expert gives his perspective on what typically went wrong:

These up-and-coming entrepreneurs, they're ... quoting about 'changing the world', and 'offering something totally new'. They believe that's so true to the core of their heart. And to have an analyst show scepticism about either their strategy or their market, it is to call their baby ugly! When [analysts] make these claims and make these judgements, it is not just talking about facts, it is striking at the very heart of how [the entrepreneurs] define themselves. (AR6, interview)

Another AR expert described how entrepreneurs approached briefings with the idea that they had to 'win the meeting' (AR3, interview). This informant describes how:

[Entrepreneurs] are very used to being leaders within these firms. They are salespeople... They sell their ideas. They sell their firm. They sell their concept. They sell themselves to investors... So, their obsession with trying to win the meeting creates bad behaviour. (AR3, interview)

A further AR expert points to how 'there is a huge difference between pitching your business and briefing an analyst' (AR4, interview). She talked about how briefings could become 'salesy' where 'the speaker is not speaking to the analyst' (AR4, interview). Instead, 'they're broad-brushing as though they're trying to pitch their business' (AR4, interview).

However, analysts did not appreciate 'being sold to' (AR4, interview). According to informants, it was common for entrepreneurs to pitch their business and for analysts, in turn, to respond negatively. The AR expert goes on:

An analyst is going to get really annoyed with this, because usually when you're selling, you're pitching, you're talking about how 'you're the best', 'you're the only one', 'you're the greatest'. And so, analysts' red flags will go up. They'll start being super-sceptical. They'll stop believing what you're saying. (AR4, interview)

Another AR expert talked us through what he described as a typical first-briefing scenario, where an entrepreneur, having received a critical response from an analyst, begins to question directly, and even disparage, the analyst: 'So at once, [the entrepreneur will] assault [the analyst's] judgement, assault their wisdom and assault their integrity' (AR3, interview). Such emotional and conflict-filled displays were far from isolated examples. According to the AR expert, 'this happens every single time' (AR3, interview). A further AR expert tells us how '[Y]ou would not believe the number of conversations we start where ...we're repairing relationships' (AR6, interview).

The above exemplifies the struggle around what we call 'selling the vision'. The entrepreneurs, who think they have a strong story to tell, act out their vision of the venture, but this audience does not appear to share their passion and enthusiasm. After these initial episodes, entrepreneurs are often persuaded to change their approach. An AR expert will 'prep' the entrepreneur, which includes telling them what the analyst is looking for and how to respond. Recollecting his difficulty in prepping one particular entrepreneur, an AR expert discusses how he tries persuading entrepreneurs to keep passion and aggression in the background:

I think that the assertive, aggressive technique, it's really interesting. What [entrepreneurs] want to do is [be] aggressive and assertive about arguing the theme of the story. So, [they] are storytellers. When somebody says, 'I will force [entrepreneurs] to be aggressive when it's about telling the story', like 'No, no, no, no, no Ted stop there'. (AR3, interview)

The AR expert encourages entrepreneurs to be open to the analyst's perspective and to modify behaviour and expectations through the course of the meeting:

I don't let them be aggressive [as] we play on this idea that [analysts] don't change their mind very often. So, there's this idea that if you come in with black when they're white, they're probably not going to come half your way. But if you come in with pink or light blue, that's closer to the white. (AR3, interview)

We have demonstrated a gap between the entrepreneur's story and that expected by the analyst. The ensuing repair work – an iterative negotiation between entrepreneurs and market gatekeepers – is part of the broader 'taming hype' process explored in this book, through which exaggerated claims are managed and recalibrated. We now consider what analysts look for by examining how they evaluate the story.

4.3 Gatekeeper Probes and Problematises the Story

In theory, what analysts attempt, namely verifying the future potential and survivability of a new venture, including the plausibility of its technology and market projections, is difficult or even impossible (Navis & Glynn, 2011). The initial challenge is to identify the most promising opportunities in the rapidly changing innovation landscape, which involves a relatively high degree of uncertainty and ambiguity. Will the venture be 'disruptive'? Alternatively, could it be a flop? How are analysts to make sense, so they can advise clients? It appears that they have well-established methods and techniques for conducting what is commonly referred to in the investor pitch as due diligence (Huang & Pearce, 2015). Below, we show that briefings are organised as an escalating process whereby analysts often *lie in wait* for entrepreneurs before *getting to the truth*.

4.3.1 Analysts Lie in Wait for Entrepreneurs

Attending briefings is a routine part of the analyst day. They listen to several in a single sitting, and it is common for them to come off one call, pause for a few seconds and scan through a new set of PowerPoint slides, before entering a further briefing. Here, an analyst describes his reasons for attending briefings: 'I want to learn what [ventures] do, so we have one-hour briefings. I had one yesterday... I had one this morning, where we are trying to understand more about their business' (A1, interview). During briefings, analysts will sit, listen, and take notes to understand what they are being told. It could be that later they will be required to relay this information to their clients: 'I have to do the research. I have to do the vetting of that vendor. And I have to be somewhat confident that they're going to deliver, because you're going to get [my clients] reading my stuff and buying IT, based on my recommendations' (A2, interview).

Briefings are organised in a temporal arrangement to produce an ever-increasing process of evaluation. As indicated, these are not one-off events. The entrepreneur will potentially build a long-term relationship with the analyst, meaning that they could be briefing them many times over the next few years. Therefore, during the initial stages, many analysts are relaxed and restrained, knowing they can return to scrutinise the story later.

An analyst describes how '[W]e are quite easy-going in the first one or two. We let people flow their own way. But usually, by the time we have a second or third one ... you go: "Wait a minute. Let's just cut to it now..."' (A1, interview).

When listening to a venture outline its vision and offering, analysts restrict themselves to questions of understanding. After this initial courtship period, the analyst begins ratcheting up the process. They will go through the story 'with a fine-tooth comb' (A1, interview). An analyst describes how:

I am trying to bet on who is going to survive to some degree — viability becomes important. I am trying to bet on who has commitment from the service providers and systems integrators. I am trying to look at the management team. I am trying to look at the product itself. (A1, interview)

Analysts were highly skilled at holding stories up to the light and talked of how easy it was to spot when a venture was inflating its position. Vendor exaggeration could be counterproductive since it only invites the analyst to 'poke around'. Here, an analyst talks about how ventures should approach briefings:

Don't overstate your competitive position ... [it] turns into again another opportunity just to poke around on that, because, if it doesn't seem believable, the analytic brain says, 'let me go figure out where that's wrong, because it doesn't seem right what I'm hearing'. (A3, webinar)

Another analyst talked of how they could quickly 'cross-check' because the venture's customers were also often *their* customers:

There was a vendor briefing and they tell me they have 500 customers and there is 50 people in the company. Who are you kidding with that? What they don't know is that most of their clients are our clients too. So, for us, it is very easy to cross-check. (A4, interview)

The robustness and veracity of a story are developed over a staged process. Each progressive stage places the ventures under more scrutiny, thus forming an escalating process. Entrepreneurs have much to gain and indeed lose from briefings. Hence, as the analysts themselves recognised, the situation could induce 'overstating' and 'misrepresentation', raising the question of how they dealt with stories that seemed implausible.

4.4 Getting to the Truth

Analysts described how they placed great importance on building good relationships with entrepreneurs but that these interactions could, at times, become practically and morally fraught. Their experience told them entrepreneurs would dress things up: 'They always want to give you an impression that they do much more than they really do' (analyst 6, interview). The analyst role, by contrast, was 'to get to the truth': 'Some of the vendors are telling the truth; some of the vendors are exaggerating' (A7, interview).

An analyst describes how: 'We are quite cynical, and the reason we are quite cynical is that most people are lying to us ... so the question is, how do you get behind the lies to find out what is really going on?' (A1, interview).

Therefore, during briefings, analysts will mobilise mechanisms to evaluate claims, which include acting out moral frames to get behind 'the façade' as they see it. Similarly, 'proof' was also a standard part of their lexicon. An analyst describes how: '[O]ne kind of value is not just being different but being able to prove it... Prove your differentiation... If we're going to say that, let's have some proof to it, let's have some metrics, let's have some facts' (A3, webinar). However, this raises the question of what counts as proof in these situations.

Upon hearing a questionable claim, an analyst may not immediately challenge the entrepreneur but instead go away and verify the information before returning to it in a later briefing. To see through stories, analysts performed something akin to 'proxy ethnographies' (Knorr Cetina, 2010). When entrepreneurs began mentioning a prestigious 'partner' or 'customer', the analyst would ask for names so that those cited could be contacted.

Customers and partners are seen to offer some validity to the emerging story, but it is not that analysts have blind faith in them, as they expect 'prepping' and 'staging'. To get around this, analysts are on the lookout for impromptu or unsupervised gatherings. An analyst discusses how, when a venture invited him to a conference event, he took the opportunity to meet informally with its partners and customers. Such casual exchanges, known as 'personal briefings', were rich in information:

I just went around talking to customers and partners... I organised some of the meetings in advance, some I did on the sly, but it was like a series of one [to one] personal briefings on channel partners which I don't think was quite what [the venture] intended. I think they were hoping to have me sit in front of [the CEO] and be bored. (A5, webinar)

The analyst portrays their role as one where they take pride in not being taken in by entrepreneurs. Thus, they will listen with interest during briefings and later hold the venture accountable for the claims made. We describe below one such episode involving a venture (V4), where analysts had uncovered what they believed was a potentially misrepresented claim, which was then relayed to the venture's CEO, prompting him to undertake corrective action.

An AR expert recounts how V4 had claimed to have established a 'strategic partnership' with [BigTech], and this helped it not only win analyst attention but make it onto a high-profile ranking: '[V4] shouldn't have made the [ranking]. They made the [ranking] because [the analysts] saw them as a disruptive technology, [but] what they're doing is they are piggybacking off a lot of [BigTech] initiatives' (V4, prep). However, the analysts were now beginning to pour water on V4's claim that it had indeed established a strategic partnership with

BigTech. When the analysts approached BigTech for confirmation of this partnership, they received a surprising response. An AR expert recounts the words of the analyst: 'You know, I asked people at [BigTech] about you, because I wanted some of that third-party validation that you do what you say you do, and no one's even heard of you!' (V4, prep). BigTech's failure to corroborate V4's claim of a strategic partnership caught the CEO off guard. The AR expert recounts the conversation:

[V4's CEO] was like: 'Well, who are you talking to, because [BigTech] is so big?' And [the analysts] poked holes in [V4's] market strategy because they said, '[BigTech] is not selling you . . . so why is [BigTech] not going to market with you in their back pocket?' and 'why are you not doing . . . joint pitches?' And so that's where [the CEO] was like, 'Erm'. . . . (V4, prep)

A few months later, in a subsequent briefing, the analysts would return to this issue. The analyst asks: '[T]he thing I'm kind of curious about is this relationship that you've formed with [BigTech], more detail about that would be good' (V4, briefing). In the preceding months, the venture had spent considerable time working to improve and repair this part of the story, which required significant effort to establish the strategic partnership discussed. The AR expert describes: '[S]o, [V4's] been working really hard on beefing their [BigTech] support so that they have that ecosystem that's helping to sell, and then [the analysts] will see that, so this is going to hopefully impress [them]' (V4, prep). During the briefing, the CEO tells the analysts how: 'We weren't necessarily that well-known within the [BigTech] ecosystem . . . so we spent really the last three or four months working closely . . . on the [BigTech] side . . . [so] that we could get to the [BigTech] executive team and talk to them' (V4, briefing). The V4 CEO points to how they will be doing joint pitches with BigTech at a forthcoming event: '[W]e are now going to be in keynote presentations and other highly-visible spots within the [BigTech] event where [BigTech] are highlighting the nature of our relationship' (V4, briefing). The repair work satisfies the analyst, and the matter is dropped.

4.5 Entrepreneur and AR Expert Adjust and Reconcile the Story

We found that, over time, the briefing process can become a source of frustration for entrepreneurs. The disappointment is that, while the evaluation is being ratcheted up, they can often be in the dark about how the analyst perceives them, which prompts them to attempt to elicit *feedback* from the analyst. Moreover, fear of attracting disapproval or losing analyst interest could tempt the entrepreneur to engage in *revised storytelling*.

4.5.1 Drawing Out Feedback from the Analyst

The briefing was a highly asymmetric process. While it was common for the analyst to probe and quiz the entrepreneur continually, this was not a two-way interaction: the analysts limited the amount of comment and feedback.

Feedback and advice are sold as part of a service called 'client enquiry'. An analyst describes this service but also how it plays out in practice: 'Briefings are not a forum for analysts to provide feedback. True, we are told not to. Most analysts, I think, will buckle towards the end, I usually do, and give a little bit of feedback, though we're not going to give very much' (analyst 5, webinar).

The lack of feedback could create problems for entrepreneurs and advisors because it meant there were few indicators, from one briefing to the next, as to how things were progressing. Did the analyst believe they were onto something? Might they be losing interest or, worse still, unconvinced by what they were hearing? For instance, after one such briefing, an AR expert admits how: 'I did not get anything, and I do not know what to talk about next' (V1, debriefing).

What should entrepreneurs do when feedback is in such short supply? Some worked this into briefing routines. For instance, those advising made clear to first-timers their one-directional nature. A neophyte is told how: 'If you hear silence on the other end of the line, it's a good thing. [The analyst] takes a lot of notes and he doesn't feel the need to say, uhuh, uhuh, uhuh.... But if he doesn't seem extremely engaged, it's actually the opposite' (V1, prep). Advisors would also coach entrepreneurs on the importance of drawing the analyst out, to solicit clues to understand whether they liked what they were hearing:

We take her time, go slow, ask for her feedback throughout. This will be a good sense of her priorities moving forward to, so there are things that she wants to see that we ... can't show. Those will probably be important in the next [ranking] moving forward, so we can inform the product team or at least build a story around those things we can't do yet. (V1, prep)

Some entrepreneurs and their advisors took this further by attempting to disrupt the standard briefing practice. In an example that shows that storytelling is a material phenomenon enacted by material practices as much as by narratives, we saw that some had developed methods for drawing the analyst out. An analyst informant describes the 'card-trick', where entrepreneurs go through their PowerPoint slide-deck at a rapid pace, hoping the analyst will ask them to return to a slide that catches their attention:

I've seen multiple companies do that where they literally have 20 slides and go shuffle, shuffle really fast, and they're pretending they're going to get to slide 20 and spend an hour on slide 20, but actually, what's really going on is they're going: 'Which one is it you want?' And then you go: 'That one'. It's laying out a menu, and you go 'that one'. (A5, webinar)

The card trick's materiality is crucial because it upsets the analyst's usual reticence and provokes a visible display of interest that can then be used to adjust stories.

4.5.2 Revising Storytelling

The importance of shifting towards the analyst was a common theme throughout fieldwork. An AR expert explains to an entrepreneur during a prep session how '[t]he number-one objective, when you are introducing yourself to analysts, is to get yourself in a box as quickly as possible' (V1, prep). A further AR expert describes how the goal is to 'create alignment with [the analyst]' (V2, prep). Advisors will gather 'intel' to understand a specific analyst's 'POV – point of view' (AR4, interview). They will then 'talk about how that [POV] either aligns or doesn't align with the [entrepreneur's] perspective and ... try to find a point of commonality [to] start the briefing with' (AR4, interview). Some tell the entrepreneur to put themselves in the shoes of the analyst:

Imagine you are an analyst with a [ranking] coming up, and you've got your [category], you're trying to do a find and fill like you're playing bingo. Do you think they are structuring the information in a way that's gonna be – obviously, it's a very easy way for them to tell their story – but is it an easy way for the analyst to consume? (AR3, interview)

During fieldwork, we observed numerous instances where ventures were encouraged to reframe their narratives to better align with audience expectations and address areas of concern. There appeared to be not one but an array of potential adjustments. One venture 'pivoted', for instance, after receiving decisive feedback from analysts. Relations with the analyst had got off to a bad start as a venture informant recounts: 'When we started talking to [analyst firm], it was like we were Martians. It would be like, 'Oh, that's interesting. It never occurred to me that somebody could do it that way. How nice of the Martians. Let us know what you think of our world'' (V16, interview). The informant goes on to recount how the analyst's feedback became a 'turning point', where he suggested they reframe entirely how they think of themselves.

Another venture maintained 'a façade' where it spoke differently to different audiences. An informant describes how they differentiated between the analyst community and the 'broader world':

How it works is that we have a concept which aligned very tightly with one of [the analyst firm's] concepts... So what we do is, when we are pitching and briefing and talking to those analysts that work in that area, we alter our language to match what they are saying, even though the concept is the same, we change our language to match theirs. But we don't necessarily do that to the sort of broader world. (V15, interview)

Because it was being passed from one analyst to another, another venture reverted to 'dressing up' (AR-G, interview) (e.g. trying out different versions of its story) to attract interest. Developing an ambitious artificial intelligence (AI) solution for the 'underbanked' (V12, briefing), its product crossed 'four or five different [analyst] categories' (AR7, interview), which meant whenever it approached an industry analyst firm, their request for a briefing was rejected. This led them to 'rewrite' their story:

We submitted it [to the analyst firm].... And it went to AI people, and they turned it down. So, then we rewrote it, resubmitted it, and it went to financial services people, and they turned it down. And then we rewrote it and resubmitted it, and it went to ... communications providers, and then it went through there. (AR7, interview)

Such rewrites required producing a credible account of their product, together with their understanding of the analyst categories. This AR expert recounts the process of adjustment necessary: 'So, rewriting the story as if you're a completely different company. In a certain sense, you have to look at the [categories] that they've declared.... And so, it's that dressing up' (AR7, interview).[2]

4.6 Discussion: Extending Storytelling to Industry Analysts

While Cultural Entrepreneurship scholarship has offered rich insights into how storytelling can persuade and enrol an early-stage audience, such as investors, there has been less focus on how entrepreneurs extend processes of storytelling to a later-stage audience group, like industry analysts (Fischer et al., 2016; Lounsbury & Glynn, 2019). Based on this, our chapter offers a model that maps and theorises how entrepreneurs revise storytelling processes to meet this new audience's demands and expectations.

We found that entrepreneurs struggle to move beyond the initial investor pitch and understand what is expected in industry analyst briefings. But they can still repair the connection with this audience through revised storytelling. Our main contribution to research on entrepreneurial storytelling is to reveal and theorise the stages through which entrepreneurs brief a later-stage audience through *presenting an initial story* that had worked well with a previous group, how industry analysts then engage in *probing and problematising the story*, which led to *collective adjusting and reconciling of the story* to meet new audience demands. Below, we describe the key stages and their various steps that lead entrepreneurs to extend and translate storytelling processes to garner the attention of a new audience group (see Figure 4.1).

We show that entrepreneurs attempt to enrol this new audience by extending the same or similar storytelling processes that had worked well with previous investor audiences, which comprised *selling the vision*. However, we found that interactions with this new audience often turned sour, theorised as *finding opposition* (see also Zilber, 2007). Driven by different goals and concerns, we identify that analysts probe and problematise stories through an escalating evaluation process that consists of two steps. Initially, they *lie in wait* for entrepreneurs, knowing that allowing them space and freedom to sell the vision would provide an opening for further interrogation. Then they carry out a second step where they expose story weaknesses and limitations, which we theorise as *getting to the truth*.

---

[2] These tactics – pivoting to new narratives or 'dressing up' to fit analyst categories – reappear in our analyses of ranking strategies (Chapter 8).

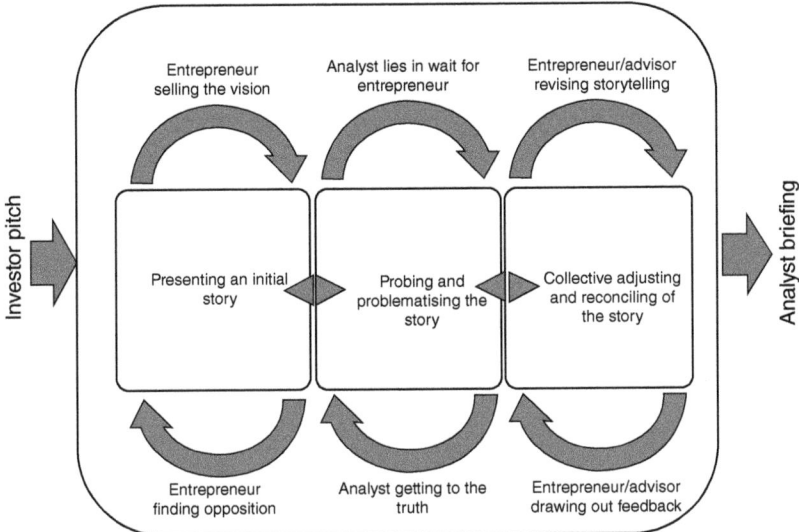

Figure 4.1 Extension of processes of entrepreneurial storytelling to a new audience group.

During the briefing process, the entrepreneur learns (O'Neil & Ucbasaran, 2016) or is counselled by advisors that it is not just a matter of selling the vision but aligning with the audience's interests (Lounsbury & Glynn, 2001). As a result, entrepreneurs attempt what we theorise as *adjusting and reconciling* to consider (and perhaps even adapt to) the analysts' prevailing view (Zuckerman, 1999). Specifically, adjusting and reconciling involves 'drawing out feedback' from the analyst and engaging in *revised storytelling* based on the entrepreneur and AR expert scrutinising and making sense of (the often limited) reaction received.

We observed how revised storytelling could take numerous forms that included: (1) 'repair work' (Bachmann *et al.*, 2015), where an entrepreneur carried out transformative changes to reverse growing analyst distrust of a potentially misrepresented claim; (2) 'pivoting' (Grimes, 2018), where a venture radically changed direction after receiving analyst feedback; (3) 'dressing up', where an entrepreneur drew on a range of similar but slightly modified stories to capture analyst attention (Giorgi & Weber, 2015); and (4) 'maintaining a façade of conformity' (Hewlin, 2003), where an entrepreneur told one story to analysts and a different one to other audiences.

Our interpretation of events is that while the investor pitch and
industry analyst briefing appeared similar enough for the entrepreneur,
the industry analyst had, in Fisher *et al.*'s (2017) terms, different
'expectations'. This audience seemed less accepting of the more
future-oriented and promissory narratives favoured by the entrepreneur (O'Connor, 2004). Our chapter captures and theorises the 'critical moment' (Boltanski & Thevenot, 1999) when the audiences'
different expectations become evident and explains why entrepreneurs
find themselves in difficulty and discord. There was initially what
Boltanski and Thevenot (1999) might describe as a 'shift' of expectations as the entrepreneurs' ported stories honed for one audience to
another group. It follows that because the investor pitch and analyst
briefing expectations were mostly incompatible with one another, the
entrepreneur was then required to shift between different expectations
to attempt to garner the support of this new audience.

Despite the importance of extending entrepreneurial storytelling processes to a new audience (Überbacher, 2014; Fischer et al., 2016, 2017),
we know relatively little about how an entrepreneur can enrol a further
audience group (Fischer et al., 2016; Lounsbury & Glynn, 2019). Our
chapter thus directly responds to calls for further research into the
processes by which an entrepreneur might modify storytelling processes
for a later-stage audience (Überbacher, 2014; Fisher *et al.*, 2016, 2017).
Even though the transfer of a story to a new audience group has been
labelled a critical entrepreneurial 'competence' (Überbacher et al., 2015,
p. 946), research to date has not yet provided a detailed examination
and theorisation of how this extension process 'actually occurs'
(Überbacher, 2014, p. 684). Nor has it examined how entrepreneurs
meet the different expectations of their audiences. Some suggest that
audiences apply different 'logics' when assessing ventures (Fischer et al.,
2017, p. 68). However, studies have not thoroughly explored the complex, evolving considerations and oppositions that govern interactions
between entrepreneurs and a new audience (Gegenhuber & Naderer,
2019; Lounsbury et al., 2019), as we have done here.

4.7 Struggling to Transcend the Initial Vendor Pitch

A key contribution is that we demonstrate how entrepreneurs struggle
to transcend the initial investor pitch. Whereas Fisher et al. (2017)
suggest that entrepreneurs can 'reframe' stories to meet different

audience expectations, our findings lead us to question their assumption that frames are 'easily adjusted' (p. 66). In our study, it was not always the case that entrepreneurs could 'quickly and easily change their frames' to attract and appeal to new audiences (p. 66). Instead, our evidence hints at the presence of 'path-dependent' processes (Garud et al., 2010). Some entrepreneurs based their storytelling to this new audience on techniques seen as successful with earlier groups (namely, investors). Our argument echoes Mauer and Ebers' (2006) analysis, which suggests that entrepreneurs can suffer from 'lock-in' (p. 277) due to their limited ability and competence to relate to later groups. Yet, we extend their focus by showing how these same path-dependency processes can apply not just to forming new audience relationships but also during storytelling processes.

4.8 Audiences of Storytelling Far from Inactive

A second contribution is demonstrating the audience's role in shaping storytelling, which contrasts with the assumption implicit in research that audiences are 'passive recipients of the entrepreneurial story' (Gegenhuber & Naderer, 2019, p. 154). However, a unique aspect of our study is that we could study *both* entrepreneurs and audience simultaneously, which provided us with evidence that market gate-keeper audiences are far from inactive. Specifically, we found that by probing and problematising narratives and moving entrepreneurs through an escalating evaluation process, where the story is placed under an increasing amount of scrutiny, this audience could bring to the surface discrepancies for which the entrepreneurs would ultimately be held accountable, leading to revised storytelling.

We are not alone in highlighting these critical audience evaluations. Some studies do give importance to how audiences 'challenge' entrepreneurs (O'Connor, 2004). Scholars (Garud et al., 2014b, p. 1485) point to how, as 'milestones are missed repeatedly', entrepreneurs can be held accountable. However, whereas previous studies have focused on how audiences become critical after entrepreneurs encounter difficulties and setbacks – what Garud et al. (2014b, p. 1483) characterise as 'commitment rather than critical evaluation' – we demonstrate how audiences probe and problematise entrepreneurs *before* forming their assessment. This finding is important because it challenges the tacit assumption of previous studies (Garud et al., 2014b) that entrepreneurial storytelling is only episodically or exceptionally exposed to audience evaluation. We instead shift attention to an ongoing evaluation process surrounding storytelling, where audiences are active and bring significant influence to bear from the outset.

4.9 How Entrepreneurs Modify Storytelling for Later-Stage Audiences

A final contribution is to develop our understanding of *how* entrepreneurs adapt storytelling processes for later audiences. While it is increasingly recognised that an audience will probe an entrepreneur, especially when they transition from an early-stage to a later-stage audience, the processes of 'replotting' (O'Connor, 2004; Garud et al., 2014b) have not been extensively studied and theorised. Our chapter contributes here by opening the 'black box' of replotting to identify the repertoire of potential revisions deployed by entrepreneurs (e.g. repair work, pivoting, dressing up, and maintaining a façade). Unpacking the replotting process is essential because it reveals the various ways an entrepreneur can modify and revise a story to manage relationships with an audience that may struggle to understand and place them within their own frames and categories.

Moreover, once we open the black box, we can demonstrate that revised storytelling can result from a direct audience challenge to a potentially misrepresented narrative. For instance, V4 revised its story following the questioning of its strategic partnership. This makes it different to entrepreneurs identified in prior work, who revised storytelling either to attract a new audience group (Fisher et al., 2017) or because they had failed to maintain earlier promises (O'Connor, 2004; Garud et al., 2014b). Importantly, while there was potential for this misrepresentation to be treated more seriously than mere 'legitimacy lies' (Rutherford et al., 2009), we also observed that it was possible to remedy the situation.

On this occasion, where censure was anticipated, we observed that the venture in question devoted considerable effort to revising its storytelling processes. Our chapter, in this respect, responds to recent calls for further research on how a new venture might 'mitigate' audience threats (Fisher, 2020, p. 19). It also moves us beyond a dualistic view that depicts entrepreneurs as either winning audience backing or not to a more dynamic perspective that shows, for instance, how they could gain initial support but then have their story problematised and be required to reverse growing audience scepticism through revised storytelling.

4.10 Research Opportunities for Studying Briefings

We join with those reconsidering the prevailing understanding of entrepreneurs as 'skilled cultural operatives' (Lounsbury & Glynn, 2001, p. 559), where it is argued that one cannot assume entrepreneurs have from 'the outset' (Überbacher et al., 2015, p. 945) the necessary competences to gain the support of a new audience group (see also Lounsbury et al., 2019). Instead, as our chapter begins to explore, entrepreneurs often start with little knowledge of a new audience and must acquire the skills and competencies to win their backing. However, more studies are required, particularly those that explore the internal dynamics within ventures as they seek to understand and meet new audience expectations. Moreover, we shed light on a case where interactions were mediated by an AR agency that guided entrepreneurs on approaching industry analysts. However, it would be helpful to study situations where no such mediation and support were available to understand whether similar or different responses would occur.

Chapter 5 extends the above analysis by shifting focus from the act of storytelling and narrative refinement to the downstream consequences of a successful briefing. Specifically, it explores how some ventures, having passed through these evaluative filters, are elevated by analysts as 'disruptors' through designations such as *Cool Vendor, Market Disrupter, Hot Vendor*, etc.

5 | Cool Vendors

'ABC', a software start-up from Estonia, was selected as the preferred supplier in a procurement contest in the UK for delivering a customer relationship management (CRM) system. However, it suddenly found itself ejected from the process after the adopting organisation approached an industry analyst firm for more information about the venture. An analyst reported back that they had 'a list of some 500 vendors of CRM, many of which [the analyst] meets regularly to track the development of their products, but [ABC] is not on the list'. The analyst suggested that if the adopting organisation bought from an 'unknown venture', it would be 'taking a risk', which led one procurement team member to ask, 'who would sign up to a company that no one has heard of?' (Pollock & Williams, 2011). This interaction underscores that industry analysts act as brokers in a market of hype – their endorsements (or omissions) effectively commodify credibility, determining which innovations gain traction in the economy of expectations.

The above example reflects a pressing problem. All ventures face the difficulty that they are unknown quantities at the outset (Fisher et al., 2021). However, they can seemingly rectify this problem in part through drawing support from 'key resource holders' (Lounsbury et al., 2019, p. 1229), such as a market gatekeeper (Plummer et al., 2016; Soublière & Gehman, 2020). An evaluation or endorsement from an influential gatekeeper, like an industry analyst, is critical because it is 'linked to the likelihood of firm survival and growth' (Navis & Glynn, 2011, p. 479). Scholars have noted that market gatekeeper coverage can reassure audiences about investing in or purchasing from a venture lacking a proven track record (Fischer et al., 2016). Others have provided evidence that when gatekeeper backing is not forthcoming, it can become a block or impediment to progress (Petkova et al., 2013). For instance, if a venture does not appear on a 'recommended vendor list', as the example of ABC above shows, the gatekeeper will caution against it (Coslor et al., 2020). As noted in

Chapter 3, digital start-ups often turn hype into a strategic asset by targeting key audiences; here, that means utilising analyst coverage to overcome being perceived as an 'unknown quantity'.

However, the process through which ventures gain the support of a market gatekeeper has not been fully addressed (Überbacher, 2014). The literature suggests a 'screening process' (Petkova et al., 2008, p. 327) involving abstract 'filtering' and 'selecting' mechanisms (Petkova et al., 2013, p. 866). Still, the specific evaluative processes used by gatekeepers remain poorly understood (Überbacher, 2014), which highlights the need for further investigation into how, in 'crowded locations' (Petkova, 2012, p. 396) with numerous ventures competing for gatekeeper attention, certain ones garner support.

The challenge of drawing gatekeeper coverage appears especially acute in the context of digital entrepreneurship. There has been a recent surge in the number of new digital ventures (Nambisan, 2017; Nambisan et al., 2019), defined as ventures that have 'digital artefacts at the core of their business model for value creation and capture' (Lin & Maruping, 2021, p. 1). *How do new digital ventures engage and benefit from market gatekeeper support?* Answering this research question is crucial. It is argued that the uncertainties surrounding digital ventures differ from those of non-digital enterprises (Ingram Bogusz et al., 2018), rendering them especially reliant on gatekeeper coverage (Von Briel et al., 2018; Elia et al., 2020).

5.1 Liability of Newness

A core insight of the new venture literature is that young enterprises suffer from the 'liability of newness' (Stinchcombe, 1965; Bruederl & Schuessler, 1990). Scholars have given significant attention to identifying how potential customers and others, because new ventures lack a track record, could be sceptical towards their performance and whether they can deliver the required quality in a timely manner (Fischer & Reuber, 2007; Fischer et al., 2016). Recently, it has been noted that this liability is more prominent in new technology areas or what Überbacher (2014) calls 'high velocity environments' as there can be a 'rapid transformation' (p. 685) of many different aspects, including what venture performance and quality mean. We focus below on digital ventures, as the liabilities surrounding these enterprise types are especially pronounced.

5.1.1 New Digital Ventures

In the emerging field of digital entrepreneurship, attention has recently turned to differences between digital and non-digital enterprises (Nambisan, 2017). An early insight of this embryonic literature is that the liability of newness may be 'manifested differently' in these contexts (Ingram Bogusz et al., 2018, p. 318; see also Srinivasan & Venkatraman, 2017). It is argued that digital ventures have a 'high propensity for radical transformation' (Von Briel et al., 2018, p. 284) because their products can be taken in new directions by, for instance, user innovation (Nambisan et al., 2019). Other studies suggest that 'pivoting', where digital technologies enable a radical change in focus, goals, or strategy, is a distinguishing characteristic of digital entrepreneurship (Ghezzi & Cavallo, 2020; Wagner & Som, 2021). Despite progress, an important issue left unaddressed concerns how digital ventures make themselves visible and understandable to potential audiences.

Scholars have drawn attention to how digital ventures uniquely rely on gatekeeper support for building market acceptance (Elia et al., 2020; Von Briel et al., 2021). It has been suggested that we are witnessing the emergence of 'an increasing number of intermediaries' who 'play the role of brokers' and help digital ventures 'reach key goals' (Von Briel et al., 2021, p. 13). Some argue that winning the support of a gatekeeper will become increasingly decisive as digital entrepreneurship continues to grow (Nambisan et al., 2019). Others point out that, as the number of new digital ventures increases (Hull et al., 2007; Hair et al., 2013), competition for gatekeeper attention will become more challenging (Nambisan et al., 2019). Others still suggest that ventures failing to win gatekeeper support will become marginalised or that hierarchies could emerge between those receiving endorsement and those ignored (Dy et al., 2016). However, notwithstanding calls for more research on the 'nature of intermediaries and their impact on digital entrepreneurship' (Von Briel et al., 2021, p. 13), scholars have stopped short of examining the process gatekeepers play in the formation of new digital ventures and what a venture can do to win and harness their support.

5.2 Gatekeeper Screening Processes

Mainstream scholarship has made much progress in showing how new ventures attempt to remedy the liability of newness through 'being selected for coverage by influential institutional intermediaries' (Petkova et al., 2013, p. 866). Gatekeeper coverage provides valuable assurances because it is assumed that the gatekeeper has conducted some evaluation and made a favourable judgement about venture qualities and viability (Hsu, 2004). Gatekeepers are defined as neutral 'third parties' (Beckert & Aspers, 2011) or 'intermediaries' (Bessy & Chauvin, 2013; Coslor et al., 2020) who evaluate phenomena in which they have no stake or interest (Beckert & Musselin, 2013; Khaire, 2017). The most well-known gatekeepers include industry analysts (Pontikes & Kim, 2017), industry media (Vasterman, 2005; Kennedy, 2008; Byrne & Giuliani, 2025; Magalhães & Smit, 2025), and critics (Coslor et al., 2020). Research shows that the gatekeeper performs essential functions such as 'enhancing the visibility' of ventures and 'mediat[ing] information flows' between it and other stakeholders (Pollock & Gulati, 2007, p. 347). Ventures that win gatekeeper attention fare better as they channel market attention to those covered (Petkova et al., 2013). Failing to attract coverage will mean ventures will 'not only be perceived as of lower quality', but they could also be 'less visible' (Pollock & Gulati, 2007, p. 347) since they are not part of industry discussions. However, the fact that gatekeepers have become an important staging post for new ventures echoes the puzzle we highlighted in the previous chapter. In Chapter 4, we showed that analyst briefings are a crucial site where start-ups repair their narratives to meet analysts' criteria. Here we pick up on that by asking how, in practice, an analyst chooses one venture over another.

Studies have noted how gatekeepers have an internal 'screening process' (Petkova et al., 2008, p. 327) where they figure out 'which firms merit their attention, for what reasons and to what extent' (Rindova et al., 2007, p. 34). Others similarly describe how gatekeepers 'filter information about new developments' and 'select a relatively small subset of issues, events, and organisations to focus public attention on' (Petkova et al., 2013, p. 866). However, beyond these abstract screening processes, the actual mechanisms and evaluation processes remain poorly understood (Überbacher, 2014). How, in situations where there are hundreds or, as with digital entrepreneurship, thousands of ventures vying for attention, does the gatekeeper decide to cover one venture and not another?

5.3 Valuation Studies

To help specify the gatekeeper evaluation process, we turn to recent Valuation Studies, a body of work that has shifted conceptions of evaluation from simple outcomes based on filtering and selection to more 'processual' understandings (see Millo et al., 2021). Two key insights are relevant from this literature. First, it acknowledges that venture performance or qualities are not given. Instead, they must be enacted as part of an evaluation. This is not an abstract or cognitive evaluation but rather one that involves distinctive socio-technical evaluation processes (Helgesson & Muniesa, 2013, p. 23). Here, we will focus on the briefings provided by new digital ventures to industry analysts and the latter's efforts to comprehend venture viability and distinctiveness.

Second, this research also highlights how evaluation can be transformative (Antal et al., 2015; Kornberger et al., 2015). In tracing the etymology of the concept of 'value', for instance, the French sociologist Vatin (2013) distinguished between 'evaluating' and the more generative notion of 'valorising', where the latter conception captured how the work of evaluation is not merely about appraisal but can also be additive towards the phenomenon under review. To evaluate 'corresponds with a static judgement attributing a value to a good, a thing, a person', whereas to valorise 'has a dynamic meaning – increasing a value, adding an increment to it, a surplus value' (Vatin, 2013, p. 33). The view of evaluation as concerned with identifying and creating value has begun having currency within management scholarship and broader social sciences (Karpik, 2010). For instance, in their study of the evaluation of art, Plante and colleagues (2020, p. 3) discuss how art evaluators do more than identify the value of a particular artistic asset. In defending and rationalising their assessment to others, they actively enhance its value (see also Barman, 2015; Bidet, 2020; Frenzel & Frisch, 2020).

When considering how gatekeepers screen new ventures, existing scholarship describes the first conception, appraisal (Pollock & Gulati, 2007; Petkova et al., 2013), but not the second, valorising. Inspired by the idea that digging further into gatekeeper screening processes reveals potentially more profound value-creating mechanisms, we highlight the role of valuation and valorisation in screening processes as new ventures brief gatekeepers to win their backing.

5.4 New Ventures: An Unknown Quantity

To understand how new digital ventures engaged with and benefited from gatekeeper support, we surfaced three processes that enabled ventures to move from being an *unknown quantity* in the eyes of the gatekeeper to *engaging the gatekeeper*, to *being valorised* by it.

We found that analyst firms are expanding their coverage as they attempt to map and categorise the start-up community. This is a significant departure point. Previously, they only focused on the more prominent and significant/established players. This shift, we found, involved them in *crafting a new venture focus* and *building developmental screening*.

5.4.1 Crafting a New Venture Focus

The interest in creating specific categories and processes for identifying new ventures started when Gartner launched its 'Cool Vendor' reports. Each year, this firm chooses several hundred ventures from various technology areas for coverage. An analyst specialising in the customer relationship management (CRM) area describes this focus:

We do a Cool Vendor report across the whole of Gartner where we look at Content Management, Web Analytics, and all sorts of different subjects, and we look for Cool Vendors in that area. It could be networking technologies, or mobile technologies or broadband or whatever; it doesn't really matter. But in the area of CRM, we'll routinely find 30 to 40 vendors easily, and we pick about 15 to write up and say that is quite cool or even different. (A1, interview)

The analyst defines what is different about new ventures compared to the more established players usually covered:

Our Cool Vendor reports are really vendors that have been trading for three or four years, maybe five, unlisted. Most people haven't got a clue who they are, but we know that they have got some really good customers. The customers say they are good, and that is what we think is cool about them. They have got something unique, and they got real customers. (A1, interview)

From the earliest stages of industry analyst formation, Gartner often leads the way in developing new types of promissory products (Pollock & Williams, 2016). Thus, other industry analyst firms have followed suit, in many cases, borrowing and remaking the Cool Vendor appellation. For instance, the CEO of Analyst Firm B describes the provenance of his 'Hot Vendor' designation: 'I was at Gartner for a long time. So, I started [Analyst Firm B] seven years ago. We said it's not cool to be Cool, it's cool to be "Hot"! We just took that phrasebook and reinvented it' (A2, interview). The new venture focus was further augmented recently when another major analyst firm launched its 'Innovators' label. An informant from Analyst Firm C explains what they are doing to build a focus on new ventures:

We're investing in the market around the 'Innovators', around the emerging vendors. We've got the analyst teams now supporting emerging vendors a lot more than what we've done in the past. We're wanting to write about them a lot more. We want to get them visibility a lot more. (A3, interview)

Two reasons were given for this expansion of coverage. The first point to shifts in digital innovation: 'Most of the really innovative technologies are not coming from the big companies that always occupied [analyst research], it's coming from the small vendors. They're very innovative.... [And] seem to account for most of the innovation' (A4, interview). Another cited reason was the changing interests of technology adopters, the main clients of industry analyst firms. Recent technological developments, such as Software-as-a-Service (SaaS) and cloud-based services, meant new ventures could offer attractive solutions to technology adopters:

The thing that we notice.... in SaaS software and in a lot of cloud-based applications, is you wonder if the product works and if [buyers] can sign up and they can cancel. A lot of business buyers say: 'Look that [start-up] looks pretty good to me. I think I'm going to sign up for that'. (A2, interview)

Analyst informants specified how clients no longer avoided new ventures. Seemingly, the buyer's assessment is, 'If it works, and it will help my business, then I'm going to take a chance, and I'm going to go for it' (A2, interview). Since ensuring clients maintain subscriptions is an immediate priority, this means analyst firms are increasingly focusing on new ventures.

5.4.2. Building Developmental Screening

Building on our earlier notion of analysts crafting 'promissory products' (Chapter 2), Gartner launched its Cool Vendor reports to spotlight young, innovative firms. Crafting this new venture focus required the industry analysts to create different, more developmental screening processes. As existing evaluation mechanisms were geared towards assessing the larger more established players with significant and enduring market presence, they contained high 'entry thresholds' that new ventures could not meet: '[W]e do a lot of reports or syndicated research that evaluates [ventures] that cross the threshold of like four to five million [dollars] at least in revenue. So, a lot of the smaller vendors just won't qualify to be evaluated. They don't have enough customers and enough revenue' (A2, interview). Another analyst describes how 'most vendors aren't on anything published by Gartner at all .... The small ones' (A1, interview), which, in his view, was not necessarily a bad thing because the evaluation criteria would show them in a negative light: 'I am a big believer that if you are small, you don't really want to be on [a major analyst ranking] at all. You are not going to look good' (A1, interview).[1]

An analyst describes how the decision by his firm to cover new ventures required two moves. First, this was selectively drawing evaluation criteria from existing assessments: 'We got [ranking 1] and [ranking 2], which are different market evaluations. So, when we evaluate, let's say a product, we use some of the criteria for innovation from those reports to actually look and evaluate some of the younger, smaller vendors' (A2, interview). Second, they developed a developmental screening process where analysts engaged with ventures in a more open and advisory manner, which included, for instance, offering 'feedback'. Direct feedback is unusual in these settings as briefings are typically structured as a 'one-way conversation' (Analyst webinar). Analyst input and feedback are sold as part of a different service called 'client inquiry'. However, analysts told us they make an exception to this rule when dealing with smaller ventures. An analyst described how:

Sometimes we give them some free feedback. The technique is called Pattern Recognition: what does the vendor have, and can they explain it. Sometimes even they can't explain it. Like: 'Wow! That's great. That's a huge capability. You should talk about that more.' (A2, interview)

---

[1] These practices prefigure what we will analyse in Chapter 8, which explores related competitive dynamics as vendors vie for spots in influential rankings.

A further analyst made a similar point about how, when he found 'confusing' the material a new venture had sent him, he provided them with direction:

I had to admit, the first time I read [new venture's] material, I said, 'Well, this is really interesting'. And my second question was, 'What do you do? What's your deliverable? What's your service?' So I'm big on the economy of words or phrase. Tell me what you do in as few words as possible. And they found out that using my research was easier to explain what they did. (A4, interview)

As analysts expand their coverage to include newer ventures, this provides opportunities for these ventures to engage more and benefit from the attention.

5.5 Engaging Gatekeeper Screening Processes

Our analysis identified a second process whereby the venture engaged with gatekeeper screening processes *through a briefing*. Our investigation captured how the briefing involved a series of mechanisms that included *keeping them interested, understanding expectations,* and *navigating categories.*

5.5.1 Keeping the Gatekeeper Interested

As noted in the previous chapter, briefing industry analysts is not easy – it is marked by several hurdles. The first is finding an analyst. Because of the 'volume of vendors participating in the marketplace' (Analyst webinar), these experts are inundated with requests from promising ventures. Thus, there was a need for a venture to be proactive and to set out to 'win analyst attention' (V1, interview). Some ventures reported that they 'didn't have a targeted approach to the analysts', and they 'would bump into them at conferences' (V1, interview). Others talked of more directed strategies: 'We targeted specific analysts that we felt were commenting on the space to tell them about who we were and what we did and our points of view about how we felt that this market space was evolving' (V2, interview).

A second hurdle is finding the analysts who cover a venture's product area. These experts are divided into 'primary' or 'referral' analysts. The former is the analyst who directly covers the area and 'who knows you the best', while the latter is the analyst more on the periphery but who could potentially 'make mention of you' (Analyst webinar). Working out primary from referral analysts was complex (for reasons we unpack more fully below) and often required multiple briefings. One venture describes how: 'I have probably spoken with 20 analysts at Gartner, some of them more than others. Most of them, multiple times.... You either have 15- or 30-minute calls or one-hour calls. I bet we've had 100 hours of analyst interaction calls' (V3, interview). Another described how they approached cohorts of analysts at a time: 'You start with about six [analysts].... You see how it's going. And then you start with the next six. So, we have talked to probably close to 18 or 20 analysts, maybe 24, over the course of the two years' (V4, interview).

Once identified, the next significant hurdle is keeping the analyst interested. These briefings are not a one-off event but a process where ventures must brief the analysts continuously – 'maybe every quarter' (Analyst webinar). Ventures are thus encouraged to build a 'relationship' with the analyst. This is to avoid their losing interest but also to move the affiliation to the next level. Specifically, a particular informant, having already 'worked with analysts' in a previous role, knew it was about 'developing relationships of trust and collaboration' (V4, interview). She describes how: '[W]e found a few who were interested in us quite early and having an internal analyst champion is absolutely critical' (V4, interview). The 'analyst champion' is described as the 'set of analysts who will then start talking about you and take the big leap to starting to write about you' (V4, interview).

5.5.2 Understanding Gatekeeper Expectations

What do these briefings look like? How should the venture approach them? Ventures learnt that gaining industry analyst attention required assembling more than one set of skills; it was not just a matter of pitching but also understanding what analysts wanted. In thinking about the briefing, a venture CEO asks, '[w]hat's the hook that most analysts are interested in? Is it because ... it's their space, and they're interested in all the vendors and all the technologies? Is it because they want to understand what's happening at the lower end, the earlier stage?' (V6, prep). Ventures were often unsure why analysts had suddenly become interested in them. For instance, the same CEO asks:

Why would they care about what we're doing? I'd get why they would care if we'd launched in January and we now had 50 customers, and we were beating [rival 1] and [rival 2] out of customers. You know, there's certain start-up companies that get on a path and a traction where it's like you can't not care. But ones like us where it's sort of that early stage. (V6, prep)

Ventures worked hard to understand how to present themselves, that is to say, construct their 'stories' and 'pitch deck' to make themselves attractive to the analyst. AR experts would prep ventures on how the analyst is a 'different audience', that the process was unlike 'pitching to clients', and thus required ventures to 'switch their tone from a pitch tone to an analyst focused tone' (V7, prep). This echoes Chapter 4's finding that start-ups must tailor their stories specifically for analysts.

During briefings, ventures tended to highlight technical features and had more difficulty conveying their products in a way that analysts understood. For instance, an analyst explained the briefing structure: '[i]t's a pretty tight story, it follows a pretty visible logic structure: what does the marketplace look like, what are the complications affecting that market, and how can your solution solve it or undo this complicating factor' (Analyst webinar). Ventures were advised to focus on how their product resolved significant customer problems (V7, prep). An AR expert explains to a venture:

So, [explain] what is [the venture], what does it do and how does it solve these [customer] issues. So, if we think of the lion's share of our expository, right, I think.... We should just get [the analyst] to start thinking about, 'Wow, this is something that I didn't pay attention to, and I should be paying attention to. I would like to land that as the primary thing, right? I want [the analyst] to go, 'Wow, I didn't know this was that big of an issue'. (V7, prep)

5.5.3 Navigating Gatekeeper Categories

Pitching also required periods of socialisation, whereby ventures would learn about these experts and, as one informant described it, 'analyst curiosities' (V2, interview). As this venture CEO saw, the critical aspect of developing and improving a briefing was to understand how:

[Analysts] have [an] established market model.... If you don't necessarily fit.... Within an established category of business or activity.... They can be a bit resistant.... Because they are 'Are you ... this? Or a[re] you ... that?' ...

And if the answer is 'Well, we're neither of those things'. . . . Then [there] can be a little bit of difficulty in the conversation. (V2, interview)[2]

Failing to present the venture in a way the analysts recognised was risky. An AR expert recounts how analysts were reluctant to schedule further briefings with a venture as they found its product challenging to understand: 'They haven't used Gartner's language to describe the market category that they were in. And so, [the analysts have] misunderstood what the company does. And they've responded to say, "I don't follow you"' (V6, prep). Ventures were advised to 'create alignment' with the analyst, which means thinking about 'how you speak to them' and responding in 'the same tone and the same way to these people' (V5, prep). A venture informant describes how '[y]ou can look at what each analyst is writing about, and the sort of terminologies and the models and so on that [they] have developed. . . . And in that way, you can sort of align language' (V8, interview). Contained in analyst research would often be explicit mention of entry criteria: '[A]nd the trick', one venture described, 'is to be able to customise your brief request to show that you know the analysts' research, that you understand how far you meet their criteria, so that you can show relevance, and you can show that you are helpful' (V6, prep) – a point we emphasised in Chapter 4 when discussing how entrepreneurs must align their pitches to analysts' frameworks.

However, our empirical data show that aligning with a specific analyst category could be problematic for many ventures. For instance, when an AR expert asked a venture CEO to tell him which analyst category his 'platform' belonged to, he responded that he no longer knew. This was because the platform had become something of a 'Swiss army knife' (V6, prep) – that is, something that can be used in multiple different ways by customers – and thus did not easily fit into one analyst category:

Part of the challenge I think we have. . . . You can do a multitude of things with [the platform]. . . . So, the use cases we're finding actually in the market tends to be actually cross organisation data sharing. . . And it's a totally side use case we hadn't really thought of when we first started building the platform. (V6, prep)[3]

---

[2] Chapter 7 will show how analysts actively create and adjust those categories to shape attention.

[3] This ambiguity is precisely the challenge explored in Chapter 7: how multipurpose products struggle to fit analysts' evolving category definitions.

5.6 Being Valorised by the Gatekeeper

Those ventures that successfully proceed through the screening process would expect to benefit from gatekeeper attention in some way. In our analysis, we identified a third process that included *giving spontaneous reactions*, *talking up*, and *advocating for*.

5.6.1 Giving Spontaneous Reactions

In the briefing, many ventures hoped to provoke 'feedback'. Whilst we heard above how 'comment' and 'input' is not formally a part of these settings, we also saw that analysts might provide 'a little bit of feedback' (A1, interview), especially if the venture briefing is a start-up. For instance, one venture CEO told us that he approached the briefing with the explicit aim of provoking a reaction:

> What I wanted to do was approach it from the standpoint of: is my idea, is this product that the three of us have dreamed up great? Is it truly unique? Or is it my own naivety because it's the first time I've thought of it, but surely someone else has thought about tackling the problem this way. (V10, interview)

This informant particularly appreciated the analysts' broader perspective: '[Analysts] see all the technology. They understand it way better than I do. And where [the briefing] was beneficial was, as a learning experience for me, because as I'm verbalising what my thoughts are, they're giving me feedback, which is making me smarter, right' (V10, interview).

Indeed, during debriefing sessions, it is customary for venture staff and AR experts to spend time reviewing the analysts' comments and questions to identify what can be gleaned. After one briefing, for instance, an analyst's remark about a venture's product being the 'holy grail' was latched onto. This was first welcomed, then, a few moments later, discussed, as doubt began to creep in about whether the comment was positive or negative: '[The analyst] did mention that the metric piece was the "holy grail." Does that mean that she doesn't believe it or that we're really onto something?' (V11, debrief).

Analyst comments – even if spontaneous and cryptic – were seen as crucial for a developing venture. For instance, one informant told us how after being briefed by a particular analyst, he suggested they rethink their entire identity, which seemingly provided a breakthrough in their development. As we saw in the previous chapter, the analyst told them:

'Look, you're not a networking company. You do networking, but you want to be a security company And it took us over a year to really appreciate what he meant. But he's absolutely right, and we are a security company now. What we say is 'security is what we do, and networking is how we do it'. . . . Suffice to say, it was the most important advice this company has ever gotten. (V5, interview)

5.6.2 *Talking Up Ventures*

Industry analyst coverage was viewed as a positive development. In some cases, a very good thing: 'It was a great honour to be named a Cool Vendor' (V12, interview) said one venture; it 'helped in building our credibility' (V2, interview) described another; it was 'very powerful; it's probably one of the best awards we've ever received' (V13, interview), said a third. For some, this initial analyst attention is viewed as a stepping stone to further, perhaps more substantial, analyst coverage. One venture told us how there was talk 'potentially of Gartner moving us up into a [major analyst ranking] this year' (V14, interview). Direct acknowledgement of the coverage received was common among informants: 'It's like a stamp of quality that we are not just another product but a product who is in the right space' (V15, interview). Some described having achieved 'industry acceptance':

As you build a business, particularly in tech environments, you know. . . . That people want to have a sense that. . . . There is a technology which is kind of going in the right direction. . . . And has an industry acceptance. . . . So that kind of associational branding. . . . brings that endorsement to you. (V2, interview)

Industry analyst coverage was seen to allow entry into a market that was otherwise obstructed: 'When you're trying to break into the enterprise market, it's very important to be recognised by an enterprise analyst firm' (V16, interview). Informants discussed using this coverage to attract buyers and secure funding. A venture covered by an analyst firm very quickly received further attention from others, including investment analysts:

451 . . . covered us, Forrester covered us. . . . First Analysts have covered us, and then you know JP Morgan and Goldman have both covered us and so

forth... I think that you know the fact that we've had that ... coverage by Gartner has helped you know, putting us on their radar. (V16, interview)

Many reported increased numbers of venture capitalists (VCs) cold calling them: 'We got all these VCs calling us, and I kept saying, "Well, where have you heard about us?" ... "You're on the Gartner's Cool Vendor list"' (V1, interview). Another analyst informant described examples of ventures he had covered that secured further investment: 'We know one from a couple of years ago, that no-one knew, who was from Australia, they said it helped them get some major deals because [Analyst Firm B] research thought that they were innovative, and that was enough to convince some big banks to invest in them' (A2, interview).

It is analysts who open doors for new ventures. Analysts achieve this indirectly by serving as a source of relevant information. They could provide advice to a new venture on how to approach prospects. One venture describes how: 'So, I'm trying to leverage other Gartner analysts so that they can give me insight so I can make better-informed sales calls on my prospects by knowing more of my competition in those individual industry verticals' (V14, interview). They may do this more directly through, for example, facilitating critical introductions for ventures:

I would say there were a couple of analysts that did approach us that way, and what's interesting is that while they didn't specifically reach out to me in advance of me saying making an enquiry into them, what they did do, was take it upon themselves to go above and beyond the call and introduce me to people in the industry that would be important to the success of my company. (V14, interview)

Alongside gatekeeping, analysts also provide the all-important introductions to potential customers. These direct recommendations influenced bottom-line decisions:

They would use their position, and they say, 'Oh, this company is struggling with something like this, why don't you reach out to, you know, their head of technology or their CEO or whatever? Use my name, tell them I said it might be worth a phone call and see what you can do'. And they've done that. There's probably been a handful, three or four analysts that have done that multiple times for me. (V14, interview)

Informants explained that analysts would help ventures stand out from the crowd, but this was only part of it. For instance, an analyst explains to a group of ventures how they will 'talk them up' if they win their backing:

We will talk about you if we think you've got an interesting story. We will speak of you with clients. We'll talk about you in presentations. We'll present case studies of what your clients are doing because that solves the need of our end-user organisations our end-user clients to understand the marketplace and to understand where their solutions are coming from.... There are different ways of getting to us so that we are as passionate about your solutions and capabilities as you are. (Analyst webinar)

5.6.3 Advocating for Ventures

In the vernacular of these settings, analysts provide 'lead generation'. Although ventures could achieve these leads themselves, it was widely recognised that contacting the lead 'cold' would have been of little use. The analyst not only provided them with an introduction but also crucial information regarding the specific problem they faced. Another informant gives a similar example where it was the analyst who provided the break needed, pointing them to a particular client problem and then smoothing over reservations they had of working with a start-up:

Gartner has been very influential to us.... One of the big things that happened to our company is we have a relationship with a security company called [Big Vendor], one of the biggest security companies.... And [Big Vendor] had a problem... But we could fix that problem with them. But, you know, they didn't really want to work with a start-up. The problem is they couldn't find anybody else who could solve their problem. (V17, interview)

While reluctant to go with a new venture, the more prominent vendor agreed because the industry analyst's recommendation provided this possibility. She recounts how the conversation between Big Vendor and the analyst firm went:

But, you know, [Big Vendor] is a big customer of Gartner, and I'm sure it helped when [Big Vendor] talked to Gartner about us and said, 'Hey, can we work with these people or are they going to be total flakes?' And Gartner said, 'Well, you know, they have this weakness and this weakness. But, yeah, they do what they say they do, and we know a lot about them', and so on and so forth.... So, it helped us establish the most important partner rela-tionship that this company has had, and it was a turning point for us because once we could say that we worked with [Big Vendor], then we were real. (V17, interview)

Above, we heard about the 'analyst champion'. Others used similar terms. For instance, an AR expert explained how analysts could become 'advocates'. Moreover, once enrolled as an advocate, the person could be 'leveraged':

What you can do with an analyst who is an advocate for you, in a lot of ways, is more valuable than being written in a report or being in a [ranking].... Once we have them as an advocate, what strategies can we use to better leverage that advocacy in sales, marketing, product development. (AR webinar)

The language of 'championing' and 'advocacy' appeared no overstatement. It was routine to hear analysts speak enthusiastically about ventures covered. Some even used words like 'my' venture and 'buy-in'. For instance, we heard how analysts would compete internally to write about selected ventures. An analyst informant describes the selection process for ventures defined as 'Cool Vendors': 'Let's say there are ten analysts on a team and there are only five vendors that are going to be written about, and everybody is encouraged to submit a Cool Vendor' (analyst webinar). The results are 'some back and forth saying my Cool Vendor is different and more unique or impactful than yours' (Analyst webinar). Once included in the research, it was common for analysts to talk about the ventures with clients and others: 'So an analyst nominates and successfully publishes a vendor as a Cool Vendor. Well, then there is a psychological buy-in to the business problem that they are trying to solve and the uniqueness that they bring. So they would come to the lips of the analyst a little more' (Analyst webinar).

These effects exemplify the shift we describe in Chapter 1 from 'hype in the wild' to more institutionalised, expert-mediated hype – or 'tamed hype'. The case of Cool Vendor demonstrates how hype is being integrated into formal market structures.

5.7 Discussion: Model of the Gatekeeper Evaluation Process

This chapter sought to answer how new digital ventures engage a market gatekeeper and benefit from its coverage in helping solve a critical problem, being an unknown quantity. In doing so, we develop

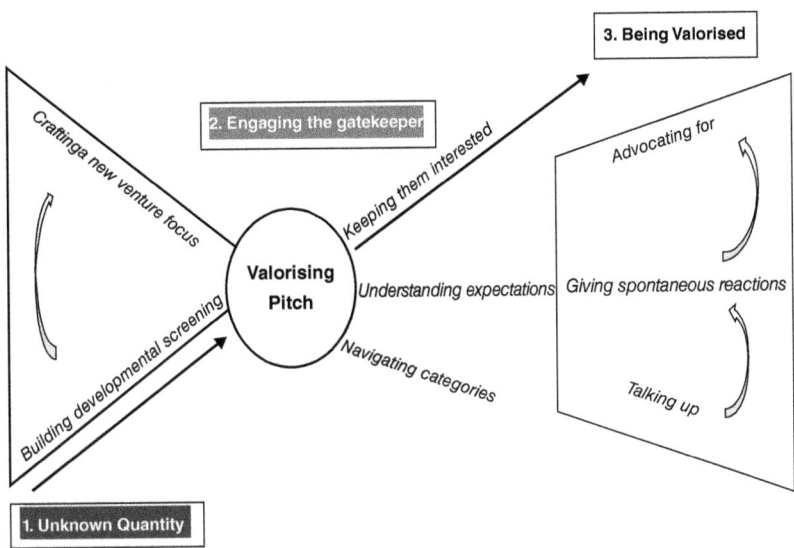

Figure 5.1 Model of the gatekeeper evaluation process.

a process model of gatekeeper evaluation, revealing how ventures were required to perform a new kind of pitch, theorised as a valorising pitch, to move from being an *unknown quantity* to *engaging the gatekeeper* and *being valorised*. Figure 5.1 illustrates the mechanisms and challenges associated with briefing the gatekeeper and securing its support.

From Unknown Quantity to Engaging the Gatekeeper: The starting point for our process model is how, identifying the growing significance of new digital ventures (Nambisan et al., 2019), the gatekeeper went about *crafting a new venture focus* and, because these ventures rarely met 'established scales of evaluation' (Aspers, 2018), 'building developmental screening'. We show that to move from being an *unknown quantity* to *engaging the gatekeeper* required ventures to mobilise three mechanisms: *keeping them interested*, where, similar to 'entrepreneurial storytelling' (Lounsbury *et al.*, 2019), ventures attempted to convince why gatekeeper coverage was warranted; *understanding expectations*, whereby ventures become socialised in gatekeeper practices and worldview; *navigating categories*, where ventures needed to consider and take into account gatekeeper categorisations (see Chapter 7). While these mechanisms helped ventures progress to the next phase of gatekeeper evaluation, we emphasise that this was far from inevitable, given high levels of competition for analyst coverage and exacting briefing demands.

From Engaging the Gatekeeper to *Being Valorised*: If successful in briefing, a venture may potentially receive more detailed consideration, perhaps making it onto a ranking or procurement list. However, the nub of our argument is that the briefing triggered more than inclusion in the formal gatekeeper evaluation system. Specifically, it led to *being valorised*, which comprised the gatekeeper *talking up*, where it explained and justified to gatekeeper clients and others why certain ventures received coverage, including providing further detailed evidence of positive attributes and innovative characteristics; *advocating for*, where, having discovered a promising venture, gatekeeper staff might then enthuse about it during client meetings, on stage when making a presentation, or when writing up a case study; *giving spontaneous reactions*, where advice was offered to a venture struggling to spell out its more innovative attributes or identity. These were typically not deep reflections but unprompted and knee-jerk.

However, this raises the puzzling question of why the gatekeeper might support or promote a venture, especially considering its role as an 'impartial' assessor (Beckert & Musselin, 2013; Pollock & Williams, 2016; Khaire, 2017). As we see it, the gatekeeper promoted ventures not in a prescribed or designed way but as a 'consequence' of its evaluation process (Kruger & Reinhart, 2017; Frenzel & Frisch, 2020). This interpretation is reinforced by Valuation Studies scholarship, which views gatekeeper screening as involving evaluation and a more generative process of 'valorising' (Kornberger et al., 2015; Aspers, 2018). As Vatin (2013) theorises, evaluators play an active role in not just identifying but 'enhancing' value through explaining and justifying assessments (see also Bidet, 2020). However, in our case, the gatekeeper did more than elaborate and define a venture position – what we theorise as *talking up* – it also sought to 'improve' that position through *advocating for* and *giving spontaneous reactions*.

These findings resemble Karpik's (2010) analysis of the competition between evaluators, where, because evaluators vie with others for the attention of audiences, they strive to make the things they assess 'more visible and more desirable than their competitors' (p. 46). Hence, as shown in our case, the gatekeeper devoted considerable effort to help ventures prosper in the market, that is, going as far as to provide suggestions ('You want to be a security company'), introductions ('We will speak of you with clients'), and even affective responses ('We are as passionate about your solutions and capabilities as you are'). We suggest that valorisation should be conceptualised as involving both these aspects (justifying and advocating), which brings together what the extant literature treats as separate or does not account for. It also allows us to theorise another aspect in our study – how ventures sought to trigger and leverage this broader gatekeeper role.

Valorising Pitch: The notion of the valorisation pitch should capture the idea that ventures were often mindful that, underlying the gatekeeper evaluation system, there were other mechanisms to be leveraged. This aspect resembles the 'strategic valorisation' described by Plante and colleagues (2020, p. 3), showing how actors, often purposefully and expertly, exploit the connection between evaluation and valorisation. For instance, some ventures viewed briefing not simply as a means to enter a ranking but as a way to elicit spontaneous feedback, which could then have an 'editing' effect (Überbacher et al., 2015, p. 943) on their venture. Others realised the potential for the briefing to build more significant gatekeeper engagement – similar to the 'soft power tactics' described by Santos and Eisenhardt (2009, p. 663) – which could then be subtly exploited. Others still saw the potential for a venture to enter a ranking but then for the two processes – evaluation and valorisation – to shape each other in a 'bootstrapping manner' (Plante et al., 2020, p. 15) where, because of gatekeeper coverage, it receives further valorisation, which enables entrance to other higher prestige rankings.

These insights illuminate how ventures could engage the gatekeeper to overcome some of the damaging aspects of being an unknown quantity. Valorisation appeared as powerful as other influences that stem from the formal gatekeeper evaluation system. Indeed, for some, gatekeeper valorisation was thought to be more powerful. Ventures that proactively leverage gatekeeper valorisation appear more likely to build market acceptance, that is, successfully engage with potential customers and other resource providers. Our analysis suggests that leveraging gatekeeper valorisation requires all three mechanisms – *keeping them interested, understanding expectations,* and *navigating categories.* We, therefore, reveal and theorise an enhanced model of gatekeeper evaluation that offers ventures the potential to mitigate some of the liabilities of venture adolescence (Stinchcombe, 1965; Bruederl & Schuessler, 1990).

We now discuss how this new theorisation of the gatekeeper evaluation process and valorising pitch contributes to research on new venture development, gatekeepers, and digital entrepreneurship.

5.8 How New Ventures Brief Market Gatekeepers for Endorsements

There is broad recognition of the importance of gatekeepers in the development of new ventures (Navis & Glynn, 2011). They can perform a significant role for ventures that find it challenging to gain a foothold in the marketplace (Überbacher, 2014). Our chapter thus directly responds to Petkova's (2012) call to build conceptions of 'what exactly a young firm can do to become selected by prestigious affiliates' (Petkova, 2012, p. 394) by offering a rare empirical study of interactions between gatekeepers and ventures at the moment when they become more structured and formalised around a briefing. Our exploration of relationships forming around this distinct briefing type is novel; to our knowledge, we are the first to study and establish the importance of these valorising pitches and the micro-processes enacting them.

It is widely recognised that pitching is a core 'cultural competence' (Überbacher et al., 2015). However, most attention has been given hitherto to pitches related to starting and financing (Clarke et al., 2019) rather than to audiences, such as gatekeepers, for broader assets, such as an endorsement (Fischer et al., 2016). Scholars posit that it is necessary to distinguish between pitches to early- and later-stage audiences as the challenges will likely differ (Lounsbury & Glynn, 2019). Fisher and colleagues (2021) identified six pitch types with unique features and functions, but none directly reflect the dynamics and audience identified in this chapter. Our account complements the above studies by revealing a further pitch – the valorising pitch – which we have defined as a device to enrol a market gatekeeper to help build market presence. For instance, while investment pitches are characterised as a 'singular transaction-based exchange' (Teague et al., 2020, p. 336) involving 'simple relationship[s]' (p. 334), the valorisation pitch requires longer-term interactions where ventures must not only 'engage the gatekeeper' but 'keep them interested' over many years, which requires new skills and expertise. Furthermore, our theorisation of the valorising pitch would seem to complement Überbacher and colleagues' (2015) call for further research on the 'strategic cultural actions' those in new ventures must engage in when 'legitimising their ventures' (p. 947).

5.9 Gatekeeper Evaluation Processes Are Value-Creating

Our theorisation of the market gatekeeper evaluation process is also novel. Despite being theorised as 'expert evaluators' (Hsu, 2004), 'evaluative institutions' (Überbacher, 2014), and 'evaluators' (Bessy & Chauvin, 2013), there are as yet no fine-grained models (Überbacher, 2014) that tell us how gatekeepers evaluate ventures vying for their attention and what influence this has on their development. This chapter provides this more granular analysis in the form of an enhanced theoretical model of gatekeeper evaluation, which depicts evaluation processes as not simply 'value-identifying' but also *value-creating*. To date, researchers have advanced the debate by examining the 'screening processes' (Petkova et al., 2008, p. 327) used by gatekeepers to help figure out 'which firms merit their attention, for what reasons and to what extent' (Rindova et al., 2007, p. 34), where gatekeepers are depicted as making 'judgments about the presence and level of specific [venture] attributes' (Petkova et al., 2013, p. 866). However, this focuses on static value-identifying processes, the first part of our model, but not the second. The more value-creating mechanisms we reveal here are important because they are fundamentally generative of venture attributes and capabilities. Our enhanced theorisation, therefore, articulates mechanisms not fully accounted for in the existing concept of gatekeeper screening. It also deepens our understanding of how gatekeepers influence the development of new ventures.

Specifically, existing research has highlighted two prominent roles the gatekeeper plays towards new ventures. First, this is Pollock and Gulati's (2007) suggestion that it 'enhance[s] the visibility' of ventures (p. 347). Second, it is Petkova and colleagues' (2013) finding that gatekeepers funnel 'public attention toward some [ventures] and away from others' (p. 866). However, by revealing how gatekeepers have value-creating and not just value-identifying mechanisms, we theorise them as more than simply amplifying pre-existing venture characteristics or popularising ventures with audiences. For instance, we show that the gatekeeper can shape the narrative surrounding venture identity and attributes ('That's a huge capability, you should talk about that more'). This insight that the gatekeeper can make ventures more understandable and attractive aligns with Überbacher's (2014) call for research on the evaluative institutions that enable ventures to become 'comprehensible and meaningful in the first place' (p. 688). It also complements Lounsbury and colleagues' (2019) discussion of the 'judgement processes' surrounding new ventures and how it is these that drive the activity whereby ventures 'acquire their attributes' rather than simply residing in the 'hands of the entrepreneur' (p. 1225).

5.10 Gatekeepers Are Central in Realising Digital Entrepreneurship

Our chapter fosters an understanding of digital entrepreneurship by examining the unique role gatekeepers play in digital ventures (Elia et al., 2020; Von Briel et al., 2021). Scholars suggest the liability of newness is revealed differently in digital entrepreneurship (Srinivasan & Venkatraman, 2017; Ingram Bogusz et al., 2018). Specifically, this is because digital technologies embody 'traits that allow [ventures] to evolve their identity' (Recker & Von Briel, 2019, p. 2). While the process of transforming identity through a 'pivot' (Ghezzi & Cavallo, 2020; Wagner & Som, 2021) can help survival and growth (Von Briel et al., 2021), it can also make it difficult for ventures to be clear about questions relating to 'who [they] are' and 'what [they] do' (Navis & Glynn, 2011, p. 479), which can be damaging when approaching resource providers.

Our generative model of gatekeeper evaluation complements existing research by showing how industry analysts are crucial actors in realising and shaping digital entrepreneurship, working as both 'evaluators' and 'valorisers'. Our chapter suggests they play an especially significant role for some ventures more than others – specifically, those still developing significant aspects such as identity. Surprisingly, it did not seem to be the case that confusion around identity was wholly damaging in these settings (see McDonald & Gao, 2019; Fisher, 2020). Indeed, the gatekeeper took a 'developmental' rather than policing (Zuckerman, 1999) approach. However, this finding does not sit easily with mainstream gatekeeper literature. Scholars suggest that a venture lacking clarity around identity would be 'screened out' (Zuckerman, 1999, p. 1415). Yet, our chapter showed this was not always or inevitably the case (Durand & Paolella, 2013). We thus complement the body of scholarship that seeks to move beyond the depiction of ventures as either 'screened in' or 'screened out' (McDonald & Gao, 2019; Fisher, 2020). This is particularly important, given that we show that the gatekeeper adopted more 'developmental screening' and ventures themselves appear more expert and strategic in leveraging such coverage.

5.11 Research Opportunities for Studying Valorisation

Our chapter points to further research opportunities. We investigated how the valorising pitch benefits new digital venture development, but we glossed over whether this is a 'tide that lifts all boats' (Lounsbury et al., 2019, p. 1226). An essential vein of research would highlight the differences between those receiving gatekeeper coverage and those failing to win such endorsements. It is also necessary to identify the adverse consequences surrounding these briefings, including aspects such as what happens if the gatekeeper develops a negative assessment and how the venture might 'shield' (Überbacher et al., 2015, p. 945) if valorisation turns out to be 'reductive' instead of additive.

A further aspect for future research would be capturing the tension in our model between 'value-identifying' and 'value-creating' mechanisms. Both are important in supporting new ventures, but each works differently. Scholars may develop a richer understanding of how these mechanisms interrelate and whether there can be clashes, such as when one mechanism overrides or subsumes the other. For instance, further research might seek to understand whether there are limits to valorisation and any measures evaluators must take to ensure their evaluation systems and outputs continue to be seen as 'impartial' rather than 'puff pieces' (Silberstein-Loeb, 2011).

Finally, we suspect that our insights surrounding the valorising pitch could be further elaborated upon and incorporated into Valuation Studies (Kornberger et al., 2015; Aspers, 2018; Plante et al., 2020). Studying these briefings suggests a new type of evaluation practice – a 'valorisation practice' – that captures actors' strategies and tactics to leverage the valorisation mechanisms underlying evaluation systems. Further research could investigate practical techniques as well as challenges across a variety of settings – rankings (Ringel et al., 2021), third-party certifiers (Gehman et al., 2019), investment analysts (Arjaliès et al., 2017), auditing firms (Power, 2021), rating agencies (Rona-Tas & Hiss, 2010) – as actors seek to benefit from this not much studied but fundamental evaluator role.

PART III

The Promissory Products that Make Hype Actionable

Part II examined how industry analysts evaluate and amplify individual vendors' claims. In this part, we explore how analysts engage not with single ventures but with broad technological trends – assessing, categorising, and making sense of emerging innovations. They do this work to help market actors move beyond passive responses to proactive, strategic engagement with hype. Rather than merely reacting to the latest trends, organisational managers are encouraged to interpret hype, time their engagement with it, and leverage it as part of their innovation and investment decision-making.

Chapter 6, *Navigating the Hype Cycle*, explores the construction of the Gartner Hype Cycle Chart (HCC), a trend analysis tool designed to structure and operationalise hype. While scholars have examined the role of consultants and tools in market-making, limited attention has been given to tools specifically designed to navigate hype and their influence on shaping hyped markets. Prior research highlights the challenges market actors face when engaging with hype: they must simultaneously leverage its momentum while mitigating its risks, balancing calculative assessments with affective dynamics.

However, how analysts develop and operationalise tools to support market actors in managing these tensions remains unexplored. This chapter proposes a model of 'hype purification', demonstrating how analysts design and operationalise the HCC and attempt to transform hype from unstructured noise into an interpretable market force. It introduces the concept of 'hype tools' and shows that hype is not merely an emotional phenomenon but also incorporates calculative dimensions.

Chapter 7, *Categorising the Sea of Hype*, examines how industry analysts help market actors navigate the digital economy by introducing 'categories'. Categories are one of the primary mechanisms by which hype is channelled (and ultimately tamed). Analysts attempt to make sense of the 'sea of hype' (van Lente, 2012) from vendors regarding the changing innovation landscape, identify the most promising narratives, and translate these into categories that their clients can understand. These categories help constitute an innovation arena, as they often encourage a swarm of offerings and create 'protected spaces' (van Lente & Rip, 1998; Smith & Raven, 2012), where nascent innovations can flourish.

Drawing on insights from Information Systems Research and Category Studies, this chapter reveals how and why industry analysts decide to create, segment, or retire a category. It demonstrates that these categories are not simply passive reflections of technological or market changes, as conventional interpretations might suggest. Instead, analysts actively and selectively create categories tailored to align with their clients' perceived needs – a process the chapter theorises as 'client-induced categorisation'. In doing so, analysts have turned category creation into a commodified service – actively shaping market taxonomies as part of the business of hype management.

6 | *Navigating the Hype Cycle*

WITH NAJMEH HAFEZIEH AND MARIAN
GATZWEILER

Few visual models have attracted as much attention in the digital economy as the Gartner Hype Cycle Chart (HCC). With its now-familiar double curve – rising toward the 'Peak of Inflated Expectations' before dipping into the 'Trough of Disillusionment' – it offers a stylised yet compelling depiction of the volatile rhythms of technological innovation. Hailed as 'one of the most brilliant insights in the history of technology' (Brinker, 2018), its continued influence speaks not only to its visual clarity – 'the shape just resonates', notes its creator Jackie Fenn – but also to its ability to influence how market actors perceive and respond to technological change. Fenn insists the HCC is not a prophecy or invention but 'a mirror held up to reality'. 'You may hate the reality that hype cycles happen', she quips, 'but it is a recognition of something that occurs naturally in the wild', pointing out that there have 'been booms and busts for as long as history has been recorded – be it tulips, railroads, or any of the other big historical examples'. The real innovation of the HCC lies not in simply noticing these volatile rhythms, but in rendering them visible, structured, and actionable – something executives can point to in meetings, or investors can use to guide planning. By creating a recognisable curve, the HCC transformed hype from something seen as risky or even 'dangerous' into a calculable input for decision-making.[1]

Scholars have widely explored the role of consultants and tools in market-making (Chiapello & Gilbert, 2019; Gond & Brès, 2020), highlighting how markets do not emerge in isolation but are actively shaped by various instruments and frameworks (Ahrne et al., 2015; Geiger et al., 2024). Research emphasises the performative effects of such tools, particularly in how they structure decision-making and influence market trajectories (Muniesa et al., 2007; Callon, 2021). One increasingly influential but underexamined force in this process is *hype*. Hype has become a defining feature of market-making,

---

[1] Adapted from our interviews with Jackie Fenn, ex-Gartner analyst and creator of the Hype Cycle Chart.

particularly in new technology markets, where it amplifies attention, fuels expectations, and directs investment flows (Grodal & Granqvist, 2014). It channels market actors toward 'hot markets' (Pontikes & Barnett, 2017) – fields perceived as highly promising and potentially lucrative – while amplifying their fear of missing out (FOMO). However, while scholars have explored the role of tools in structuring markets, the specific tools designed to interpret and navigate hype – and their influence on market-making – remain largely unexamined.

Navigating hype, as Chapter 3 argued, has become a crucial yet complex challenge for market actors across industries (Garud et al., 2021). The difficulty stems from the rapid rise of hyped markets and their inevitable downturn, a pattern commonly referred to as a 'hype cycle' (van Lente et al., 2013). Moreover, hype operates at the intersection of calculative and affective dimensions, shaping decision-making by introducing new information while simultaneously triggering strong emotions such as excitement and fear – what Beckert (2016), following Keynes (1936), terms 'animal spirits'. For example, a manager evaluating an emerging technology may feel exhilarated by the potential for first-mover advantage, driven by the promise of competitive gains. At the same time, the manager may hesitate, fearing premature investment in an unproven innovation (Arnold et al., 2022). This tension highlights the central challenge of timing market entry. As Kumaraswamy et al. (2018, p. 1030) observe, determining when and whether to enter a hyped market requires actors to 'cultivate the capacity' to interpret the 'weak signals' embedded within hype and act 'before it is too late'.

The growing significance of hype in market-making has led consultants and analysts to develop specialised tools – what, in this chapter, we term 'hype tools' – to help stakeholders navigate hype cycles and strategically respond to hype as a market-making force. These frameworks have also become commercial offerings, showing how the task of taming hype is packaged and sold as part of a business of future-oriented advice. Hype tools are an example of the kind of promissory product described in Chapter 3 – crafted frameworks that structure uncertainty and market expectations. Yet, despite their increasing influence, the design and operationalisation of these tools remain largely unexplored, particularly the tensions that arise at the intersection of hype's calculative and affective dimensions. Existing research has examined how hype fuels market momentum, creating high-growth markets while simultaneously rendering others 'passé'

(Pontikes & Barnett, 2017). Yet, little is known about how these cycles are actively mediated by the very tools that claim to map them. As Beckert (2016) suggests, examining these tools is crucial, as they do not merely reflect hype but actively shape how it unfolds, influencing market actors' perceptions, decisions, and strategies.

To advance this enquiry, we theorise how analysts transform hype into a structured market-shaping framework that market actors can interpret and act upon. By developing hype tools, consultants and analysts aim to strike a balance between excitement and calculation, enabling technology adopters and investors to navigate hype cycles effectively. However, in designing these tools, consultants themselves must contend with the tensions inherent in hype's dual nature – its affective intensity and its calculative dimensions. To examine how they manage this challenge, we draw on Latour's (2012) concept of 'purification', which captures the effort to reconcile and structure the interplay between hype's emotional and more calculative aspects. This perspective leads us to ask: *How do consultants design and operationalise tools to enable market actors to leverage hype in markets for novel technology?*

To address this question, we conducted a qualitative study of the original design and subsequent production and maintenance of the Hype Cycle Chart (HCC), a widely recognised tool for assessing how emerging technologies progress through a hype cycle and shaping how market actors evaluate the timing of investment in new technology markets (van Lente *et al.*, 2013). The HCC has 'gained substantial attention from practitioners' (Dedehayir & Steinert, 2016, p. 34), 'facilitated strategic investment decisions' (van Lente et al., 2013, p. 1615), and particularly influenced 'large companies' R&D decisions' (Steinert & Lefier, 2010, p. 2). Based on this analysis, we propose a model that highlights three mechanisms – *balancing, reconciling*, and *timing* – through which analysts frame hype not as speculative noise but as a structured and staged phenomenon that market actors can engage with. We term this 'hype purification', illustrating how analysts manage the interplay between excitement and calculability to help market actors navigate hyped markets.

6.1 Tools and Market-Making

Scholars widely acknowledge that 'markets do not emerge out of a vacuum' (Ahrne et al., 2015, p. 9) but are actively 'made and shaped by actors of all kinds' (Geiger et al., 2024, p. 6). Specifically, research has highlighted how tools, defined broadly as 'frameworks, concepts, models, or methods' (Jarzabkowski & Kaplan, 2015, p. 538), often play a leading role in facilitating market-making processes through 'equipping' actors (Callon, 2021) with the means to navigate markets (MacKenzie & Millo, 2003) and structuring decision-making, particular decisions aimed at the future (Miller & O'Leary, 2007). Building on this foundation, several key themes have emerged. One prominent theme explores how tools do more than support rational decision-making; they engage in 'qualculation' (Cochoy, 2008) – a process that blends qualitative judgements with numerical calculations to shape market realities (Callon & Law, 2005). Another theme has explored how tools act as 'market devices', defined as the 'material and discursive assemblages that intervene in the construction of markets' (Muniesa et al., 2007, p. 2). A further theme has developed around the 'performative' role of market devices, where tools are not merely passive representations of markets but actively shape and influence them (Callon, 1998; Muniesa et al., 2007). For example, MacKenzie and Millo (2003) examined the mathematical models underpinning financial derivatives, demonstrating that such tools are not external to markets but fundamental to their very construction.

However, while researching tool performativity remains important, scholars caution that focusing exclusively on performative effects risks neglecting the equally critical question of how tools are initially designed and constructed in the first place. As MacKenzie and Spears (2014) argue, prioritising performativity alone 'occludes attention' to the processes through which tools are developed, potentially obscuring the underlying assumptions embedded in their design and designers' intentions in shaping market dynamics. Following this approach, Gond and Brès (2020), studying the development of the Corporate Social Responsibility (CSR) market, highlight consultants' dual role as both 'tool designers' and 'market builders', demonstrating how they crafted tools to reframe concerns initially seen as 'peripheral' within markets and organisations (CSR products and services), ultimately transforming them into 'mainstream' priorities. This shift from tool deployment to tool construction is also evident in Pollock and D'Adderio's (2012) examination of Gartner's Magic Quadrant tool. While their research underscored the tool's performative role in shaping market behaviour, it also revealed how its 'format and furniture' – the design principles and classificatory mechanisms embedded within it – were deliberately engineered to structure market competition from the outset.

6.2 Hype and Market-Making

Scholars have long linked hype to adjacent ideas – passionate interests (Hirschman, 2013), fads and fashions (Abrahamson & Fairchild, 1999), contagious stories (Shiller, 2019), projective storytelling (Garud et al., 2014), speculative bubbles (Goldfarb & Kirsch, 2019), and fictional expectations (Beckert, 2016). Earlier chapters reviewed this foundational work in depth; here we focus on what that literature leaves unexplored: the role of hype in early market formation.

Recent studies highlight hype's pervasive role as an 'integral part of the life' of all emerging technology markets (Rip, 2006, p. 355) and an 'important element' of market emergence (Grodal & Granqvist, 2014, p. 142). Innovators and entrepreneurs often employ hyperbolic claims to generate enthusiasm among investors and early adopters, with van Lente (2012) theorising hype as a 'resource' that legitimises emerging technology markets and justifies their support. In this sense, hype builds excitement and channels the movement of key actors – such as investors and innovators – into a market (Valliere & Peterson, 2004). As Wüstenhagen et al. (2009, p. 123) note, '[a]ttracting both talent and capital seems to be easier in industries or firms where expectations are high', a dynamic echoed by Valliere and Peterson (2004, p. 15), who found that investors are 'drawn to where the largest growth opportunities could be found', with 'hype serv[ing] as an indicator of these areas'.

Hype derives its effectiveness from its 'collective' nature (van Lente, 2012). The more diverse the stakeholders who engage with and amplify hype, the more momentum it gains as a persuasive force, shaping market perceptions and attracting investment. When hype attains widespread attention, it fosters what Grodal and Granqvist (2014, p. 143) describe as 'collective excitement', where self-perpetuating promissory narratives 'give rise to fads, hypes, and bubbles'. Moreover, Pontikes, and Barnett (2017) highlight how the rapid escalation of hype can fuel the emergence of 'hot markets' – nascent industries that gain widespread attention due to their perceived potential and profitability. These markets serve as 'attractive points of entry', drawing in market actors particularly enticed by the surrounding 'buzz' (Pontikes & Barnett, 2017, p. 147).

Navigating hyped markets is inherently challenging, as hype can distort decision-making by blurring the line between genuine opportunities and inflated promises. As Grodal and Granqvist (2014, p. 143) observe, hype constrains market actors' ability to 'make decisions', particularly in the early stages of an emerging technology market when uncertainty is at its peak. To mitigate risk, some actors adopt a 'waiting game' strategy (Robinson et al., 2012; Endenich et al., 2022), delaying investment to avoid what Kumaraswamy et al. (2018) term 'errors of commission' – prematurely investing in over-hyped technologies that ultimately fail. However, while early-stage investments carry the highest risk of failure, they also offer the greatest potential for profit and growth (Knight, 1921). To avoid 'errors of omission' – missing out on transformative innovations (Kumaraswamy et al., 2018) – early adopters must often commit before clear evidence of a technology's success emerges. These competing risks underscore hype's dual role in market decision-making, raising a critical question: Does it obscure judgement or provide valuable strategic insight?

Research has begun to examine hype as a key driver of decision-making, yet its role remains highly contested. Many studies link hype to irrationality and incalculability, arguing that it distorts decision-making processes. For instance, Shi and Herniman (2023, p. 6) highlight that while hype can be 'instrumental in decision-making', it often presents 'less accurate information about an innovation', making it difficult for actors to make well-informed choices. Similarly, Wüstenhagen et al. (2009) argue that hype fosters non-reflective thinking and 'herd behaviour', where actors follow market trends without rigorous evaluation. As a result, hype is frequently positioned in opposition to rational decision-making, often dismissed as 'communications that lack factual, rational substance' (Kiefer & Hunt, 2017, p. 168).

Despite its association with uncertainty and speculation, a recent study in the Market Studies literature (Geiger et al., 2024) has highlighted the powerful affective reactions that hype can generate, demonstrating that it remains a significant force in shaping markets and driving technology investment. With its ties to passionate interests (Hirschman, 2013), excitement, and future-oriented expectations rooted in technological promises, hype can be seen as a crucial yet underexplored mechanism in the 'vascularisation' (Gond & Brès, 2020; Callon, 2021) of the economy – pumping energy, attention, and resources into emerging fields. For instance, scholars argue that hype fuels economic activity by creating an 'evocative overload' of what Beckert (2016, p. 13) terms 'fictional expectations' – projected futures that drive present-day investment decisions. Drawing on Keynes' (1936) concept of 'animal spirits', it is suggested that emotions such as 'excitement' and 'fear' can spur bold decision-making and high-stakes risk-taking in uncertain environments, even when such actions might appear irrational.

6.3 Role of Consulting Tools in Navigating Hype

Despite growing recognition that hype is not just a by-product but a crucial driver of market-making, existing research has largely overlooked how consultants actively mediate hype through specialised tools. To manage the challenge of navigating hype, market actors increasingly turn to tools like the HCC, which claim to structure hype by offering frameworks for distinguishing between exaggerated expectations and genuine opportunities. While the Sociology of Expectations has emphasised the impact of tools in shaping technological expectations (Borup et al., 2006; Konrad & Alvial-Palavicino, 2017), far less attention has been given to their actual design and operationalisation. Existing studies acknowledge that tools like the HCC provide structured mechanisms for action (Dedehayir & Steinert, 2016). However, while these studies highlight the role of hype tools in shaping expectations, they do not examine how these tools are developed, maintained, and refined in response to market dynamics.

To address this gap, our research shifts the focus from merely acknowledging the existence of these tools to examining their design and operationalisation. To explore this, we draw on Latour's (2012) concept of 'purification', which describes the attempt to categorise and separate domains – such as science and society, or in this case, calculation and affect – to maintain the illusion of distinct, independent spheres of action. Purification is central to how consultants frame their role in managing hype. For instance, consultants claim that the HCC can 'separate hype from the real drivers of a technology's commercial promise' (Gartner, 2018), positioning it as an instrument of neutral evaluation.

However, Latour's (2012) thesis is that purification is never entirely successful – in an enduringly non-modern 'hybrid' world, purification efforts are constantly confronted by a parallel process of 'hybridisation', where there is the simultaneous mixing and entanglement of domains that purification attempts to separate. Little empirical research has explored how consultants grapple with this duality – balancing the affective pull of hype with its calculative dimensions – when designing these tools. This leads us to ask: *How do consultants design and operationalise tools to enable market actors to leverage hype in markets for novel technology?*

6.3.1 A Note on the Hype Cycle Chart (HCC)

The concept of a 'hype cycle' is a relatively recent innovation, first introduced in 1995 by Jackie Fenn, a Gartner consultant, during her first year at the firm. Fenn coined the term and developed the tool to illustrate the dramatic rise in excitement and subsequent disillusionment surrounding emerging technologies, framing it as a predictable and repeatable process. She observed a recurring pattern among emerging technologies and 'drew a graph illustrating the ups and downs of this cycle' (Fenn & Raskino, 2008, p. 8). She then mapped out each stage of the process and populated the curve with examples of technologies (Burkhardt, n.d.).

In developing the HCC, Fenn drew inspiration from two key sources. To name the cycle's stages, she turned to theological fiction, particularly John Bunyan's The Pilgrim's Progress (Fenn, interview). She compared the trajectory of hype cycles to a journey, beginning with an 'Innovation Trigger', that sparks attention and generates hyped, often unrealistic expectations. When these expectations fail to materialise, they collapse, moving from the 'Peak of Inflated Expectations' into the 'Trough of Disillusionment'.

Fenn also drew on economic theories, particularly Kondratiev Waves and Schumpeterian creative destruction (Grodal et al., 2023). While traditional economic cycles involve a series of 'consecutive up and down movements' (Fenn & Raskino, 2008, p. xiv), Fenn argued that hype cycles feature a distinct stabilisation phase. As technologies mature, they enter the 'Slope of Enlightenment', where gradual improvements accumulate through experience. Finally, when the broader benefits of these innovations become widely recognised, they achieve the 'Plateau of Productivity' (see Figure 6.1).

The HCC evolved organically as other Gartner analysts 'used the framework to put their own sets of technologies, their own domains on

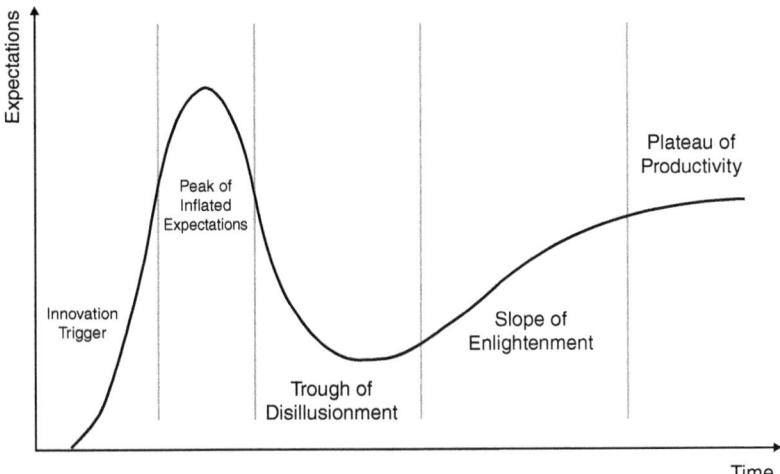

Figure 6.1 The Hype Cycle Chart (HCC).
Source: Author representation

it' (Fenn, interview). Its visibility surged when Alexander Droibik, a fellow Gartner analyst, incorporated the HCC into his 1999 e-business analysis to 'predict the 2001 dotcom bust' (Fenn, interview). Fenn describes this as a 'really nice validation' of the tool and a pivotal moment that propelled the HCC into global prominence (Fenn, interview).

The HCC is primarily designed for Gartner clients, particularly organisational technology adopters, who seek to navigate the evolving business solutions landscape and identify the most promising opportunities among emerging innovations that remain untested or underdeveloped. Gartner faces the challenge of effectively engaging this audience and demonstrating the value of the HCC and its advisory services in guiding strategic investment decisions. Given that Gartner's business model relies on expanding its subscription services through personalised advisory support, client retention becomes a critical priority (Pollock & Williams, 2016). As a result, ensuring continued subscriptions directly influences how Gartner analysts develop and refine tools like the HCC, shaping them to align with clients' decision-making needs and feedback, thus reinforcing the perceived value of their insights.

Today, the HCC has become one of the most recognisable and widely referenced tools in the digital economy and beyond. With over 100 distinct iterations mapping nearly 2,000 technologies (Hashemi et al., 2021), it has evolved from a proprietary tool for Gartner's clients into a broadly circulated and influential benchmark. As Bourne (2024, p. 757) notes, the HCC is 'now deeply embedded in promotional knowledge, reproduced in client pitches, industry presentations, and textbooks'.

Each HCC is updated annually, with new technologies added, existing ones repositioned, and others phased out. While designed for enterprise decision-makers, its online accessibility means it is used by technology vendors, venture capital investors, and other market actors seeking to position and evaluate emerging innovations. The release of a new HCC is eagerly awaited, and any adjustments send strong signals to investors, vendors, and market analysts, aligning adopter communities, vendors, and other experts, reinforcing the idea that a technology's placement on the tool 'can help make or break a given sector of the technology industry' (Woodie, 2014).

Producing and updating an HCC involves a combination of quantitative and qualitative data, interpreted through a process that blends calculation with qualitative judgement – what Cochoy (2008) terms 'qualculation'. Quantitative data includes financial forecasts evaluating innovations' impact and market penetration. Meanwhile, qualitative data is drawn from vendor briefings and use cases (A1, interview). Analysts also routinely engage with clients, exploring their strategies for adopting emerging technologies and gaining insight into investment considerations. The final decision on where to position technologies within the HCC is described as a 'judgment call' (A1, interview) – one that reflects not only formal analysis but also the more nuanced, qualculative process of making sense of complex and often ambiguous signals. This process integrates insights from internal technology vendor assessments, media coverage, and even 'looking at Google Trends' (A1, interview).

6.4 Purifying Hype as a Market-Making Force

Deciding to invest in hyped markets was once a wholly unspecified process. Before the release of the HCC, no comparable tools, methodologies, or frameworks existed to help market actors navigate and interpret hype in emerging technology markets. Moreover, hype was perceived as random or relentless, moving in unpredictable waves rather than following a structured trajectory (Edgerton, 1997).

According to Jackie Fenn, it was disorganised 'noise' without much of a discernible pattern – there were merely constant 'waves of hype' (Fenn, interview). This situation began to change in the late 1990s. Initially published as a one-off research note, the HCC quickly gained traction with Gartner clients, who would approach Fenn during conference events to ask, 'Hey, are you going to update that [HCC]?' (Fenn, interview). Fenn attributes the HCC's widespread appeal to its visual simplicity: 'The shape just resonates.' Once she sketched the HCC, its meaning required no extensive explanation. 'Some models you need to present and say, "Well, this is how you use it." But with the [HCC], people just saw it, and they get it' (Fenn, interview).

6.5 Balancing: Bringing Together Different Rationales in One Tool

The HCC invites market actors to consider two very different curves – a process we characterise as *balancing*. First, a bell curve depicts 'initial enthusiasm and disappointment driven by positive and negative hype' (Fenn & Raskino, 2008, p. 26), foregrounding how the projected claims surrounding emerging technology may not be fulfilled, which we label *managing animal spirits*. Then, an S-curve portrays 'how an innovation's performance improves slowly at first, then picks up steadily, and finally yields diminishing returns' (Fenn & Raskino, 2008, p. 26), labelled as *encouraging calculative rationalities*. We begin by discussing the HCC's left-hand side (see Figure 6.2).

6.5.1 Left-Hand Side: Managing Animal Spirits

When analysts first assess a newly released innovation, they adopt a cautious stance, working under the assumption that hype is widespread. They frequently warn market actors about a recurring pattern in which technology vendors and other stakeholders exaggerate the potential and applicability of innovations – describing the HCC as being 'judgmental against [this] trend' (A3, interview). As Jackie Fenn herself explained, 'these very large waves of hype that move quite rapidly' can lead some adopter organisations 'to move in before all the lessons have been learnt' (Fenn, interview). As Fenn explained, '[w]hen

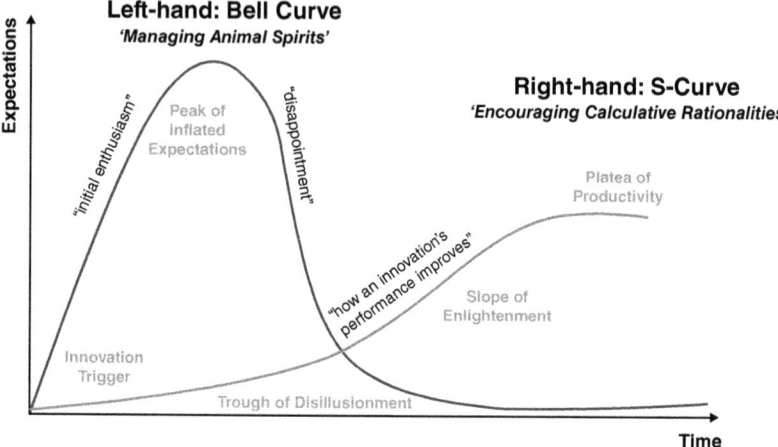

Figure 6.2 Bringing together different rationales in a single picture.
Source: Author representation

it first came out, it was more of a statement, the recognition that this is a pattern that happens ... an adopter beware type of message' (Fenn, interview). Organisations were warned not to 'fall victim to the hype cycle', as premature adoption of unproven technologies could result in catastrophic failure.

Analysts frequently use cautionary language, warning market actors about the risks of premature investment. One described the tendency as 'bright shiny object syndrome', advising clients to 'beware' of its pull (A1, interview). Another noted that 'the vendors are always trying to manipulate you into thinking that everything is wonderful, which of course it isn't' (A2, interview). A third emphasised that '[a]t the end of the day, it's all about dispelling the enthusiasm that is not justified' (A3, interview). The same analyst explained that 'the primary purpose of [HCCs] is to remind people that early-stage investments carry significant risks' (A3, interview). He continues:

You're potentially buying into a technology and probably companies, many of whom are probably start-ups, who simply are probably not going to be around to see that technology come to a mutual market sense. So, I think there is a bit of a caveat emptor intention in [HCCs], not necessarily to scare people away but certainly to remind them to do their due diligence very carefully. (A3, interview)

According to this informant, analysts aim to temper expectations, advising market actors: '"Don't necessarily get your hopes up too high about this." I think that's probably the number one message that any analyst would want ... if you're a buyer, to walk away with' (A3, interview). For example, when discussing the current excitement surrounding Blockchain technologies, another analyst illustrates this cautionary approach by saying:

There's all types of hype around Blockchain.... Hard to tell which is true and which is not true unless you actually get hands-on with stuff.... Once a vendor or a concept or space gets past The Peak, then, because the journalists and all the trades are all hyping up, 'Oh man, this is going to solve everything. Blockchain is the answer to every problem we ever have in IT. You know culpability is not a problem, we've got Blockchain.' (A4, interview)

This scepticism is frequently a result of their extensive familiarity with new successive technologies over a lengthy period. Based on their experience, analysts advise market actors to exercise caution to avoid disappointment, noting that:

We have always been, as a culture, sceptical. We have seen a lot of these things come to the market, and we get clients coming back and saying that 'I stuck my neck out in the organisation, I invested the money, I got a business case, [and] we didn't get the business return.' (A5, interview)

6.5.2 Right-Hand Side: Encouraging Calculative Rationalities

Now, we turn to the right-hand curve, where the objective shifts. While analysts use the left-hand side to highlight risks, they are careful not to discourage market actors from engaging altogether. Jackie Fenn warned against the dangers of excessive caution. Waiting too long can be just as consequential as acting too early. 'Serious threats to survival', she stressed, 'are probably cases when companies don't move soon enough' – leading to irrelevance or missed opportunity. As Fenn explained, some market actors may dismiss a technology as 'no good' or fail to recognise that competitors are already adopting it (Fenn, interview).

The right side signals when benefits can be gained from investing and adopting early. As Fenn points out, 'so when something's Peaking, adopters could say, 'Ok, this may be of interest, and we should look at it, but let's not invest at all costs just because everybody else is. Let's really understand what it means for us' (Fenn, interview). Her message to market actors is to capitalise on the opportunities presented within the HCC, even when things turn sour: 'And then when the issues hit, and things start to be difficult, and people are telling you all the times it didn't work, if it's valuable to you, then you can and should pursue it anyway, even while it's in The Trough' (Fenn, interview).

Furthermore, drawing on well-established criteria for stock market orientation (Chiapello, 2015; Birch & Muniesa, 2020), the internal HCC methodology encourages analysts to categorise market actors as 'Type A, B, or C' based on their risk tolerance. A central message of the HCC is that entering a market should align with the adopter's risk profile. 'Aggressive' adopters may explore and adopt emerging technologies earlier, as they are more willing to take risks, whereas 'conservative' adopters are advised to adopt early only if the potential benefits outweigh the uncertainties. Jackie Fenn explains the reasoning behind these classifications:

I found it in talking with companies to be a very simple way that organisations are prepared to self-identify. So, if you say, 'well, you do think you're Type A, B, C, you're aggressive, moderate, conservative?', they can immediately say, 'Oh, yes, we're definitely a Type C'. Or, 'well, our Product Department is a Type A, but in IT we're Type B or C' or vice versa. So, it's a very simple way that people identify where they are in terms of how willing they are to take the risk of new technologies and also the mismatches within their own companies. (Fenn, interview)

Another analyst describes how he needs to find the correct balance between optimism and caution when providing recommendations to different market actors. As they see it, some should expect to reap significant rewards, whilst others should stay in line with best practices:

[I]f you're Type A, stuff that's early in the [HCC], that's the kind of stuff you might want to be an early adopter of to create competitive advantage. But, if you're Type B or Type C, we would probably say, 'You want to stay away from that unless it's absolutely transformational, and you're going to lose out by not being part of it.' (A1, interview)

For instance, Type Bs are told to invest at 'The Trigger mid-point, right before it quite reaches The Peak' (A1, interview). Investing after The Peak is considered a safer investment because,

We're going to look at something as it's fed out of the hype, so it's made it through that. But we know now it's going to be refined [and] bugs are going

Figure 6.3 When to invest?
Source: Author's representation of an image witnessed at an industry conference

to be fixed as it goes down through The Trough of Disillusionment - maybe that's where some companies want to invest. (A1, interview)

Another analyst uses the example of Software-as-a-Service (SaaS), an emerging phenomenon at the time, to talk us through the way he advises market actors:

When you talk to a client, the Type B and Type C will say, 'Should we go SaaS?' And you can go, 'No, it's not for you, yet'. But for the Type As, you might say, 'Yes, SaaS Financial Management or SaaS HR, it's over The Peak, it's going into The Trough of Disillusionment, so if you know what to watch out for then, yes, you can be an early adopter.' (A4, interview)

The image above, widely disseminated in industry circles, illustrates this segmentation of market actors based on their capacity/willingness to support risk (see Figure 6.3).

6.6 Reconciling: Engaging Hype without Succumbing to It

We now examine how analysts determine when technologies enter, progress through, or exit a hype cycle. A key challenge for analysts in constructing the tool is engaging with hype without becoming over-influenced by it. To maintain critical distance, they must engage in a *reconciliation process*, where, to avoid *falling prey to hype*, analysts balance individual judgement with collective peer review. This process, which we theorise as *negotiating where the dots go*, ensures that decisions are not solely driven by speculative enthusiasm but are instead tempered through structured evaluation and collective deliberation.

6.6.1 Falling Prey to Hype

Individual analysts devote much effort to investigating technology sectors, but it is recognised that they struggle to maintain analytical distance. Before commencing this role, many were seasoned technology specialists, meaning they had extensive professional experience and had often made time and personal/emotional investments in the specific fields covered. However, they face the challenge of becoming overexcited by technology. Informants told us that one of the most damaging errors an analyst can make is to fail to see through overstated vendor promises and to produce a 'vendor puff piece' that is 'too biased in one direction' (interview, A2). In other words, analysts must counter the overenthusiasm of innovation actors and communities by 'not falling prey to … the vendor hype' (A4, interview). According to one analyst's description,

It is a hype cycle, and the vendors tend to define markets by virtue of their own strength. And some of them are very good at it: very good marketing material, very good at supporting arguments they want to support, rather than looking where the evidence is taking you. So, you have to resist that. (A4, interview)

Another analyst makes a similar argument: '[y]ou need a certain amount of cynicism and experience, essentially, to be able to cut through vendor claims' (A1, interview). Indeed, according to this analyst, it is through their long-term career and emotional investments in learning about the technology and trends that they can see through vendor hype:

This does require folks who have some experience and background [and] understand the application of the technology, and can do their own research, right, in terms of [developing a] better understanding [about] these technologies and how they're applied. Where the experience comes in is, really, being able to look at all the current information about something like that and be able to not just plot it on a [HCC] … but be able to say, 'And this is the impact it's going to have.' (A1, interview)

However, more seasoned analysts would admit that this closeness and familiarity could also make it difficult to stay impartial: 'It's human nature to think that the things that you're studying are more advanced than they really are, and you have a tendency to move those dots quicker than they should' (interview, A4). As another informant saw it, neophyte analysts have the propensity to become 'enamoured' with technology:

The biggest thing we [tell] our analysts ... is 'not to get enamoured with the technology. Don't admire the technology. Understand it so that you can help the client to understand whether it's relevant or not'. And that's probably the reason ... a lot of ... inexperienced people ... don't work on these [HCCs] ... it's not just a function of age, right? It can be just the interest in technology. We can get blinded ... by what is described with the technology itself and ... be so enamoured with it that we lose sight of what its real impact is going to be. (A1, interview)

A direct consequence of becoming enamoured is prematurely moving technologies forward in the HCC, regardless of whether there is evidence to support the move:

As an experienced analyst, I've been doing this a long time, I can resist those urges. The younger, the less experienced analysts have a tendency to feel like they need to move the dots year every year – some without real evidence that there's actually increased adoption or a more vibrant vendor community. So, I check all those things out. So, I make sure I'm not falling prey to those proclivities that you tend to do. (A4, interview)

6.6.2 Negotiating Where the Dots Go

Because individual knowledge and judgement are inherently limited and prone to error, the development of HCCs is not the responsibility of a single analyst but the result of a collective process. HCCs are shaped through collaboration among multiple contributors. As one informant explains, HCCs typically 'go out of the door with maybe three or four [author] names' (interview, A6). However, these authors 'don't own all the dots in the [HCC]' (A7, interview). Instead, 'every single one of those dots would have possibly a separate owner' (A3, interview), reflecting the highly distributed nature of the process. Creating an HCC requires synthesising and aligning the perspectives of dozens – and, in some cases, hundreds – of dot owners, a task one author described as a 'pain to do' (A6, interview) and another likened to 'herding cats'. (A2, interview)

An analyst explains a characteristic example: 'So, I do the [HCC] for [tech area 1], so I need the dot from the guy who does [tech area 2], and

I need the dot from the guy who does [tech area 3]. I need the stuff from the [tech area 4] guy' (A6, interview), and so on. Moreover, they must coordinate with them about where their dot should appear and whether it has moved since the previous year. For some HCCs, this coordination effort could be massively expanded: '400 people would play a role in really negotiating where these different dots go and creating the document that gets published' (A3, interview). The process of bringing these actors together is described by the same analyst as follows:

So in a typical year when the [specific HCC] relevant to me was being produced, I would be in this periodic phone, WebEx conversation, providing my point of view of what I think this should be here and that should be there, and these are the anecdotal reasons why I think so, typically based upon the ongoing conversations you're having with end-users and vendors and balancing the two, and in a [HCC] that may have had 25 dots, I would probably end up being the [dot owner] for about four or five of them. (A3, interview)

However, there is more to these events than mere coordination of actions. For example, during meetings, analysts vigorously dispute and occasionally 'fight' with each other: 'If you look at any [HCC], it's the result of probably 50 or 60 analysts debating and infighting to position where those various dots live', says one analyst (A3, interview). The HCC, according to this informant, is a 'methodology' for encouraging debate and negotiation:

Negotiate is a good word. I would have to basically haggle with all of these other people in terms of why I think it should be towards the bottom of 'The Trough' or wherever I've decided it ought to be. So, [the HCC], to me, is the rather important methodology for the internal negotiating and debating that takes place within the analysts. And a [HCC] which finally sees the light of day … can be seen to represent a very broad quern of opinion. (A3, interview)

Placing dots required extensive collaboration and 'a lot of arguing' among community members:

You try to get consensus from your peers … they demand evidence even though it's difficult to find. They want you to launch a good argument, and they want you to defend your placement of that dot. It's a lot of collaboration, a lot of communication, a lot of arguing, [and] a lot of meetings before everyone feels comfortable that, if challenged, they can defend it. (A4, interview)

By, for example, pushing analysts to not only crystallise and polish opinions but also 'defend' them, the frequent (and at times intense) conversations that ensue aided the production and testing of judgements. As another analyst characterises, 'if you can convince somebody that this [dot] deserves to be right up on the right-hand side of that [HCC], then [the innovation] has truly arrived, and it's ready to be a mainstream product' (A3, interview).

6.7 Timing: Shaping Market Actors' Investment Decisions

A final challenge for analysts is positioning technologies within the HCC in a way that aligns with evolving market dynamics – a process we term *timing*. However, this plotting process involves an ongoing balancing act as analysts navigate the risks of responding too quickly to speculative enthusiasm or delaying recognition of technological shifts. When hindsight reveals misjudgements, analysts must be adept at *addressing missteps* and *performing repair acts*.

6.7.1 Addressing Missteps

6.7.1.1 Too Late: Overlooking Transformative Technologies

The placement of technologies on the HCC has wide-ranging consequences, structuring vendor strategies and technology adoption rates and influencing broader industry expectations. Analysts recognise that adjustments to the HCC are not just descriptive but actively shape how market actors engage with new technologies. The idea that tools like the HCC actively influence market dynamics has become so deeply embedded in their practice that it is now 'not much of a discussion point' nor considered 'controversial' within the analyst community (interview, A2). This recognition reinforces their awareness that misjudgements in plotting HCCs are not merely analytical errors but can have significant implications for market dynamics.

As one analyst observed, while their primary goal is 'trying to measure and get a sense of an emerging technology,' they also acknowledge they have a 'certain amount of influence' over which technologies make it onto the [HCC]' (A3, interview). The plotting process is not neutral; it involves deliberate 'filtering', where only a select group of technologies – those considered most 'relevant to [their] audience' (A3, interview) – are included. Rather than attempting to map all innovations, analysts prioritise those they believe will resonate with their clients.

A key risk in this filtering process is that analysts may overlook or underestimate the importance of specific vendor claims. This can result in the omission or delayed recognition of technologies that later prove to be critical, ultimately causing their clients to miss out on emerging opportunities. For instance, an informant recalls how they initially dismissed the 'smartphone's' potential and consequently did not include it in the HCC at all:

Did anybody really assess [the smartphone] correctly? I mean the smartphone starting with what Nokia came out with, with the N95s and whatnot back in the late '90s, early 2000? See, that's an interesting example. Did we or anybody actually call [out] how important or significant that was?... When the iPhone got introduced ... did anybody really go 'this is going to change the world?' ...Well yeah, it did. And I honestly ... can't remember if we or anybody actually called out ... how much impact the smartphone was going to have on consumers, marketing [and] society. (A1, interview)

Another factor that shapes how technologies appear on the HCC is the persistence of certain long-standing entries – what analysts refer to as 'perennial favourites'. Analysts invest considerable time and effort in establishing themselves as recognised experts in the field – making a personal investment in their status. The high standing of a specialist analyst depends on their ability to identify and position themselves as a leading authority. Thus, because analysts invest time and professional credibility in evaluating specific technologies, there can be a reluctance to remove or downgrade those which have been prominently featured for extended periods. As one analyst noted, this reluctance can lead to stagnation in the HCC's representation of emerging technologies, preventing clients from being informed about the full spectrum of potential opportunities:

In terms of the [HCC] for [technology area, we] saw that there were a number of technologies that had become 'perennial favourites'.... So, right at the beginning, I could not actually go for emerging technologies for 13 years, and because, you know, others have been on for long periods of time as well, and because we have limited 'real estate' on the [HCC]. (A3, interview)

6.7.1.2 Too Early: Advancing Technologies Prematurely
Conversely, there is also the challenge of positioning a technology too early within the HCC, signalling that it is more advanced than market

evidence suggests. Premature repositioning can shape vendors' allocation of resources and influence how market actors perceive a technology's trajectory. Analysts acknowledged that 'sometimes the
vendors ... will change what they're doing to adapt to the [HCC]'
(A4, interview). For example, vendors may prioritise certain technologies over others, accelerate development efforts, or scale back investment based on their placement within the tool (A4, interview).

Another consequence of premature repositioning is that it can generate excessive market optimism. One analyst described how market
actors like technology adopters primarily use the tool to compare their
current strategies with projected technology trajectories: '[they] compare what [they're] currently doing to what is in the [HCC] to see if
[they] can do a kind of current and future gap study' (A3, interview).
This includes determining: 'What do [they] need to decommission?
What do [they] keep? And what others should [they] look at?' (A3,
interview). Another informant describes how he worked with 'big
banks in the US' who 'would spend their innovation budget based on
some of the [HCCs] they saw out there for their specific industry or for
specific technology' (webinar 1).

In some cases, market actors have interpreted premature movements
in the HCC as confirmation that a specific technology was ready for
large-scale adoption, leading to investment decisions that later proved
problematic. One analyst recounted an instance where premature
movement within the HCC created unintended market effects:

I've had clients say.... 'You said this would move at a certain speed, and it's
languished, and we bought into it early, and we haven't been able to deploy
that as a result'. That's happened, but earlier in my career. As I got wiser,
with a little more diligence and a lot more trying to figure [out] whether or
not that movement was real or imagined. (A4, interview)

6.7.2 Performing Repair Acts

6.7.2.1 Too Late: Correcting Oversights and Rebuilding Credibility
As market observers and interpreters, analysts rely on the perceived
reliability of the HCC to maintain their credibility. This credibility can
be undermined when they overlook important technologies. For
instance, when they failed to anticipate the rise of the smartphone,
one industry commentator dismissed the HCC as a 'complete waste of
time' (Goodwin, 2023). Another noted that 'every single truly

transformative technology wasn't ever tracked by the [HCC]' (Molander, 2023).

   To mitigate the impact of such omissions, analysts engage in repair acts, adjusting the tool to account for past oversights. A key strategy involves incorporating previous misjudgements, such as missing the smartphone, into internal training, using these cases as cautionary lessons for newer analysts:

One of the things we kind of try to inculcate and kind of beat into our ... new analysts' heads is ... 'remember the smartphone'. Because I will tell you ... a lot of people made fun of them: 'Who's going to pay [for] that; Who needs that?; I just want to make a phone call; 'I just want to text; Who cares'? And well ... almost 15 years later, we've seen what the impact has been of that. And so that's the example I use a lot with our newer analysts: 'Don't look past that ... keep an eye on that'. ... You're never going to be right with the [HCC] 100%.' (A1, interview)

To prevent the HCC from becoming overly static with 'perennial favourites', analysts introduced a 'shelf life' rule, capping the duration a technology can remain on the tool before being removed. One analyst explained that this change aimed to prevent outdated entries from dominating the tool: 'Technologies now have a maximum three-year shelf life on the [HCC]' whereafter they are removed 'and that is to free up real estate to introduce more technologies that our clients should be aware of' (A3, interview). However, removing a technology from the HCC can create confusion – or even signal concerns – about its trajectory to the broader market. When, for example, the 'Big Data' dot was abruptly dropped from the HCC, many in the specific industry were 'mortified' (Ellis, 2015), and market commentators speculated whether this indicated that 'the technology has not progressed as fast as initially expected' (Woodie, 2014) and that its projected market potential was not being realised (Ellis, 2015).

6.7.2.2 Too Early: Managing Premature Advancements without Undermining Trust

What happens when analysts realise – or are informed – that they have prematurely advanced a technology, misrepresenting its maturity beyond what market evidence supports? As one analyst explains, 'You don't move [the technology] forward unless there's real evidence of market changes, increased adoption, or other clear indicators'

(A4, interview). However, one rule remains firm if this misjudgement occurs: while a dot can progress along the curve, it cannot be moved to an earlier point. 'We never go backwards', the analyst stated. 'You might let the market catch up, but you don't move anything backwards' (A4, interview). This practice aims to maintain the credibility of the HCC by creating the illusion of forward momentum, ensuring that every placement appears deliberate and informed. As the analyst elaborates:

> You don't move anything backwards. That's admitting you're wrong, I guess. Since you spent so much time putting it in the right place to begin with, and there's so few new ones introduced every year – usually two every year – you spend so much time getting consensus about where to put it. (A4, interview)

Yet, in practice, this rule is not consistently upheld. Our research reveals instances where technologies have indeed been moved backwards. In the HCC for artificial intelligence (AI), for example, Edge AI and Cloud AI Services advanced in 2023, creating some excitement, but were repositioned backwards in 2024, leading to some confusion in the market (Ramel, 2024). However, when challenged, analysts rely on narrative adjustments rather than explicitly acknowledging errors, strategically framing these movements as refinements rather than reversals (Jaffri & Khandabattu, 2024). By incorporating additional commentary and new insights into subsequent iterations, they subtly recalibrate expectations while maintaining the perception of methodological rigour.

6.8 Discussion: Towards a Processual Understanding of Hype Purification

How analysts create tools to help market actors interpret and respond to hyped markets plays a vital role in emerging new technology industries. Yet the extant literature on market-making has paid scant attention to how analysts construct and operationalise these tools. We conducted a qualitative study of the original design and subsequent production and maintenance process for the HCC, where our findings show that analysts attempt to transform hype from unstructured noise into an interpretable market force, theorised as a process of 'hype purification'. This new understanding contributes to research on tools and market-making, adds to the hype literature, and extends the emerging concept of hype management.

Our notion of hype purification refers to analysts' attempts to distinguish between hype's affective and calculative dimensions when creating tools like the HCC. We identify three mechanisms that help analysts contend with the complexities, tensions, and contradictions of purifying hype – *balancing*, *reconciling*, and *timing* (see Figure 6.4).

The first mechanism, *balancing*, refers to how analysts structure the relationship between hype's emotional (excitement, speculation) and calculative (evidence, feasibility) dimensions in a two-sided graph. Rather than fully separating these elements, they seek to balance two rationales – what we label 'animal spirits' and 'calculative rationalities' (Beckert, 2016) – and navigate the tension that arises from their interaction. The left-hand side of the tool is dominated by animal spirits – the surge of excitement and speculation accompanying emerging technologies. This curve indicates the volatility of early-stage hype and the potential risks associated with premature investment. As enthusiasm and attention build, market actors are prompted to view emerging technologies as 'hopeful monstrosities' (Mokyr, 1990) and reflect on the risks and consequences of entering a market too soon.

Conversely, the right-hand side of the tool illustrates the transition to calculative rationalities as more evidence accumulates regarding a technology's feasibility and commercial potential. This shift encourages market actors to adopt an investor mindset (Chiapello, 2015; Birch & Muniesa, 2020), weighing risks and opportunities in a more structured manner. By visually distinguishing between these two dimensions, the tool does not eliminate hype but reframes it as an interpretable and structured phenomenon.

However, as Latour (2012) argues, purification efforts are always associated with multiple hybrids – messy interconnected realities that require management by deploying several complementary mechanisms.

The second mechanism, *reconciling*, shows that analysts are embedded in the promissory forces they seek to manage and could, for instance, become emotionally 'attached' (Hochschild, 2011) to technologies, which we label as *falling prey to hype*. For example, analysts consistently retained specific technologies in the tool year after year ('perennial favourites'), thereby delaying the recognition of newer innovations and leading to 'errors of omission' (Kumaraswamy et al., 2018), which caused market actors to overlook emerging

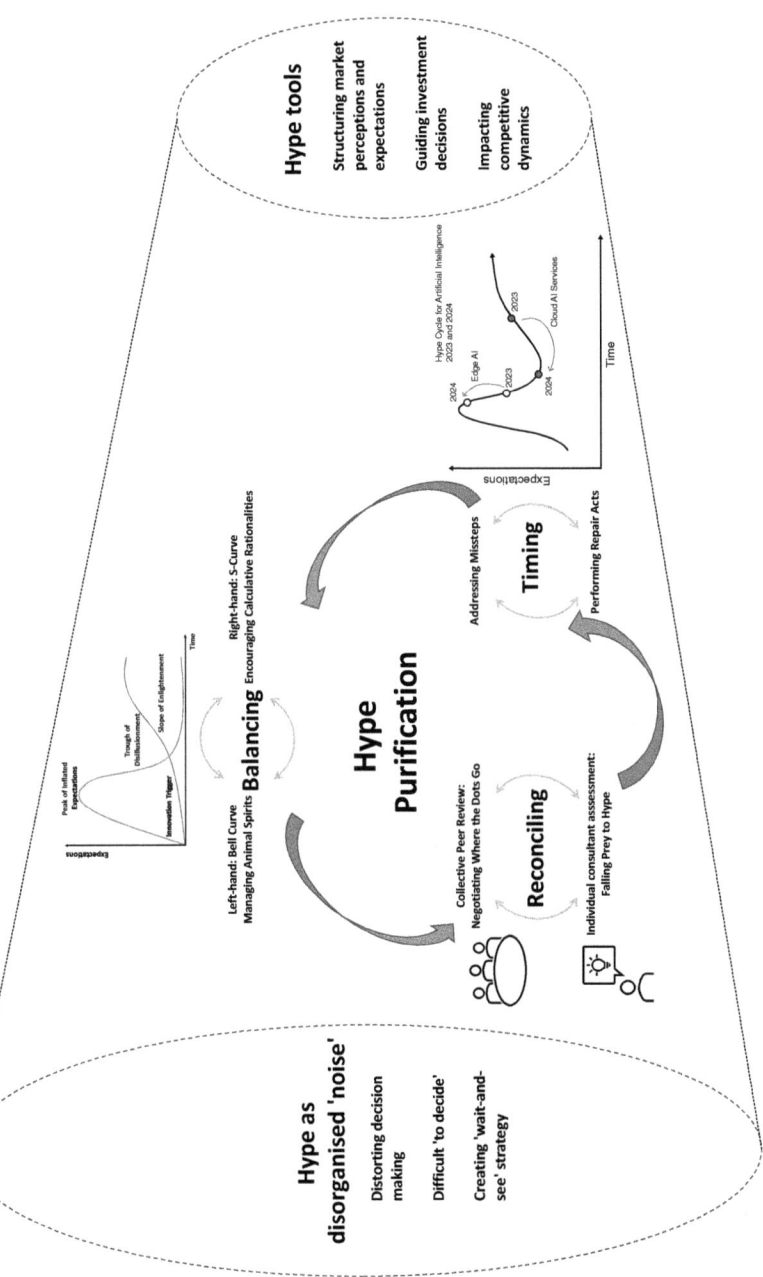

Figure 6.4 Model of hype purification.

opportunities. To remedy this, the analysts' judgements were subjected to collective scrutiny – a process we label as *negotiating where the dots go*.

The final mechanism, *timing*, involves moving technologies strategically from left to right on the tool, flagging technologies that may be transitioning between phases. However, while analysts sought to reinforce the idea that there are more and less favourable moments to invest, they could sometimes advance technologies through the tool too soon, contributing to 'errors of commission' (Kumaraswamy et al., 2018), which encouraged market actors to enter markets prematurely.

We show that *addressing missteps* was critical as errors could become visible and consequential. Supporting prior findings that the tool's 'plausibility' (Rindova & Martins, 2022) is essential for sustaining legitimacy, analysts engaged in *repair acts*, which involved codifying and refining 'tool-based practices' (Gond & Brés, 2020). This suggests that while the HCC presents itself as a structured forecasting tool, it is, in reality, an evolving framework – one that adjusts to market shifts but does so silently and selectively, ensuring that its authority remains intact.

6.9 Theorising Hype Tools as a Market-Making Force

Our chapter contributes to the Market Studies literature (Geiger et al., 2024) by introducing a distinct and previously unexplored category of market device (Muniesa et al., 2007) – 'hype tools'. We defined hype tools in Chapter 2 as material and technical frameworks that shape hyped markets by guiding the timing of decision-making processes and market actions. Prior research has established that markets do not emerge autonomously (Ahrne et al., 2015; Geiger et al., 2024) but are actively constructed by various actors, including consultants and their tools, which play a pivotal role in organising and structuring markets (Pollock & D'Adderio, 2012; Gond & Brès, 2020).

However, while scholars have explored how tools shape market emergence and organisation, far less attention has been paid to how hype – an important market force – is structured, mediated, and sustained through tools. Specifically, we examine the HCC, one of the most influential and widely referenced tools in technology markets, which Beckert (2016, p. 12) suggests is a 'constitutive element of capitalist dynamics'. While previous studies have acknowledged the HCC's role in shaping how market actors engage with and respond to hype (Pontikes & Barnett, 2017; Logue & Grimes, 2022; Wadhwani & Lubinski, 2025), the tool itself has yet to be systematically examined in terms of how it is constructed, maintained, and adjusted over time. In this chapter, we address these gaps by providing an in-depth analysis of the HCC, shedding light on its development, adaptation, and influence on market dynamics.

Moreover, prior research has pointed to the performativity of tools, suggesting that they do not merely describe market trends but actively produce and reinforce them (Callon, 1998; MacKenzie & Millo, 2003). However, rather than focusing solely on their performative effects, we have argued for a closer examination of how hype tools are designed and operationalised to exert influence in the market. As MacKenzie and Spears (2014, p. 394) suggest, '[tools] do indeed have effects, but ... exclusive attention to their effects occludes attention to the processes that shape [tools] and their development'. We extend this argument by shifting attention from the presumed performativity of hype tools to examining how they are continuously redesigned, thus offering one of the first empirical studies to capture the iterative, negotiated, and often contested processes involved in embedding, shaping, and reconfiguring a key tool to ensure that it remains performative by sustaining the attention of market players.

Scholars have highlighted that hype – and its institutionalisation through structured hype cycles – is expanding (Garud et al., 2023), creating a pressing need to understand better the mechanisms that govern how market actors navigate hyped markets (Pontikes & Barnett, 2017; Garud et al., 2021; Logue & Grimes, 2022). While existing research has explored how hype acts as an engine of economic dynamism (Beckert, 2016), a critical unanswered question remains: how do market actors interpret the 'high hopes' (Beckert, 2016) surrounding new markets and determine when they are 'hot' and when they are 'passé' (Pontikes & Barnett, 2017)? Previous studies have primarily explained these dynamics through 'herding behaviour' (Wüstenhagen et al., 2009) or 'self-perpetuating' promissory narratives (Grodal & Granqvist, 2014; Beckert, 2016).

However, these perspectives largely overlook the critical role of hype tools in structuring market perceptions. They do not fully account for how analysts actively monitor, categorise, and selectively amplify hype, shaping expectations, guiding investment decisions, and constructing trajectories of market development. Our chapter shows how the HCC introduces a shared language, framing hyped technologies within a structured trajectory that encourages early-stage caution while positioning later phases as business opportunities. Through directing attention and expectations, the HCC actively helps market participants navigate hyped markets by getting actors to consider their risk appetite in judging when to respond to market signals.

Finally, we highlight that, rather than a neutral mapping of techno-logical trends, the HCC operates as a selective and highly curated tool, in which analysts deliberately 'filter' and 'prioritise' which technologies to include (Pollock & D'Adderio, 2012). This filtering process ensures that only technologies deemed strategically relevant to clients are included. In other words, we show that hype is a 'business issue' that analysts actively manage and monetise, transforming the tool into a 'sellable product' that sustains client engagement and advisory services (Gond & Brès, 2020, p. 721).

Furthermore, we reveal how analysts themselves are not immune to the forces of hype and may prematurely advance certain technologies, reinforcing promissory cycles or developing attachments to 'perennial favourites', keeping them on the tool well beyond their relevance. These tendencies can lead to feedback loops that shape investor senti-ment and technological momentum, fostering what Patvardhan and Ramachandran (2020) term 'artificial evolution' – a process that pro-pels market trajectories in unexpected, sometimes contradictory, direc-tions. By conceptualising these dynamics, our chapter responds directly to Gond & Brès' (2020, p. 721) call for deeper engagement with how consultants and their tools actively structure and recalibrate the 'tra-jectory of markets'.

6.10 Hype Tools Balance Calculative and Affective Aspects

Our concept of hype tools advances existing research on hype by showing that it is not solely an emotionally charged phenomenon but also one in which distinct 'calculative' dimensions are constructed and enacted. Existing literature has prioritised accounts of hype's affective dimensions, mainly the excitement and speculative fervour surround-ing emerging technology markets (Grodal & Granqvist, 2014; Geiger & Gross, 2017). For instance, Beckert (2016, p. 32) describes hyped expectations as a 'cognitive and emotional force that helps orient and animate the capitalist economy', while Geiger and Gross (2017, p. 451) highlight the 'strong affective valence of hype', noting how it fosters 'feverish anticipation, expectations, and hope'. Yet, other research points to the tension between speculative enthusiasm (animal spirits) and structured decision-making (calculative rationalities) (Hirschman, 2013). For instance, as Zaloom (2009, p. 246) argues, much contemporary business knowledge is organised around the dual influences of calculation and affect. However, existing research offers limited insight into how these two influences are managed and mediated in practice.

Our chapter addresses this gap by examining how analysts actively construct, operationalise, and sustain the interplay between affect and calculation – not as opposing forces but as co-constitutive elements that shape market dynamics. Rather than merely visualising hype cycles, the tool creates a negotiation space where affective excitement and calculative assessments are present and strategically balanced. By visually separating and contrasting hype's emotional and calculative aspects in a structured framework such as a two-sided graph, the hype tool studied plays a critical role in framing hyped technology markets as viable spaces for intervention and investment. While the emotive dimension of hype fuels enthusiasm, it could also generate scepticism among decision-makers, perhaps leading to a wait-and-see approach (Endenich et al., 2022).

However, the hype tool does not simply reflect this tension but actively shapes it by introducing a structured distinction between affect and calculability, which serves a dual rhetorical function. First, hype tools establish 'affective credibility' (Comer, 2024) by recognising the emotional force of hype as a key driver of engagement with emerging technologies. Excitement, anticipation, and the imaginative dimensions of technological futures are crucial for resonance. A hype tool may struggle to connect with its audience without these elements. It risks losing relevance and credibility among market participants if analysts 'over-purify' their tools – stripping away speculative energy in favour of pure calculability. Second, it confers 'calculative legitimacy' (Doganova, 2024) by incorporating structured, measurable, and commensurable elements that frame hype as a navigable and structured phenomenon. By introducing notions of calculability, these tools reframe hype from speculative noise into an organised and interpretable process that market actors can strategically engage with.

6.11 Hype Tools Extend Processes of Hype Management

Scholars typically characterise hype and hype cycles as 'unbounded' and emerging spontaneously and unfiltered from within innovation communities (Garud et al., 2014). However, recent scholarship has introduced the concepts of 'expectations management' (Konrad & Alvial-Palavicino, 2017) and 'hype management' (Logue & Grimes, 2022), reflecting a shift in how hype is understood – not merely as a destabilising influence but as a force that, under certain conditions, can be shaped and leveraged. As research on hype management gains prominence (Ometto et al., 2023; Heupel et al., 2024; Wood et al., 2024; Wadhwani & Lubinski, 2025), scholars increasingly recognise the need to examine how market actors engage with hype and channel it as a strategic resource. While existing studies primarily focus on entrepreneurs as primary articulators of hyped expectations (Logue & Grimes, 2022), our chapter broadens this perspective by examining analysts and their role in designing tools that actively structure hype trajectories. This shifts the focus of hype management beyond individual and organisational actors to the industry-wide tools that sustain, regulate, and legitimise hype.

Our chapter builds on the hype management perspective by examining how analysts develop tools and practices that provide a 'threshold of institutionalisation' (Power, 2015, p. 48) to hype cycles. By framing hype as a staged and repeatable process, these tools embed a prevailing interpretation of hype cycles into market discourse, shaping how market actors perceive, engage with, and respond to hype, reinforcing expectations that hype cycles follow a structured trajectory – even though, in practice, technological developments remain contingent and uncertain (see van Lente et al., 2013).

However, while analysts seek to impose structure on hype, our findings reveal that hype management is anything but straightforward. Rather than working as authoritative guides (Porter, 2004), hype tools are precarious instruments (Jackson, 2017). Errors, misjudgements, and 'discrepancies' (Dedehayir & Steinert, 2016) frequently emerge in the classification and positioning of technologies, requiring ongoing adjustments to sustain their credibility. This aligns with research on 'invisible work' (Justesen & Plesner, 2024), highlighting how seemingly stable systems and frameworks rely on continuous, often unseen maintenance work. Our findings suggest that hype management is not solely about predicting technological trajectories; it is equally about repairing and recalibrating expectations to sustain the 'plausibility' of these tools (Rindova & Martins, 2022). (We return to the hype management concept in Chapter 9.)

6.12 Research Opportunities for Studying Hype Tools

We have only begun to scrape the surface of hype cycles and their role in market-making. While this chapter and book expand our understanding of how analysts and their tools actively shape the trajectory of hype in new technology markets, they also reveal opportunities for further research. Future studies could investigate further how hype tools actively shape competitive dynamics by channelling attention and investment into specific areas while marginalising others. This asymmetry in speculative interest warrants closer scrutiny, particularly in its role in market structuring. Research should more fully explore the extent to which those who judge the timing of a technology's entry or exit from a hype cycle wield significant influence over industry resource allocation. Future work might examine in more detail how powerful consultants, in constructing and disseminating a 'coherent field frame' (Lo & Rhee, 2022), strategically amplify or suppress innovations – decisions that can have far-reaching consequences. Studies might throw more light on whether analysts, by prematurely promoting a technology in a tool like the HCC, may fuel excitement and drive speculative investment, or by quietly 'removing' it, might introduce doubts about its viability – potentially leading to its 'stigmatisation' (Garud et al., 2023).

Future research could expand the scope of enquiry to encompass the broader ecosystem of actors and mechanisms involved in generating, filtering, and evaluating hype. A key area of interest is the role of other hype tools that shape organisational decision-making in uncertain technological landscapes. While the HCC remains the most prominent, other influential tools – such as McKinsey's Tech Trends, WEF's Top Ten Emerging Technologies, and Forrester's Top Emerging Trends to Watch, to name a few – may also play a crucial role in shaping market expectations. Digitalisation has also given rise to algorithmic tools that track and quantify hype in real-time, including Google Trends, Brand24, HypeIndex, and Buzz.

Our study only had limited engagement with market players regarding how they utilise these tools. We explored how vendors respond to these tools but have not yet studied extensively how technology adopters act on them. Future research might address an intriguing range of issues. For example, how do these tools shape adopters' perceptions of opportunities for action? What new practices and strategies emerge as market actors develop more sophisticated responses to hype? Exploring the extent to which the development of hype tools encourages market actors to build proactive or reactive approaches to hype would offer valuable insights into the evolving dynamics of hype tools and market-making.

The HCC is just one example of how analysts attempt to reshape market actors' disposition towards hype. Chapter 7 builds directly on the above analysis by turning to another critical dimension of this taming process: the categorisation of emerging technological trends. If Chapter 6 demonstrated how analysts guide market actors on *when* to act, Chapter 7 addresses how they help them decide *what* to act upon. Analysts provide a structured map of the innovation landscape by developing, revising, and retiring technology categories. These category frameworks, much like the HCC, are not passive reflections of technological developments but active devices for shaping market attention and organising vendor narratives.

7 | *Categorising the Sea of Hype*

Market categories matter. In 1998, when industry analyst firm Gartner launched the Enterprise Resource Planning (ERP) category, it did more than label a group of software products – it heralded a new class of computer solution that set the market's direction for the next decade. However, two years later, it would suddenly declare ERP dead and introduce its new ERP II category. Yet, a few months later, and somewhat surprisingly, Gartner would then withdraw the ERP II category (Bond et al., 2000). Similarly, in 2008, following the launch of Facebook and LinkedIn, the same industry analyst firm introduced the Social Software category. When Facebook released its Facebook at Work product, it added further sub-categories to Social Software, including Externally Facing Social Software (EFSS). However, Gartner would soon withdraw the newly introduced EFSS category (Mann et al., 2016). The above cases raise a puzzle. Why do powerful gatekeepers like Gartner introduce bold new categories, only to discard them more or less rapidly afterwards? What kind of market work is being done through these acts of naming, renaming, and erasing? And how do such fleeting categories still exert influence in shaping hype and structuring markets?

The introduction – and often rapid adjustment or abandonment – of market categories has become a defining feature of the digital economy. In a context marked by extraordinary technological change, industry analysts have created hundreds of market-defining categories over the past few decades to help clients navigate shifting landscapes. While some categories endure for years, many prove far more transient (Wang, 2010), with some disappearing after only a few months (Pontikes & Kim, 2017).

There is a clear gap in Information Systems (IS) research regarding why a market gatekeeper, such as an industry analyst, launches a category and subsequently adjusts or abandons it shortly after. When IS researchers and others discuss these ephemeral terminologies and classifications, they depict them as part of the rhetoric accompanying new technologies (Barrett et al., 2013), as fads and fashions (Baskerville & Myers, 2009; Hirschheim et al., 2012; Cram & Newell, 2016; Piazza & Abrahamson, 2020; Heusinkveld et al., 2021), or organising visions (Swanson & Ramiller, 1997; De Vaujany et al., 2013; Davidson et al., 2015; Liao, 2016; Wang, 2021). Yet, these broad-brush approaches tend to leave the complex topology of digital economy product markets underspecified and tell us little about what prompts this gatekeeper to permit, and in some cases, foster an ever-changing category system. However, it is essential to understand these developments, as even short-lived categories herald significant technological and market changes (Wang, 2010).

To shed light on this puzzle, we turn to Category Sudies, which has provided deeper insights into how market gatekeepers categorise technologies (Durand et al., 2017). Scholars have begun to ask what spurs a market gatekeeper to create a category in the first place (e.g., Durand & Khaire, 2017; Delmestri et al., 2020). However, there are still crucial gaps in this literature, particularly on the question of 'how categories emerge and fall out of use' (Kennedy & Fiss, 2013, p. 1139). Specifically, Category Studies has 'overemphasised the stability of categories and the inertia of classificatory systems' (Durand & Paolella, 2013, p. 1109). Moreover, the mechanisms and forms of organisation within gatekeepers that launch, modify, and truncate the career of the category have not been thoroughly investigated (Kennedy & Fiss, 2013). This prompts our research questions: *How and why do gatekeepers continuously introduce, adjust, and abandon categories?*

This chapter addresses these questions by drawing on empirical evidence from a long-term, in-depth qualitative study of the 'Big Three' industry analyst firms. Examining these firms provides insight into how they develop and promote categories that clients find helpful, and then modify or abandon those that detract from this goal. Furthermore, we link IS research with developments in practice-based category discussions (Granqvist & Ritvala, 2016; Durand et al., 2017; Granqvist & Siltaoja, 2020). This allows us to demonstrate how industry analysts attempt to make their expertise relevant to client decisions through a set of material and visual processes, which we theorise as *category-work*, *figuring-work*, and *client-mapping*. Together, these create 'client-induced categories', defined as temporary-probing mechanisms devised to help technology adopters navigate complex digital markets (Khaire & Wadhwani, 2010).

7.1 Market Gatekeeper Priorities during Category Creation

Market categories have been depicted as 'disciplining standards' (Kennedy & Fiss, 2013, p. 1139) and defined as 'devices that create order in markets' (Beckert & Musselin, 2013, p. 7). Categories channel how consumers search for and evaluate products (Rosa et al., 1999; Lounsbury & Rao, 2004). For instance, when an industry analyst issues a report on a new technological category, buyers will use it to find and compare vendors (Pontikes & Kim, 2017). Consequently, because they guide adopters in deciding what and where to buy, vendors must consider (and perhaps adapt to) categories to avoid illegitimacy discounts (Zuckerman, 1999).

For instance, when Gartner introduced its Enterprise Resource Planning (ERP) category, software vendors had little choice but to rebadge and redesign offerings under the ERP banner, as these solutions were sought by adopter organisations (Swanson, 2020). Alternatively, research has shown that if a vendor does not identify as part of a category, it could be 'screened out' of consideration (Zuckerman, 1999, p. 1399). For instance, Pollock and Williams (2011) discuss the case of a software producer that failed to actively position itself in Gartner's emerging customer relationship management (CRM) category and subsequently lost out in a procurement contest.

Technology vendors are especially keen to be included in categories produced by a market gatekeeper, such as an industry analyst, as these receive the most attention from technology buyers (Pontikes & Kim, 2017). Such gatekeepers emerge to help technology adopters choose and evaluate complex products. Conceived as neutral third parties (Aspers & Beckert, 2011), gatekeepers are viewed as possessing the necessary expertise and having no stake or interest in market categories (Khaire, 2017). When a gatekeeper launches a new category, it is thus assumed that they are providing consumers with a comprehensive and inclusive picture of market offerings (Rosa et al., 1999, 2005; Lounsbury & Rao, 2004); that they faithfully represent the market. For instance, Lounsbury and Rao (2004) hypothesise that a gatekeeper is spurred to launch a new category when 'new entrants' flood into an area, therefore expanding the 'variety of product models' and stretching the category boundary (p. 976). Such surges of new entrants typically reflect intense excitement around a technology, suggesting that gatekeepers launch categories to capitalise on that moment of heightened attention.

In contrast, more recent work describes gatekeepers as not passively reflecting markets (Lounsbury & Rao, 2004) but actively constituting them (Carruthers & Stinchcombe, 1999; Beunza & Garud, 2007). Evidence has emerged that shows gatekeepers categorise vendor offerings around the decision-making concerns of clients, rather than providing complete pictures (Kodeih et al., 2018). For instance, in her examination of film critics, Hsu (2006) provides evidence that intelligible categories are 'awarded attention and legitimacy by consuming audiences' (p. 489). Similarly, Pontikes and Kim (2017) describe how, because their clients 'favour category clarity', an industry analyst could 'exclude a firm from a report' that 'complicates their narrative' (p. 85).

Together, these studies support the notion that market gatekeepers shape category systems in response to client concerns. However, the processes through which gatekeepers use these concerns to construct categories remain poorly understood. For example, the creation of more selective or meaningful pictures (Hsu, 2006; Khaire, 2017), where producer developments are excluded (Pontikes & Kim, 2017), contrasts with previous assumptions that gatekeepers built exhaustive knowledge of producer offerings (Carruthers & Stinchcombe, 1999; Rosa et al., 1999, 2005; Lounsbury & Rao, 2004). Indeed, a gatekeeper's decision to omit significant technological developments could appear as an oversight, for which it could be challenged (Lounsbury & Rao, 2004; Navis & Glynn, 2010).

In this context, there are growing calls to study the pragmatic circumstances surrounding category construction (Durand et al., 2017; Grodal & Kahl, 2017), including the work practices and artefacts that produce categories (Blanchet, 2017). Indeed, while Pontikes and Kim (2017) note the specificity of industry analyst category formats – for instance, they are incorporated in 'visual' reports – they do not give this importance. However, it might be assumed that when the gatekeeper foregrounds client concerns, the figures utilised will have some bearing on the categorisation process (Delmestri & Greenwood, 2016; Blanchet, 2017). Thus, to move forward, we must focus on the material and, specifically, visual processes gatekeepers enact in the process of building categories to serve client requirements.

7.2 Material and Visual Processes for Foregrounding Client Concerns

For this purpose, we build on recent calls for research on what market gatekeepers do when they categorise entities in markets (Durand et al., 2017) and aim to identify categories and categorisation processes (Kennedy & Fiss, 2013). While earlier research considered categories as 'theoretical constructs' (Rosa et al., 1999, p. 64) or 'conceptual tools' (Negro et al., 2010, p. 4), we build on later scholarship, which calls for practice-based investigations (Granqvist & Ritvala, 2016) that forge an understanding of the various 'acts of categorisation' (Durand et al., 2017, p. 13). Early literature suggested that simply 'listing products' (Lounsbury & Rao, 2004, p. 1974) was sufficient to spark a category system, but later contributions have described a more structured progression. For instance, Beckert and Musselin (2013, p. 2) describe categorisation as involving processes of framing (i.e. the 'construction of categories to which goods can be allocated'), allocation (i.e. how particular goods are 'defined as belonging to this category'), and discrimination (i.e. 'the establishment of quality differences within a product category').

However, the sociomaterial mechanisms underpinning categorisation processes (see Wagner et al., 2018) are still under-researched. Such mechanisms include how categories are tied to material processes, directing our focus towards the visual character of schemata – a topic attracting increasing attention among category scholars (Delmestri & Greenwood, 2016; Blanchet, 2017). For example, Espeland and Stevens (1998) have demonstrated the importance of visualisations in related market processes, such as 'commensuration'. Delmestri and Greenwood (2016) see 'appearance' as part of a more extensive process of 'visual framing', which is crucial in the social valuation of a category (p. 34). Further studies of visualisation complement Category Studies, which conceives category turnover as driven only by 'linguistic' (Vergne & Wry, 2014) or 'discursive' (Grodal & Kahl, 2017) interventions. Delmestri and Greenwood (2016) argue that the 'persuasive rhetoric of visuals' may be more potent than the linguistic, as it provides for immediate kinds of visual apprehension (p. 34; see also Puyou & Quattrone, 2018). While these studies help us understand how figures persuade, they throw little light on our quest to uncover how gatekeepers go about making categories more valuable to clients.

Building on the above studies, we can refine our initial research question. First, if the market gatekeeper views its primary goal as increasing the value of categories for clients, what categorisation acts (Durand et al., 2017) are involved? Second, to what extent are the resulting processes of material and visual display performing as constitutive elements in the construction of categories?

7.3 Helping Clients Understand the Complex Market of Offerings

Industry analyst informants from the 'Big Three' – Gartner, Forrester, and IDC – viewed their primary goal as creating categories to support and help their clients understand the complex market of offerings. In prioritising value categories given to clients, we found that industry analysts conducted three sets of processes. The first concerned how analysts constitute the market for offerings through category-work. These processes include *framing*, *allocating*, *discriminating*, and *figuring*.

7.3.1 *Framing: Defining an Emerging Technology Field*

Framing captures how analysts participate in helping define and develop a shared understanding of emerging innovation. The process starts when they seek to identify growing fields where their interventions, such as giving a name to a product market, help catalyse its formation. Framing interventions play a historical role here. As noted by an analyst discussing his firm's role in shaping the now well-established ERP category, '[We] sometimes define the terminology that gets used to describe a particular innovation. Many people claim ERP, but Gartner was one of the original players behind the ERP term and trying to make that more widespread in use' (A1, interview). In framing a competitive space, analysts engage in a specific type of category-work. As another analyst described, 'It puts a stake in the sand' (A2, interview). Thus, framing interventions help focus attention on a promising area and help mobilise the resources needed to develop and exploit that innovation. The same analyst continued, '[It] puts a box around what we consider a particular market, which we can then put revenue dollars around, market sizes around, growth rates around' (A2, interview). Framing interventions also create a space where another kind of category-work can be undertaken: *allocating*.

7.3.2 Allocating: Putting Vendors into the New Category

At the next stage, specific vendors are *allocated* to the new category. One informant stated: 'The role of analysis is to categorise things … analysts do try to pigeonhole into categories to understand where we cover, where we don't cover, to some degree' (A3, webinar). A new category encourages a swarming of offerings in the early stages, with multiple vendors attempting to enter with diverse offerings. An analyst described how, as soon as a new category is created, vendors will approach them: 'So vendors are coming now to us to present their offering. They say, "You know what, that's very good, what you produced in terms of the description. We think that we are fitting to your category, and we want to participate [in] the next update"' (A4, interview). Other analysts described similar processes: 'Once you publish a report about a new sector that's emerging and that it's high growth, my God, the phone doesn't stop' (A5, interview).

7.3.3 Discriminating: Creating Evaluation Criteria for Category Entrance

As time continues, an emerging category begins taking shape, and more and more solutions are developed. As further evidence becomes available about the effectiveness of these solutions, analysts establish tools to *discriminate* between different producer offerings in their category. One informant, reflecting on many years of experience as an analyst, discussed how: 'In being able to compare apples against apples and understanding … whatever technologies are growing the fastest in which organisations, that's critical to our base business' (A2, interview). In discriminating between products, the idea is not merely to compare technologies but also to identify notable differences between vendors. To this end, analysts develop a set of evaluation criteria. As another analyst explained, she will: 'Try and define a measurable set of criteria but also a reasonable number, so not too many. You might have five key criteria and various sub-criteria, maybe 25 or something in total' (A6, interview). The analyst plays around with these different approaches to achieve the kind of discrimination they think is helpful. As one analyst put it, 'It's not also just a matter of defining criteria, it's also understanding, obviously, what can be measured, but also what will give ... a degree of diversity' (A6, interview). The same analyst highlighted the problems that would arise if no such discrimination strategy was implemented: 'It's important that you get things that have a degree of diversity. It would be a fairly poor measurement if [all vendors] were "lumped in the middle" because your measurements were not specific enough' (A6, interview). Through discriminating, analysts produce lists of vendors and ultimately figurations that enable technology buyers to select between the leading providers.

7.3.4 Figuring: Incorporating Categories in a Graphical Figuration

Figuring the category is a decisive process in these contexts. Attached to many industry analyst categories is a graphical figuration. For example, Gartner produces its Magic Quadrant, and Forrester and IDC author similar instruments, called the Forrester Wave and IDC MarketScape. These figurations further discriminate between vendors. For instance, the IDC MarketScape will rank vendors along two axes, labelled capabilities and strategies, and place vendors in one of four segments: leaders, niche vendors, contenders, and participants. Those vendors set further to the right are seen to have comprehensive strategies, while those placed towards the top have a high capability. Vendors thus seek to ensure that their products are 'up and to the right' (Stiennon, 2012).

7.4 Client-Friendly Pictures Lead to Category Segmentation

The second set of processes we identified in our data captures creating figurations, theorised as figuring-work, which involves *depicting, splitting*, and *drawing in*.

7.4.1 Depicting: Creating Figurations in a Way that Helps Clients Make Decisions

Depicting, primarily by creating figurations that told a story, was vital in helping the client towards a decision. Below, we examine the circumstances in which these figurations are seen to be optimally designed to provide information that can assist clients in procurement decisions. Here, there is a lifecycle element in that the influence of figurations varies across different moments in the evolution of a category. In the early stages, when scores of vendors are attracted to a promising application field, there are too many vendors to draw a meaningful figuration. A figuration with two hundred vendors on it, an analyst told us, would be 'unreadable' (A7, interview). Another analyst said: 'If you look at the Magic Quadrant as it stands today ... it can get a little bit cluttered, and ... people have to spend a bit of time scrutinising it to read it' (A8, webinar).[1] Later, when a field is mature, with some products prevailing, and where applications are well characterised, procurement becomes less uncertain, and there may ultimately be little need for a figuration.

Over the years, however, analysts have recognised an ideal range or number of vendors that enhance the effectiveness of categories for clients. For example, according to analyst A7, the optimal number of dots on a Gartner Magic Quadrant was about 15 to 25. A similar heuristic existed surrounding the Forrester Wave, where they looked to have '10 to 12 vendors' (A11, internal meeting). Likewise, according to A6 at IDC, MarketScape should contain around 10 to 15 vendors. An analyst described the rationale for why they sought to avoid 'crowding' on the figuration:

By providing more relative space between [dots], it's much easier to read and view and take a snapshot of which vendor is where. You can see clearly the dot positions, and you can actually see the distances and the deltas between the dots a little bit more. (A8, webinar)

Analysts are guided not only by a number range; there is also a market picture drafted for directing categorisation work. Two types of market pictures enhance the category construction process. One analyst told us how, when constructing figurations, they wanted to capture the 'good market' (A6, interview) and another how they sought 'beautiful pictures' (A7, interview). The words 'good' and 'beautiful' were a framing mechanism that pointed towards producing aesthetic figurations that were not so crowded as to confuse the client and not so sparse that they

---

[1] This challenge parallels the Hype Cycle Chart's need to simplify complex innovation trajectories (Chapter 6) – too much clutter undermines any strategic visual.

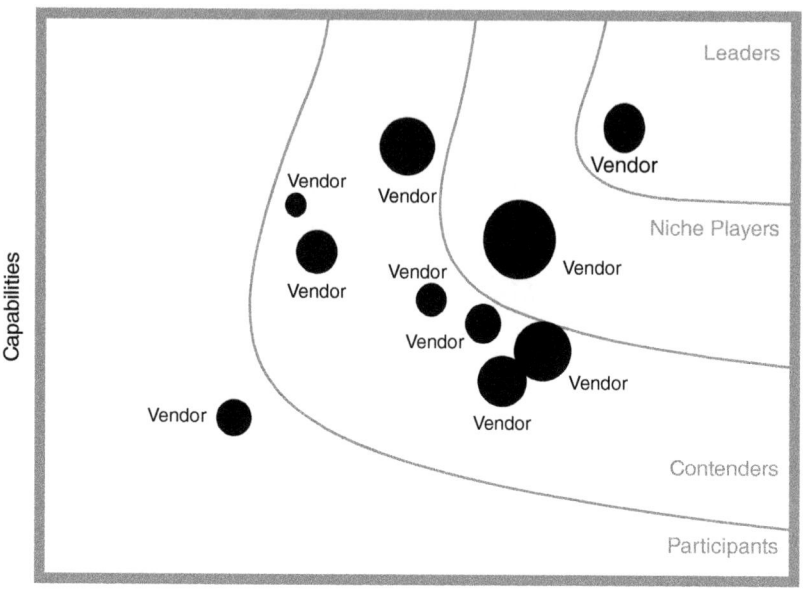

Figure 7.1 The 'good market'.
Source: Author representation

lacked complexity (see Figure 7.1). Additionally, it was necessary for the figuration to have a reasonable number of vendors and for there to be a clear message for the decisions faced by would-be adopters.

There were also diagrammatic devices to enhance how vendors appear on a figuration. For instance, analysts sought to arrange vendors within Waves to create a 'rugby ball' or 'torpedo shape' (A7, interview), which suggested a desire not just to fill the figuration randomly but also to discriminate between vendors in a way that gave it a structure with an implicit narrative of improvement: a torpedo meant vendors were not bunched within one part of the diagram (see Figure 7.2). Instead, there would be vendors with an even spread of capacities (e.g., challengers, contenders, strong performers, and leaders). In other words, the figurations were fashioned to allow analysts to create a set of ordered associations that helped guide clients, similar to how an artist leads a viewer's eyes through a painting, which served to give the figuration significance so that the picture would indeed tell a story about the different capacities of vendors.

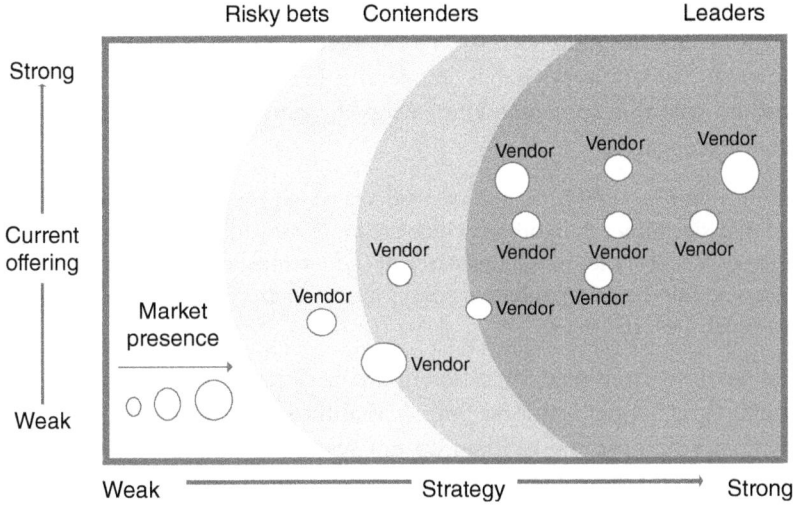

Figure 7.2 The 'torpedo shape'.
Source: Author representation

7.4.2 Splitting: Segmenting the Category

Splitting the category is where the analyst sought to manufacture the desired market picture. Our data show that these market pictures mattered. If the circumstances did not deliver them, analysts would actively attempt to create these pictures. For example, an analyst explains how he segmented a category when the Forrester Wave became 'overly crowded' (A4, interview). He started by explaining what overly crowded meant: 'We have more than 15 vendors in a category [which is a problem] because our Wave process cannot get a good representation in terms of positioning of those 15 vendors. [This is] more than 15, meaning 20, 30, 40 vendors in our graphic ... so we are limiting [the Wave] to 15 vendors' (A4, interview). He then describes what limiting meant: '[When] we are getting too many vendors, which is the case for one of the categories that I am studying currently ... we are getting too many vendors, so, I decided, in that case, to split the category in two' (A4, interview).[2]

---

[2] As with our Hype Cycle Chart discussion in Chapter 6, here the analyst is intentionally shaping a simpler, legible narrative from complexity.

To clarify, one might assume that if an analyst decides to split a category, notable differences have emerged between vendor products. However, this is not what is happening here. The analyst described how he sees this split emerging while showing that it is not easy to achieve in practice:

I try to split [through] getting some products which are more for SMEs, small and mid-size rather than others which are more for [the] large enterprise. So, more a tactical choice in the first place or more strategic choice in the second category. But I am struggling anyway, just to share with you some of the problems. (A4, interview)

The analyst attempted to differentiate between products offered to smaller and larger vendors. Still, it is difficult to create two distinct categories because the vendors do not want to conform. He reported that after he created the split, he hoped vendors would offer products for both categories, but this did not happen and '[Some] of the vendors want to participate in only one [category]' (A4, interview). Thus, the analyst wondered whether he should persist: 'We are facing some problems of deciding how we should split or not split' (A4, interview).

Crucially, if the category split does not resolve itself organically, analysts have other means at their disposal to help encourage it. For example, the analyst could modify the category entrance criteria to include only those vendors who follow his lead and differentiate their products: 'I try to limit [category entrance] to vendors who are participating in both [categories]' (A4, interview). The analyst continued: '[We decide] which are the most representative vendors in that category, and that's our decision, so we have some sort of criteria to discriminate which one should participate, which one should not participate' (A4, interview). Of course, this begs the question of why industry analysts split categories in this way. To answer, we show how the basis of these categorisations revolves around efforts to draw in clients.

7.4.3 Drawing In: Creating Categories That Enrol Clients

Analysts devise their categories to *draw in* those who buy and consume this research, specifically, their clients. Analysts were clear how, when categorising nascent fields, discriminating between vendors, and creating these market pictures, they were doing this for clients and not vendors: 'We are an advocate for the end-user' (A8, interview) (recall

Chapter 4's theme that analysts position themselves as advocates of technology adopters). Another described how this imperative to bring value to their clients permeated everything they did: 'If we try and look at the vendors and say "oh yes, let's come up with a term," it doesn't work that way. Can't work because you have not got the customer in mind' (A7, interview). Ensuring clients maintained their subscriptions was the immediate priority, requiring analysts to respond to queries and provide advice that offered practical help:

If you have got the customer in mind, you are thinking what the customer wants to do is this, this, this, and this, and [if] that's the direction everything is consolidating in, then we can name something. So, when push comes to shove, and there [are] deadlines to be met and customers are screaming at us and wanting something ... you are going [to] go and serve the client. (A7, interview)

7.5 Building Categories around Client Concerns

The third and final set of processes we identified in our data captures how industry analysts directly build categories around client concerns, theorised as client-mapping, which involves probing, cycling, and killing off.

7.5.1 Probing: Launching and Adjusting Categories to Understand Client Buying Preferences

When categorising an emerging technology, the industry analyst must answer a fundamental question – how many categories to create? The difficulty is that they do not know how the technology will play out in the market: will it develop and sell as a broad 'suite' of solutions or fragment into many smaller, more specialised applications? They attempt to understand this through *probing* their client base. The industry analyst will launch an initial categorisation and probe for a reaction. Where this yields a negative response, it becomes the basis for further interventions such as adjusting or adding to a category. We investigate this further by examining Gartner's categorisation of CRM.

Gartner started with a single broad category – the 'CRM Suite' – but as an analyst describes, this did not last long: 'Back in 2002, we had a CRM Suite [category, but] we got rid of it because it was mindless as far as we were concerned' (A7, interview). It was mindless because their probing revealed that clients were not interested in buying the broad CRM suite but only specialised applications:

The problem was that nobody bought [a CRM suite]. 90% of our questions [from clients] were: 'I want to buy a Marketing Campaign solution; what is this CRM Suite thing?' You go: 'Well, most of it is irrelevant to you if you only want to buy a Marketing [campaign solution]'. [Clients go] 'Why don't you just tell me about the Campaign Management vendors?' [You go] 'Well, you need these other vendors who are not on that Magic Quadrant'. 'Well then, what is the point in the Magic Quadrant?' the clients ask. (A7, interview)

Since it was recognised that the single categorisation was unhelpful, the analysts decided to segment CRM further to capture the areas where clients were spending money. The same analyst describes how the CRM category went from one to sixteen categories overnight: '[We] have 16 Magic Quadrants, [where] each one is describing a market' (A7, interview). How did they choose which sixteen specific areas to cover? Again, probing the client base was key: these were '[t]he 16 [specialist applications] that we get most asked about [by clients]' (A7, interview).

Adjusting and augmenting categories based on client probing was an effective means to locate client purchase dynamics. Yet, it could create another problem – proliferating categories. Industry analysts must balance the need to inform clients of new developments whilst avoiding over-burdening them with too many market pictures. Presenting selective and meaningful pictures in highly dynamic areas like CRM is challenging, however, as there are constantly new specialist applications coming on stream about which clients need to know.

7.5.2 Cycling: Moving between Front and Backroom Categories

Industry analysts sought to overcome the problem of overloading clients through an internal innovation: *cycling* between front and backroom categories. There were two aspects to this. The first was to identify a threshold number of categories that could be communicated publicly to clients. An analyst describes how hundreds of vendors continue to enter the CRM category: '[Most] people think [CRM] is all standardised on a few vendors, but we track 300 vendors, and we know that we don't track them all' (A7, interview). As another analyst describes, however, they could not just continue to segment the CRM category as 'the problem for the buyer then is ... [y]ou've got these segments which are sub-segmented and sub-sub-segmented ... which [sub-category] do [they] look in?' (A9, interview). Since a separate analyst could own each category, the result would be that '[buyers] might have to speak to 8 different Gartner analysts to find out what they should be doing' (II, interview).

Therefore, when Gartner expanded the number of CRM categories, it calculated that this could be no more than '16'. These would become the categories published and communicated to clients and others. Yet, as analysts revealed, this 16 represents only a fraction of the market: 'There [are a further] 48 sub-markets that we look at' (A7, interview). These 48 categories have similarities to the 16, but there is a significant difference. They are not communicated to clients the same way. Whereas the 16 are given publicity, the 48 are deliberately hidden from public view and catalogued internally – thus, we might think of the former as 'front room' and the latter as 'backroom' categories.[3]

The second aspect, to ensure clients are kept abreast of changes, was that frontroom and backroom categories are not fixed but could be upgraded or downgraded. An analyst describes what caused an upgrading: 'At least once every 18 months or so we kind of have a pow-wow, and we sit down like we are now to say, "This doesn't really quite work, does it, guys! Let's tweak it around a bit"' (A7, interview). The reason there is flexibility, he suggested:

In the 48, there [are] three main [categories] – Campaign Management, Customer Care, and Sales Force Automation – and that represents 70% of packaged software spend in just three categories. So, the other 30% is split across the other 45 categories. So, they are much more smaller markets with 'nicher' players. (A7, interview)

He went on: '[It] is quite dynamic, so we watch those in ... not as much detail as the big three, but we do, on some of them ... pick them out and write the particular market where we know it has firmed up as a market; we know who the 20 players are' (A7, interview). The notion

---

[3] The emergence of 16 Magic Quadrants will be shown in Chapter 8 to create intense rivalry effects.

of 'firming up' and the number '20' are highly significant in these contexts. It means that the desired number of vendors has emerged for a Magic Quadrant to be drawn, and a meaningful story could be told to the client about the category. This is also a trigger to tell the analyst that a frontroom category has emerged.

It is also possible that the reverse will happen; that is, some of the frontroom categories will be downgraded:

For example, we're in a conversation that is going on this week, actually, where we will tweak around our 48, where we will probably create a couple, kill a couple, merge a couple of these sub-markets.... We'll say, 'these vendors are actually sort of competing against each other all the time', so we'll put those two little sub-markets together, and this group over here, really that is not a very good way of viewing it, so we have to be quite flexible. (A7, interview)

We have shown how industry analysts constantly cycled between what might be thought of as front and backroom categories when client-buying patterns were found to be moving in a different direction. In the next part, we delve further into how and why an industry analyst might downgrade or abandon a category.

7.5.3 Killing Off: Abandoning Categories that No Longer Offer Client Value

Our informants identified the factors that encouraged industry analysts to introduce and then – at times – *kill off* categories. These actors gear their research processes to determine areas where something is changing. One analyst told us: 'We try to identify the future of [the] market rather than the past of the market' (DD, interview). They must sustain the perception, as another analyst stated, 'We are always ahead of you, we are always more on the button about what is going on in our area' (A7, interview). As another analyst saw it,

from a commercial point of view, [industry analysts] are incentivised to keep [adjusting categories], and the problem is that you get to a point where you have named everything: What do you do? You have to rename it. And that is what you find more and more. (A9, interview)

Analysts can be damaged if they miss a significant trend or arrive in an area that a rival has already framed. It is common, however, for analysts to propose a category too prematurely that does not take off. Washouts are an inevitable aspect of their category-work: 'We sort of take for granted that we are going to be wrong' (A10, interview). It might seem safer to wait until patterns are more evident, but this would run the risk of allowing others to take the initiative – such as a competitor analyst organisation or consultant. For instance, an analyst recounted the story of how an industry analyst firm attempted – prematurely in his view – to modify the 'Software Oriented Architecture' (SOA) category. This caused 'a bit of a backlash' (A10, interview) amongst the client base, forcing the abandonment of the new category:

[The analyst firm] attempt[ed] to define a new trend, not to uncover a new trend but to define a new trend – and I use my words quite carefully – which they called SOA 2.0. So, the idea was everyone out there in the industry, you've heard of SOA, you love SOA, but now we've got this thing called SOA 2.0, which is blah, blah, blah. (A10, interview)

Surprisingly, analysts can sometimes kill off categories unintentionally – as a simple consequence of creating a category. For instance, an informant describes the process an analyst went through when introducing the 'Work-Force Optimisation' (WFO) category and how this led to other, more established categories becoming redundant:

A colleague of mine ... came up with the term WFO – Work-Force Optimisations. What he was picturing, and was quite right, was that there [were] four markets consolidating... And all he was pointing out was, look at these different vendors, they were all aiming for the same thing.... So he coined that term, but in doing that, he killed three other terms that were submarkets. (A7, interview)

Analysts can also be damaged if they retain for too long a category that becomes uninteresting for clients. Areas of technological opportunity will, for various reasons, become exhausted. How would the analysts know in practice when a category is in decline? A category could be killed off when the allocated vendors drop below a specific number:

Because if [the market picture] drops to five dots, there's five vendors in this market, it's highly consolidated, so why would [clients] ring us? So, for example, Operating Systems, what's the point of having a Magic Quadrant for Operating Systems? Let's take Operating Systems on Desktop PCs ... there is about three or four. It is a religious war.... Likewise, another one is Desktop Productivity Applications. We used to have [a category] for that back in '94, '95. Once Microsoft killed everybody, we just dropped them. (A7, interview)

Falling numbers of vendors in a category is a problem because '[w]here you have got down to just a handful like five vendors in a market' there is no longer a 'market that can be evaluated here' (A7, interview). This would mean there would be little distinction between vendors, and the category would struggle to maintain a community of interest. Critically, if there is no longer a meaningful story to be told to clients, why would they ring the analysts? Client disinterest would be the final nail in the coffin, and the category would be killed off.

7.6 Discussion: Fostering a Changing Category System

In addressing how and why industry analysts foster an ever-changing category cycle, we find that they want to ensure their expertise is seen as relevant to client decisions. Bringing together insights from IS research and Category Studies and studying the Big Three industry analyst firms, we found that analysts created and maintained categories that clients find valuable and adjust or abandon those no longer attracting attention. Furthermore, by deploying a practice-based category focus (Granqvist & Ritvala, 2016; Durand *et al.*, 2017; Blanchet, 2017), we show that analysts maintain a category system that seeks to engage clients through *category-work*, *figuring-work*, and *client-mapping*.

Category-work consists of framing, allocating, discriminating, and, by extending Beckert and Musselin's (2013) framework, figuring (i.e. creating a graphical figuration). *Figuring-work* reveals the constitutive elements of these figurations where the gatekeeper splits (i.e. segments) a category to allow the drawing of market pictures that tell the client a story. *Client-mapping* is where the gatekeeper probes for buyer preferences, cycling between frontroom and backroom categories and adjusting or abandoning categories no longer attracting client attention (see Table 7.1 for a summary of our findings). Together, these processes produce 'client-induced categories', defined as temporary-probing mechanisms devised to help technology adopters navigate complex markets in the digital economy. We will revisit this concept in Chapter 9, which reframes categories as part of moving from 'hype in the wild' to more managed hype systems.

In short, client-induced category creation exemplifies how hype interpretation has become part of the business of hype. The client-induced category should capture how the gatekeeper attempts to make

Table 7.1 *Client-induced categories*

Process definition	Example quotes	Implications for category change
Process 1: Category-work *Framing* an emerging technology by giving it a name *Allocating* vendors to the new category Discriminating between vendors in the category *Figuring* the category through incorporating it in a graphical figuration	'[We] sometimes define the terminology that gets used to describe a particular innovation. Many people claim ERP, but Gartner was one of the original players behind the ERP term and trying to make that more widespread in use'	Analysts attempt to constantly detect and categorise new technological developments to help their clients understand technical change, which includes identifying and ranking major vendors in the category
Process 2: Figuring-work *Depicting* figurations in a way that helps clients make decisions *Splitting* categories when figurations become overcrowded *Drawing in* clients when creating categories	'[When] we are getting too many vendors, which is the case for one of the categories that I am studying currently ... we are getting too many vendors, so, I decided, in that case, to split the category in two'	Analysts sought to make categories understandable for clients by incorporating them in graphical figures, which included splitting categories to allow more meaningful market pictures to be drawn
Process 3: Client-mapping *Probing* the client base to see if a category intervention is helpful *Cycling* between categories that are more/less of interest to clients *Killing off* categories no longer attracting client attention	'Because if [the market picture] drops to five dots, there's five vendors in this market, it's highly consolidated, so why would [clients] ring us? So, for example, Operating Systems, what's the point of having a Magic Quadrant for Operating Systems?'	Analysts would 'frontroom' categories that clients appeared most interested in and 'backroom' or abandoned those receiving less attention

things easier for its clients by providing them with selective and meaningful market pictures (Hsu, 2006; Pontikes & Kim, 2017). Although one might imagine that categories are created on their own terms – that is, separate from consumption – the notion of client-induced category captures how the gatekeeper introduces or adjusts categories to capture attention and client interest. If a category does not gain traction (and thus market value), it is quickly retired in favour of a new narrative. In other words, a category's survival depends on its commercial relevance – analyst firms do not sustain a classification that fails to engage their paying audience. Instead, they pivot to new categories better aligned with client demand.

By continually tailoring and refreshing these classifications to match client interests, analysts ensure that hype is not only managed but also monetised – its interpretation packaged as a product in its own right. Thus, category creation is not merely an analytical exercise but a cornerstone of the business of hype, where interpreting and structuring hype for clients becomes a commodity. We therefore depict these categories as shaped by the dynamics of consumption. In practice, this means that as client interest (and hype) in an area swell, analysts carve the market into categories that reflect that excitement. This conception differs markedly from the accounts offered by Lounsbury and Rao (2004) and Rosa et al. (2005), for instance, who see gatekeepers as creating categories that are comprehensive and inclusive of innovation, simply reflecting the market.

Even though client-induced categories can be short-lived, this does not mean they are insignificant. Their fleeting nature does not make them insignificant – on the contrary, even brief client-induced categories help anchor moments of hype. As Kennedy and Fiss (2013) argue, transient categories act as 'disciplining standards', directing attention towards which technologies are considered promising at a given moment. In doing so, they help shape the 'social realities' of innovation economies, even if only for a time (p. 1139).

We throw new light on how client-induced categories constitute markets in the digital economy. For instance, our study revealed that when there are many vendors in up-and-coming application areas, the gatekeeper will 'split' the category to allow meaningful market pictures to be drawn. In other words, we show that categories can be segmented not just because notable differences have emerged between vendor technologies but also to attract and capture clients (Cochoy, 2007).

Finally, building on Khaire and Wadhwani (2010), the concept should capture how category emergence is 'not always followed by stabilisation' as client-induced categories endure only as long as they provide utility for primary audiences (p. 1283). After a short period, many of the categories no longer seem to achieve the same level of purchase with their intended audiences. When this happens, the gate-keeper will either backroom or abandon the category.

Below, we articulate how this theorisation of client-induced categories allows us to integrate and build bridges between IS and category scholarship and open up new research opportunities for studying markets in the digital economy.

7.7 How Organising Visions Relate to Category-Work

Few markets are as dynamic as that for digital solutions (Chiasson & Davidson, 2005). There is an almost continuous flow of new terminologies and classifications (Swanson & Ramiller, 1997). We contribute to this conversation by incorporating insights from Category Studies into our understanding of how the digital economy is constituted by 'relatively transitory collective beliefs' (Abrahamson & Fairchild, 1999, p. 709). IS scholars and others have usefully theorised transient terminologies as 'organising visions' (Swanson & Ramiller, 1997; De Vaujany et al., 2013; Davidson et al., 2015; Liao, 2016; Wang, 2021), defined as a 'focal community idea for the application of information technology in organisations' (Swanson & Ramiller, 1997, p. 460). While some (e.g., Wang, 2021) conceptualise the industry analyst categories described here as the same or similar to organising visions, we think it essential to differentiate these concepts as the former reveals processes not captured by the latter.

Industry analyst categories are not generic visions that attract and orient diverse players in forming new technological areas, like organising visions do. Instead, they are knowledge products that (re)make product-market boundaries as part of outputs designed to inform the actions and decisions of technology buyers. Our identification and theorisation of client-induced categories, therefore, articulate mechanisms not fully accounted for by existing concepts. We thus echo and give a new direction to the call by De Vaujany and colleagues (2013) to bring the abstract study of organising visions down to earth by showing how they relate to the concrete operation of markets and innovation alongside and in tandem with categorisation work, inviting further study of how the digital economy is constituted through the enactment of client-induced categories.

We consider the insights offered here necessary, not only because we identify the different dynamics underpinning client-induced categories but also because doing so deepens our understanding of how gatekeepers influence markets. Research in this space has usefully characterised organising visions as having 'a career', where many struggle to gain ascendancy before eventually being displaced (Ramiller & Swanson, 2003, p. 13). However, scholars have been less effective at explaining why specific organising visions take hold and others fade away (Liao, 2016; Wang, 2015). Our category lens suggests that scholars in this area have left underspecified the complex topology of digital product markets and have not given sufficient weight to the emergence of gatekeepers like industry analysts who exercise increasing influence over transient terminologies. The concept of the client-induced category moves this form of analysis forward and also responds to calls for more attention to be given to the role of 'influential gatekeepers' who 'patrol' category boundaries (Wang, 2021, p. 414).

7.8 Creating Categories to Deliver Benefits to Clients

Our chapter further contributes by shedding light on a key but understudied question in the Category Studies literature: how and why categories emerge and fall out of use (Kennedy & Fiss, 2013, p. 1139). We identify and explain how this market gatekeeper creates, adjusts, and abandons categories and how this relates to their primary goal of delivering benefits to clients. Moreover, our chapter offers empirical depth and nuance to this conversation by revealing the different processes that shape industry analysts' course of action. For instance, in theorising the notion of client-induced category, we build on the suggestion by Pontikes and Kim (2017) that what matters to the gatekeeper is to provide clients with categories that they find valuable, and to this end, they will eliminate information and develop specific methods to manipulate categories.

While offering a point of departure for our study, we also provide a more nuanced theorisation of how and why gatekeepers might conduct these kinds of interventions, including revealing aspects that contrast with Pontikes and Kim's (2017) analysis. For instance, we find that the gatekeeper does not simply omit data during category creation, as they suggest, as this may appear as an oversight for which they could be challenged by clients and others (Lounsbury & Rao, 2004; Navis & Glynn, 2010). Instead, it operates a more dynamic system where new vendor developments and technologies are accounted for in further layers of the gatekeeper organisation and where specific categories are front and back roomed as client interests and buying patterns dictate.

7.9 How Figurations Impart New Dynamics to Categories

Our final contribution is to demonstrate how incorporating a category into a graphical figuration intensifies this cycle of category creation, adjustment, and abandonment. In our chapter, client-induced categories are linguistic, material, and, most importantly, visual (Delmestri & Greenwood, 2016). We reveal how attempts by the gatekeeper to create market pictures that told a story for clients became a powerful mechanism shaping the creation and abandonment of a category. The Category Studies literature has not seriously examined how categories and graphic figurations interrelate and whether figurations might impart different dynamics to category systems. For instance, Category Studies suggests that shifts in 'linguistic' (Navis & Glynn, 2010) and 'discursive' (Grodal & Kahl, 2017) frames intensify the cycle of category generation and exhaustion (see also Granqvist & Siltaoja, 2020). However, because in the contexts described in this chapter, the picturing of a category is seen to draw in an audience in ways that linguistic formats do not (Delmestri & Greenwood, 2016), some categories might be considered 'prelinguistic' (Comi & Whyte, 2018). A further understanding of how a category develops through incorporation in a graphical figuration is essential because emergence through a market picture chronologically precedes linguistic developments, such as the introduction of new terminology (Comi & Whyte, 2018).

7.10 Research Opportunities for Studying Categories

The dynamics of markets in the digital economy take on a new hue when seen through a category lens, especially the notion of a client-induced category. Some assume it is simply innovation by technology vendors that intensifies the cycle of generation and exhaustion of categories (Kohli & Melville, 2019). However, our research reveals that this cycle is also a product of the gatekeeper category system and the business of hype. Our chapter invites future research to explore how the gatekeeper process of introducing, adjusting, and abandoning a category evolves. For instance, as recent research indicates (e.g., Pontikes & Kim, 2017), the lifespan of the categories described in this chapter is short – and getting shorter all the time. The interval between the industry analyst introducing and then adjusting or abandoning a category is diminishing from cycles measured in years to cycles measured in months, and future research might investigate why this is the case. For instance, one conjecture worth exploring is whether this faster category turnover results from the emergence of new industry analyst firms (Pollock & Williams, 2016), forcing the Big Three to compete more aggressively for the attention of audiences through launching evermore distinctive forms of categorisation (Bessy & Chauvin, 2013).

Further research is needed on the implications for technology vendors when categories are backroomed or abandoned. For instance, Pontikes and Kim (2017) write that technology vendors have much to gain from becoming a 'category king', that is to say, dominating an industry analyst category. In such cases, the outcomes for a vendor are likely to be significant if an industry analyst decides to discontinue that category. Brandtner (2017), for instance, has written about the potential for powerful incumbents to suffer 'status anxiety' when there is no longer the same certainty about their category, as it will not be apparent 'who is on top of the status order' (p. 214).

Scholars could investigate whether client-induced categories have political ramifications (Bowker & Star, 2000) or whether they disrupt traditional kinds of entrenchment (Durand & Khaire, 2017). For instance, it is widely thought that gatekeepers are 'receptive to the interests of powerful incumbents', such that they avoid 'category reconstitution if a few incumbents dominated a category' (Lounsbury & Rao, 2004, p. 991). Evidence presented here, however, indicates that the gatekeeper would no longer promote (and could even abandon) a category dominated by a few powerful incumbents, as it would be perceived as offering little value to its clients. Future research, therefore, might seek to understand whether client-induced categories act for or against influential vendors with entrenched product markets and if this invites hostility or resistance. It could also investigate whether these categories lead to a potential reordering of the composition and structure of markets, for instance, by killing off the competition between established vendors (Arora-Jonsson et al., 2020) or generating opportunities for other vendors to enter a category (Durand & Khaire, 2017).

Finally, a further potential theme for development concerns how a focus on the socio-materiality of categories can be revealing. We found striking, for instance, that seemingly essential questions – when has a market emerged? – were prompted or settled through 'small' graphic props (e.g., analysts felt justified in launching a new category when there were fifteen to twenty-five dots in a figuration). This insight echoes research by McKendrick et al. (2003) on the number of vendors required before an area is recognised as a legitimate market. Similar issues arise as to when a category should be abandoned (e.g., fewer than five dots). This offers the 'paper trail' sought by Grodal and Kahl (2017) to study category decay, inviting further studies of how the competitive space is constituted through the material and visual enactment of categories.

PART IV

Competing for Ranking and Recognition

Part III of the book examined how industry analysts help technology adopters navigate hype by evaluating, visualising, and forecasting technology trends. We now turn to the other side of this dynamic and examine how technology vendors respond to increasing numbers of analyst evaluations. As hype in the digital economy has grown, the number and variety of promissory products, especially rankings-based assessments, have proliferated (Fourcade & Healy, 2024). Vendors now operate in a highly structured environment in which they are routinely asked to articulate their 'vision' and provide evidence of their 'ability to execute' it. This section examines the rise of rankings, and the increasingly sophisticated hype strategies vendors employ to maintain their positions within these rankings.

In Chapter 8, *Managing the Metrics*, we discuss not only a transformation in how hype is produced but also a shift in hype's role. Vendors are compelled to craft substantiated, realistic narratives and invest in specialised expertise – such as analyst relations (AR) – to secure favourable rankings. We will show that hype is now deeply embedded in the digital economy, governed by structured processes and professional actors. AR experts have become instrumental in crafting these narratives, preparing for evaluations, and strategically positioning vendors. As such, hype is redefined as a professionalised, credible process of narrative construction, rather than as mere exaggerated claims. Vendors with sophisticated AR teams engage more proactively with industry analysts, translating naive promissory narratives into ones that directly address industry analysts' concerns. This dynamic aligns with research showing that rankings can encourage 'reactivity' (Espeland et al., 2016). We extend this notion by demonstrating how vendors can gain substantial opportunities by developing promissory strategies that industry analysts can readily assimilate and adopt. As we will see in this chapter, vendors are not only learning to respond to rankings but also actively shaping them. They refine narratives to match evaluative criteria, strategically position themselves to stand out in crowded markets, and even lobby for the creation of new market categories.

8 | Managing the Metrics

In today's digital economy, the fiercest battles are no longer fought on factory floors or in research labs but, according to Beckert (2016), waged in the realm of imagined futures. 'Because decisions about innovative activities are themselves creating the future', Beckert (2016, p. 170) writes, 'competition in capitalist economies is in no small measure a struggle over imaginaries of future technologies'. This chapter explores a crucial yet often overlooked aspect of this struggle: industry analyst rankings. As hyped expectations blur with formal assessments, rankings have become strategic battlegrounds where the future is not just predicted but actively shaped. Vendors are no longer just constructing promissory narratives to sell products – they are developing narratives to shape the very criteria, narratives and categories by which their products are judged.

We live in a 'society of rankings' (Eposito & Stark, 2019). Organisations are required to respond to increasing numbers of rankings, ratings, and other reputational indices (Espeland & Sauder, 2016; Pollock et al., 2019). The organisational response has been widely studied, with strategies of 'conformance' (Martins, 2005), 'gaming' (Espeland & Sauder, 2007), and 'lobbying' (Wedlin, 2006) foregrounded. In recent years, the conversation has shifted from considering the issue of organisational change towards understanding how rankings create rivalry effects. Scholars are providing increasing empirical evidence of how rankings form new 'competitive battlefields' (Kornberger & Carter, 2010), which include intensifying existing competitive relationships (Brankovic et al., 2018) and creating new rivalries (Mehrpouya & Samiolo, 2016). It is also conjectured that competitive rivalries may be shifting more generally from those between products and services in the market to those being enacted in rankings (Karpik, 2010; Kornberger, 2017).

If, as proponents argue, rivalry today is played out as much through rankings as any other means, then this requires the reconsideration of competitive strategies. However, research sheds little light on how the effects of competitive rivalry stemming from rankings unfold at the strategic level (Arora-Jonsson et al., 2020). Even though studies intimate that rankings engender significant shifts in strategy practice (e.g. Rindova et al., 2018), the literature remains somewhat narrowly focused on identifying 'gaming strategies', defined as 'symbolic responses' located at the 'margins of organisational practice' (Sauder & Espeland, 2009, p. 77).

To explore this issue, we provide a rich empirical account of the way a group of digital economy vendors engage with rankings. The rivalry effects surrounding rankings in the digital economy perhaps represent an extreme case (Eisenhardt, 1989) in that this sector has evolved characteristics and mechanisms that propel ranking-based competition, which may not, at least not yet, be as evident in other ranking fields. However, such cases throw significant dynamics and practices into stark relief that might invite comparison and inform theorising. We show that digital vendor organisations respond to rankings not just to improve their own ranked positions but to weaken those of a competitor. These strategic practices include *leapfrogging a rival, depositioning a competitor, owning the market*, and *encouraging a breakout*, which together make up what we theorise as *ranking strategy*, defined as a set of strategic practices that actors engage in to shape rivalries.

8.1 How Rankings Create Rivalry Effects

The argument that rankings facilitate and promote rivalries between organisations predates current discussions (Karpik, 2010; Kornberger & Carter, 2010; Mehrpouya & Samiolo, 2016; Kornberger, 2017). Early studies laid the foundation for a view of rankings as more than just 'signals' that brought attention to organisational actions, accomplishments, and prospects (Fombrun & Shanley, 1990, p. 234). Because rankings provided 'definitions of success' (Rindova & Fombrun, 1999, p. 700) and facilitated competitive benchmarking, it became evident that they could go beyond signalling an organisational competitive position to encouraging the organisation to compare itself to others. In particular, studies noted how rankings created 'exemplars and role models', which could then inform 'strategic planning' (Rindova & Fombrun, 1999, p. 700). Though the potential of rankings to do more than simply represent competitive rivalries was recognised in early work, it is only in more recent studies that the consequences of bringing organisations into the same evaluative space have been foregrounded.

It has been argued that 'comparability leads to competition', that is to say, what was supposed to be a 'descriptive measure' providing information about quality of a product or service 'tends to become an assessment that puts it in competition with other items' (Esposito & Stark, 2019, p. 7). For example, in one of the first explicit formulations of how rankings create rivalry effects, Wedlin (2006) showed how the introduction of MBA rankings augmented existing competition between rival business schools (p. 11; Sauder, 2008). Kornberger and Carter (2010) further developed this idea in their discussion of Anholt's City Brands Index, arguing that rankings not only enhanced but also created new forms of rivalry (p. 236). They demonstrated, for instance, how the cities of Sydney and London had become rivals, even though they had not previously considered themselves in competition with one another.

Recent empirical work has directly shifted attention from how competition appears as an unintended consequence of rankings to how rankings can be purposefully designed and introduced to create and operationalise competitive rivalries. For example, Mehrpouya and Samiolo (2016) discuss that 'inciting competition' between drug companies was the 'programmatic ambition' of the Access to Medicine Index (p. 13). Brankovic et al. (2018) theorise university rankings 'as tools used by third parties to construct competition', which, through their 'repeated publication', can 'create a continually shifting environment for universities' that creates and maintains an 'audience' hungry for ranking products to understand the changing environment (p. 9).

In short, studies support the idea that rankings are implicated in the rivalising of organisations because they influence the scope and depth of the competitive dynamics between them (Mehrpouya & Samiolo, 2016; Esposito & Stark, 2019). This has led some to speculate whether rivalries arising as a consequence of rankings might equal, or even outstrip, those enacted in other ways, such as through the launching of new products, entering one another's markets, and attempting to wrestle away customers (see Kilduff, 2019, for a review). Scholars argue, for instance, that competition is shifting from confrontation between products and services to confrontation in and through rankings (Karpik, 2010; Kornberger, 2017). This raises an important question: if rankings engender rivalising effects, does it mean that organisations will deploy specific strategic practices in response (Rindova et al., 2018)?

8.2 How Organisations Respond to Rivalry Effects

Despite growing interest in the rivalry effects created by ranking, how organisations respond to these effects remains poorly understood. Studies have focused on the pressures' rankings generated within organisations but less on those *between* organisations (Elsbach & Kramer, 1996). For instance, prior work has shown how rankings are 'engines of status anxiety' that 'incentivise' ranked organisations to 'focus their efforts on improving their relative position' (Sauder & Espeland, 2009, p. 74). Although discussions vary on how organisations might progress their position, they commonly coalesce around a few key strategic moves. One common response discussed in the literature is *conformance* with the criteria imposed by the ranking. As Martins (2005) suggests, conformance is a widespread response because rankings 'push organisations to change in accordance with the criteria used by the rankings' (p. 715).

Another common response is that of *gaming* the ranking to maximize one's position (Corley & Gioia, 2000). Gaming responses are often depicted as 'symbolic' and include efforts at 'managing appearances' (Espeland & Sauder, 2007, p. 29). Where with a conformance response we would typically expect the shifting of the organisation and its practices towards those imposed by the ranking, gaming strategy includes attempts to 'improve ranking factors without improving the characteristics the factors are designed to measure' (Espeland & Sauder, 2007, p. 29) and to 'manipulate appearances in ways that leave internal practices intact' (Sauder & Espeland, 2009, p. 77).

Whilst gaming is a more proactive concept than conformance for understanding how organisations mitigate the pressures brought about by rankings (Sauder & Espeland, 2009), less is known about how rankings might provide organisations with a competitive opening and how they might capitalise on that opportunity (Rindova et al., 2018). Moreover, because gaming is a concept that turns attention towards symbolic responses, it also suggests a decoupling between ranking regime and organisational practice. For instance, Sauder and

Espeland (2009) indicate a dilemma between internalising (conformance) and externalising (gaming). They discuss decoupling taking place via gaming strategies but also stress 'tight coupling' between ranking and those ranked, leading to internalising pressures and (Foucauldian) self-discipline within organisations, and subsequently organisations oscillating between two unreconcilable and extreme responses.

Indeed, recent studies suggest conformance and gaming are only some of the possible strategies adopted (Brandtner, 2017; Pollock et al., 2018). This marks the point of departure for our chapter: if one accepts that rankings are increasingly central for competition, then they are likely to provoke a whole set of nuanced, differentiated strategic responses (Rindova et al., 2018). Indeed, some have begun to differentiate forms of strategic agency, defined as the organisations' 'capacity to cope with and influence' rankings (Kornberger, 2017, p. 1753). Other studies mention how a ranked organisation might embark upon a process of 'lobbying' (Wedlin, 2011, p. 205) or 'petitioning' (Chelli & Gendron, 2013, p. 200). Likewise, some have argued that increasing numbers of professionals, such as public relations (PR) experts, have become involved in the process, suggesting that rankings are 'prone to manipulation' (Sauder & Fine, 2008; Rindova et al., 2018, p. 2191). Recent research suggests the need to develop a more fine-grained, systematic, and empirically grounded understanding of the strategic practices that organisations use to engage with rankings. Thus, in this chapter, we ask: *what strategic practices are employed by organisations to improve their competitive position vis-à-vis a rival in a given ranking?*

8.2.1 A Note on Rankings

The most important ranking in the digital economy is the Magic Quadrant (Pollock & Williams, 2016). Produced by Gartner, it has become the key 'battlefield' between vendors (Gyurko, 2009). This is because technology buyers foreground this ranking over all other information sources. It is common, for instance, for buyers to draw up their shortlists solely based on those vendors appearing on this ranking (Gyurko, 2009). Made up of four quadrants, labelled Leaders, Visionaries, Challengers, and Niche Players, those placed further to the right are seen to have more 'complete visions', whilst

Figure 8.1 An analyst presents a new ranking at an industry event.
Source: Author archive

those placed towards the top have an elevated 'ability to execute' on that vision (see Figure 8.1). In his popular book *Up and to the Right*, Stiennon (2012) encourages vendors to do everything not just to get into the Magic Quadrant but to be placed in the top quadrant as 'being one of the three or four vendors in the Leaders Quadrant almost guarantees your inclusion in product selection process'.

Whilst, as we will show, competitive rivalries between vendors are increasingly played out on the Magic Quadrant, inclusion in the ranking is influenced by contradictory impulses. There is, first, a 'scarcity' (Brankovic et al., 2018) of potential ranking positions. Rather than being produced in the common format like ordinal scale tables, it is a practice or convention in the digital economy that rankings are graphical, constructed to be 'visually appealing' and never 'overcrowded' lest this makes them difficult to read. Magic Quadrants, therefore, normally contain between twenty and twenty-five vendors, as compared with twelve to fifteen vendors respectively for Forrester Waves and Decisionscapes (Pollock & Campagnolo, 2015). One consequence is that they can only ever capture a small fraction of the market, which means that in particularly buoyant technology markets where there might be hundreds of vendors vying for inclusion, competition for entrance can be fierce (Pollock & D'Adderio, 2012).

Second, rankings in the digital economy lack an 'ultimate quality' (Davies, 2016). There are now hundreds of different Magic Quadrants, Waves, and Decisionscapes in circulation, each capturing a different technology category or market, but, due to innovation, this number is changing all the time as new ones are added and older ones retired (Gyurko, 2009). In a study tracking the longevity of Magic Quadrants, for instance, it was shown that many last as little as twenty-four months before they are either withdrawn or reconfigured (Pontikes & Kim, 2017). This means that if a vendor does not make it onto a ranking, it may find further opportunities to enter just a few months later in a new or updated version. Likewise, for those having successfully secured a placement, this might only be temporary as their ranking could well be retired or adapted down the line.

Taken together, these two factors have engendered in digital vendors the understanding that while the ranking environment is high stakes, it is also highly volatile. This has required them to take major steps to help their response to rankings, including creating the expertise of analyst relations. Analyst relation (AR) experts have done two things: they (directly) foster the rivalry effects surrounding rankings through directly helping organisations respond to rankings by providing them with information about analysts and strategies to approach them, but they also (more indirectly) nurture and intensify the idea that rankings have become the key competitive battlefield where rivalries are played out.

8.3 Responding to How Rankings Create Rivalising Effects

Existing research suggests that rankings do not merely represent competitive rivalries between organisations but have also become new spaces of rivalry (Karpik, 2010; Kornberger, 2017). The goal of this chapter is to understand how ranked organisations respond to the fact that rankings create rivalising effects. What we add to the literature is a detailed analysis of how this new space is animated through various strategic practices. During fieldwork, we observed the intensity of competition that can emerge just before and shortly after the launch of a new ranking. Vendors that appeared near or above another ranked organisation were increasingly treated as close competitors. Progress against rivals was measured in terms of movement within the ranking. Before describing the practices organisations take against rivals, we first set out the internal vendor strategies used by ranked organisations to engage with rankers.

8.4 Internal Vendor Strategies to Engage Analysts

In this section, we demonstrate that as rankings have become increasingly important for competitive positioning, vendors have sought to establish closer relationships with analysts. As we saw in Chapter 4, analysts already probe and reshape emerging venture narratives; here, established vendors institutionalise those interactions through dedicated AR teams. The rankers, in turn, appear to require similarly close interactions with vendor AR teams.

8.4.1 Battle That Goes on Internally

In the digital economy, vendors and rankers often cultivate unusually close and ongoing relationships – closer, in fact, than those typically found in other sectors. From the point of view of the ranked organisations, it is the AR expert who is tasked with leading and coordinating the response. The AR expert will attempt to build 'personal relationships' with individual analysts, which includes engineering periods of 'social time', often 'over a meal' or 'drink' (Webinar 1). An experienced AR expert describes the need for this relationship building: 'You need to know what are the characteristics of these analysts: Are they approachable? Are they people who we have a strong relationship? And exactly how am I going to work with these analysts?' (Webinar 1). Such interactions enable the gathering of information not yet publicly available, including whether the ranker is currently considering introducing a new ranking and which vendors they are considering including within it. An AR expert describes how, when the analyst approaches their organisation for a 'briefing' on a new technological topic, they typically respond positively, even though they may lack the necessary information. He hopes to gain further insights about upcoming rankings:

If the analyst asks you something, for instance, [she is] researching on bitcoin currency, 'Do you cover that?' 'Yes'. 'Could you brief me on that?' 'Yes'. You should always ask why and then see where that fits in. 'Why?' 'Because my client's asking'. 'Why?' 'Because I'm researching about it'. 'When are you going to publish it?' 'Why are you going to publish it?' and so on. (AR1, interview)

The analysts, in turn, were not naive about these kinds of interactions. They knew the AR expert would probably subject them to some pressure or even try to change what they were thinking. Analysts told us how such advances could occur in the baldest of ways:

It is in their interests ... to influence it basically. In fact, they call it 'influencer marketing' .... So that is what they care about. If you ask a vendor AR person, what they ask the analyst .... 'Is there anything with our name on?'. 'Yes, that one there in about three months' time'. 'Right, OK. That is what I need to plan for'. So, they don't care about anything else that I am writing about... They care about: 'Is our name going to be on that document?'. 'Right, what do we need to do to stop you saying anything bad about us?' So, it is a PR exercise. So that is the battle that goes on internally. (A1, interview)

Surprisingly, perhaps, the rankers were not disdainful but open to these kinds of channels. This was because they, too, benefited. Analysts informed us that they required 'regular contact with the vendor' (A2, interview) because the ideas and information exchanged would help them interpret the direction of complex and fast-moving technologies and markets, which was particularly useful in the research they produced for their clients and in emerging or evolving markets. Analyst informants confided to us that the more interactions they carried out with ranked organisations, the better their own client insights. Some even lamented how AR experts would limit access to other ranked organisations by acting as gatekeepers: 'Obviously an analyst would love to have diary access to [vendor] executives and many things. So, at times, AR can be a positive, be almost an interface conduit into an organisation, but also, can be almost a gatekeeper' (A3, interview).

What we see here is that fostering interactions was in the interests of all parties concerned. In the sections that follow, we demonstrate that these close relationships enabled ranked organisations to influence the shape of rankings.

8.4.2 Tools to Influence a Ranking

Influencing a ranking requires mustering more than one skillset. Ranked organisations have developed an understanding of the process of creating and building opportunities for changing an analyst's opinion, and AR experts have created formal methods for achieving this. We listened to many AR experts as they described the various instruments they had at their disposal: 'How do I use all the tools within my toolbox in order to change that analyst's opinion? So, that's what we call "AR 1.01," that's what we do day in and day out' (Webinar 2). These tools were not vendor-specific but similar across the ranked organisations studied.[1]

The first step was to initiate the process of shaping a ranking well in advance of publication. For instance, a document on influencing rankings describes how: 'Building credibility with a [ranker] is a process that can take years' (Internal document 1). Seasoned AR experts would gently admonish more junior colleagues who thought improving a ranked position could be done immediately. As the document goes on to say: 'Many AR managers are tasked with the challenge to move [up the ranking] in the timeframe of a year .... Anyone who's looking for a quick jump [upwards] clearly is confusing AR and PR' (Internal document 1).

Another tool was to understand specifically 'who', that is to say, which analyst was to be influenced. An AR expert tells an audience: 'Don't think of [the ranking organisation] as "a firm" but think of it as the "individual analyst," and the relationship that you're trying to build with that analyst' (Webinar 1). However, many rankings are constructed by teams, with each team led by an analyst, as well as those who play other roles, such as data collection. A document unpacks the key interactions that need to be taken around the lead:

Identify the analyst who leads the creation of [the ranking], (they do change), and engage the analyst to learn more about the criteria used for vendor evaluation in previous [rankings]. Engaging the analyst in a discussion, (e.g. a briefing or phone inquiry), should uncover any possible changes in the planned criteria for a forthcoming report. (Internal document 1)

A further tool was identifying those aspects that might be influenced. AR experts typically interrogated analysts around a core set of questions: 'What is their set of assumptions? What [are] their criteria? What's their scoring mechanism?' (Webinar 1). A final, and perhaps

---

[1] These formalised tactics are analogous to the standardised promissory products like the Hype Cycle Chart (Chapter 6) we saw analysts use to tame hype. In both cases, uncertainty is managed through an organised set of techniques.

critical, question was: 'What [do] they think about you?' (Webinar 1). These were the aspects AR experts anticipated they might be able to change. Analysts are increasingly open about evaluative criteria and publicise this information on websites.

Another part of the toolbox was to be judicious about which point in the lifecycle of a ranking to apply pressure. It was commonly understood, for instance, that there were more opportunities to influence the ranking at the birth stages of a new technological phenomenon or market. This aligns with our Chapter 3 argument that early-stage hype periods are when vendors must act, treating hype peaks as opportunities for influence. This is when the ranking is being put together. As this analyst describes:

The interesting bit is when a market is in flux, when it is in the first year or two. After a while, after two or three years, it is pretty much understood on both sides. And [the ranking criteria] will nudge around a little bit, and the analyst will weight it slightly differently each year, move things around a bit each year, to try and reflect what they think is going on. (A1, interview)

AR experts recognised how, during the initial stages, 'Very radical shifts can occur in both the underlying assumptions and the [ranking] criteria' (Webinar 1). But they also expressed uncertainty about whether and how to approach the analyst. It was recognised that, on the one hand, 'Sometimes [analysts] don't want to tell you about [the ranking criteria] because they haven't got it thought out in their head' (Webinar 1). On the other, informants saw how this offered opportunities: 'It's actually not a bad idea [to approach the analyst] because if it's not thought out in their head, you have a chance to potentially influence it. If it's really firm and firmly set in their head, those are the ones that are going to be more difficult for you to change' (Webinar 1).

Certain AR experts had determined that it made sense to approach an analyst at a particular moment or 'season'. The 'on' season is the period just before the launch of a ranking when most if not all of the decisions about ranking criteria have been taken; the 'off' season, alternatively, is the period following the ranking launch and before the work for the new, annually updated ranking has begun:

At [AR Agency] we're constantly trying to figure out methodologically speaking what we do to make the biggest impact and what we found is... You must also run your 'off-season' well. So, I just want to introduce this word and this concept and talk a little bit about it .... The reason why we call the off-season is, just this straightforward sports analogy, champions are made in the off-season. By the time the game starts, you've already lost a huge opportunity to make a difference. (Webinar 2)

This informant stressed that: 'This off-season we believe is the best time to shape criteria. It is the best time to change weighting and it's the best time to completely inform the analyst about changing their perception about what they think about you' (Webinar 2). The AR expert goes on: 'During this off-season, it is the best time to say, "Hey, can I ask you to think about the problem in a different way?"' (Webinar 2).

We have provided evidence that vendor organisations have developed sophisticated internal expertise and strategies to respond to the new competitive battlefield tendered by rankings. Changing a ranked position was a very real possibility in these circles. Our informants sought to improve their own organisation's ranked position. In addition, they indicated that they were increasingly in a situation where they could influence the ranking of a competitor. We now turn to describe the various strategies they deployed to do this.

8.5 Strategic Practices Organisations Take against Rivals

Vendors were as focused on each other's ranked position as they were on their own. A seasoned AR expert described how it had become like a 'chess game' (Personal email). The goal was not simply to work out your own response, but it required 'anticipating competitors' moves' (Personal email). According to this informant, there was a 'widespread and constant chess-game of one vendor trying to de-position a competitor by supplying the analysts with information, insights, and intelligence that puts the competitor in a bad light' (Personal email).

Analysts also deployed similar kinds of analogies to describe how vendor organisations were attempting to organise the competitive encounter through them: 'The vendors know exactly how the game is played, and they are "using" the analysts' (Analyst 1, interview). He tells us what 'using the analyst' means:

It is an interesting two-way battle. The firms don't talk to each other, the vendors – not in a direct fashion, they might off the record – but they are working through the analyst and trying to pull it a little bit in their direction, of course, how we view their products. We are aware of that. We are aware that we are being manipulated to some degree. (A1, interview)

The competitive encounter between organisations has today been extended onto the new terrain of rankings. As this analyst informant sums up: 'That is where the conflict comes, on those documents, and [rankings] are the epitome of those conflicts' (Analyst 1, interview).

This extension of the competitive encounter onto rankings has also propelled the rise of a new, powerful strategic actor. This AR expert can claim a tactical role (as opposed to a mere technical assistance or professional expertise) because they control, or promise to maintain, these relevant 'zones of uncertainty' (Friedberg & Crozier, 1980). Because, in this study, rankings were channelling the encounter between competitors, it was recognised how their practices could become strategically important. Some saw the AR expert role as merely about arranging meetings with rankers, described pejoratively as a 'diary booking service', but there was also a growing sense that this actor could, or should, be 'driving strategy' (Internal presentation 1). Some advocated for how the AR expert was in a position to leverage, 'the unique insights of the industry analysts within their value chain to drive superior strategy' (Internal presentation 1), to work upstream and, 'support the explanation of a business strategy', to 'assist with short- and long- term planning' (Internal document 2) and, to offer the organisation a significant 'competitive advantage opportunity' (Webinar 1).

But what are the concrete strategy practices through which organisations engage with rankings? In Figure 8.2, we summarise the different ways an organisation might attempt to counter a competitor through a ranking. First, vendors enacted strategic practices to *leapfrog a rival*. Second, vendors deployed strategic practices to *de-position a competitor*. Third, vendors enacted strategic practices to shake up an area by *creating a breakout*. Finally, there were strategic practices that allowed a vendor to set the rules of the game or *own the market*. We will now describe these practices in more detail.

8.5.1 Strategic Practices to Leapfrog a Rival

Vendors embraced strategies to *leapfrog a rival* – to push, as one informant described, a 'competitor's dots either down or to the left or both' (Webinar 1). This meant practices were not simply conceived of as stratagems for improving one's own position but were imbued with the sense that you could make a move against a rival organisation.

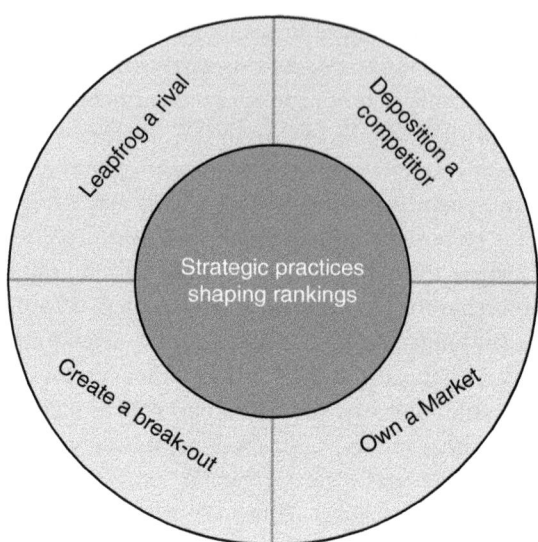

Figure 8.2 Inventory of strategic practices through which actors shape rankings.
Source: Author's Depiction

For instance, an AR expert advises others on the different ways they might go about leapfrogging a rival: 'Now, if you're on the [ranking] ... where do you fit in comparison to your competitors, to all the other people ...?' (Webinar 1). If a vendor finds itself unable to move itself up, the advice given is to consider how it might push its competitors down. The reason being: 'If I had the ability to push my competitor down, then by inference, I've pushed myself up' (Webinar 1). This particular AR expert goes on: 'If I happen to have a competitor who's in the [top spot on the ranking], what can I do to de-position them, move them into the [bottom spot] and perhaps put myself into the [top spot]?' (Webinar 1).

To push a rival down, a vendor organisation will apparently supply analysts with information 'that puts the competitor in a bad light' (Webinar 1). An analyst talked us through such a scenario. Here, the vendor was briefing him on their own products but took the opportunity to criticise a rival:

When we are preparing a [ranking], when we are having interactions with the vendors, we have to have regular contact with the product managers and the product leaders .... Obviously, in those sessions, they'll be saying, 'I can't believe that you've got [rival 1] here or you have got [rival 2] here [on the ranking]? You know they are complete rubbish. You know that we have just won this customer from them who had to throw them out because they were completely useless'. So, we get that all the time, you know. They are constantly hectoring us and badgering us and saying: 'You really don't know what is going on out there.' (A4, interview)

There was the very real possibility that a rival was working to highlight your weaknesses, which 'could impact your dot' (Webinar 1). An informant gives an example where a rival successfully argued for a modification to the ranking's original evaluative criteria, which saw his organisation 'drop' to a weaker position:

I was [well placed] in the original [ranking], and actually not too bad a position [in the top spot]. But because the criteria changed in the new release .... Not because I changed, but because the way in which I'm being measured has changed, I'm suddenly dropped to a [lower] position, indicating, for example, that I don't have the [attributes] anymore that [the ranker] has now put into the criteria for this [ranking]. (Webinar 1)

Informants recounted anecdotes about vendors who had become complacent after moving into the top position. Successfully moving up in a ranking could apparently motivate a rival, especially a close competitor, to double its own efforts to 'de-position you':

I did have a client once say, 'We have moved into the [top] section, on the [ranking]: we're done!'. And that's a really important thing to understand, that to say, 'You're done', and not move ahead can be very, very dangerous. Because remember, your competitors are trying to de-position you. So, one of the reasons why we see vendors fail is that they're not staying on top of these evolving criteria and assumptions and they didn't continue to improve the communications with the analyst. (Webinar 1)

The work of analyst relations is both a matter of improving your own position and stopping a rival from leapfrogging you. This comprised the reflexive task of paying close attention to others' practices, including carrying out research to understand a rival's knowledge or expertise of rankings. There were several tell-tale signs to indicate a rival's preparedness and ability to influence a ranking. For instance, an AR expert advises organisations to: 'Go out and look to see if your competitors have posted any of these [rankings] as reprints' (Webinar 1). Buying 'reprints', which would cost several thousand pounds, not only allowed a ranked organisation to advertise its improved placing to a prospective customer but would also indicate: '[Their] understanding of [ranking strategies], and their level of influence, and likewise, how much effort they may be putting into trying to change [rankings] as well' (Webinar 1). In these settings, such skills and knowledge provided vendors a competitive edge, especially if rivals did not yet possess these skills.

8.5.2 *Strategic Practices to De-Position a Competitor*

There were many ways to dent the ambition or progress of a close competitor, but none was as damaging as 'killing-off' their ranking. An ex-analyst told us, rankings 'do have a life' and that over time they 'become stale', such that they 'Eventually become killed off or they morph into something very different' (A5, interview). Killing-off a ranking was not common as a competitive strategy for vendors and their AR advisors, as it required very high levels of expertise and detailed knowledge of the inner workings of analyst firms. An AR expert described how: '[The ranker] does retire old ones and create new ones .... Working with the analyst that has two [rankings], you might be able to alter the characteristics. Working with an analyst that has lots of [rankings], you might be able to kill a [ranking]' (Webinar 1).

Why might an organisation attempt to kill-off a ranking? A vendor might be incentivised to attempt this when its rival is dominating a ranking in the hope that it would fare better under a new category that would be formed to replace the retired one. One AR expert told us how its main rival was ranked in the top section on one ranking, but his organisation was in the bottom section. When his efforts to reverse the position proved unsuccessful, he set about an alternative strategy:

[The ranker] had two [rankings] for [technology]: One for [product 1] and the other for [product 2]. My employer ... was consistently a leader in the [ranking] for [product 1], but [in the bottom section] in the [ranking for product 2]. Not for lack of trying or significant Research and Development investment, but [my organisation] did not have a snowball's chance in hell of catching the [best placed vendors] on the [product 1 ranking]. (Personal email)

Our informant brought together evidence to convince the analyst that the initial market specialisation, which warranted two rankings, had been replaced by more encompassing 'multi-product' vendor solutions, which required just one ranking. He goes on to explain:

So, I worked to get [the ranker] to create a new [ranking] focused on [Multi-products]. It worked! For the 2016 [ranking] refresh cycle, [ranker] retired the two legacy [product 1 and 2] rankings, 2015 was the last year of publication, and launched a new [ranking] for [Multi-product Solutions]. (Personal email)

This was highly beneficial as he recounts: 'For all three years, [my organisation] has not just been a leader on this [ranking], but the clear leader' (Personal email).

Encouraging the retirement of a ranking could have significant disruptive effects. Analysts told us that killing-off a ranking: 'Does make vendors very angry' (A1, interview). Often, this is because it means their products are no longer visibly part of the market of offerings. As one ex-analyst describes: 'Vendors often take the view, "Oh my God! What are we going to do?" There is no [ranking] for us to use as our main mouthpiece' (A5, interview). The same informant goes on: 'If the [ranking] goes away, it is going to hurt. We are not pretending it won't. If you're a leader in a [ranking], it is definitely going to win you business. And you will have to find new ways to make up for the loss of that [ranking]' (A5, interview).

We also came across less obvious effects from killing-off a ranking. For instance, it was not just that vendor products lose their visibility in the marketplace, there could be other more 'in-house' implications. Apparently, 'at many vendors, [rankings] have more impact internally than externally' (Internal document 3). As an AR expert explained, if a particular vendor product was well-positioned in a ranking, the particular internal 'business unit' producing it would typically be held in high regard. The reverse also seemed to be true:

Imagine an organisation like [Vendor A] or [Vendor B] for whom it is very important that they are the number one or number two in every market, using the [ranking]. Imagine you are running a line of business inside an organisation and the [ranking] maybe might close. That will be a disaster for you because your work currently is feeding up to some corporate scorecard where the organisation strategically is trying to align its resources to the organisation's performance in [rankings]. (AR2, interview)

Because rankings are often used as internal performance measurement systems, this means that if killed off, the performance information about the specific product no longer feeds into or makes a difference to more organisation-wide measures. From then on, as our informant points out, 'Your performance doesn't matter to your boss in the same way' (AR2, interview). As a result, that part of the business could be treated differently: 'And if one [business unit] stops being in the [ranking] ... you are going to have nine most important business units rather than ten' (AR2, interview). Potentially, as this informant makes clear, this could mean that the ones, 'No longer in [rankings] will be spoken about differently. They will be spoken about as "mature organisations"; they will be treated like "cash cows" rather than "growth markets"' (AR2, interview). It was not uncommon, we were told, for an organisation to 'retire' a product if its ranking was killed off.

8.5.3 Strategic Practices to Own a Market

There were several strategic practices that a ranked organisation could potentially 'own a market' (Webinar 1). Owning a market could be enacted through lobbying for a new ranking or market category. An internal document explains how 'categories are vital to validating a technology's value to companies' as they make it 'possible for buyers to understand where different solutions fit, and help vendors to reduce confusion about whether their solutions complement or replace others' (Internal document 3). The document goes on: 'In the same way that technology vendors co-create industry standards, influencing categories is crucial for the success of firms that are leading markets, and thus might not fit pre-existing schemas' (Internal document 3). Creating a category 'could be done within [rankings]' (Webinar 1).[2]

For instance, one AR expert describes how he played a role in how a ranker viewed and created its 'Web Services' category and ranking: 'It was before Web Services was the big area it is now, and it sort of changed in its definition slightly' (AR3, interview). Creating a new ranking or category was potentially highly advantageous. As an internal document describes: 'Because few firms attempt it seriously, the benefits accrue massively to those who do' (Internal document 3). As another AR expert explained: 'You can own a market if you redefine the category, so you're the leader' (Webinar 1). It meant, for instance, that everyone else, that is to say your rivals, must compete

---

[2] This effort parallels the category creation we saw in Chapter 7, where analysts and vendors co-create new market schemas. Here, too, influencing the category boundary via a new ranking is a way for a vendor to secure leadership.

according to the criteria in which you have had a hand in shaping: 'You're unique in this category; everybody else is an also-ran. And you're going to be the leader' (Webinar 1).

Category creation campaigns represent a significant endeavour, however. They take a long time, possibly up to 'one or two years' (Internal document 3) and require 'extensive, prolonged investment', 'serious executive commitment' (Internal document 3), and high levels of knowledge and expertise. In shaping the Web Services category, for instance, the AR expert drew upon his understanding and often direct involvement in the practices of ranking organisations to craft his interventions in a way that resonated most strongly with the ranker. As the AR expert describes:

And with analysts we have to educate them to say, 'No, we are actually looking at things differently'. And we have managed to get them to change the way they approach the scenario. It is harder, you have to get some metrics to get them to change the way they think. But it can be done, and I have done it. (AR3, interview)

Our AR informant understood the internal processes for ranking creation. This includes establishing that there is a market with enough players for the ranker's work of assessment to be pertinent to its own clients: 'We knew that for it to become a [ranking] in its own right it had to have a certain amount of revenue within it, it had to have a certain number of vendors competing within it, lots of different scenarios' (AR3, interview). The AR expert supplied this information: 'And it worked. They actually developed a new way of looking at things' (AR3, interview).

8.6 Strategic Practices to Encourage or Exploit a Breakout

A final strategic action is to try to *encourage or exploit a breakout*. Ranking breakouts were highly disruptive and could have complex consequences. They could place an incumbent under pressure and also provide vendors previously excluded from a ranking the opportunity to enter. We encountered two types of breakouts: geographical breakouts and technical breakouts. They resemble the disaggregation of hype fields we described in Chapter 6, where splitting categories (such as geographical or technical breakouts) creates new hotspots of attention.

Geographical breakouts are where a global ranking is divided into multiple regional versions. Large incumbents tend to dominate international rankings since they sell into numerous geographical markets. However, it was also these vendors who could be most negatively impacted by a breakout, as they are not automatically included in all new regional rankings unless they have a physical presence in the region. As an AR expert describes: 'Imagine you have a global market segment that shows [a French vendor] as the world's number six IT firm, and shows [a Japanese vendor] as being the world's number two IT firm, and you segment that into North America, Europe and Asia' (AR3, interview). What happens then is that these vendors who 'are in the top 10 of IT firms globally' might 'just disappear off the North America [ranking]' (AR3, interview). If this happens, these vendors will then find it difficult to sell into the North American market and could be forced into quite radical action, such as striking partnerships with vendors in North America.

Technical breakouts are where a product covered in one ranking is divided into several more specialised versions. For instance, we observed the case of a ranking for security software which went from one to eight rankings overnight. Technical breakouts put incumbents in difficulty because their products are now subject to more scrutiny. According to this informant, this offered a rival the potential to highlight weaknesses:

> If you have got [IT security] solutions that are able to do the core things, [but] there are eight [rankings] now. Let's say that there are eight things that these solutions could do, but probably most of them will only be really, really excellent at two or three of these pieces of functionality. They won't need to be great at all of them. But suddenly you break it out into separate [rankings] and then it becomes visible that you are weak. (AR3, interview)

Breakouts could be used to identify weaknesses or gaps in a rival's solutions, which could then be brought to the attention of buyers and others. As this informant describes: 'Suddenly you break it out into separate [rankings] and then it becomes visible that you are weak and then that becomes a "proof point" for your competitors' (AR3, interview). Our informant describes how these proof points could be used in sales discussions. A prospect is interested in a rival vendor, but despite being well-positioned in the original IT security ranking, it is not ranked in the new 'Firewalls' ranking. The vendor makes the prospect aware of how its rival is absent from the ranking and its imputed deficiencies: 'You are using a Firewall System, a system that doesn't have Intrusion Detection. And OK, at the moment, you are not worried about Intrusion Detection. But what if you do become worried about Intrusion Detection?' (AR3, interview). A technical breakout could also prompt an incumbent to implement large-scale remedial measures similar to those described above.

By contrast, for those initially excluded from a ranking, a breakout could be highly positive. As an analyst described, this is because 'where you have more [rankings], you have more chance of being on one' (Analyst 1, interview). Similarly, as another analyst describes, the sudden entrance of new rankings 'provides a stimulus for the vendors to go after the analyst afresh' (A4, interview). This informant tells us how 'I will find myself talking with vendors who maybe feel the [ranking] is very unfair to them or maybe they struggle to even get eligibility to even be in a [ranking]' (A4, interview). Or, as this inform-ant goes on: 'If you have got a very dated [ranking] that has been there for many years, it probably doesn't change much from one year to another, the mind-set of the analyst may be closed and myopic as well' (A4, interview). So, when rankings are broken up this provides open-ings: 'The fact is when the analysts are forced to rethink the way they assess the market, they are more open-minded. They are more open to suggestions and ideas' (A4, interview).

8.7 Discussion: How Rivalry Effects Unfold at the Level of Organisational Strategy

Whilst there is growing evidence that rankings engender competition between vendor organisations (Wedlin, 2006; Espeland & Sauder, 2016; Brankovic et al., 2018), we know little about how such rivalry effects unfold at the level of organisational strategy (Kornberger, 2017; Rindova et al., 2019). Based on our ethnographic study of how digital vendors engage with rankings, we have provided insights into the strategic practices developed by ranked organisations, not just to improve their own position but to confront rivals and weaken their position. Our data suggests that organisations are making a high number of strategic moves against one another, identified through the field-inspired labels of *leapfrogging a rival, deposing a competitor, owning a market,* and *encouraging a breakout,* which together we theorise as *ranking strategy*. We have defined ranking strategy as the strategic practices developed by organisations to shape rivalries.

8.8 Ranking Strategy

The first strategic practice, *leapfrogging a rival*, points to how rankings create a 'system of stratification', where 'one [organisation's] ascent requires another's descent' (Sauder & Espeland, 2009, p. 77). The second strategic practice, *de-position a rival*, foregrounds how competitive relations between vendors have become so intense that they might be motivated to invest (often significant) resources to 'undermine' a rival's position (Rindova et al., 2019, p. 2195). Killing-off a rival's ranking could be beneficial because losing one's position on a ranking can be a source 'status anxiety' as there will no longer be the same certainty about 'who is on top of the status order' (Brandtner, 2017, p. 214). The third strategic practice, *own a market*, sheds light on how rankings are created in the first place and the role of powerful stakeholders in that process (Rindova et al., 2019, p. 2191). The fourth strategic practice, *encourage or exploit a breakout*, offered excluded organisations further opportunity to enter or excel on a ranking because in a more 'plural' ranking system, 'there can be more than one winner' (Brandtner, 2017, p. 201). These strategic practices demonstrate the professionalisation of hype management. We return to this point in Chapter 9, which frames these developments as part of the shift to 'tamed hype' in the digital economy.

Constructing a ranking strategy allowed organisations to modulate the competitive rivalry effects stemming from rankings, which might include increasing or decreasing competitive rivalries. The concept builds on previous studies of rankings, which have also attempted to characterise organisational attempts to have a say in setting 'the rules of the game' (Corley & Gioia, 2000, p. 322) and have employed notions like 'lobbying' (Wedlin, 2006) and 'negotiating' (Chelli & Gendron, 2013). In so doing, our chapter shares in a general shift beyond the idea of the ranking as a 'black box' (Esposito & Stark, 2019) towards conceptualisations that recognises how, in specific contexts, organisations can form close 'interactions' with rankers (Sauder & Fine, 2008; Rindova et al., 2019), which allows them to shape rankings (Pollock et al., 2018). In articulating ranking strategy, we do not wish to convey the impression that organisational actors can drive or control a ranking. Instead, the concept sheds light on how they achieved success in moulding the 'cycle of influence' (Analyst 6, interview), as the informant put it. In other words, they could establish channels with rankers and provide ideas and information to inform their evaluation process. Previous work in the sociology of markets has noted similar forms of influence around market categories, which, because there is 'flexibility in how people construct categories', 'opens opportunities for category strategy to influence how people conceive of markets' (Pontikes, 2018, p. 628).

8.9 Gaming Process Giving Way to Strategic Responses

Our chapter challenges the narrowly focused *gaming* analysis in which organisations are seen to embark on 'symbolic responses' located at the 'margins of organisational practice' (Sauder & Espeland, 2009, p. 77). Though the notion of gaming remains a valuable concept that illuminates critical resistance to the internalisation of rankings, in suggesting that there is a 'decoupling' (Sauder & Espeland, 2009, p. 74) between the ranking regime and organisational practice, it inadvertently implies that ranked organisations are accepting of the evaluation regime. That is to say, they attempt to avoid their adverse effects, but they do not necessarily challenge or reshape rankings. We found, by contrast, that ranked organisations, with the help of the new forms of ranking experts described above, were not accepting but attempted to reconfigure the evaluation scheme they were subject to through encouraging the ranker to create, rework, or retire a ranking.[3] In this respect, we answer calls to throw light on the 'strategic actions' undertaken to influence rankings (Brandtner, 2017; Rindova et al., 2019, p. 12). We also echo recent discussions of the shift from 'push' to 'pull' stratagems surrounding evaluation and ranking processes, which were initially not thought 'a priority' as they bear 'little relation' to existing organisational practices but increasingly organisational actors 'welcome and desire' them, especially if they can shape and benefit from them (Power, 2021).

8.10 Rankings Pattern Competitive Rivalries in New Ways

Our chapter offers new insights into the critical question of why organisations might become rivals in the first place (Porac et al.,

---

[3] This proactive reconfiguration of hype channels illustrates the transition to managed hype – a theme we explore in depth in Chapter 9.

1995) and provides indications of how rankings could shape competitive rivalries in new ways (Durand & Paolella, 2013; Pontikes, 2018). In this respect, we answer calls by strategy and organisation theory scholars to build an understanding of 'when and why organisations compete' (Arora-Jonsson et al., 2020). As Samiolo and Mehrpouya (2021) similarly note, the consequences of competition are studied more often than the conditions that give rise to it. There is also growing interest in understanding whether and how competitive rivalries might die out. In particular, how a situation that has 'been constructed as competitive becomes uncompetitive' (Arora-Jonsson et al., 2020, p. 18).

In the fields of strategy and organisation theory, the question of rivalry has been framed around a discussion of market categories. Our chapter is relevant here because scholars have identified how rankings are a key trigger in category formation (Durand & Paolella, 2013). But category scholars often approach the study of rivalries as either resulting from managerial cognition or broader institutional and cultural factors. In terms of the former, for instance, Porac et al. (1995) argued that the question as to who might be considered a rival was the 'product of managerial minds' (p. 224). As for the latter, in discussing the *US News & World Report* and other rankings, Durand and Paolella identify how it is ultimately 'audience interpretations' that decide rivalry (2013). However, we have demonstrated that rivalry is not solely the result of managerial cognition or audience interpretations but is also mediated by and through rankings. There may thus be benefits in exploring rivalry through the practices of engagement that occur around rankings. Studying such strategy practices may offer alternative entry points and open up new possibilities for research on rivalries.

In particular, our chapter not only invites greater integration between discussions of rankings and market categories but also raises the question of whether ranking strategies realise unique kinds of competition. Are rivalries enacted by rankings likely to be different from those surrounding a category? While our insights align with Pontikes' (2018) discussion of how organisations leverage strategy to influence a market category, for instance, our focus on rankings contrasts with her inference that shaping a market category requires organisations to 'band together' and pursue 'collaboration over competition' (p. 626). For instance, Pontikes (2018) argues, 'sound category strategy focuses on influencing the category boundary such that the firm is in a favourable position with respect to competitors', but this does not extend to keeping 'all competitors out of the category' (p. 625). We show, by contrast, that the competitive rivalry effects surrounding rankings do appear to encourage struggle and confrontation and that organisations actively attempt to exclude their rivals from particular markets.

Moreover, rankings appear to afford different temporalities with regard to rivalries. We contrast, for instance, the constantly changing ground of rankings with the relatively long-lived nature of market categories (Durand & Paolella, 2013). Because rankings in the digital space are continuously created and retired (Pontikes & Kim, 2017), our data suggest that rankings create 'episodic' forms of rivalry (Arora-Jonsson et al., 2020). Organisations are brought together for intense periods of rivalry but may no longer desire the same level of competition once their ranking has been killed off. Thus, in contrast to the market category literature that assumes rivalries are enduring over years and decades (Durand & Paolella, 2013), our chapter suggests they can potentially have a much shorter lifespan.

8.11 Illuminating and Theorising a New Set of Strategy Practices

Our final contribution is to the strategy practices literature, where we provide an inventory of the strategy practices through which organisations engage with these new competitive battlefields. This new inventory has the potential to advance the Strategy as Practice (SAP) agenda in two specific ways. We extend the focus of this literature into the increasingly important but not yet identified domain of 'strategising' (Vaara & Whittington, 2012). As Vaara and Whittington (2012) note, the literature has generally ignored the topic of how strategies emerge. In our chapter, we witness the birth of a new domain or category of strategising in response to changing external environments. Indeed, our data show that while these practices were not always formally or universally expressed as a strategy (Jarzabkowski et al., 2007), they can be thought of as strategic because they were consequential in creating a competitive advantage (Vaara & Whittington, 2012). Furthermore, this chapter highlights the role of 'strategies of engagement' defined as those 'plans and actions that aim at influencing and changing the calculation of another actor in one own's favour' (Kornberger & Vaara, 2022, p. 15). The literature has recognised the importance of strategies of engagement but has not explored them in depth, tending instead to focus on internal strategic practices, which, as Kornberger and Vaara (2020) argue, has meant that it has lost sight of how organisations engage with each other. A ranking strategy goes some way to readdressing this imbalance by shedding light on the moves organisations are making against one another.

8.12 Research Opportunities for Studying Ranking Strategy

Our chapter highlights how rankings should be considered as not simply the enabling mechanism for strategy analysis but the object of strategy itself. We provide insights into how developing and implementing a well-crafted ranking strategy is becoming a requirement for organisations in certain areas like the digital economy, where those not devoting often significant resources to such strategies are being outmanoeuvred by competitors who are. An empirical programme is needed to build a better understanding of what it takes to develop and execute a ranking strategy from one sector to another, while noting that in different contexts, the intensity, modalities, and extent of these strategy practices will differ. Though not exhaustive of all possible practices, our inventory provides a focus for empirical enquiry into ranking strategy and its relation to general competitive strategies. We do not necessarily think that organisations will engage in all the strategy practices described above. Strategies are likely to be more developed in specific contexts than others. We should also be careful to pay attention to the limitations of ranking strategy. As acknowledged by Sauder and Fine (2008), influencing a ranking is a time-consuming and challenging process that requires bringing together multiple sets of skills. Accordingly, future work could focus on the kinds of limits that those constructing and deploying ranking strategies encounter.

Overall, these competitive practices around rankings demonstrate the increasing institutionalisation of hype, setting the stage for the final chapters' broader analysis of how hype has become 'tamed' and what that means for markets (Chapter 9) and future research (Chapter 10).

PART V

What Comes after Hype?

In this final part of the book, our focus shifts from presenting empirical findings to analysing the broader evolution of hype in the digital economy. Parts II to IV provided empirical evidence of a significant change in how hyped expectations are created, managed, evaluated, and disseminated since the dotcom era. Chapters 9 and 10 aim to elaborate on these changes. Chapter 9, *Managed Channels in the Wild Sea of Hype*, describes how hype has transitioned from a primarily spontaneous and chaotic phenomenon to a more managed and institutionalised one. This chapter rearticulates the book's central thesis – that hype is no longer fully disorganised – and characterises a critical shift marked by the emergence of 'tamed' forms of hype alongside more unregulated, 'wild' forms. It outlines various channels that have emerged to tame hype as experts and specialists moderate the vendor-adopter nexus. It examines how the business of hype and market for promissory products and expertise has evolved through a dynamic spiral. The chapter concludes by situating this discussion within broader debates on hype management (Logue & Grimes, 2022) and fictional expectations (Beckert, 2016).

Chapter 10, *Towards Hype Studies*, calls for establishing a dedicated academic focus on hype to systematically analyse its creation, evolution, evaluation, and influence within the digital economy and beyond. The chapter demonstrates why dedicated scholarly attention to hype is necessary, arguing that Hype Studies might develop as an interdisciplinary area that examines the hype lifecycle across innovation ecosystems. It outlines several key aspects that require further investigation, including expertise, reflexivity, competition, stratification, and speculative cycles. Together, these aspects offer a foundation for future research directions. It also reflects on the implications of hype's institutionalisation for sectors beyond the digital economy and for policymakers.

9 Managed Channels in the Wild Sea of Hype

There is a tide in the affairs of men,
Which taken at the flood, leads on to fortune;
Omitted, all the voyage of their life
Is bound in shallows and in miseries.
On such a full sea are we now afloat;
And we must take the current when it serves,
Or lose our ventures
     – William Shakespeare, Julius Caesar, Act 4, Scene 3

In today's digital economy, hype is no longer adrift and untamed – it is actively steered. Market actors increasingly seek to catch the rising tide of expectations at precisely the right moment, harnessing structured tools and expertise to avoid being swept away or left behind. We distinguish between 'hype in the wild' and 'tamed hype', a framing used throughout this book. We have argued that tamed hype now permeates the chaotic sea of unruly claims. This chapter analyses how hype's new actors have created *managed channels* within the wild sea of hype, potentially reconfiguring how market actors navigate this phenomenon. One early attempt to *structure* the chaos of hype was the creation of the Hype Cycle Chart (HCC).

9.1 A Pivotal Moment in Hype's Evolution

One key turning point in taming hype came in 1995, when Gartner analyst Jackie Fenn introduced the HCC. This trend-analysis tool would reshape how expectations around emerging technologies are visualised and managed. Before its introduction, there was no clear framework to make sense of hype's trajectory; it was considered 'random', as 'noise' and 'ever accelerating' (Edgerton, 1997), but not as cyclical and with predictable stages. Fenn, however, developed and offered a structured framework for understanding hype's temporal progression.

Initially, the HCC functioned as a cautionary device, grounded in the principle of 'caveat emptor'. As Fenn herself explained, '[w]hen it first came out, it was more of a statement, the recognition that this is a pattern that happens ... an adopter beware type of message' (Fenn, interview). Adopter organisations were warned not to 'fall victim to the hype cycle', as premature adoption of unproven technologies could result in catastrophic failure. Yet Fenn also warned against the dangers of excessive caution. 'Serious threats to survival', she stressed, 'are probably cases when companies don't move soon enough' – leading to irrelevance or missed opportunity. In short, the HCC framed the strategic dilemma at the heart of hype: act too early and risk failure; wait too long and risk being left behind.

Over time, however, the HCC's message evolved. While it first encouraged restraint, it later promoted the idea that hype could be embraced and strategically leveraged as a resource. Alongside other promissory products – categories, rankings, and Cool Vendor designations – the HCC began guiding organisations on how to time their investments and respond to emerging innovations. It thus shifted from warning against hype to embracing and capitalising on it, recognising innovation's potential to transform industrial landscapes.

This reframing highlighted not only the 'threats' posed by disruptive innovations but also the 'opportunities' available to those who can time their moves effectively. Many still interpret the HCC as a warning against speculative bubbles – an instrument to tell managers to 'get in while the hype is rising and get out before the disappointment sets in' (Rip, 2006, p. 353). However, this common interpretation neglects the more subtle strategic sensibility embedded in the HCC: it not only counsels caution in periods of accelerating hype but also reframes phases of waning enthusiasm – exemplified by the 'Trough of Disillusionment' – as potentially advantageous moments for intervention rather than simply phases to be avoided.

But the shift was not merely rhetorical. The HCC began to inform concrete practices and decisions, equipping organisations with new ways to assess and act on emerging technologies. The HCC can be seen as operationalising Levitt's (1965) 'used apple' thesis. As discussed in Chapter 3, the dilemma of when to 'bite' – whether early, at the peak of freshness, or later with greater certainty but reduced reward – was previously more theoretical than actionable. By rendering the dilemma in a visual format, the tool allows actors to 'see better' the problem, and thus to deliberate and act more effectively (Quattrone, 2015, 2017). As Fenn explained in our interviews, 'aggressive companies can investigate more technologies earlier as they are comfortable with more risk', while 'more conservative companies should only adopt early if the potential benefit justifies the additional risk' (Fenn, interview).

What began as a cautionary visualisation evolved into a cornerstone of this analyst firm's product suite, eagerly anticipated by clients each year. It functions as an organisational – and arguably industrial – change agent, prompting market actors to reconsider how they might respond to hype and position themselves in relation to emerging technologies.[1] It contributes to a reconceptualisation of the technology adopter – from a passive and cautious actor (Karahanna *et al.*, 1999) to what could be termed the 'Schumpeterian adopter' – a technology adopter behaving more like an investor: proactive, risk-taking, and opportunity-seeking. This reframing has two consequences.

First, it creates 'animal spirits' (Keynes, 1936) as a new object of managerial attention. Decision-makers are encouraged to consider their emotional responses – excitement, fear, uncertainty – and evaluate whether they are being 'lured out of their comfort zones by market hype' or prepared to move beyond them in pursuit of strategic advantage (Gartner Research, 2018). The HCC not only introduces self-awareness about hype-induced emotions, but it also attempts to tame the animal spirits by channelling them into a risk profile framework, prompting them to self-identify as Type A (aggressive), Type B (moderate), or Type C (conservative) in terms of their disposition towards hype. While such risk profiling is common in venture capital (Birch & Muniesa, 2020), the HCC extends this mindset to technology adopters, now encouraged to 'think like an investor' (Chiapello, 2023), representing a shift from the conventional view of technology adopters

---

[1] A useful comparison here is Gordon Moore's observation of a regularity in semiconductor development, 'Moore's Law', which subsequently became a prescriptive goal and strategic device, around which firms, research agendas, and industry roadmaps were organised (Mody, 2016). While we would not describe hype cycles as a pattern to be actively created and strived for in the same way as Moore's Law, they have nonetheless become the focal point for a whole set of actors and institutions – paralleling in key ways the performative effects of Moore's Law (Miller & O'Leary, 2007). Thank you to Kornelia Konrad for suggesting this comparison.

as inherently 'cautious', 'risk-averse' actors requiring 'strong evidence' before adoption (Karahanna *et al.*, 1999).

Second, Fenn reframed hype as something that not only rises and crashes but also matures over time. Unlike economic cycles, which comprise a series of up-and-down movements, hype cycles include a *resurrection* (towards the 'Slope of Enlightenment' and the 'Plateau of Productivity'). Transforming hype from a random spike into a predictable cycle is significant. It offers a more positive rendering. The focus moves from viewing hype solely in terms of its 'dangers' to recognising its 'opportunities', which influences both our present approach to it and our future understanding of hype. Where hesitation once prevailed, there now exists the potential for proactive engagement. In this way, the HCC helped shift the organisational disposition towards hype, from inaction and caution to strategic experimentation and calculated risk-taking.

9.2 Taming Hype and the Structuring of Expectations

From the viewpoint of this book, the HCC illustrates the taming of hype in the digital economy, signalling a shift from unregulated narratives towards structured and institutionalised forms of expectation. In the conventional view, the digital economy is often portrayed as a turbulent sea of hype, where charismatic entrepreneurs such as Elon Musk unleash bold visions that ripple across markets (Goldfarb & Kirsch, 2019). These figures correspond to the 'promise entrepreneur' (Joly & Le Renard, 2021) introduced in Chapter 2 – individuals renowned for crafting compelling, future-oriented narratives. Such unregulated, viral storylines – what we term 'hype in the wild' – have long dominated both scholarly and popular accounts of innovation.

This framing views hype as generic promissory narratives designed to capture attention and inspire interest. Such claims circulate through dispersed discourse coalitions (Hajer, 1995) – customers, investors, or the public – and are often described as self-fulfilling or performative (Goldfarb & Kirsch, 2019). Promise entrepreneurs typically evade accountability when their claims fail to materialise. According to this view, hype fosters radical uncertainty (Felt et al., 2007), undermines established evaluation frameworks (McBride *et al.*, 2023), and renders expectations ungovernable (Grodal & Granqvist, 2014). Market actors thus experience hype as 'difficult, if not impossible, to control'

(Bakker & Budde, 2012, p. 560), often reduced to a passive 'waiting game' (Robinson et al., 2012). Proactive responses appear rash, driven by unchecked 'animal spirits' rather than strategic calculation.

However, this picture is changing – and the HCC provides one vivid but not the only example of this shift. We have shown that similar dynamics can be seen around Cool Vendor appellations, Magic Quadrant rankings, market categories, analyst briefings, etc. This points to how hype is no longer confined to untamed, spontaneous expressions; it increasingly circulates through structured, institutionalised processes of taming. Hype's new actors have built *managed channels* that reshape how market participants engage with expectations. We present our argument about tamed hype in contrast to this dominant portrayal of hype in the wild, which, we argue, rests on an overly unitary conception of hype as a single, undifferentiated phenomenon (Goldfarb & Kirsch, 2019; Bourne, 2024). Despite its prominence, hype remains under-theorised, with little attention to its heterogeneity or modes of circulation. By foregrounding taming, we show how hype is actively structured, mediated, and made actionable.

Tamed hype arises from the work of hype's new actors – in our case, industry analysts and analyst relations experts – who design, deploy, and respond to promissory products that evaluate and steer emergent narratives. Our analysis reveals a growing interplay between these actors and the broader circulation of hype, showing that hype is no longer merely driven by entrepreneurs or vendors but is increasingly co-produced within formal systems of evaluation.

This evolving dynamic transforms the character of hype itself. It is no longer just a matter of open-ended narratives: hype is now often crafted with an eye towards recognition and validation within evaluative frameworks. From this perspective, promissory work increasingly involves cultivating 'evaluability' – narratives designed to be legible, assessable, and endorsable by market gatekeepers. Much of today's hype is strategically crafted to resonate with these evaluations. Hype is not simply speculative; it has become reflexive, shaped by the very mechanisms designed to judge it. Ventures are not only pitching a future but performing it in recognisable ways – learning *how to look like a Cool Vendor*, or how to frame themselves for the next Magic Quadrant. Innovators calibrate their claims to align with, and sometimes to influence, a market category or the journey of an innovation through the HCC. This marks a fundamental shift: hype is no longer just performative future-making but a strategic response to how future-making is itself structured and assessed.

The turn to taming can be traced to the aftermath of the dotcom bubble (Garud et al., 2021). In response, market gatekeepers developed mechanisms to stabilise and steer hype, making it more predictable and actionable. 'After Hype' thus does not mark hype's disappearance, but its reconfiguration within structured, device-mediated systems of evaluation. It signals a shift from spontaneous speculation to a formalised landscape, where actors align promissory claims with evaluative infrastructures.

Taming makes hype tractable and actionable. Promissory products do not eliminate uncertainty; they create structured channels – both analytical and practical – within the chaotic sea of speculation. These channels subject bold claims to scrutiny and evaluation, offering navigability amid uncertainty. In practice, they take the form of concrete techniques – such as rankings, Cool Vendor designations, and analyst briefings – that serve as an infrastructure for filtering and interpreting hype.

Taming is not about dampening excitement but operationalising it – transforming hype from a volatile force into a strategic resource. These processes are central to how promises and expectations are now curated and controlled in the digital economy (see Table 9.1). This table synthesises the key differences between unregulated 'hype in the wild' and institutionalised 'tamed hype', using the four taming dimensions introduced earlier. As the table shows, tamed hype involves greater scrutiny, structure, and guidance, fundamentally altering how hype is produced and consumed.[2]

Our book has introduced the concept of tamed hype as a novel framework for understanding the institutionalisation of promissory narratives in the digital economy. We have traced the transformation of hype from being dismissed as 'noise' (Jordan, 2020) or condemned as 'dangerous' (Nightingale & Martin, 2004) into a deliberately

---

[2] We do not intend our distinction between 'hype in the wild' and 'tamed hype' to suggest that the former is entirely unstructured or chaotic. We recognise that 'wild' hype also exhibits its own patterned practices, routines, and forms of order. The distinction, therefore, should not be read as a rigid dichotomy but as a heuristic device to draw attention to the growing differentiation of actors, practices, and infrastructures involved in the production and circulation of technological promises. Thank you to Kornelia Konrad for raising this point.

Table 9.1 *Comparing hype in the wild with tamed hype*

Taming dimensions	Hype in the wild	Tamed hype
Reclaiming (hype) from the wild	• Promissory claims bold, unverified, and often unchallenged. • High reliance on charisma, storytelling, and visionary rhetoric. • Accountability limited due to evidentiary delay and shifting market attention. • Prone to bubbles, crashes, and reputational damage.	• Narratives are interrogated by analysts, requiring ventures to moderate claims and provide justification for projections. • Gatekeepers constrain exaggeration, prompting recalibration and narrative repair during briefings. • Tighter scrutiny begins to emerge as ventures approach commercialisation and market traction.
Making (hype) tractable or navigable	• Claims open-ended, ambiguous, and difficult to situate within established categories. • Hype operating through affect and speculative momentum; evaluative criteria are unclear. • Lack of shared references or categorisation systems hampering decision-making.	• Ventures are encouraged to reframe offerings within recognised analyst categories. • Analysts offer formalised evaluative tools to aid navigation. • Promissory products structure hype into legible forms, allowing for cross-venture comparisons and benchmarking.
Domesticating (the evaluator)	• Evaluation informal, episodic, and largely outside vendor control. • Success or failure often judged retrospectively, long after initial claims were made. • Feedback driven by market forces, media cycles, or investor sentiment. • Evaluative criteria unclear or unstable; social proof substitutes for structured judgement.	• AR professionals coach vendors on how to present promissory narratives that align with analysts' frameworks and anticipate scrutiny. • Analysts' frameworks become more formalised and transparent but also subject to strategic influence by vendors. • Vendors no longer passively receive evaluation; they actively participate in shaping it.
Cultivating and improving (hype)	• Decision-makers overwhelmed or paralysed; hype seen as noise or distraction. • Stakeholders deferring action due to high uncertainty and lack of reliable evidence. • Hype seen as misleading and difficult to act upon; actionable insights limited.	• Promissory products help decision-makers interpret claims, assess credibility, and time their investments. • Structured guidance enables decision-making despite inherent uncertainty. • Hype is increasingly treated as a legitimate, trackable signal; analysts advise clients on how and when to engage with emerging technology.

managed and institutionalised process. This mirrors what Latour (2004) described as a shift from a debated 'matter of concern' to an accepted 'matter of fact', and echoes Martin's (2015) observation of a broader shift from a speculative 'regime of hope' to an evidence-based 'regime of truth'. In short, we are witnessing the institutionalisation of hype as a structured and governable element of the digital economy. Recognising this emerging conception of tamed hype opens up new lines of enquiry. One such enquiry is how organisations might make decisions *through* hype rather than *despite* it, as we explore next.

9.3 Making Decisions through Hype, Not despite It

We examine how the emergence of tamed hype is reshaping adoption decisions in the digital economy. A crucial question follows: Are organisations now leveraging hype as part of decision-making, rather than working around or against it?

We have argued that hype is no longer a uniform force. It varies in form, structure, and degree of institutionalisation, and these variations are consequential. If distinct forms circulate – whether as tamed hype, hype in the wild, or other emerging configurations – then each shapes how technological futures are interpreted, evaluated, and acted upon. These differences influence what actors notice, how they interpret developments, and when and how they act. In other words, they affect how innovation is governed, which futures attract investment, and how opportunities and risks are understood.

A highly institutionalised hype may prompt adopters to act sooner on a technology than they would under hype in the wild. Rather than chasing every novelty or ignoring hype, adopters may now time moves strategically – for instance, targeting technologies just emerging from the HCC's 'Trough of Disillusionment' to outpace competitors (see Chapter 6). Yet these dynamics remain under-theorised and empirically underexamined, highlighting the need for systematic comparative and longitudinal research.

There are growing signs that market actors no longer treat hype as something to be screened out or ignored. Instead, they appear increasingly inclined to make decisions through the lens of tamed hype. If so, hype ceases to be mere background noise and becomes a form of market intelligence to monitor, leverage, and act upon. This possibility invites further research into how organisations develop capabilities to interpret and use hype – and the organisational and market conse-quences that follow.

This challenges the dominant scholarly view that the distinction between hype and 'fundamentals' can only be made in hindsight, once outcomes have materialised (van Lente, 2012; Master & Resnik, 2013). We suggest that hype's new actors are reshaping how decision-makers approach, evaluate, and act on technological futures in real time (or at least within organisational decision-making cycles). As recent work shows (Beckert, 2016, 2021; Logue & Grimes, 2022), not all hype is equal: some expectations are more plausible than others or backed by more credible expertise, while others remain speculative. Building on this insight, we argue that market gatekeepers – such as industry analysts – while unable to verify promissory claims, can systematically evaluate them and offer informed judgements about which narratives are more likely to be realised.

This marks a subtle but important shift. Hype's new actors do more than temper hype: they reshape how it is consumed and acted upon, steering attention away from overblown claims and towards more grounded opportunities. As a result, decisions may increasingly be made through, rather than despite, hype. In short, hype may be trans-forming from a distraction into a decision-making tool – though the extent of this shift remains to be demonstrated empirically.

Promissory products such as the HCC, Magic Quadrants, categor-ies, and Cool Vendor reports do not merely track hype; they structure, filter, and operationalise it in ways that vary across domains and over time. Where decision-making once relied heavily on informal judge-ment and 'gut feel' (Karahanna *et al.*, 1999), it is now often decom-posed into modular, manageable steps – each supported by specific promissory products that enable continuous benchmarking, tracking, and recalibration. This 'salami slicing' of decision-making – breaking big, risky decisions into smaller, manageable ones – may not eliminate speculation, but it redistributes and repackages it.

Market gatekeepers have also created new organisational arenas – such as analyst briefings – where promissory claims can be tested, revised, and provisionally endorsed. Such spaces encourage decision-makers to act more reflexively and strategically in the face of uncer-tainty. As our analysis across the book suggests, taming has not only made hype more navigable – it is elevating it into a central object of managerial attention. In doing so, it is reshaping the very infrastructure through which emerging technologies are evaluated, legitimated, and acted upon. Mapping these infrastructures, their evaluative criteria, and their consequences for innovation outcomes is a central agenda for future research.

9.4 Wild Hype Not Diminished

Our account of taming is intended as a complement – not replacement – for the prevailing hype in the wild perspective, and we see scope for examining how these perspectives interact across different technological and organisational settings. Crucially, wild hype has not disappeared (at least in the digital economy). Tamed forms of hype now circulate within the promissory arena alongside more unregulated and charismatic narratives. The relationship between these two forms of hype – tamed and wild – remains a rich and underexplored terrain, ripe for comparative study. One might conjecture that taming could eventually shape, constrain, or even discipline wild hype. However, we have not yet found substantial empirical evidence of this dynamic, beyond suggestive anecdotes. In many respects, wild hype continues to thrive unchecked by the tools and actors associated with taming.

Nor does our focus on taming dismiss the concerns raised by hype in the wild scholarship. We do not, for instance, downplay the importance of studying sensational episodes, such as the Theranos scandal (Cheney-Lippold, 2024). These moments continue to play a significant role in shaping public discourse and institutional responses. Indeed, such scandals often catalyse the emergence or refinement of taming practices – triggering calls for greater oversight, regulation, and evaluative rigour (Zankl & Grimes, 2024). The nature and extent of tamed hype's influence on wild hype, therefore, remain open and important questions for future research, including whether scandal-induced reforms diffuse or stay local.

That said, while the prevalence of wild hype remains high, its overall effectiveness in the digital economy may be uneven (and possibly in decline). Where once it dominated unchallenged, wild hype now appears increasingly marginalised. For instance, the once-unquestioned authority of high-profile 'promise entrepreneurs' is now met with growing public criticism – the so-called 'techlash' (Weiss-Blatt, 2021). This shift suggests a subtle (and still poorly mapped) reconfiguration of the promissory landscape. Alternative valuation frameworks and evidence-based tools may now be gaining ground, enabling market actors to bypass – or at least bracket – some of the more hyperbolic claims. We might be witnessing a new hierarchy of promissory narratives, in which wild hype is increasingly devalued and tamed hype carries greater weight. Future research should examine if and how such a hierarchy is taking shape.

At the same time, our model of taming prompts further reflection on its boundaries. What cannot be tamed? What resists structuring? We do not claim that the digital economy is moving towards better, more calculated decision-making. On the contrary, our research high-lights the persistent volatility, ambiguity, and fragility of innovation evaluation – even when supported by increasingly sophisticated tools, suggesting that any attempt to tame it has its limits. It is crucial to clarify that taming does not imply more control. The mechanisms designed to manage hype – such as rankings, categories, and briefings – can themselves generate new speculative dynamics. Taming is not an endpoint but a recursive process that often creates new forms of second-order hype. As Stirling (2020) reminds us, control is frequently an illusion; what appears to be management may, in fact, be amplifi-cation under different guises.

Thus, the idea of 'purifying' hype (Chapter 6) is both epistemologic-ally flawed and practically implausible (Latour, 2012a). Uncertainty remains irreducible: no evaluative framework, however robust, can fully predict which technologies will succeed, which vendors will deliver, or which futures will materialise. Promising innovations may stall; breakthroughs may render existing categories obsolete. Start-ups, in particular, often outpace the evaluative models used to assess them, revealing the limitations of existing evaluative infrastructures and expos-ing blind spots in established analyst processes – patterns that future work could document more systematically across innovation cycles.

These potential 'breakdowns' (Jackson, 2017) underscore a crucial insight: the taming of hype is always partial and contingent. It is vulnerable to failure, overreach, and misalignment with fast-moving innovation landscapes. Future studies could examine the limits of taming more explicitly, asking: Under what conditions do evaluative frameworks break down? And what unintended consequences might arise when taming tools are over-applied or misapplied? Addressing these questions will help specify when taming moderates, magnifies, or merely redistributes hype, and with what implications for innovation outcomes.

9.5 Mechanisms of Taming Hype

The four taming dimensions in Table 9.1 offer a high-level account of how hype is progressively tamed. Another of the book's contributions has been to demonstrate how these taming dimensions are materially enacted. We identified four core taming mechanisms: *(i) briefings, (ii) calculative triaging, (iii) prerequisites for success,* and *(iv) trajectory of evidence.*

9.5.1 Briefings

The first mechanism, *briefings*, represents a critical arena for the production, shaping, and evaluation of hype, where wild claims are systematically *tamed* through scrutiny. Drawing on insights from Valuation Studies (Helgesson & Muniesa, 2013), we show how briefings create structured encounters in which vendors present their promissory narratives to market gatekeepers (Antal et al., 2015). These are not merely passive exchanges. As our fieldwork shows, briefings are often sites of active negotiation, scrutiny, and recalibration.

Analysts often approach vendors with scepticism, assuming some degree of exaggeration – if not outright misrepresentation. As one analyst noted, 'vendors were exaggerating' (A7, interview); another went further, calling some claims 'lies' (A1, interview). In response, analyst relations experts are increasingly coaching vendors to substantiate their narratives with credible evidence and to avoid making speculative claims.

As Chapter 4 demonstrates, requests for proof have become increasingly standard, and vendors must learn to speak in terms that align with analysts' evaluative frameworks. Thus, success in the briefing process depends not only on a venture's potential but also on its ability to navigate and adapt to this structured and evaluative space. Our findings hint (Chapters 4 and 5), for instance, that a vendor's willingness to incorporate analyst feedback in subsequent meetings can gradually build credibility. Future studies could investigate how such alignment is learned, negotiated, and rewarded; how coaching practices are disseminated; and whether they impact the content and credibility of hype over time.

These dynamics create a 'tension' (Boltanski & Thévenot, 1999) among vendors, analysts, and analyst relations professionals. Whilst analysts come armed with scepticism and probing claims, vendors (often coached by AR) attempt to anticipate and address these doubts. When vendor narratives fall short, AR experts often step in to 'repair' the narrative, as one noted: 'You would not believe the number of conversations we start where ... we're repairing relationships' (AR6, interview). The credibility of AR experts is also at stake, as they must carefully balance loyalty to clients with maintaining trust among analysts.

9.5.2 Calculative Triaging

The second mechanism, *calculative triaging*, can be understood as the systematic sorting and prioritisation of innovations based on criteria such as credibility, market potential, and alignment with client interests. Analysts use increasingly sophisticated promissory products to determine which technologies deserve attention and investment. We define calculative triaging as the provisional deployment of evaluative frameworks that immediately distinguish between overhyped and substantiated innovations. Examples include the HCC, which situates technologies along a lifecycle of expectations; Magic Quadrants, which translate subjective assessments into quantifiable, comparative ratings; and Cool Vendor designations, which act as signals of endorsement and redirect attention to emerging players deemed credible and promising. These tools not only structure attention – they shape it, offering interpretive and practical frameworks through which hype becomes actionable. For instance, by spotlighting certain Cool Vendors, analysts redirect industry investment towards those firms. Through such calculative triaging, analysts impose structure and order on the chaos of emerging innovations, effectively taming the hype by foregrounding some technologies and sidelining others (which may then struggle to attract attention or capital).

9.5.3 Prerequisites for Success

A third taming mechanism involves identifying *prerequisites for success* – baseline conditions that ventures must meet to be deemed credible by market gatekeepers. For instance, analysts develop checklists of credibility (e.g. does the start-up have paying customers? Have these customers experienced visible benefits? Can they be a demonstrable 'use case'?). While analysts cannot predict which innovations will succeed, they can use structured frameworks to flag warning signs of fragility (e.g. reliance on social proof or vague promises) and highlight positive indicators (e.g. proven traction, coherent vision). These prerequisites serve two functions. First, they act as filters, helping analysts and clients identify which ventures possess the necessary fundamentals to move forward and flag those that lack them (e.g. ventures relying solely on vague promises or social proof are marked as fragile). Second, they operate as implicit guidelines for vendors: knowing these criteria, vendors are encouraged to align their strategies and narratives with what evaluators expect to see. In short, these criteria tame hype by embedding evaluator expectations into the innovation process (ventures must check certain boxes to be taken seriously).

9.5.4 Trajectory of Evidence

The fourth mechanism, the *trajectory of evidence*, provides a longitudinal approach for taming hype. While industry analysts cannot predict outcomes with certainty, their tools trace the 'trajectory of evidence' (Kruse, 2015), the evolution of proof points, and credibility signals over an innovation's lifespan.[3]

For example, industry analysts – tasked with identifying potential disruptors – engage in repeated briefings with ventures over extended periods to monitor a venture's progress and consistency of story. At the outset, many ventures appear similar, as their evidence and discourse follow comparable arcs, making it difficult to discern whether a venture has genuine disruptive potential or is merely overclaiming (Garud *et al.*, 2025). Although analysts are inundated with a constant stream of new ventures, genuine disruptors remain rare (Zankl & Grimes, 2024). Yet, they cannot risk overlooking or dismissing a potential disruptor in their domain, as they can be damaged by missing a vital innovation or innovator (Chapter 6).

To navigate this, analysts evaluate the *trajectory of evidence* – they look at how a venture's story and proof points evolve over multiple interactions. Analysts look for positive momentum: Is the start-up

---

[3] Kruse (2015) introduces the concept of the 'trajectory of evidence' based on a study of forensic science to describe the dynamic and situated journey that evidence takes as it moves through different institutional and professional contexts.

backing its claims with increasingly concrete evidence each time we meet? By evaluating the trajectory, therefore, analysts identify patterns and assess whether ventures are maturing towards credible innovation or failing to substantiate their claims. Thus, venture narratives are eventually either substantiated, refined, or discredited, depending on how ventures respond to evaluation processes. Repeated briefings, follow-up calls, 'proxy-ethnographies' (Knorr Cetina, 2010), and finding and assessing 'customer use cases' (Smith, 2009) provide data points that either build credibility or raise red flags. This trajectory-based approach does not eliminate uncertainty but helps analysts make more confident judgements about who is maturing towards genuine innovation.

Together, these four mechanisms create a multi-layered system for managing hype. They channel hype in the wild into formal routines, creating feedback loops and criteria that keep hype in check and make it more predictable. Having described how hype is tamed in practice, we now ask: How did these practices arise and change over time?

9.6 The Managed Spiral of Promissory Products

Studying the digital economy for over two decades has provided a unique vantage point to observe how hype has evolved into a distinct domain of economic activity – a business in its own right. From selling hype evaluations to offering specialised advisory services to producing rankings and visual tools for navigating expectations, a commercial infrastructure has emerged around the production and governance of hype. This perspective reveals not only how this business has emerged but also how the various promissory products shift and adapt in response to new challenges, reflecting the changing dynamics of innovation and uncertainty in the digital economy.

A central question arises: How do promissory products evolve in tandem with innovation, ensuring that hype remains governable over time? The promissory products developed by analysts are not static instruments tied to a single technological moment. Instead, they have proven highly adaptable, evolving to remain relevant as new technologies emerge and older ones become obsolete. We argue that this adaptability reflects not just innovation in isolation but a *managed spiral of promissory products*, sustained through processes of *entrainment* whereby evaluative tools reinforce and extend one another across technological domains.

Here we build on the spiral metaphor introduced in Chapter 3. Whereas there we emphasised its role in explaining the proliferation of promissory products, here we develop it further to show how the spiral is actively managed – through adaptation and entrainment – to tame hype over time.

The taming of hype is best understood as a recursive spiral in which one evaluative tool opens space for the development of others (MacKenzie, 2000; Beunza, 2019). Each innovation in evaluation lays the groundwork for subsequent adaptations, creating a cumulatively emerging pattern of elaboration and refinement. Our analysis has identified three overlapping phases in this evolution, each marking a shift in how hype's new actors manage hype and tailor their approaches to technological complexity and changing client needs (see Figure 9.1):

Phase 1: Ranking Mature Technologies (Late 1990s): The first phase centred on evaluating and ranking established technologies within relatively mature and well-defined markets. At this time, the digital economy lacked mechanisms to moderate inflated claims. Hype circulated largely unchecked – a phenomenon we have termed 'hype in the wild'. The dotcom boom – and its bust – exposed the risks of unregulated hype. In response, market gatekeepers developed tools to introduce order, the earliest and most influential being Gartner's Magic Quadrant. Rival analyst firms quickly followed, and today, hundreds of similar ranking products circulate in the market, fundamentally shifting industry practices (Pollock et al., 2018). This illustrates how a single promissory product can catalyse widespread shifts in how innovation is assessed.

Phase 2: Triaging Emerging Technologies (Early 2000s): As attention shifted towards emerging and less proven technologies, existing ranking tools struggled to accommodate the uncertainty surrounding early-stage innovations. In this second phase, new evaluative instruments emerged to support technology adopters in navigating immaturity and volatility. The HCC, introduced during this period, became a central tool for helping organisations decide when and how to engage with emerging technologies (Dedehayir & Steinert, 2016). Importantly, these new tools did not replace earlier analyst frameworks but extended and modified them. The evaluative remit expanded beyond large firms to include start-ups and nascent ventures. This phase marked the beginning of a more diversified landscape, where traditional performance measures were adapted to fit the innovation dynamics of early-stage technologies.

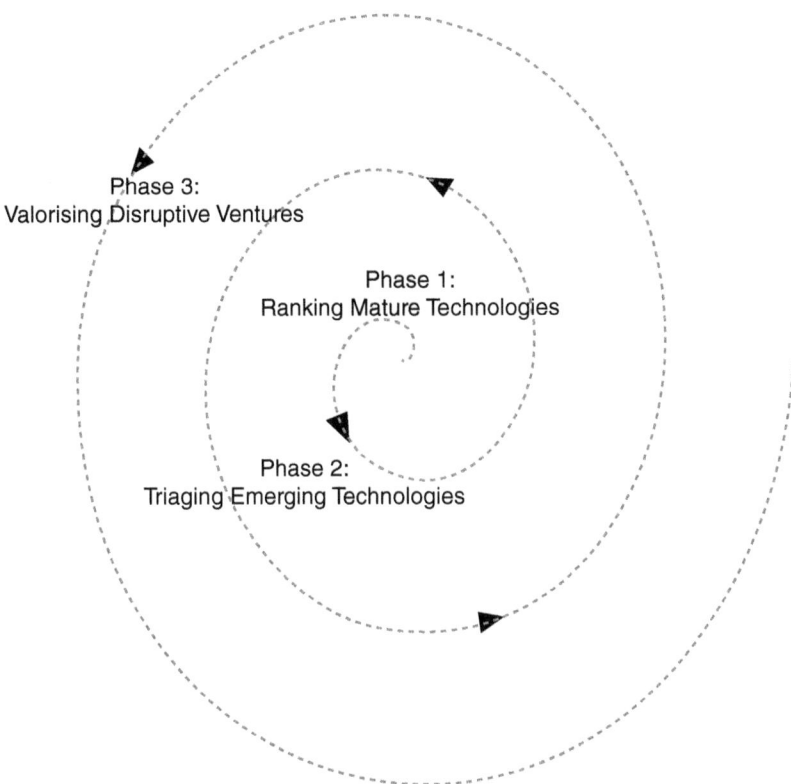

Figure 9.1 Three phases of taming hype.

Phase 3: Valorising Disruptive Ventures (2010 Onwards): The third phase focused on identifying and endorsing potentially disruptive start-ups. The introduction of the Cool Vendor label was pivotal. It allowed analysts to draw attention to ventures seen as capable of 'challenging long-held assumptions' and 'transforming business operations' (Shimel, 2013). This phase also saw the rise of dedicated evaluation formats such as start-up briefings – what we have called the 'Second Most Important Pitch' after investor presentations. These briefings were designed to capture the specific needs and capacities of start-ups while maintaining links to established evaluative frameworks. As one analyst noted, 'We use some of the criteria for innovation from [large vendor] reports to actually look and evaluate some of the younger, smaller vendors' (A2, interview). This repurposing of existing criteria allowed analysts to extend their authority to new domains (without sacrificing credibility). Since the introduction of the *Cool Vendor* designation, competing analyst firms have launched parallel labels – such as *Hot Vendors*, *Innovators*, and *Market Disruptors* – reflecting a growing emphasis on valorising early-stage innovation.

The evolving spiral of promissory products continues to adapt, signalling ongoing experimentation in the evaluative infrastructure of the digital economy. For example, this third phase remains in flux. It is unclear how stable or enduring these new evaluative forms surrounding start-ups will prove to be. What is clear is that we are still in the early stages of a broader transformation in how emerging ventures are identified, classified, and made investable.

We now consider one factor that underpins this spiral: the role of *entrainment*.

9.6.1 The Role of Entrainment

The evolving spiral of promissory products is sustained not just by innovation but by a process of *entrainment* – the synchronisation of evaluative routines across different domains. Entrainment refers to how distinct evaluation tools build upon and reinforce each other, creating a rhythm and continuity that enables further elaboration (Biesenthal et al., 2015). In this way, promissory products do not operate in isolation. Instead, their power stems from how they interact and align with existing frameworks, enabling analysts to extend their cognitive authority across both mature and emerging technology domains.

A clear example of entrainment can be seen in the development of the HCC. Jackie Fenn did not invent the model from scratch. She adapted it from the pre-existing Enterprise Technology Adoption (ETA) profiles already used within Gartner, which categorised organisations into risk types – Type A, B, or C. As Fenn explained, 'Type A, B, C actually was there when I joined Gartner . . . I found it useful to apply it . . . as a very simple way that organisations are prepared to self-identify' (Fenn, interview). This illustrates entrainment: the new HCC gained quick acceptance because it was entrained with an existing categorisation that clients already understood.

Entrainment may be central to understanding why some evaluative frameworks gain traction while others fade. Synchronisation with broader industry norms and technological shifts enhances their adoption. However, entrainment also introduces risks. Misalignment may occur when tools designed for mature markets are applied to emerging domains. Applying a Fortune-500-style ranking to a seed-stage start-up can do more harm than good. As one analyst remarked, 'I am a big believer that if you are a small venture, you don't really want to be on [a major analyst ranking] at all. You are not going to look good' (A1, interview). Such mismatches can distort the visibility and perceived viability of promising innovations.

The spiral of promissory products reflects how market gatekeepers have strategically worked to maintain their epistemic authority. Through constant adaptation – from the Magic Quadrant and categories to the HCC and Cool Vendor reports – they have responded to shifts in the innovation landscape and the rising complexity of technology markets. Yet this expansion has also opened space for other actors to gain influence, notably rival analyst firms and analyst relations specialists. What was once a closed dialogue between an analyst and a vendor has evolved into a complex evaluative ecosystem (Pollock et al., 2018) populated by diverse tools, institutions, and gatekeepers.

9.6.2 Pluralism in Promissory Products

Recognising this spiralling of promissory products is crucial for understanding how promissory economies are now sustained and institutionalised over time. As promissory products proliferate, so too do the methods and criteria for evaluating, legitimising, or contesting hype. This diversity matters. Drawing on MacKenzie's (2011) notion of *evaluative cultures*, we argue that different evaluative infrastructures generate different hype dynamics. MacKenzie's study of the subprime mortgage crisis offers a cautionary parallel: when rating agencies and investors relied on the same flawed risk models – creating a closed feedback loop – the result was systemic misjudgement on a catastrophic scale.

The same logic applies to hype. In tightly coupled systems – such as those in which 'hype in the wild' proliferates – hype enactors (entrepreneurs, innovators) and hype selectors (analysts, adopters, investors) often share assumptions, criteria, and expectations. This close alignment amplifies hype: limited evaluation standards and strong social consensus can create feedback loops that reinforce optimistic projections and foster localised bubbles of expectation (Floridi, 2024). It is in such contexts that boom-and-bust collapses are most likely, as inflated claims spiral unchecked until punctured.

By contrast, pluralistic evaluative ecosystems – characterised by diverse tools, metrics, and gatekeepers, such as those in which 'tamed hype' proliferates – introduce friction and contestation. As Stark (2009) suggests, rather than relying on a single metric, the coexistence of multiple evaluative principles can act as a check and balance. In such contexts, no single hype narrative goes unchallenged; competing perspectives disrupt groupthink and temper runaway optimism. For instance, as shown in Chapter 6, internal debates among analysts about where to position technologies on the HCC – described as moments to 'negotiate', 'haggle', 'argue', and even 'fight' – reveal that consensus is actively fought over and has to be worked out rather than assumed. These deliberative practices, while messy, ensure that evaluations are not mere reflections of dominant narratives but are subject to scrutiny, collective judgement, and recalibration.

While the spiral of promissory products cannot eliminate boom-and-bust dynamics, it does appear to reconfigure them. By establishing multiple mechanisms for testing, revising, and refining promissory claims, these products reduce the likelihood of decisions being made on predictably unreliable evidence. They do not provide absolute certainty or 'truth' (Thompson & Byrne, 2022) about the prospects of emerging technologies, but they can eliminate some foreseeable sources of error and reshape the structure of unknowns. In this way, the proliferation of promissory products is beginning to reshape speculative dynamics in the digital economy. We return in Chapter 10 to examine more closely how the HCC, in particular, participates in this reshaping.

* * *

These findings extend and complicate existing research on managing expectations and hype, as we explore next.

9.7 Hype Management

The concept of 'hype management' – recently articulated by Logue and Grimes (2022) – describes how market actors seek to shape and sustain attention, legitimacy, and credibility in the face of uncertainty. It highlights the deliberate, often strategic efforts to navigate the volatile dynamics of expectations – turning what might be fleeting enthusiasm into more durable support. How, then, do our findings on taming hype speak to and revise this concept? We develop the notion in three ways. First, we build on but complicate Logue and Grimes' (2022) distinction between 'material proof' and 'social proof'. Second, we demonstrate that evaluation unfolds longitudinally, not well captured by short-term snapshot studies. Third, we theorise 'trajectories of evidence' (Kruse, 2015) as a mechanism through which hype is tamed over time.

The etymology of 'management' – from the Italian *maneggiare*, meaning 'to handle' (Barnhart, 1999) – underscores hype management's affinity with our notion of taming: both evoke deliberate control and the careful steering of something potentially unruly. Applied to hype, the term suggests that expectations can be guided and stabilised through ongoing evaluation, as market actors decide what, and whom, to believe.

Logue and Grimes (2022) implicitly develop this taming view in their study of the impact investment sector. They demonstrate how organisations strive to convert hyped claims into 'material proof' (measurable evidence, performance metrics) and 'social proof' (endorsements, third-party validations), arguing that when 'hard' evidence is scarce, social proof becomes especially important for maintaining legitimacy and stakeholder engagement.

We build on this insight, yet we contend that treating material and social proof as a stable dualism obscures how evidentiary forms intermingle and shift in weight over time. Particularly in fast-moving domains such as the digital economy, artefacts, metrics, endorsements, and narratives migrate across the material–social divide; evidence first received as reputational markers may later solidify into performance benchmarks, and vice versa. To capture these movements, we theorise proof gradients – degrees of materialisation and social endorsement that can thicken, thin, or reverse – and we link these gradients to temporally extended 'trajectories of evidence' (Kruse, 2015) through which hype is incrementally tamed.

Chapter 4 illustrated this blurring in the case of vendor 'customer use cases'. Vendors routinely mobilise such cases to demonstrate deliverability. Yet, as Smith (2009) shows, adopter endorsements often reflect strategic positioning: a customer with sunk investments in a technology has incentives to present its deployment as successful. What appears as objective performance data (material proof) may simultaneously function as reputational evidence (social proof). Evidence, in other words, rarely fits neatly into one category. Indeed, industry analysts labour to disentangle these layers from one vendor briefing to the next – a dynamic visible in our longitudinal archive of briefing transcripts and follow-up interactions (Chapter 4).

Recognising this entanglement pushes us towards a temporally attuned account of evaluation. Prior work (e.g. Logue & Grimes, 2022) captures a 'snapshot' of evidentiary practice. Yet *hype rarely stands still*, as argued in Chapter 2. Claims are reiterated, challenged, reframed, abandoned, or re-substantiated as markets, technologies, and competitive reference points evolve. Treating hype as a short-term resource that is either validated or discarded understates the ongoing work of narrative adjustment and expectations management (Garud et al., 2014) and obscures how legitimacy can be rebuilt after early scepticism or disappointment (Hampel & Dalpiaz, 2025).

Our extension draws on Kruse's (2015) notion of a 'trajectory of evidence' mentioned above – the unfolding path along which claims accumulate, mutate, or erode supporting proof. A trajectory view treats material and social proof not as endpoints but as momentary configurations within a broader sequence of evaluation episodes. Across that sequence, indicators can be upgraded, downgraded, reinterpreted, or supplanted; what counts as credible evidence is negotiated afresh as additional actors, artefacts, and data enter the frame.

The analysts in our study routinely approach early vendor briefings as first data points, not verdicts. One analyst, after several interactions, challenged a start-up: 'I asked people at [BigTech] about you … *and no one's even heard of you!*' At that moment, the venture's claims appeared to fail both material validation (no evidence of a partnership) and social validation (no awareness among a key ecosystem player). The start-up responded by refining its narrative and producing new artefacts – evidence of 'joint pitches', publicity material, and material highlighting the relationship. Subsequent briefings registered movement along the evidentiary trajectory: from initial scepticism to contingent recognition as proof accumulated.

This episode exemplifies how evaluation unfolds as a process of mutual adjustment, narrative repair, and trajectory building (Garud et al., 2014). In this way, our taming perspective moves beyond the simple snapshot view. It shows that hype is not simply accepted or rejected but tracked, tested, and transformed over time – shaped by evolving evaluative infrastructures and the situated practices of actors such as analysts, analyst relations professionals, and vendors. Identifying the mechanisms that enable these shifts – and their consequences for adoption, investment, and legitimacy – remains an important agenda for future research (Hampel & Dalpiaz, 2025).

9.8 Fictional Expectations

Our exploration of taming hype builds on Beckert's (2016, 2021) influential concept of *fictional expectations* – the idea that expectations mobilise investment, coordinate action, and shape economic trajectories (see also Beckert & Bronk, 2018). Tracing how particular expectations travel, stick, or fade across evaluative settings remains an open empirical agenda. While Beckert captures their generative power, his account leaves key questions unresolved: How do certain expectations gain traction? What makes some narratives more plausible or persuasive than others? And through what mechanisms are these visions translated into action or held accountable?

We extend Beckert in two moves. First, although Beckert (2021) recognises that expectations must be judged credible, he does not trace how such judgements are operationalised in practice. We show that structured evaluative systems actively sort, filter, and reshape fictional expectations. Promissory products create selective visibility: they define what counts as credible, timely, and investable. As discussed in Chapter 5, the Cool Vendor designation and its associated analyst briefing process filter ventures through explicit criteria. Many technically promising start-ups fail to qualify because their narratives do not fit the required evaluative format; ventures that do align are flagged and valorised, gaining broader attention and market legitimacy.

Second, we argue that fictional expectations are not merely 'imaginative projections' – as emphasised by Beckert – but increasingly *formatted futures*. While Beckert foregrounds narrative creation, we add the formats that render those narratives legible and actionable. Promissory products encode expectations into routinised evaluative frames (Thévenot, 1984) that structure how futures can be articulated, compared, and acted upon.[4] For instance, to be flagged as a Cool

---

[4] Thévenot's (1984) concept of 'investment in forms' explains how standardised tools – such as classifications, benchmarks, and labels – facilitate coordination in uncertain environments by embedding conventions into material and institutional formats. These forms, once established, extend across time and space, shaping interactions and governance by making certain actions and evaluations more feasible and legitimate than others.

Vendor, a start-up must fit its story into the template analysts expect – framing its innovation in terms of market relevance, differentiation, and potential impact, while supplying just enough evidence to make the promise appear both credible and exciting. To appear in a Magic Quadrant, a vendor must present both its 'vision' and proof of its 'ability to execute' – for example, through client references, product demonstrations, and other credibility markers. Thus, ventures can no longer simply invent their own future stories: the projection of futures has become increasingly standardised. To be taken seriously, one must project in an accepted format – otherwise the vision will not even register on the evaluative radar. This helps explain why some narratives, no matter how compelling, never gain traction.

Investments in form (Thévenot, 1984) are not only stabilising; they are generative. The institutionalisation of promissory formats has produced a class of specialists – analyst relations experts – meaning that a whole new professional class now thrives on teaching ventures how to fit their story to these formats. As hype work becomes professionalised, analyst relations specialists coach vendors on crafting claims that satisfy formal tools and evidence protocols. In this way, fictional expectations are not simply narrated; they are *formatted into being* – the shape of the story can matter as much as its substance for an expectation to take hold. Ventures must learn to perform to these schemas not only to attract attention but also to become legible within an evaluatively saturated marketplace. This formatting work is central to our broader argument about taming hype: it shows that expectations thrive only when they can be encoded, evaluated, and iteratively adjusted via promissory infrastructures. In short, hype in the wild must enter these managed channels to gain traction.

* * *

The transformation from wild to tamed hype signals a broader institutionalisation of promissory narratives in the digital economy. As hype becomes more structured, evaluable, and routinised, new forms of expertise, legitimacy, and strategic influence emerge. In Chapter 10, we argue for a dedicated research agenda – *Hype Studies* – to investigate this institutionalisation and its implications for innovation and the economy.

10 | *Towards Hype Studies*

In this concluding chapter, we call for the establishment of *Hype Studies* as a programmatic research agenda focused on the phenomenon of hype. We seek here to consolidate the insights of this book into a clear set of principles and directions for future enquiry. Rather than a traditional summary, this chapter serves as an invitation, outlining why hype merits serious scholarly attention, proposing methodological approaches to study it, and highlighting key dimensions – such as expertise, reflexivity, competition, stratification, and speculative cycles – that future hype research should address. Importantly, our call for Hype Studies is offered not as a rigid blueprint but as a starting point for debate. It presents one possible framework for understanding how hype is created, institutionalised, and contested across different contexts, open to refinement and extension by other scholars.

Our enquiry began by examining the work of 'promissory organisations' (Pollock & Williams, 2010) and experts – particularly industry analysts and analyst relations (AR) professionals (Pollock & Williams, 2016) – and tracing how these actors were developing tools and practices to engage with emerging innovations (Chapple et al., 2022; Pollock et al., 2023). Through this lens, we observed a shift from 'hype in the wild' to more structured and strategic forms of 'tamed hype', exemplified in practices such as the Hype Cycle Chart (HCC). As we studied how this tamed hype was being mobilised alongside more spontaneous forms of expectation work, it became clear that industrial actors were acquiring new capacities to navigate volatile innovation landscapes.

This empirical journey gradually brought us into conversation with what now appears to be a burgeoning, cross-disciplinary field – what we here term Hype Studies. In the course of our research, we encountered scholars from other empirical and disciplinary settings who were engaging, often implicitly, with similar questions: how hype is shaped (Garud et al., 2023), how it is institutionalised (Konrad & Alvial-

Palavicino, 2017; Ometto et al., 2023), and how it functions as a strategic and evaluative force across different domains (Martin, 2015; Logue & Grimes, 2022). We propose the establishment of Hype Studies as a way to unify these disparate research strands that currently touch on hype only indirectly – such as those found in Sociology, Science and Technology Studies (STS), Organisation and Management Theory (OMT), Economic Sociology, Market Studies, Media Studies, and beyond – yet stop short of analysing hype as a discrete, evolving object of governance and strategy.

In what follows, we first argue why hype must be treated as a serious object of study; then, we suggest methods for studying it; and finally, we propose core themes and questions for future research. We conclude with a call to action, inviting scholars to engage with this emerging agenda.

10.1 Developing a Symmetrical Sociology of Hype

Why study hype at all, given its ambivalent status? For many, perhaps the majority, hype remains profoundly problematic (Vinsel & Russell, 2020; Funk, 2024; Min, 2024; Bender & Hanna, 2025). Yet despite its frequently maligned status, other scholars contend that hype is integral to innovation ecosystems (Konrad & Alvial-Palavicino, 2017; Logue & Grimes, 2022) and economic dynamism (Beckert, 2016, 2021).

These contrasting perspectives point to a deeper and more persistent issue: *the constitutive ambivalence of hype.* It is at once enabling and distorting, generative and destabilising. This dual character is not incidental – it is central to how hype operates. Because the outcomes of radical innovation are inherently uncertain, actors must rely on promissory narratives to make decisions and mobilise resources. Hype becomes a necessary vehicle for action in the absence of settled evidence. But the same speculative quality that allows hype to catalyse innovation also makes it vulnerable to exaggeration, disappointment, and critique.

Hype draws its power from precisely this duality: it can coordinate futures while deferring judgement. This ambivalence is not a flaw to be corrected but a condition to be understood. Rather than marginalising it, we argue that ambivalence is constitutive of hype and should be explicitly thematised as such. This recognition underscores the need for a more nuanced analytical stance. We propose that researchers adopt a symmetrical and non-binary perspective on hype, consistent with long-standing social science commitments to tracing the co-production of knowledge, technology, and social order (Jasanoff, 2004).

Following the principle of symmetry from the Sociology of Scientific Knowledge (Bloor, 1976), hype can be studied without presupposing it to be inherently 'true' or 'false'. This requires treating hype not as inherently deceptive or valid but as a social phenomenon enacted in specific contexts, producing effects that are uneven, contingent, and open to empirical investigation. Sometimes hype may indeed mislead and create bubbles; in other instances, it may stimulate constructive action, cooperation, or institutional alignment. A symmetrical approach urges us to trace empirically how and when hype becomes consequential, rather than evaluating it in advance or relying on retrospective judgements.

Adopting hype as an object of study also requires moving beyond the idea that it is uniform or monolithic. As we show throughout the book, hype constitutes a stratified and contested field of promissory claims – a domain in which actors project visions of the future that are evaluated, challenged, or sustained through specific mechanisms. As Beckert (2021) notes, future-oriented claims do not circulate on an even footing; some are deemed more plausible or credible than others. This *hierarchy of credibility* is itself a critical object of study. We invite scholars to investigate how such distinctions are constructed, stabilised, and contested. Which actors or institutions separate credible promises from implausible ones? How do certain narratives come to be accepted as 'realistic' expectations, while others are dismissed as 'mere' hype?

While our primary focus has been the work of industry analysts and AR professionals, many other gatekeepers shape these dynamics: the media (Vasterman, 2005; Byrne & Giuliani, 2025; Magalhães & Smit, 2025), investors (Spivack et al., 2025), governments (Christian et al., 2025; Veneziano & Gerli, 2025), research funders (Konrad & Alvial-Palavicino, 2017), entrepreneurial support organisations (Bergman & McMullen, 2022), and so on. Together, these actors participate in the ongoing calibration of hype by parsing its claims and differentiating between what is rendered actionable and what remains speculative.

Recognising this complex ecosystem of actors leads us to consider how our approach aligns with and differs from existing scholarly traditions that have examined futures and expectations.

10.2 Hype Studies and Its Disciplinary Affinities

We are not alone in making these arguments about hype and associated taming processes (though we may be among the first to explicitly foreground them and draw together these disparate elements into a cohesive analytical framework). Our call for Hype Studies has affinities with several emerging and established research strands – notably the Sociology of Expectations, Future Studies, the Sociology of the Future, etc. There are clear affinities with Martin's (2015, p. 440) account of how 'the promissory is transformed into the real', where he highlights the role of promissory organisations – such as analysts and investor advisors – in converting speculative assets into tradeable ones. Rather than counterposing 'promissory' and 'real market' valuations, his framework draws attention to the processes through which distinctions between the two are negotiated, and how transitions from the 'regime of promise' to the 'regime of truth' are actively managed. This example illustrates how Hype Studies could extend such work by focusing on the active management of that transition.

Our contribution aligns with a broader shift across multiple disciplines that treats the future as a site of *practical engagement* rather than a distant abstraction. Scholars in STS and Sociology have begun investigating how futures are constructed and governed in real time, challenging older assumptions that we can only understand expectations in hindsight (Tutton, 2017; Adam, 2023; Halford & Southerton, 2023). It also challenges the legacy of logical positivism (Clardy, 2022), which holds that future claims are inherently unverifiable until retrospectively confirmed – and are therefore a form of 'non-knowledge' (Aligica, 2003). Such a perspective is inadequate in contexts of innovation, where decisions must be made under radical uncertainty. The critical question is not whether the future can be known, but how it is rendered actionable in the present (Chapter 3).

In response, scholars have begun to explore the concrete practices through which near-term technology futures are constructed, contested, and institutionalised. Idoko and MacKay (2021) identify a shift within Future Studies towards a practice-oriented perspective. Ethnographic research by McDowall (2012) demonstrates that innovation roadmaps are not simply predictive artefacts but living instruments, revised over time to manage divergences between expectation and outcome. Garud et al. (2014) introduce the concept of 'projective stories' to understand how entrepreneurs mobilise commitment and navigate disappointment. Birch (2023) extends this analysis by emphasising the reflexive dynamics of expectation work: futures are not only projected but are continuously revised, reinterpreted, and contested in light of unfolding developments.

Hype Studies does not attempt to displace existing traditions. Instead, it aims to offer a more integrated, conceptually nuanced, and empirically detailed account of how hype is structured, mediated, and tamed over time. Where Future Studies and the Sociology of Expectations have often focused on early-stage promises or addressed hype only implicitly, our approach drills down into hype as an evolving, institutionalised, and empirically traceable object of study. At the same time, we recognise that drawing sharp boundaries around Hype Studies may risk appearing somewhat artificial. Hype can indeed be seen as one particular form of anticipatory dynamic, naturally linked to broader processes of expectation and anticipation. Our aim, however, is not to separate but to foreground hype as a distinctive configuration within these broader dynamics, thereby consolidating and deepening the empirical study of the phenomenon. These affinities and distinctions suggest that the moment is right for a dedicated Hype Studies approach that brings these strands together. Our next task is to consider how one might systematically study hype as such an object.

10.3 Constructing a Methodological and Analytical Lens for Studying Hype

If we are to treat hype as a serious object of study, we must also consider *how* to study it. We anticipate that Hype Studies should examine the full lifecycle of hype – from its genesis and amplification, through its operationalisation and evaluation, to its eventual impacts and outcomes. This means developing methods that capture hype in action, rather than reducing it to a feature of 'start-up culture' (Wadhwani & Lubinski, 2025) or theorising it in the abstract. Research that ranges too broadly across multiple spheres and temporalities without clear empirical grounding risks producing overgeneralised accounts and obscuring the fine-grained processes at stake. Armchair theorising risks reifying hype as an 'unbounded resource' (Logue & Grimes, 2022), detached from the organisational practices that produce and manage it. Our agenda, therefore, calls for systematic, empirically grounded studies that trace how hype is generated, channelled, and evaluated within specific organisational and institutional settings. This involves treating hype not as abstract 'buzz' (Pontikes & Barnett, 2017) but as a structured set of practices that can be observed, analysed, and compared across contexts.

Despite hype's evident influence in innovation processes, few empirical studies place it at the centre of analysis. More often, hype is addressed only tangentially – treated as a by-product of entrepreneurship or technology ventures rather than as a driving force in its own right (see Bourne, 2024). This reflects a broader methodological challenge: we currently lack approaches for examining hype in action. While our book has laid some groundwork – for example, by suggesting the study of *tamed hype* – much more remains to be done.

Studying hype means engaging with an amorphous and elusive set of practices. Hype is not confined to a single site; it unfolds across multiple (ultimately unbounded), overlapping promissory arenas, producing effects that ripple across domains, actors, and formats. We found that the most consequential hype work often occurs in liminal spaces opaque to outsiders – closed-door meetings, analyst briefings, pitch sessions, strategy discussions, and so on – where actors actively shape and respond to hype. Its distributed, liminal character makes hype difficult to study using conventional social-science methods. In this sense, applying the concept of hype in empirical research is not only methodologically demanding and perhaps also in consequence analytically underdeveloped.

This elusiveness is not unique to hype – it reflects a broader paradox familiar in social science: the more powerful a phenomenon is, the harder it often becomes to study directly – a 'black box', as Latour (1987) would say. The most consequential social forces are frequently the most opaque, operating across sites. Hype, when effective, is subsumed into institutional routines and infrastructures, with its origins disappearing into the machinery of markets, policies, and innovations it helped bring about. This means Hype Studies must be especially innovative methodologically and analytically.

10.3.1 Studying Traces

While hype is diffuse and slippery, it is not invisible – it leaves 'traces' (Power, 2022). The challenge for researchers is to find ways of following those traces and capturing the patterned effects of hype.

In today's digital economy, the abundance of digital traces generated through our online interactions offers significant scope for analysing hype at scale. These new digital tools and information resources also open up scope to examine large corpus of information arising in a digitised world. This has several distinctive features: for example, the ability to analyse variations within a community; the capacity to study long-term processes; and the potential to rapidly detect changes as they occur. Researchers can now measure patterns of attention and communication flows using tools such as Google Trends (Jun et al., 2018) or large language models (LLMs) to track attention cycles. Computational techniques enable the analysis of media coverage, social media content, and industry reports to identify longitudinal patterns in hype (Wang et al., 2021). Sentiment analysis of large textual datasets – ranging from news articles and social media posts to conference presentations – can reveal shifts in tone over time, helping to pinpoint when and why collective disillusionment sets in. More targeted metrics, such as user responses to advertisements (MacKenzie & Caliskan, 2025), are also increasingly used in fields like marketing (Boegershausen et al., 2022).

Yet despite the availability of these real-time digital indicators, their value alone is limited. They can measure the *volume* of hype, but not the *significance* or *force* of particular claims. Our research suggests that decision-makers continue to rely heavily on artefacts like the HCC and other promissory products. This underscores a key distinction: while digital data tracks hype's visibility, it misses the social and organisational processes – and the behind-the-scenes negotiations – that imbue hype with institutional force. Thus, computational approaches may need to be complemented with qualitative and process-oriented methods.

10.3.2 Beyond Snapshot Studies: Longitudinal Perspectives

A central challenge in studying hype lies in its *temporal* character: hype unfolds unevenly across time. Hype is not a singular event but a process whose rhythm, acceleration, and deceleration vary across contexts and moments. This uneven development renders problematic existing research, which captures hype only in fleeting moments or early-stage episodes, obscuring its longer-term trajectories and institutional consequences. Simply put, snapshot studies of hype miss the full story (in both senses of the term). To address this, researchers need approaches that trace how hype evolves and becomes institutionalised across different phases of innovation. Applying such a longitudinal lens is demanding, but it can yield distinctive insights.

Ethnographic approaches offer one way to achieve this extended perspective, though they must be adapted to follow hype as it circulates across media, markets, and institutions. Our own long-term ethnographic research programme provides an example of how one might access these elusive spaces of hype. This sustained engagement with hype's new actors has given us a privileged view of how hyped claims circulate, are evaluated, and are consumed in the digital innovation space. Through a series of detailed field studies, we identified a number of interstitial spaces – or nexuses (Furnari, 2014) – such as analyst briefings and the Institute for Industry Analyst Relations, where innovation promises are articulated and assessed. Studying these spatially and temporally localised sites over time allowed us to track evolving institutional changes in the promissory economy – for instance, the establishment of new specialised roles (such as AR professionals) and the emergence of longer-term trends, like a growing future orientation in promissory products as adopter organisations pivot towards emerging technologies.[1]

By contrast, many existing studies offer more limited 'snapshots' of hype, and risk overlooking hype's longer-term trajectory and later-stage impacts by focusing exclusively on early bursts of enthusiasm. Such a perspective obscures the temporal dynamics and evolving nature of innovation claims. For example, Min (2024) examined the immediate implications of entrepreneurs' idealistic statements – terming them 'near-lies' – but did not explore how such claims develop or shift over time. While there is considerable value in studying specific moments and contexts, the danger of purely snapshot approaches is that they overlook the interpretive flexibility and ongoing evolution that characterise many innovation processes (van Lente, 1993). This includes tracing how early claims are subsequently reinterpreted, validated, or refuted (as illustrated in Chapter 4). Hampel and Dalpiaz's

---

[1] Some of this access was serendipitous. As Swedberg (2014) reminds us, serendipity is often a necessary, if underacknowledged, element in research design. We were thus fortunate to be already embedded in a related project at the time the new form of analyst relations expertise emerged. This enabled us to become the first to study how analyst relations professionals assist vendors in preparing for analyst briefings.

(2025) extended case study further underscores this point: they follow an entrepreneur who initially engaged in what they term 'morally reckless' hype practices and a 'growth at all costs' strategy, but whose early excesses were later subjected to narrative repair – ultimately reframing the venture's trajectory as a story of 'virtuous growth'. Such longitudinal research reveals how initial hype can be rehabilitated or recontextualised over time.

By extending our focus beyond snapshot accounts, we can better appreciate that hype practices are not confined to the early stages of innovation but rather operate across the entire arc of technoscientific change, shaping both the emergence and the consolidation of new technology fields. In the early stages, hype generates excitement, attracts investment, and assembles provisional discourse coalitions (Hajer, 1995). However, as technologies move towards adoption and routinisation, hype's role shifts: it becomes a tool for structuring relationships, aligning expectations, and managing credibility in more established market settings (Swanson et al., 2025). In other words, hype not only sparks early enthusiasm but, if successfully managed, can also help sustain momentum and legitimacy as innovations mature.

Yet much of the existing literature remains compartmentalised – focusing either on early-stage excitement (as in the Sociology of Expectations tradition) or on later-stage sensemaking (as in work on organising visions or market categories), with little attempt to connect these phases, as we do here. Early contributions have tended to celebrate the narrative, imaginary, and affective features of promissory claims, often portraying rational, evidence-based evaluation as infeasible in the earliest hype-filled stages (see Grodal & Granqvist, 2014). The transition to more mature later stages of innovation – when bold promises have become routinised, codified, and operationalised – frequently remains under-explained or inadequately theorised. Too often, these transitions are depicted as if they were the automatic, inevitable outcomes of initial hype (cf. Goldfarb & Kirsch, 2019), thereby obscuring the complex, contested, and often laborious processes that actually give promissory narratives traction in practice.

While existing work has richly documented how promissory claims mobilise interest and resources in nascent phases of innovation, it often stops short of examining what happens as innovations mature (an exception is Alvial-Palavicino & Konrad, 2019). Promissory processes play critical roles in both the upstream creation of hyped expectations (around which scientific 'blue-sky' research agendas are formed, and funding is allocated) and the downstream construction of markets for particular new applications, including their implementation and use. In doing so, we align with a small but growing number of scholars who likewise seek to develop cross-temporal accounts of promissory dynamics (e.g. Joly, 2010; Martin, 2015; Birch, 2023).

Our study advances a cross-temporal perspective on hype, making two key points. First, we show that hype does not simply dissipate after a product's market entry; instead, it becomes recontextualised, professionalised, and woven into promissory product and associated practices. For instance, once products are on the market, hype endures through the competition for positioning within analyst rankings. Vendors invest heavily in shaping their placement (Leader, Challenger, etc.), and these rankings then influence procurement by enterprise clients. Here, hype is strategically modulated into calculative, comparative form while retaining its capacity to mobilise excitement, prestige, and rivalry. Thus, hype can be strategically modulated over time to build legitimacy, shape procurement processes, and underpin field-level stability (Park & Grundmann, 2025). Understanding these dynamics is vital for explaining how promising technologies eventually become durable market realities.

Second, we demonstrate that hype's emotive and calculative elements are not restricted to distinct phases (Beckert, 2016) but co-present throughout the innovation arc, combined in different ways at early and late stages. Even at the first analyst briefings, entrepreneurs are required to supplement bold narratives with adoption metrics and market sizing, bringing the scope for calculation into play from the outset. Conversely, in later phases, ranking devices such as the Magic Quadrant continue to trade on affect – generating excitement, pride, and anxiety among vendors and competitors (Espeland & Sauder, 2016). Hype's durability lies precisely in this interpenetration: calculation never arrives without emotion, and emotion is never entirely expunged by calculation (Zaloom, 2008).

Taken together, these two points highlight hype not as an ephemeral prelude to innovation but as a dynamic and evolving force that sustains influence across time. Hype Studies, as an emerging perspective, could offer a framework for examining how early enthusiasm is not only sparked but also deliberately sustained and translated into enduring influence.

10.3.3 *Methodological Innovation and Cross-Disciplinary Insights*

Initial work in this area has struggled to develop truly cross-temporal empirical insights (Borup et al., 2006). The early Sociology of Expectations literature, for instance, emphasised that compelling visions of a technoscientific future could frame and shape how that future emerges – but this created the risk of presuming that these framings would simply be performative. In these accounts, compelling visions articulated by committed actors could help bring about the futures they anticipated, a dynamic often characterised as a self-fulfilling prophecy (Brown & Michael, 2003; van Lente, 2012; see also Chapter 2, Tenet Five). Many accounts tended to assume the successful realisation of promissory narratives, rather than examine empirically how and why certain narratives are enacted, fail, morph, or only partially succeed.

Contemporary studies from the Sociology of Expectations have in fact faced a methodological problem: it has proven difficult to explore empirically how deviations might emerge between prior promises and what is eventually delivered, and how such discrepancies are handled. This is paradoxical, given that the Sociology of Expectations originated from an attempt to capture the dynamics through which promises are articulated by innovators and then assessed by selectors or funders (van Lente, 1993). Van Lente's (1993) foundational concept of the 'promise-requirement cycle' drew attention to sponsors' tolerance for limited progress in early R&D projects. Subsequent studies acknowledged the possibility of disappointment if promises are not fulfilled and note that promise-makers may be held to account by sponsors (Borup et al., 2006). Yet, by and large, we still lack empirical approaches that show how the inevitable gaps between promise and outcome are negotiated in practice.

This weakness should encourage hype scholars to consider the performativity of methods (Abbott, 2001) – for example, how some research designs can better capture the negotiability surrounding hype, while others constrain our view. Encouragingly, we are beginning to see calls for more nuanced, longitudinal research designs. Logue and Grimes (2022), for instance, propose a *longitudinal* investigation of specific expectations around an innovation, examining how a venture's sponsors and investors respond over time to discrepancies between projected outcomes and actual performance. Swanson and Ramiller's (1997) concept of *organising visions* similarly argues for extending the temporal and societal scope of enquiry by examining the 'career' of such visions (Ramiller & Swanson, 2003). Organising visions evolve much like product life cycles: a new vision is articulated in an uncertain, contested period; it may achieve ascendancy and stabilise as a dominant frame; and eventually it can lose momentum and be displaced by new challengers. These proposed approaches push researchers to follow the evolution of hype-related narratives beyond the initial buildup, through phases of institutionalisation and potential decline or replacement.

However, calls for longitudinal extension of studies are easier to make than to implement (Van de Ven, 1992). Resources are rarely available to continue studies over the many years (or decades) that truly extended hype trajectories can span – most funded research and doctoral projects last only two to three years. Moreover, proposals to simply 'study longer' miss a crucial practical point: organisational decision-makers cannot wait for evidence to arrive. They are required to make judgement calls on emergent technologies *in advance* of consensus or clear evidence about those technologies' prospects. This raises vital questions about how they can act in such uncertain settings, and it challenges researchers to devise methods that capture decision-making *in real time*, under uncertainty.

In response, a productive strand of analysis has emerged across disparate fields that combines ethnographic and *historical* methods to achieve an extended temporal scope of enquiry, along with a detailed focus on particular contexts and practices (Hyysalo et al., 2019). Much of this work, broadly constructivist in orientation, shares elements of the recent 'practice turn' (Gond *et al.*, 2025), influenced in particular by performativity discussions in new economic sociology (Callon, 1998a; MacKenzie *et al.*, 2007). It focuses on detailed processes – the tools and models deployed by actors in specific settings and the work these perform (Gond & Brès, 2020). By blending in-depth qualitative observation with historical tracing, such approaches manage to capture both fine-grained practice and longer-term evolution.

One consequence of the intellectual impact of this practice-oriented, longitudinal work has been a pre-alignment of analytical attention across several cognate research strands. For example, scholars in Market Studies (Geiger et al., 2024), OMT (Logue & Grimes, 2022),

Cultural Entrepreneurship (Thompson et al., 2020), and Marketing (Bourne, 2024) have all, in different ways, engaged with promissory processes. Similarities in epistemic style have made it easier to link insights between these partial engagements. The related field of Valuation Studies (Hutter & Stark, 2015) provides another valuable lens. While Sociology of Expectations focuses on how innovation is animated by the hopeful visions of scientists or engineers, Valuation Studies shifts attention to the *sociomaterial processes* through which value is constructed, contested, and stabilised (see Chapter 5).

Martin (2015, p. 440), drawing on this approach, extends the Sociology of Expectations by showing how life science start-ups with 'promissory assets that cannot be traded' gradually become integrated into a 'real economy' with tangible assets that are traded in established financial and technology markets. His analysis usefully traces how individual firms and technologies navigate between promise and disappointment. Notably, in Martin's view, there is no single moment of resolution or verification; the transition from speculative promise to realised value is gradual, mediated by a growing repertoire of tools, metrics, and evaluative techniques designed to make uncertain claims more concrete.

However, even these studies (including Martin's) remain relatively bounded when compared to the increasingly dynamic and diffuse sea of expectations that characterises today's digital economy (van Lente, 2012). In such settings, hype does not operate at a single level but instead circulates through multiple nested social arenas. It moves fluidly between local interactions, organisational practices, and broader market and societal narratives. This recognition sets the stage for our next analytical step.

10.4 The Multi-Scalar Life of Hype

Our investigation thus adopted a *multi-scalar* perspective on hype. We traced how hype is produced, mobilised, and consumed across different levels of social and organisational life. Our starting point was sustained empirical engagement with promissory organisations (Pollock & Williams, 2010) in the digital economy and new forms of expertise, tools, and practices that are deployed in concrete market arenas (Pollock & Williams, 2016). The pivoting of analyst attention, responding to client interest, from established towards emerging products led us to study hype itself, extending the Sociology of Expectations into downstream domains where the speculative becomes economically actionable. As we began to track the creation, circulation, assessment, and consumption of hype, we quickly encountered evolving forms of expertise, shared vocabularies (such as the stages of a HCC and product categories), and representational formats across new tools.

Crucially, this multi-level, multi-temporal engagement allows us to connect the multiple (nested and overlapping) promissory arenas in which hype is circulated, assessed, and consumed (Smets et al., 2012). We observed, for example, how micro-level interactions – such as a vendor reconfiguring its pitch in response to an analyst's feedback – feed into meso-level patterns like industry rankings and categories, which in turn accumulate into macro-level shifts in market perception. In doing so, we extend Beckert's (2013, p. 323) claim that the 'management of expectations' is central to contemporary capitalism, while contributing to his call for connecting micro-level practices with macro-level transformations.

We foreground the multi-scalar character of hype by examining its variation across both time and organisational scope – from short-term cycles of attention and adaptation to longer-term processes of institutionalisation and market restructuring. Rather than treat hype as a single, static phenomenon, we show that it operates on multiple levels. Specifically, hype plays out in:

- *Everyday interactions*, where hype is locally produced, tested, and consumed;
- *Short-term adjustments*, including how actors recalibrate in response to gatekeeper scrutiny and how they develop tactics to shape and channel expectations;
- *Longer-term shifts*, such as the emergence of new evaluative infrastructures and specialised forms of expertise.

This dynamic interplay brings into focus how hype circulates through, and shapes, different layers of the digital economy. For example, our analysis of the HCC reveals it to be not just a neutral mapping tool but an influential promissory product that appears to actively co-produce the innovation landscape. At one level, the HCC is an everyday market device for organisations trying to gauge whether to invest in a technology now or later. At another level, it represents a short-term cycle of collective adjustment: by publicly designating certain technologies as peaking or troughing in hype, Gartner's analysts influence how market actors recalibrate their expectations and plans. At a broader level, the HCC itself has become an obligatory point of passage – it codifies a patterned way of thinking about the sea of hype, effectively guiding the allocation of attention and capital in the digital economy. In our study, we found that tools like the HCC do more than reflect the state of excitement; they actively shape the trajectory of innovation by signalling when to be sceptical and when to invest.

Similarly, micro-level interactions supply much of the content that populates these promissory products. In vendor–analyst briefing meetings, for example, plausibility and credibility are continually negotiated. We documented how start-ups (like Juvo) went through repeated rounds of narrative refinement in conversations with industry analysts. Over time, those iterative pitches and feedback loops helped crystallise a new market category – 'Financial Identity as a Service' – which repositioned the venture and signalled to the broader market how this innovation should be understood. Such episodes show that local narrative work can scale up, contributing to shifts in how entire sectors define and evaluate emerging technologies.

Our multi-scalar view also highlights the rise of powerful gatekeeping actors, particularly analyst firms – the 'professional evaluators' (Mützel, 2022) of the promissory economy – and the new expertise of AR. Analyst firms collectively represent a multi-billion-pound market, and AR professionals have carved out a thriving consulting niche, all profiting from the cultivation and steering of promissory narratives. Far from being passive observers, these firms now function as what Giorgi and Weber (2015, p. 357) call 'conversation makers', shaping how entire sectors and vendors are evaluated. They underwrite a managed, industrial-scale form of hype circulation that is distinct from the more chaotic dynamics of 'hype in the wild'.

This layered, multi-scalar analysis of hype marks a distinctive contribution of our work. Whereas existing accounts often rely on isolated anecdotes (Bourne, 2024) or single-point observations (Logue & Grimes, 2022), our analysis maps the circuitry of hype over time and across space. We show that what happens in the short term ultimately shapes longer-term outcomes. Below, we summarise these insights in Box 10.1, which contrasts short-term adaptations and longer-term institutionalisation in the hype process.

Box 10.1 The circuitry of hype over time and across space

10.4.1 Short-Term Adaptations

Rather than simply being swept up in hype, actors now engage in its ongoing calibration:

Entrepreneurs refine early narratives, aligning them with the evaluative infrastructures of gatekeepers.

Evaluative tools like the HCC help adopters translate hype into manageable risk strategies.

Analysts test, mediate, and curate claims, weighing enthusiasm against scepticism.

10.4.2 Longer-Term Learning and Institutionalisation

Over time, these interactions contribute to more enduring transformations:

Hype becomes tamed, funnelling grand promises through increasingly standardised evaluative routines.

Adopters grow more strategic, treating hype not as noise but as calculable input for planning and investment.

Hype itself becomes a resource, embedded in organisational strategy and used to influence perception and positioning.

A new professional class emerges, with AR experts institutionalising hype navigation as a core function.

All parties become more reflexive: vendors anticipate how claims will be judged, while analysts adapt their evaluative frameworks in response to their market-shaping role.

Together, these processes reveal a maturing promissory economy, where hype is not only produced but governed – reflexively managed by actors who recognise their mutual role in shaping its trajectory. In the next section, we draw these insights into a framework for analysing how hype has become institutionalised within the digital economy.

10.5 Elements for a Future Research Agenda

We propose some elements for a research agenda to deepen understanding of how hype functions as a structured element of economic coordination. This is not a definitive or exhaustive set of questions. They emerge from our empirical material in the digital economy, identifying five interrelated elements through which hype is stabilised, contested, and rendered actionable. The enquiry is bound to be incomplete. Nonetheless, we hope it provides a helpful starting point for exploring how hype is not only structured by institutional processes but also actively reshapes the dynamics of innovation and markets.

10.5.1 The Professionalisation of Hype

A core contribution of this book is to demonstrate how the production and governance of hype have become increasingly reliant on new forms of *expertise*. Our findings underscore the role of professionalised actors who now shape, mediate, and legitimate promissory claims. Where hype was once the domain of individual 'promise entrepreneurs' (Joly & Le Renard, 2021), it is now managed by hype's new actors.

Specifically, we identified an 'expertise arms race' (Glode et al., 2012), meaning analysts and vendors are constantly upping their game to outdo each other in narrative control. Historically, this dynamic was most visible in the sharply asymmetric relationship that arose between analysts and vendors, crystallised in powerful rankings and evaluations. In response, vendors invested heavily in AR functions, developing internal expertise to decode these once-opaque evaluative processes. These investments enable vendors to engage proactively with these gatekeepers, allowing them to respond to, challenge, and strategically leverage their assessments. In short, vendors professionalised their approach to hype because analysts had professionalised their evaluation – each side had to level up.

This growing complementarity of roles benefits both parties. Vendors with mature AR teams are better equipped to provide analysts with targeted, high-quality information. Analysts, in turn, use this input to refine their understanding of emerging technologies and market trends. These interactions can shape how analysts identify emerging innovation categories and develop future-oriented narratives (Chapter 7). Analysts and vendors effectively co-produce innovation futures, even as they maintain an outward appearance of independence.

This reflects broader transformations in expertise structures. As Eyal (2019) argues, expertise is no longer confined to fixed professional jurisdictions; it is increasingly interstitial, adaptive, and relational.

Our findings demonstrate how the boundaries between industry analysts and AR experts have become increasingly blurred. While they occupy formally distinct roles, their activities are deeply interdependent. AR teams can be seen as a form of 'loyal opposition' – they push back on analysts even as they ultimately validate the importance of analysts' evaluations. While AR teams work to advance their vendors' interests, their engagement with analysts' reports ultimately reinforces the analysts' authority. Analysts often draw on narratives presented by vendors. Savvy AR professionals understand this reciprocal dynamic and aim to cultivate what they term 'advocates in the channel' (Chapter 5).

Thus, we see a shift from a simple vendor–gatekeeper model to a more complex ecosystem of mutual influence. Hype Studies should investigate these evolving structures of authority and their implications for how innovation futures are defined. This requires attention to the role of emerging forms of expertise and intermediation in shaping the trajectory of hype, as well as to the processes through which certain claims come to be recognised as 'promising'. A key task is to examine how expertise is being reconfigured: who is regarded as credible, how authority is enacted and negotiated, and how legitimacy is distributed across innovation ecosystems.

10.5.2 Reflexivity around Hype Practices

Contemporary hype is marked by a heightened *reflexivity* among market participants. Actors are increasingly aware of the role hype plays in shaping innovation trajectories. Rather than treating hype as a by-product of innovation, they actively monitor, manage, and respond to it, tailoring their claims and conduct in anticipation of how they will be received. This represents a shift from earlier eras, when vendors might issue generic claims – now they carefully script them with analysts' criteria in mind.

Drawing on Birch's (2023) concept of *reflexive expectations*, we argue that promissory narratives are not fixed endpoints but strategic instruments – constantly adapted, recalibrated, and fine-tuned to meet shifting expectations among analysts, investors, clients, and others. This focus moves beyond static or linear models of hype's performativity, such as the self-fulfilling prophecy notion of early Sociology of Expectations literature (Brown & Michael, 2003; van Lente, 2012).

Vendors do not just launch bold claims – they calibrate those claims to align with what they expect analysts will find credible, relevant, and timely. Market actors are learning to anticipate how their narratives will be evaluated. This shift introduces a new level of reflexivity in hype management, with AR experts coaching vendors to align their claims with key evaluations. Hype Studies should trace how this reflexivity reshapes the very tools and expectations used to measure innovation.

Actors across the innovation ecosystem learn from experience, generating a new anticipatory dynamic: start-ups and their AR advisers now actively anticipate gatekeepers' evaluations, prompting vendors to refine their promises to better align with analysts' criteria. As ventures become more adept at navigating these assessments, they also become participants in what we might describe as second-order hype – they strategically re-package promises to fit established evaluative frameworks. Hype-making thus becomes reflexive: ventures actively craft narratives to be *recognisable* and credible to market gatekeepers, rather than just exciting to themselves.

A key protagonist in this reflexive turn is the AR expert. AR specialists have emerged as a distinct community of practice, dedicated to equipping vendors with the knowledge and techniques needed to navigate complex evaluative environments. In this context, reflexivity is not merely an abstract orientation; it is, as Beunza and Stark (2005, p. 369) put it, part of their 'tools of the trade'. It enables them to anticipate shifts in market sentiment, calibrate promissory narratives, and strategically position their organisations in relation to powerful gatekeepers such as industry analysts.

We propose a framework adapted from Cusworth et al. (2023, p. 18), which theorises how prominent evaluations spark an 'awareness-raising dynamic', wherein actors begin to anticipate future evaluations and modify their promissory behaviour in advance (see Box 10.2).

Each of the above points to a rich vein of enquiry for Hype Studies. Scholars could investigate, for example, how widespread these reflexive practices are beyond our case. How are market actors becoming more reflexive in their handling of hype, and with what consequences for innovation outcomes and the dynamics of hype itself? Does greater awareness of hype as a strategic force encourage caution and responsibility, or does it instead enable more sophisticated manipulation and orchestration? Another line of enquiry is the institutionalisation of

---

Box 10.2 How vendors modify promissory behaviour to anticipate evaluation

- **Vendors engage in mapping influence** by investing significant effort in identifying who matters in the promissory arena – tracking analysts, understanding their preferences, and building targeted engagement plans. Vendors are no longer simply making unbounded promissory claims but are actively charting the evaluative terrain so they can perform innovation in ways that match the expectations of powerful gatekeepers.
- **Vendors build promissory narratives to align with the language and expectations of analysts.** By adopting the evaluators' idiom, they engage in what Garfinkel (1967) terms 'recipient design' – shaping promissory narratives to enhance the chances they will be recognised, understood, and taken seriously by gatekeepers. AR coaching and pre-briefing rehearsals are central to this process. Ventures study analysts' own terminology, criteria, and visual frameworks, ensuring their pitch mirrors these cues.
- **Vendors attempt to influence wider industry narratives.** AR teams proactively offer success stories, forward-looking visions, or even proposed category definitions to shape how technologies – and the vendors offering them – are positioned. Such efforts can yield powerful effects: redefining a category or shifting its boundaries can recast a vendor's offering in a more favourable light, while simultaneously disadvantaging competitors.
- **Third-party evaluations are treated as strategic assets.** Vendors actively leverage a Cool Vendor award or high analyst ranking third-party evaluations to sustain and amplify their own promissory narratives. In this way, the tools designed to regulate hype also generate new hype – fuelling a 'promissory product spiral' in which vendors compete to excel within evaluative frameworks, further entrenching second-order hype as a dominant mode of market positioning.

---

reflexivity: Do vendor organisations establish formal processes for managing hype, and how do they collectively learn from past successes or failures? When projected claims fall short, do they seek to maintain legitimacy by, as some informants suggested, asking for the 'forgiveness' of market gatekeepers?

10.5.3 How Rivalry Plays Out through Hype

We have argued that hype has become a site of *competition* – not just over who can generate the most compelling promissory narrative but over who can perform best in the proliferating landscape of evaluation.

Conventionally, competition is viewed as a direct contest for market share, customers, or resources (Kilduff, 2019). However, as Beckert (2016, p. 170) observes, 'competition in capitalist economies is in no small measure a struggle over imaginaries of future technologies'. From this perspective, vendors today are effectively competing through hype. Each can be seen as participating in an 'expectations race' (Hoppmann et al., 2020), vying to capture the imagination of investors, analysts, and other stakeholders.

But we extend this idea further: vendors are not only competing over whose promises are most compelling – they are also competing over the frameworks through which those promises are judged. Competition has intensified not just in generating hype but in influencing the metrics, rankings, and categories that determine hype's impact. In other words, competition increasingly unfolds through the evaluator. Vendors do not just construct generic promissory narratives; they carefully tailor these narratives to resonate with market gatekeepers. Evaluative infrastructures – rankings, appellations, categories – have become the terrain on which rivalry plays out.

This dynamic is clearly visible in the digital economy; for example, as shown in Chapters 5 and 8, inclusion in a Gartner Cool Vendor list or a high position in a Magic Quadrant ranking significantly enhances a vendor's credibility and market position. In other words, success in the hype game (e.g. being labelled a 'Leader' in a Magic Quadrant) translates into competitive advantage in the market. These evaluations have become central to how hype is validated. Market gatekeepers now use them to differentiate between vendors based on their projected ability to deliver on promises. This introduces new forms of rivalry among vendors – not through direct competition but through contestation over how they are evaluated.

If rankings produce rivalrous effects, then vendors' reactions to those are inherently competitive as well. Vendors skilled at crafting promissory narratives that resonate with evaluators gain opportunities to navigate and even reshape the competitive landscape. We showed that some vendors develop expertise in crafting compelling stories about the trajectory and scope of emerging innovations that can redefine category boundaries in ways that advantage their products while sidelining those of rivals.

This gives rise to a new kind of rivalry, not traditional head-to-head competition but on winning the favour of third parties. It is a mediated contest – what Stark (2020, p. 4), drawing on Simmel (2008), calls a 'rivalry for the favour of a third party' – in which vendors vie to gain the approval of analysts by crafting promissory narratives that align with ranking criteria. Vendors, then, are not simply targeting customers with their messaging; they are actively courting analysts, rankings providers, and other market gatekeepers. As one industry analyst informant observed, '[vendors] are working through the analyst and trying to pull it a little bit in their direction … how we [the analyst] view their products' (A1, interview).

We propose that 'competition through the evaluator' – rivalry waged by influencing third-party judgements rather than directly outperforming competitors – has become a defining feature of vendor strategy in the digital economy. This form of mediated rivalry deserves closer attention within Hype Studies. Research should examine how competition unfolds in the arena of evaluation, the tactics vendors deploy to shape judgements, and the extent to which these tactics are accessible to all firms or skewed towards those with greater resources and experience. Equally important is attention to evaluators themselves. Analysts are not passive arbiters: they recognise, and in some cases embrace, their role as a competitive battleground, as it reinforces their authority. Yet this reflexive awareness can alter how evaluations are produced and how claims are substantiated. Understanding these dynamics is crucial for analysing the co-construction of hype and authority in innovation ecosystems.

10.5.4 Hype's Winners and Losers

Our book shows the *layered* and *uneven distribution* of hype, in which specific claims and actors gain visibility and legitimacy, while others are excluded or subordinated. Indeed, not all vendors can compete equally in this new hype game. Those who lack the expertise, connections, or resources to manage hype effectively may be excluded from recognition and investment. Hype Studies should analyse how hype reinforces or mitigates inequalities in market visibility and

opportunity. We demonstrate how hype's transformation into a pro-
fessionally mediated resource has created new forms of innovation
inequality, privileging those who can harness it.

Hype circulates most powerfully through dominant innovation clus-
ters – such as Silicon Valley, London's Tech City, or Shenzhen – and
around major platform firms like Google, Facebook, or Amazon
(Shestakofsky, 2024). By contrast, peripheral regions and smaller
vendors often struggle to attract the same levels of promissory attention. As Belsunces (2024) puts it, hype may increasingly 'overstimulate
the visibility of certain ventures and consequently overshadow others'
(see also Potts, 2017). Following MacKenzie (2018), we might describe
this as *the material political economy of hype*, a system where hype
increasingly 'benefits the already privileged' (Belsunces, 2024), reinforcing what one informant described as a world 'where the rich get
richer' (Chapple, 2024) – that is, hype begets more hype for those
already in the spotlight.

Early scholarship highlighted how hype is not evenly distributed
(Brown, 2003). Ventures attracting and sustaining hype often gain
privileged access to resource providers (Pontikes & Barnett, 2017)
and benefit from operating within 'protected spaces' (van Lente &
Rip, 1998; Smith & Raven, 2012), where the risks of failure are
buffered and the prospects of innovation are more readily materialised.
Conversely, ventures unable to generate or sustain hype face disadvan-
tages. Yet, we challenge the idea that these asymmetries are fixed or
immutable. By approaching hype as a business and showing how its
new actors have reconfigured the rules of the game, we reveal how
these experts mediate and channel hype – establishing promissory
products that can both open up and shut down opportunities.

This means that while hype is not a level terrain (and may indeed
become more unequal), this landscape is changing. Moreover, increasingly reflexive actors can better orient themselves within it – hype now
opens up new scopes for strategic intervention. For example, vendors
that craft promissory narratives aligned with gatekeeper expectations
will likely gain visibility and endorsement. Designations such as *Cool
Vendor* provide significant amplification, propelling start-ups into the
mainstream and enhancing their perceived legitimacy.

In this new environment, access to specialised expertise, particularly
AR, becomes critical. Vendors with strong AR capabilities are better
equipped to shape and align their narratives with evaluators'

frameworks, increasing their chances of recognition. Learning to *speak the language* of gatekeepers and to *look like* a Cool Vendor emerged as a key tactic for gaining attention and endorsement. AR professionals coach vendors on how to frame evidence, fit their story into existing categories, and engage effectively in analyst briefings. Throughout our study, we document cases where such expertise enabled vendors to shift analysts' perceptions and influence broader industry promissory narratives.

By contrast, vendors lacking these capabilities cannot compete on equal terms. Participation in analyst evaluations requires time-consuming preparation, carefully curated evidence, and alignment with specific frameworks – all of which demand resources. Without AR support, smaller or less-resourced firms may find their innovations overlooked, even when those innovations are as promising as those of better-supported competitors.

Therefore, this analysis highlights how the professionalisation of hype generates both new opportunities and new exclusions (see also Byrne & Giulani, 2025). While some ventures can navigate and benefit from this system, others risk being left behind, reinforcing emerging forms of innovation inequality in the digital economy. Future research should examine the economics of hype production: crafting narratives, engaging gatekeepers, and participating in high-profile evaluations all require significant investments of time, expertise, and capital. Recognitions such as the Cool Vendor designation may be formally merit-based, yet in practice they depend on costly activities – targeted marketing campaigns, intensive briefing preparation, and careful narrative refinement. Analysing these costs can illuminate the barriers facing smaller actors and expose the structural inequalities embedded in the innovation landscape. (We return to the policy implications of these inequalities under the 'Responsible Hype' section below).

10.5.5 Managing Speculative Cycles

Scholars have long sought to interpret speculative cycles such as hype cycles or bubbles, yet existing framings remain contested and incomplete. Some see them as symptoms of malfunctioning capitalist systems (Goldfarb & Kirsch, 2019). Others view them not as side effects but as the defining condition of our time (Bear, 2020; Komporozos-Athanasiou, 2022). Despite their recurring presence in innovation markets, we still lack a robust understanding of how speculative cycles form, evolve, and persist (Garud *et al.*, 2025).

Our study highlights the importance of developing a more comprehensive understanding of speculative cycles and recognising the growing attempts to manage them. Where speculative cycles were once seen as natural or inevitable features of capitalism, recent work in the 'sociology of bubbles' (Carruthers, 2009) has emphasised instead how they are actively shaped and organised (Weber, 2016, 2019). This perspective redirects attention from abstract models of rise and fall to the concrete techniques, evaluative infrastructures, and sociomaterial practices through which markets are, in Weber's phrase, 'set up to cycle' (2016, p. 588; see also Tvede, 2013). Our analysis extends this line of enquiry by showing how promissory products do not merely depict speculative cycles but actively configure and recalibrate them.

We extend this line of enquiry by showing how speculative cycles are increasingly moderated through promissory products such as the HCC. The HCC functions not only as a visualisation of hype's rise and fall but also as a mechanism for disciplining speculative enthusiasm. By framing the trajectory of emerging technologies, industry analysts use it to guide market actors in recognising the conditions under which bubbles are likely to form.

A telling illustration of this dual role is Gartner's retrospective claim to have foreseen the 2001 dotcom crash. As Jackie Fenn recalled, 'Gartner analyst Alexander Droibik forecast the bubble bursting in his 1998 e-business [HCC]' (Fenn, interview). She emphasised that this claim of early detection became a crucial form of public 'proof' of the HCC's credibility and practical utility – an instance of what Hildebrandt et al. (2008) and Latour (2012b) describe as the visible demonstrations that stabilise and legitimise evaluative infrastructures. The dotcom episode thus helped cement the HCC as a cornerstone of the digital economy's evaluative infrastructure, consolidating its authority not merely to map hype but to manage it.

Speculative cycles feed on the narrowing of evaluative perspectives. When many actors share the same hype narrative, echo chambers form and bubbles inflate. As we argued in the previous chapter, cycles emerge most forcefully when evaluation is narrow or homogenous (Stark, 2009; MacKenzie, 2011). Inflated claims gain traction within tightly interconnected groups that share interests and biases, reinforcing one another's views. Droibik himself described this dynamic as an 'echo system' – a self-reinforcing hype loop with little accountability until collapse. He offered an analogy: 'It is a bit like a political party. If you ask your supporters what you should do, and you get a sub-weird caucus – if your supporters are in the majority, you tend to focus on a very small view on what you should do' (Droibik, interview). In such environments, positive assessments amplify each other until punctured by dissenting perspectives or hard constraints, often culminating in dramatic bursts. These are precisely the conditions under which boom and bust cycles flourish.

Yet the proliferation of promissory products now arguably modifies and complicates this dynamic, producing products that recalibrate expectations. Industry analysts have developed tools to intervene in these potentially self-reinforcing cycles. The HCC is a prominent example: a promissory product that systematically conveys the shifting credibility of emerging technologies. It helps identify both promising developments and potential pitfalls by tracing the 'trajectory of evidence' (Kruse, 2015) – mapping how credibility evolves and signalling when caution is warranted.

Gartner's dual achievement – creating the HCC as an evaluative infrastructure and using it to demarcate phases of speculative momentum – represents a sophisticated intervention into innovation markets. The tool is designed to help determine whether enthusiasm around a technology signals collective exuberance or genuine opportunity. This is an inherently difficult distinction: both are accompanied by similar claims and forms of supporting evidence. Our earlier research (Pollock & Williams, 2016) showed how analysts are primed to act on such signals, likening their sensitivity to a spider detecting vibrations in its web. In this role, analysts do not simply record adoption trends but also issue warnings about potential bubbles, particularly when endorsements come from reputable but vendor-aligned actors who may face conflicts of interest.

Despite its relatively recent introduction, the HCC has achieved a near-axiomatic status within the digital economy. Yet we know surprisingly little about how such hype tools shape the very dynamics they purport to measure. Some scholars suggest they act as an early warning system, mitigating excess (Floridi, 2024). Others argue they entrench and normalise speculative momentum, amplifying rather than curbing it (Joly, 2010). Our analysis suggests a further possibility: promissory products increasingly operate as *dampening mechanisms*. Rather than allowing what Pontikes and Barnett (2017, p. 141) call 'dramatic boom and bust cycles', these tools smooth the height of speculative peaks and depth of troughs – reducing the severity of swings without eliminating their underlying rhythm. In this sense, they act less like fire alarms that warn of imminent danger and more like shock absorbers that modulate and recalibrate enthusiasm over time.

Viewing promissory products as dampening mechanisms also connects to our broader argument about the taming of hype: volatility is no longer left entirely 'in the wild' but is increasingly channelled through institutionalised evaluative infrastructures. The proliferating promissory products can help mitigate (though not eliminate) the risk of destructive swings, suggesting that speculative momentum may now circulate through more contained oscillations of adaptation and recalibration. Yet whether this represents a fundamental reconfiguration of the digital economy – where catastrophic collapses are less likely – or whether risks are instead displaced and redistributed in new, less visible ways, remains uncertain. These are precisely the kinds of questions that mark out a fertile agenda for future Hype Studies.

* * *

Taken together, these five elements offer a provisional roadmap for enquiry into the anatomy of hype. Each highlights a different layer of its institutionalisation – from who performs it, to how it is contested, scaled, and judged. Yet this agenda is necessarily incomplete, especially as attention shifts to sectors beyond the digital economy, where different institutional constellations and dynamics of hype are likely to emerge.

Having explored hype within the digital domain, we now broaden our focus to examine hype dynamics in other fields beyond the digital economy.

10.6 Hype beyond the Digital Economy

While our analysis has focused on the digital economy, we regard this sector as exemplary for understanding hype dynamics more widely. Our broader aim is to open the way for comparative work. We conjecture that the deliberate practices of taming hype identified here – professionalised expertise, reflexive management, competition structured through evaluation, processes of stratification, etc. – are also evident in other fields. A research programme on hype should therefore compare and generalise across domains, rather than remain anchored in a single context. *Hype Studies*, as we envision it, offers a lens applicable wherever promissory narratives and imagined futures organise innovation, mobilise investment, and shape decision-making.

Such comparative work should investigate how institutionalised forms of hype migrate across sectors, and how different fields adapt, adopt, or resist practices of evaluation and future-making. We conjecture that organisations across diverse industries – not just in the digital economy – are increasingly developing structured approaches to navigate hype. Indeed, one might begin from the premise that hype is a distinctive corollary of all discontinuous innovation. We posit that any sector characterised by rapid, discontinuous innovation will exhibit high levels of hype and the emergence of hype-management institutions.

Historical and contemporary cases – from nanotech and hydrogen to artificial intelligence (AI) and most recently quantum computing augmented by Large Language Models (LLMs) – illustrate how successive waves of enthusiasm, investment, disappointment, and recalibration unfold (Bakker & Budde, 2012). Yet the form hype takes, and the degree to which it can be structured or 'tamed', varies widely. For instance, compare the relatively short hype cycles in smartphone apps to the decades-long promissory horizons of nuclear fusion. In the latter case, researchers have been observed generating excitement around relatively modest advances in order to sustain attention and attract investment over time (Funk, 2019; Minkkinen et al., 2023). This kind of long-term promissory work exemplifies what Powers (2019) calls the 'strategic calibration' of hype – keeping expectations alive while avoiding 'fatigue' or 'backlash'.

These variations reflect the different exigencies of the 'promissory game': the time horizons of the innovation journey, its degree of uncertainty or capital intensity, and the scale of anticipated payoff. Radical, long-horizon innovations such as nuclear fusion or hydrogen energy demand continuous hype work to maintain attention and legitimacy over decades, whereas more incremental domains like consumer apps rely on carefully timed bursts of enthusiasm calibrated to market cycles. Across these domains, actors mobilise ideas of 'technological maturity' (Roussel, 1984) to codify progress, but innovation pathways diverge widely in scientific and technical difficulty, investment requirements, institutional buy-in, and infrastructure demands.

The digital economy is characterised by a vast and constantly evolving market of business technologies that cut across sectoral boundaries. In this environment, industry analysts have become pivotal in constituting arenas of evaluation and comparison, providing the coherence and benchmarks needed to navigate such a fragmented and fast-moving space. This stands in contrast to specialised fields such as healthcare or the life sciences, where analysts coexist with sectoral-specific organisations like 'industry associations' (Martin, 2015). These latter organisations may lack the breadth and visibility of an industry analyst firm like Gartner, but they offer in-depth, domain-specific expertise and often operate within established professional or regulatory frameworks. Another distinctive feature of the digital economy is the relatively limited role of the state. Unlike sectors such as energy, defence, or pharmaceuticals – where policy intervention, regulation, and public funding strongly shape expectations – the digital economy has developed mainly outside formal governance (Malerba, 2002). This has left a vacuum of coordination, which analysts and related experts have been able to fill by structuring expectations, defining categories, and taming hype. AI and quantum computing may be partial exceptions, but even in these cases, public initiatives operate alongside the powerful evaluative influence of analysts.

From this vantage point, *tamed hype* appears as part of a broader reconfiguration of how futures are organised. Organisations across sectors increasingly rely on routines and tools to interpret, manage, and act upon hype in real time, rather than adopting a passive 'wait-and-see' stance (Robinson et al., 2012). Promissory products, roadmaps (Miller & O'Leary, 2007), investment schedules (Mallaby, 2022), and evaluative frameworks render the future more calculable without making it certain. As Appadurai (2021) argues, this reflects the progressive 'socialisation' of the future: expectations are shaped and circulated through professional practices, institutional conventions, and infrastructures of valuation. In parallel, Mützel (2022) points to the growing 'market of expectations', in which diverse actors exchange, evaluate, and institutionalise future imaginaries. Wenzel *et al.* (2020, 2025) describe this as the 'commodification' of the near future, whereby expectations are packaged, priced, and systematically appraised.

Comparable figures to industry analysts can be found well beyond the digital economy. In finance, financial analysts construct visions of future returns (Leins, 2018), while rating agencies discipline rather than register speculation, moderating dynamics through their ratings (Feher, 2021). In the pharmaceutical industry, experts actively manage and channel hype (Mützel, 2022). In the life sciences, industry associations operate as collective evaluators (Martin, 2015). And in healthcare, specialist firms such as Klas explicitly style themselves as the 'Gartner for healthcare'. More broadly, consultants, think tanks, and funding bodies all play central roles in producing, legitimising, and evaluating promissory narratives.

Importantly, practices of taming are not confined to one sector but travel across domains. Professionals carry evaluative tools, repertoires, and frameworks with them, reshaping how hype is organised and contained in new contexts. The founder of Gartner, for example, imported techniques from his earlier career as a financial analyst into the emerging computing industry when establishing the firm (Pollock & Williams, 2016).

Organisations across sectors now routinely scan for signals, threats, and opportunities, triggering proactive action (Kumaraswamy et al., 2018). This reflects a cultural and strategic orientation in which the future is increasingly populated with tools – roadmaps, investment schedules, benchmarks – that make it manageable without making it certain. These tools do not provide foresight in a deterministic sense (Thompson & Byrne, 2022), but they enable action and adaptation as futures unfold. As Urry (2016, p. 192) observes, the future is no longer fixed or fated but a contested, 'murky world' that we must 'enter, interrogate, and hopefully reshape'.

Understanding these sectoral variations in hype practices will be crucial, especially as we consider how hype's institutionalisation intersects with broader societal and policy concerns (as we discuss next).

10.7 Responsible Hype

Hype's consequences extend well beyond organisational strategy and adopter attention. Its institutionalisation carries far-reaching implications for public funding, regulation, and the governance of innovation. Hype influences how governments allocate resources, shapes the construction of policy agendas, and determines which futures become thinkable. If hype is now, in part, a structured resource that directs attention and capital, policymakers can no longer treat it as background noise.

Some critics have called for curbing hype altogether (Funk, 2019; Vinsel & Russell, 2020), but this position is both reductive and infeasible. As this book has argued, hype is not simply a problem to be solved; it is a persistent feature of innovation ecosystems, particularly in the digital economy. This persistence places a greater burden on public actors, who must become literate in the mechanisms of hype – able not only to navigate but, when appropriate, to harness it. Hype Studies can contribute to this task by offering public institutions a more nuanced understanding of hype, and of the tools and strategies deployed by hype's new actors. Such knowledge is essential for leveraging hype's mobilising potential while mitigating its distorting effects.

Governments and public agencies are increasingly implicated in hype – not only as funders or regulators but also as customers, partners, and architects of innovation-led growth (Mazzucato, 2011). They are swept up in global innovation races, responding to international rankings and anticipatory narratives. When public institutions support R&D, they often amplify hype to justify investment and stimulate action, invoking the risk of falling behind or missing out.

A formative example is the US response to Japan's Fifth Generation Computing programme in the 1980s, when the Department of Defence raised alarms about a looming AI capability gap. This was the first of several high-profile episodes of techno-nationalism – followed by genetic engineering, nanotechnology, big data, and supercomputing – that illustrate how hype becomes entwined with geopolitical and industrial strategy (Smith, 2020). More recently, governments worldwide have launched ambitious AI R&D programmes, often invoking similar narratives of urgency and competitive threat (Minkkinen et al., 2023).

Yet this entanglement is not without risk. Governments can become too caught up in the excitement, mirroring private investors in triggering speculative bubbles. Public funding surges, start-ups proliferate, and vendors and intermediaries eagerly attach themselves to the momentum. The result is often public investment that mimics speculative markets, complete with cycles of enthusiasm, disillusionment, and even crashes.

Policymakers often feel pressure to back frontier technologies. As Nordmann (2007) argues, hyped expectations can trigger an 'if and then' syndrome: once speculative futures are accepted, debate shifts to how best to prepare for them, rather than whether they should be pursued at all. Hype can thus foreclose deliberation, making speculative trajectories feel inevitable and narrowing the range of considered alternatives.

Distinguishing genuinely transformative innovation from overhyped speculation is far from straightforward (Kriechbaum et al., 2018). Enthusiasm can distort priorities: public actors may overestimate technological maturity, underestimate barriers to scale, and direct resources towards areas already saturated with private-sector interest. In the absence of counter-narratives, commercial excitement is often taken as a proxy for opportunity or social need – meaning that alternative innovation pathways, including those with potentially greater societal value, may remain underfunded or ignored (Tracey & Stott, 2017; Gray & Purdy, 2018; Beckman *et al.*, 2023).

The state's responsibility goes beyond competitiveness. Public institutions must also consider the directionality of innovation – its social and ethical aims, not merely its market potential. Responsible Research and Innovation (RRI) frameworks urge that innovation be anticipatory, inclusive, and reflective (Owen *et al.*, 2020). By extension, *Responsible Hype* is a stance in which stakeholders actively channel hype's energy towards socially beneficial outcomes while mitigating its risks (Simakova & Coenen, 2013).

Hype is more than rhetoric: it is also a structuring mechanism and resource (van Lente, 2012; Logue & Grimes, 2022). In its tamed form, hype creates 'protected spaces' (van Lente & Rip, 1998) where emerging technologies can develop under the shelter of optimism and commitment. Such spaces can be valuable, but they also raise questions of equity: who benefits from hype, and whose futures are being legitimised? As this book has shown, attention and legitimacy are increasingly allocated through professionalised mechanisms involving hype's new actors – actors who can amplify, dampen, or redirect expectations, shaping the boundaries of these protected spaces. These processes determine not only which innovations succeed but also where and for whom they succeed.

If tamed hype is central to how ventures are legitimised and resourced, then policymakers must confront the question of distribution: How evenly is this resource spread across geographies, organisations, and communities? Who controls the hype – and by extension, who controls the future being imagined?

Governments could use hype proactively to foster a more inclusive innovation economy. Innovation support programmes, for instance, might include mechanisms to help underrepresented ventures engage with hype's new actors – by offering guidance on working with analysts, crafting strategic narratives, or preparing for high-impact evaluations.

Governments could also strategically recast hype, aligning neglected domains with dominant technological narratives. Framing social issues such as elderly care (Christian et al., 2025) or environmental challenges (Downs, 2016) as promising innovation frontiers could mobilise private-sector engagement. Through structured initiatives such as competitions and targeted calls, public actors can bring overlooked problems 'onto the agenda' (Protess & McCombs, 2016), transforming diffuse concerns into coordinated investment and development (Christian et al., 2025).

While hype functions as a vital resource for innovation, it remains unevenly distributed. Advancing a more inclusive innovation economy will require sustained attention to the sites and mechanisms through which hype is articulated and tamed. Democratising hype entails greater transparency in evaluative processes, broader access to evaluation arenas, and targeted capacity-building for ventures and organisations in underrepresented contexts to engage with – and benefit from – the business of hyped expectations.

* * *

Overall, *After Hype* has shown that we live in a world where hype is no longer entirely wild but in part tamed – and has become a business in its own right. This concluding chapter argues that recognising and scrutinising this evolution is crucial for understanding contemporary innovation and capitalism. Hype Studies offers a critical lens for examining and navigating this shift. We see it as a framework for developing more informed and reflexive approaches to technological change, and we invite scholars from across disciplines to join us in shaping this emerging area.

Appendix
Research Design and Methods

A.1 Studying Hype's New Actors

Many of the key insights in this book are grounded in detailed ethnographic research and follow-up interviews conducted over more than a decade. Our work builds on an extensive program of participant observation of analyst briefings, complemented by in-depth interviews with industry analysts, analyst relations (AR) experts, start-up ventures, and clients of analyst firms. Through the long-term relationships developed during this extended fieldwork programme, we gained access to spaces that are typically difficult to observe and largely closed to outsiders.

Part of the reason why hype remains understudied is the relative invisibility of hype's new actors. Although they have been active since the early 2000s, industry analysts and AR experts have often operated behind the scenes. Their work has largely been ignored or dismissed as too peripheral for academic study, with a few exceptions, such as Bernard and Gallupe (2013). While these actors are occasionally visible at public events, such as industry conferences, the bulk of their activity unfolds in private or liminal settings, making them elusive to conventional research methods (Pollock & Williams, 2016).

Gaining access to these domains posed a considerable challenge. Our initial efforts to contact industry analysts and to observe their briefings were often met with polite interest but ultimately declined. This outcome is understandable, given that such briefings frequently involve sensitive content, such as unreleased product roadmaps or strategic positioning. As a result, we had to adopt a strategic and adaptive approach to fieldwork (Marcus, 1995).

As part of this adaptive approach, two pivotal developments proved instrumental in expanding our access to these actors and practices. The first occurred during our early engagements with industry analysts, when we encountered an emerging group of professionals who were

---

Box A.1 The Institute of Industry Analyst Relations (IIAR)

The Institute of Industry Analyst Relations (IIAR) is a member organ-isation founded over a decade ago by UK-based AR experts to bring together technology vendors that engage with industry analysts. Today, the IIAR represents approximately sixty of the world's largest technology vendors. Its mission is to build and strengthen the fledgling AR community, enabling members to act in unison and to share knowledge and expertise. To this end, the IIAR hosts monthly meetings and webinars that assemble a broad range of participants – including industry analysts themselves – for both formal discussions and informal exchanges.

---

equally interested in the evaluative processes we were studying: AR experts. Recognising the central role of these AR experts in the evolving hype ecosystem, we expanded our research to include AR experts and the broader ecosystem they help orchestrate.

The second pivotal development came when one of the authors (Pollock) discovered the Institute of Industry Analyst Relations (IIAR), which was then a nascent professional network (See Box A.1). He travelled from Edinburgh to London to attend the IIAR's Christmas event and, beer in hand, introduced himself to AR experts while explaining his interest in industry analyst practices. Unlike the confusion or scepticism that often greeted such explanations at academic conferences, the IIAR members responded with enthusiasm and curiosity. This encounter led to an invitation for Pollock to give a talk at a subsequent IIAR meeting, followed by further invitations and ultimately his regular participation in IIAR events, both online and in-person. Thus, what began as simple event attendance eventually evolved into active participation. We initially attended these IIAR gatherings as observers; later, as our project's stakeholder participation strategy developed, we even assisted in organising and running them.

A.2 Participant Observation

Between 2009 and 2019, we conducted approximately 800 hours of physical and virtual participant observation at IIAR events. Initially, the lead author's role was that of a traditional observer – attending events and taking notes. But as relationships deepened and trust developed, his participation grew more active. Over time, he was invited to present talks on his research into industry analysts, to co-author IIAR white papers and blog posts, and to collaborate on a major initiative called the 'ranking of the rankers' (an evaluative project examining analyst influence). This growing integration culminated in an invitation for him to stand for election to the IIAR board – a position he won.

Joining the IIAR board provided unrestricted access to private IIAR meetings and strategic activities within the organisation. In this role, he took on responsibilities such as organising the annual IIAR Industry Analyst Awards. These awards evaluated and ranked leading analysts and firms, making the awards ceremony a key moment in the field's self-understanding. As a board member, he also helped coordinate and present regular AR webinars, further embedding our research within this evolving professional network.

Membership in the IIAR granted us unprecedented access to a new domain of expert practice at a formative stage in its development. It allowed us to observe gatherings where industry analysts, AR experts, venture representatives, and analyst clients came together to negotiate the framing and evaluation of emerging technologies. Many of the practices we document – though routine for participants – remain largely invisible to social scientists studying hype and the digital economy. Yet these practices take place in some of the most consequential arenas where promissory narratives are shaped, authorised, and contested.

In 2019, we further extended our ethnographic reach through an immersive four-week study (approximately 300 hours of observation) at an AR agency we refer to pseudonymously as 'Sunshine'. During this fieldwork, we observed ten live analyst briefings involving digital entrepreneurs, industry analysts, and AR experts, and we were also granted access to seven previously recorded briefings from the agency's internal repository. Together, these observations provided a unique longitudinal view of narrative evolution in the briefing process.

We are especially grateful for the high-trust relationships that made this level of access possible. In some cases, our interlocutors effectively became co-researchers, generously sharing their insights, experiences, and strategic reflections developed over years in the field. Special thanks are due to Duncan Chapple – former industry analyst turned

AR expert – whose collaboration was instrumental in helping us negotiate access to this highly significant yet previously overlooked interface.

Additional insights were gathered at industry events. We attended three Gartner conferences and two Forrester seminars, where we sat in on formal presentations and conducted informal conversations with analysts during breaks and social events. We also participated in over fifty webinars, where analysts and AR experts discussed industry trends, evaluation practices, and the formation of new technology categories.

A.3 Semi-structured Interviews and Focus Groups

Between 2009 and 2024, we conducted over 140 semi-structured interviews as part of our extended ethnographic research. Our initial focus was on current and former Gartner analysts, with whom we conducted more than twenty-six interviews. This core group was complemented by interviews with analysts from other major firms: nine at IDC, five at Forrester, and twenty across various smaller analyst organisations. While most of these were one-time interviews, we re-interviewed some Gartner analysts across multiple years to capture longitudinal shifts in their perspectives and practices. In addition, we spoke with several pivotal figures in the history of the industry analyst profession, including Gideon Gartner (founder of Gartner Inc.), Jackie Fenn (creator of the Hype Cycle Chart), and Alexander Droibik (who famously forecasted the bursting of the dotcom bubble).

In parallel, we conducted forty-four interviews with AR experts working within technology vendor organisations. We also interviewed twenty consultants from marketing or specialist AR agencies who advise vendors on how to navigate relationships with analyst firms. These additional perspectives helped to further contextualise our insights from the analyst interviews.

We also interviewed thirty-five start-up ventures that had engaged with, or were in the process of engaging with, industry analysts. While we began by focusing on ventures that had been awarded Gartner's 'Cool Vendor' status, we soon broadened our scope to include other start-ups seeking visibility through analyst channels. This broader sample provided a more comprehensive view of how such ventures attempt to position themselves within these promissory circuits.

Finally, we conducted three focus groups with early-stage ventures in the UK. Each group consisted of founders or staff who were either actively considering briefings with analyst firms or had already begun such engagements. In total, these sessions involved forty-five participants, providing a collective perspective on how smaller ventures interpret and approach engagement with industry analysts.

A.4 Archival Research

We had access to the private archives of the IIAR, from which we obtained recorded webinars, PowerPoint presentations, and internal reports. The IIAR archives included documents and minutes from past meetings, as well as recordings of presentations and webinars spanning several years. We also visited the Gartner archive at the Charles Babbage Institute (University of Minnesota), which houses documents on Gartner's tools dating back four decades. One notable artefact from the Gartner archive was the company's internal 'blue book' from 1988, which set out the tool authoring principles still in use today (Gartner, 1988).

We extensively reviewed Gartner's primary research database, which stores historical materials on the firm's evaluation tools, such as the Magic Quadrant and the Hype Cycle Chart. The database includes original descriptions of these tools, as well as recordings of presentations and webinars that document methodological changes and new version launches over the past twenty-five years. These sources provided valuable insight into how Gartner's evaluation frameworks have evolved. Additionally, we obtained eight internal documents that detail the methodology behind the Hype Cycle Chart (HCC).

A.5 Media Articles

To further inform our study of the Hype Cycle Chart, we examined a variety of published sources. We began by studying Jackie Fenn's 2008 book *Mastering the Hype Cycle*, co-authored with Mark Raskino, to gain historical context on the Hype Cycle concept. We also collected dozens of industry documents and blog posts on the HCC, including transcribed interviews with Jackie Fenn. Additionally, we reviewed social media posts and commentaries on new releases of the HCC, which provided insight into how these updates were received and interpreted by market actors.

References

Abbott, A. (2001) *Time matters: on theory and method*. Chicago: University of Chicago Press.

Abernathy, W. J. and Clark, K. B. (1985) Innovation: mapping the winds of creative destruction. *Research Policy*, 14, pp. 3–22.

Abrahamson, E. and Fairchild, G. (1999) Management fashion: lifecycles, triggers, and collective learning processes. *Administrative Science Quarterly*, 44(4), pp. 708–740.

Adam, B. (2023) Futures imperfect: a reflection on challenges. *Sociology*, 57(2), pp. 279–281.

Ahrne, G., Aspers, P. and Brunsson, N. (2015) The organization of markets. *Organization Studies*, 36(1), pp. 7–27.

Akerlof, G. A. and Shiller, R. J. (2010) *Animal spirits: how human psychology drives the economy, and why it matters for global capitalism*. Princeton, NJ: Princeton University Press.

Akrich, M. (1992) The de-scription of technical objects. In Bijker, W. and Law, J. (eds.) *Shaping technology/building society: studies in sociotechnical change*. Cambridge, MA: MIT Press, pp. 205–224.

Akerlof, G. A. and Shiller, R. J. (2010) *Animal spirits: how human psychology drives the economy, and why it matters for global capitalism*. Princeton, NJ: Princeton University Press.

Aldridge, A. (1994) The construction of rational consumption in *Which?* magazine: the more blobs the better? *Sociology*, 28(4), pp. 899–912.

Aligica, P. D. (2003) Prediction, explanation and the epistemology of future studies. *Futures*, 35(10), pp. 1027–1040.

Alvial-Palavicino, C. and Konrad, K. (2019) The rise of graphene expectations: anticipatory practices in emergent nanotechnologies. Futures, 109, pp. 192–202.

Antal, A. B., Hutter, M. and Stark, D. (2015) Pragmatist perspectives on valuation: an introduction. In Antal, A. B., Hutter, M. and Stark, D. (eds.) *Moments of valuation: exploring sites of dissonance*. Oxford: Oxford University Press, pp. 1–14.

Appadurai, A. (2021) The scarcity of social futures in the digital era. In Kemp S. and Andersson, J. (eds.) *Futures*. Oxford: Oxford University Press, pp. 280–295.

Arjaliès, D.-L., Grant, P., Hardie, I., MacKenzie, D. and Svetlova, E. (2017) *Chains of finance: how investment management is shaped*. Oxford: Oxford University Press.

Arnold, F., Breitenmoser, P. P., Röth, T. and Spieth, P. (2022) How do technological frames feel? Business model innovation in pre-digital companies and the emotional impact of digital technologies. *International Journal of Innovation Management*, 26(9), p. 2240021.

Arora-Jonsson, S., Brunsson, N. and Hasse, R. (2020) Where does competition come from? The role of organization. *Organisation Theory*, 1(1), pp. 1–24.

Arrow, K. J. (1962) The economic implications of learning by doing. *The Review of Economic Studies*, 29(3), pp. 155–173.

Aspers, P. (2018) Forms of uncertainty reduction: decision, valuation, and contest. *Theory and Society*, 47, pp. 133–149.

Aspers, P. and Beckert, J. (2011) Value in markets. In Beckert, J. and Aspers, P. (eds.) *The worth of goods: valuation and pricing in the economy*. Oxford: Oxford University Press, pp. 3–38.

Bachmann, R., Gillespie, N. and Priem, R. (2015) Repairing trust in organisations and institutions: toward a conceptual framework. *Organisation Studies*, 36, pp. 1123–1142.

Bakker, S. and Budde, B. (2012) Technological hype and disappointment: lessons from the hydrogen and fuel cell case. *Technology Analysis & Strategic Management*, 24(6), pp. 549–563.

Bakker, S., Van Lente, H. and Meeus, M. (2011) Arenas of expectations for hydrogen technologies. *Technological Forecasting and Social Change*, 78(1), pp. 152–162.

(2012) Credible expectations – The US Department of Energy's Hydrogen Program as enactor and selector of hydrogen technologies. *Technological Forecasting and Social Change*, 79(6), pp. 1059–1071.

Bareis, J. and Katzenbach, C. (2022) Talking AI into being: the narratives and imaginaries of national AI strategies and their performative politics. *Science, Technology, and Human Values*, 47(5), pp. 855–881.

Barlevy, G. (2015) Bubbles and fools. *Economic Perspectives*, 39(2), pp. 54–77.

Barman, E. (2015) Of principle and principal: value plurality in the market of impact investing. *Valuation Studies*, 3, pp. 9–44.

Barnhart, R. (1999) *Chambers dictionary of etymology*. London: Chambers.

Barrett, M., Heracleous, L. and Walsham, G. (2013) A rhetorical approach to IT diffusion: reconceptualising the ideology-framing relationship in computerisation movements. *MIS Quarterly*, 37(1), pp. 201–220.

Bartel, C. A. and Garud, R. (2009) The role of narratives in sustaining organisational innovation. *Organisation Science*, 20, pp. 107–117.

Baskerville, R. and Myers, M. (2009) Fashion waves in information systems research and practice. *MIS Quarterly*, 33, pp. 647–662.

Bazzani, G. (2023) Futures in action: expectations, imaginaries and narratives of the future. *Sociology*, 57(2), pp. 382–397.

Bear, L. (2020) Speculation: a political economy of technologies of imagination. *Economy and Society*, 49(1), pp. 1–15.

Becker, H. S. (1984) *Art worlds*. Berkeley: University of California Press.

Beckert, J. (2013) Imagined futures: fictional expectations in the economy. *Theory and Society*, 42(3), 219–240.

(2016) *Imagined futures: fictional expectations and capitalist dynamics*. Cambridge, MA: Harvard University Press.

(2021) The firm as an engine of imagination: organisational prospection and the making of economic futures. *Organisation Theory*, 2(2), pp. 1–24.

Beckert, J. and Aspers, P. (eds.) (2011) *The worth of goods: valuation and pricing in the economy*. Oxford: Oxford University Press.

Beckert, J. and Bronk, R. (eds.) (2018) *Uncertain futures: imaginaries, narratives, and calculation in the economy*. Oxford: Oxford University Press.

Beckert, J. and Ergen, T. (2021) Transcending history's heavy hand: the future in economic action. In Maurer, A. (ed.) *Handbook of economic sociology for the 21st century*. Cham: Springer, pp. 79–94.

Beckert, J. and Musselin, C. (2013) *Constructing quality: the classification of goods in markets*. Oxford: Oxford University Press.

Beckman, C. M., Rosen, J., Estrada-Miller, J. and Painter, G. (2023) The social innovation trap: critical insights into an emerging field. *Academy of Management Annals*, 17(2), pp. 684–709.

Bell, W. and Mau, J. (1971) Images of the future: theory and research. *The Sociology of the Future*, pp. 6–44.

Belsunces, A. (2024) What are critical hype studies? LinkedIn post. www .linkedin.com/posts/andreubelsunces_what-are-critical-hype-studies-last-week-activity-7221079741531906048-WJL2?utm_source= share&utm_medium=member_desktop. Accessed 9 May 2025.

Bender, E. M. and Hanna, A. (2025) *The AI con: how to fight big tech's hype and create the future we want*. London: Penguin Books.

Benner, M. J. and Beunza, D. (2025) The influence of analysts on innovation: an evolutionary view of evaluative frames. *Academy of Management Review*, 50(2), pp. 318–341.

Bergek, A., Jacobsson, S., Carlsson, B., Lindmark, S. and Rickne, A. (2008) Analyzing the functional dynamics of technological innovation systems: a scheme of analysis. *Research Policy*, 37(3), pp. 407–429.

Bergman, B. J. and McMullen, J. S. (2022) Helping entrepreneurs help themselves: a review and relational research agenda on entrepreneurial support organizations. *Entrepreneurship Theory and Practice*, 46(3), pp. 688–728.

Berkhout, F. (2006) Normative expectations in systems innovation. *Technology Analysis & Strategic Management*, 18(3–4), pp. 299–311.

Bernard, J. G. and Gallupe, R. B. (2013) IT industry analysts: a review and two research agendas. *Communications of the Association for Information Systems*, 33(1), pp. 275–302.

Bessy, C. and Chauvin, P. M. (2013) The power of market intermediaries: from information to valuation processes. *Valuation Studies*, 1(1), pp. 83–117.

Beunza, D. (2019) *Taking the floor: models, morals, and management in a Wall Street trading room*. Princeton, NJ: Princeton University Press.

Beunza, D. and Garud, R. (2007) Calculators, lemmings or frame-makers? The intermediary role of securities analysts. *The Sociological Review*, 55, pp. 13–39.

Beunza, D. and Stark, D. (2005) How to recognize opportunities: heterarchical search in a trading room. In Knorr Cetina, K. and Preda, A. (eds.) *The sociology of financial markets*. Oxford: Oxford University Press, pp. 84–101.

Bidet, A. (2020) Economising as exploring valuations. *Valuation Studies*, 7, pp. 123–150.

Biesenthal, C., Sankaran, S., Pitsis, T. and Clegg, S. (2015) Temporality in organization studies: implications for strategic project management. *Open Economics and Management Journal*, 2(1), pp. 45–52.

Birch, K. (2023) Reflexive expectations in innovation financing: an analysis of venture capital as a mode of valuation. *Social Studies of Science*, 53(1), pp. 29–48.

Birch, K. and Muniesa, F. (2020) *Assetization: turning things into assets in technoscientific capitalism*. Cambridge, MA: MIT Press.

Blanchet, V. (2017) Performing market categories through visual inscriptions: the case of ethical fashion. *Organisation*, 25(3), pp. 374–400.

Bloor, D. (1976) The strong programme in the sociology of knowledge. *Knowledge and Social Imagery*, 2, pp. 3–23.

Boegershausen, J., Datta, H., Borah, A. and Stephen, A. T. (2022) Fields of gold: scraping web data for marketing insights. *Journal of Marketing*, 86(5), pp. 1–20. https://doi.org/10.1177/00222429221100750 (Original work published 2022).

Boltanski, L. and Thévenot, L. (1999) The sociology of critical capacity. *European Journal of Social Theory*, 2(3), pp. 359–377.

Bond, B., Genovese, Y., Miklovic, D., Zrimsek, B. and Rayner, N. (2000) *ERP is dead – long live ERP II (Strategic Planning Assumption SPA-12-0420)*. Stamford, CT: Gartner Group.

Borup, M., Brown, N., Konrad, K. and van Lente, H. (2006) The sociology of expectations in science and technology. *Technology Analysis & Strategic Management*, 18, pp. 285–298.

Bourne, C. (2024) AI hype, promotional culture, and affective capitalism. *AI and Ethics*, 4, pp. 757–769.

Bower, J. L. and Christensen, C. M. (1995) Disruptive technologies: catching the wave. *Harvard Business Review*, 73(1), pp. 43–53.

Bowker, G. C. and Star, S. L. (2000) *Sorting things out: classification and its consequences*. Cambridge, MA: MIT Press.

Brandtner, C. (2017) Putting the world in orders: plurality in organizational evaluation. *Sociological Theory*, 35(3), pp. 200–227.

Brankovic, J., Ringel, L. and Werron, T. (2018) How rankings produce competition: the case of global university rankings. *Zeitschrift für Soziologie*, 47(4), pp. 270–288.

Breschi, S., Malerba, F. and Orsenigo, L. (2000) Technological regimes and Schumpeterian patterns of innovation. *The Economic Journal*, 110(463), pp. 388–410.

Brinker, S. (2018) The one thing everybody forgets about Gartner's hype cycle, even in martech. https://chiefmartec.com/2018/01/one-thing-everybody-forgets-gartners-hype-cycle-martech/. Accessed 30 July 2025.

Brown, N. (2003) Hope against hype-accountability in biopasts, presents and futures. *Science and Technology Studies*, 16(2), pp. 3–21.

Brown, N. and Michael, M. (2003) A sociology of expectations: retrospecting prospects and prospecting retrospects. *Technology Analysis & Strategic Management*, 15(1), pp. 3–18.

Bruederl, J. and Schuessler, R. (1990) Organisational mortality: the liabilities of newness and adolescence. *Administrative Science Quarterly*, 35, pp. 530–547.

Byrne, J. and Giuliani, A. P. (2025) The rise and fall of the girlboss: gender, social expectations and entrepreneurial hype. *Journal of Business Venturing*, 40(4), P. 106486.

Callon, M. (1984) Some elements of a sociology of translation: domestication of the scallops and the fishermen of St Brieuc Bay. *The Sociological Review*, 32(1_suppl), pp. 196–233.

Callon, M. (1998a) An essay on framing and overflowing: economic externalities revisited by sociology. *The Sociological Review*, 46, pp. 244–269.

(1998b) Introduction: the embeddedness of economic markets in economics. *The Sociological Review*, 46, pp. 1–57.

(2021) *Markets in the making: rethinking competition, goods, and innovation*. Princeton, NJ: Princeton University Press.

Callon, M. and Law, J. (2005) On qualculation, agency, and otherness. *Environment and Planning D: Society and Space*, 23, pp. 717–733.

Carruthers, B. G. and Stinchcombe, A. L. (1999) The social structure of liquidity: flexibility, markets, and states. *Theory and Society*, 28, pp. 353–382.

Carruthers, H. (2009) Using PEST analysis to improve business performance. *In Practice*, 31(1), pp. 37–39.

Cellan-Jones, R. (2001) *Dot.bomb: the strange death of dot.com Britain*. London: Aurum Press.

Chapple, D. (2024) Mind the gap: the growing divide in analyst relations. LinkedIn post. https://www.linkedin.com/pulse/mind-gap-growing-divide-analyst-rela tions-duncan-chapple-4ouzc/?trackingId=YvFdrG9kT02sQyAmSaeUlQ%3D%3D. Accessed 9 May 2025.

Chapple, D., Pollock, N. and D'Adderio, L. (2022) From pitching to briefing: extending entrepreneurial storytelling to new audiences. *Organization Studies*, 43(5), pp. 773–795.

Chelli, M. and Gendron, Y. (2013) Sustainability ratings and the disciplinary power of the ideology of numbers. *Journal of Business Ethics*, 112(2), pp. 187–203.

Cheney-Lippold, J. (2025) The silicon future. *New Media & Society*, 27(7), pp. 4164–4180.

Chiapello, E. (2015) Financialisation of valuation. *Human Studies*, 38(1), pp. 13–35.

(2023) Impact finance: how social and environmental questions are addressed in times of financialized capitalism. *Review of Evolutionary Political Economy*, 4(2), 199–220.

Chiapello, E. and Gilbert, P. (2019) *Management tools*. Cambridge: Cambridge University Press.

Chiasson, M. W. and Davidson, E. (2005) Taking industry seriously in information systems research. *MIS Quarterly*, 29, pp. 591–605.

Chiles, T. H., Bluedorn, A. C. and Gupta, V. (2007) Beyond creative destruction and entrepreneurial discovery: a radical Austrian approach to entrepreneurship. *Organisation Studies*, 28, pp. 467–493.

Christensen, C. M. (1997) *The innovator's dilemma: when new technologies cause great firms to fail*. Boston, MA: Harvard Business School Press.

Christian, A., Pollock, N., Gatzweiller, M. and D'Adderio, L. (2025) Getting on the agenda: channeling hype to address overlooked social innovation problems. Manuscript under review at *Academy of Management Journal*.

Clardy, A. (2022) What can we know about the future? Epistemology and the credibility of claims about the world ahead. *Foresight*, 24(1), pp. 1–18.

Claridge, C. (2010) *Hyperbole in English: a corpus-based study of exaggeration*. Cambridge: Cambridge University Press.

Clarke, J. S., Cornelissen, J. P. and Healey, M. P. (2019) Actions speak louder than words: how figurative language and gesturing in entrepreneurial pitches influences investment judgements. *Academy of Management Journal*, 62, pp. 335–360.

Cochoy, F. (2007) A brief theory of the 'captation' of publics: understanding the market with Little Red Riding Hood. *Theory, Culture & Society*, 24(7–8), pp. 203–223.

(2008) Calculation, qualculation, calqulation: shopping cart arithmetic, equipped cognition and the clustered consumer. *Marketing Theory*, 8(1), pp. 15–44.

Colyvas, J. A. (2012) Performance metrics as formal structures and through the lens of social mechanisms: when do they work and how do they influence? *American Journal of Education*, 118(2), pp. 167–197.

Comer, J. (2024) #HoldTight: neoliberal affects, embodied hopes, and anticipatory chronotopes in corporate LGBTQ diversity discourse. *Language in Society*, 53(4), pp. 731–754.

Comi, A. and Whyte, J. (2018) Future making and visual artefacts: an ethnographic study of a design project. *Organisation Studies*, 39, pp. 1055–1083.

Constant, E. W. (1973) A model for technological change applied to the turbojet revolution. *Technology and Culture*, 14(4), pp. 553–572.

Corley, K. and Gioia, D. (2000) The rankings game: managing business school reputation. *Corporate Reputation Review*, 3(4), pp. 319–333.

Cornelissen, J. P. and Clarke, J. (2010) Imagining and rationalising opportunities: inductive reasoning and the creation and justification of new ventures. *Academy of Management Review*, 35, pp. 539–557.

Cornford, J. and Pollock, N. (2003) *Putting the university online: information, technology, and organizational change*. Open University Press.

Coslor, E., Crawford, B. and Leyshon, A. (2020) Collectors, investors and speculators: gatekeeper use of audience categories in the art market. *Organisation Studies*, 41(7), pp. 945–967.

Cram, W. A. and Newell, S. (2016) Mindful revolution or mindless trend? Examining agile development as a management fashion. *European Journal of Information Systems*, 25, pp. 154–169.

Croissant, J. L. (2014) PowerPoint, communication, and the knowledge society. *Contemporary Sociology: A Journal of Reviews*, 43(3), pp. 383–385. https://doi.org/10.1177/0094306114531284cc.

Cusworth, G., Brice, J., Lorimer, J. and Garnett, T. (2023) When you wish upon a (GWP) star: environmental governance and the reflexive performativity of global warming metrics. *Social Studies of Science*, 53(1), pp. 3–28.

Davidson, E. J., Østerlund, C. S. and Flaherty, M. G. (2015) Drift and shift in the organising vision career for personal health records: an investigation of innovation discourse dynamics. *Information and Organization*, 25, pp. 191–221.

Davidsson, P. (2015) Entrepreneurial opportunities and the entrepreneurship nexus: a re-conceptualisation. *Journal of Business Venturing*, 30, pp. 674–695.

Davies, W. (2016) *The limits of neoliberalism: authority, sovereignty and the logic of competition*. London: Sage.

De Togni, G., Erikainen, S., Chan, S. and Cunningham-Burley, S. (2024) Beyond the hype: acceptable futures for AI and robotic technologies in healthcare. *AI and Society*, 39(4), pp. 2009–2018.

Deuten, J. J. and Rip, A. (2000) Narrative infrastructure in product creation processes. *Organization*, 7(1), pp. 69–93.

De Vaujany, F. X., Carton, S., Dominguez-Péry, C. and Vaast, E. (2013) Moving closer to the fabric of organising visions: the case of a trade show. *The Journal of Strategic Information Systems*, 22, pp. 1–25.

Dedehayir, O. and Steinert, M. (2016) The hype cycle model: a review and future directions. *Technological Forecasting and Social Change*, 108, pp. 28–41.

Delmestri, G. and Greenwood, R. (2016) How Cinderella became a queen: theorising radical status change. *Administrative Science Quarterly*, 61, pp. 507–550.

Delmestri, G., Wezel, F. C., Goodrick, E. and Washington, M. (2020) The hidden paths of category research: climbing new heights and slippery slopes. *Organisation Studies*, 41, pp. 909–920.

Dennington, C. and Leforestier, L. (2014) Who are industry analysts and what so they do. A primer on industry analysts, IIAR Best Practice Paper, Institute Of Industry Analyst Relations, The IIAR Blog. Available online at: http://Analystrelations.Org/2013/08/27/New-Iiar-Best-Practice-Primer-Paper-Who-Are-Industry-Analysts-And-What-Do-They-Do/.

Doganova, L. (2024) *Discounting the future: the ascendancy of a political technology*. Princeton, NJ: Princeton University Press.

Doganova, L. and Eyquem-Renault, M. (2009) What do business models do? Innovation devices in technology entrepreneurship. *Research Policy*, 38, pp. 1559–1570.

Dorobat, C. E., McCaffrey, M., Foss, N. J. and Klein, P. G. (2025) Knightian uncertainty in entrepreneurship research: retrospect and prospect. *Entrepreneurship Theory and Practice*, 49(5), pp. 1392–1430.

Dosi, G. (1982) Technological paradigms and technological trajectories: a suggested interpretation of the determinants and directions of technical change. *Research Policy*, 11(3), pp. 147–162.

Dow, A. and Dow, S. C. (2011) Animal spirits revisited. *Capitalism and Society*, 6(2), pp. 1–25. https://doi.org/10.2202/1932-0213.1087.

Dow, S. C. and Dow, A. (2012) Animal spirits and rationality. In *Foundations for new economic thinking: a collection of essays*. London: Palgrave Macmillan UK, pp. 33–51.

Downs, A. (2016) Up and down with ecology: the 'issue-attention cycle'. In Protess, D. and McCombs, M. E. (eds.) *Agenda setting: readings on media, public opinion, and policymaking*. London: Routledge, pp. 27–33.

Durand, R., Granqvist, N. and Tyllström, A. (2017) From categories to categorization: a social perspective on market categorization. In Durand, R., Granqvist, N. and Tyllström, A. (eds.) *From categories to categorization: studies in sociology, organizations and strategy at the crossroads* (Vol. 51). Bingley: Emerald Publishing Limited, pp. 3–30.

Durand, R. and Khaire, M. (2017) Where do market categories come from and how? Distinguishing category creation from category emergence. *Journal of Management Studies*, 43, pp. 87–110.

Durand, R. and Paolella, L. (2013) Category stretching: reorienting research on categories in strategy, entrepreneurship, and organisation theory. *Journal of Management Studies*, 50(6), pp. 1100–1123.

Durand, R. and Thornton, P. H. (2018) Categorizing institutional logics, institutionalizing categories: a review of two literatures. *Academy of Management Annals*, 12(2), pp. 631–658.

Dwivedi, Y. K., Hughes, L., Baabdullah, A. M., Ribeiro-Navarrete, S., Giannakis, M., Al-Debei, M. M. ... and Wamba, S. F. (2022) Metaverse beyond the hype: multidisciplinary perspectives on emerging challenges, opportunities, and agenda for research, practice and policy. *International Journal of Information Management*, 66, p. 102542.

Dy, A. M., Marlow, S. and Martin, L. (2016) A web of opportunity or the same old story? Women digital entrepreneurs and intersectionality theory. *Human Relations*, 70, pp. 286–311.

Edgerton, D. (1997) Ever accelerating hype. Prospect. www.prospect magazine.co.uk/magazine/everacceleratinghype. Accessed 20 September 2023.

Edwards-Schachter, M. (2018) The nature and variety of innovation. *International Journal of Innovation Studies*, 2(2), pp. 65–79.

Eisenhardt, K. M. (1989) Building theories from case study research. *Academy of Management Review*, 14, pp. 532–550.

Elia, G., Margherita, A. and Passiante, G. (2020) Digital entrepreneurship ecosystem: how digital technologies and collective intelligence are reshaping the entrepreneurial process. *Technological Forecasting and Social Change*, 150, p. 119791.

Ellis, D. (2015) The great escape: big data breaks Gartner's hype cycle model. www.linkedin.com/pulse/great-escape-big-data-breaks-gartners-hype-cycle-model-david-ellis/. Accessed 10 March 2025.

Elsbach, K. D. and Kramer, R. M. (1996) Members responses to organisational identity threats: encountering and countering the business week rankings. *Administrative Science Quarterly*, 41(3), pp. 442–476.

Endenich, C., Hahn, R., Reimsbach, D. and Wickert, C. (2022) Wait-and-see-ism as partial adoption of management practices: the rise and stall of integrated reporting. *Strategic Organization*, 21(3), pp. 566–595.

Espeland, W. N., Sauder, M. and Espeland, W. (2016) *Engines of anxiety: academic rankings, reputation, and accountability*. New York: Russell Sage Foundation.

Espeland, W. N. and Stevens, M. L. (1998) Commensuration as a social process. *Annual Review of Sociology*, 24(1), pp. 313–343.

(2008) A sociology of quantification. *European Journal of Sociology/ Archives européennes de sociologie*, 49(3), pp. 401–436.

Esposito, E. and Stark, D. (2019) What's observed in a rating? Rankings as orientation in the face of uncertainty. *Theory, Culture & Society*, 36(4), pp. 3–26.

Eyal, G. (2019) *The crisis of expertise*. John Wiley and Sons.

Faxon, H. O., Fields, D. and Wainwright, T. (2024) Beyond the hype: digital transformations in global land, housing, and property. *Environment and Planning D: Society and Space*.

Feher, M. (2021) *Rated agency: investee politics in a speculative age*. Princeton, NJ: Princeton University Press.

Feldman, A. (2016) For world's unbanked people, Juvo turns cellphones into an entry point for loans. Forbes. www.forbes.com/sites/amyfeldman/2016/11/17/for-worlds-unbanked-juvos-steve-polsky-is-turning-cellphones-into-an-entry-point-for-loans/. Accessed 26 July 2025.

Felt, U., Wynne, B., Callon, M., Gonçalves, M. E., Jasanoff, S., Jepsen, M., Joly, P.-B., Konopasek, Z., May, S., Neubauer, C., Rip, A., Siune, K., Stirling, A. and Tallacchini, M. (2007) *Taking European knowledge society seriously*. Luxembourg: Office for Official Publications of the European Communities.

Fenn, J. and Raskino, M. (2008) *Mastering the hype cycle: how to choose the right innovation at the right time*. Boston, MA: Harvard Business Press.

Fincham, R., Fleck, J., Procter, R., Scarbrough, H., Tierney, M. and Williams, R. (1995) *Expertise and innovation: information technology strategies in the financial services sector*. Oxford: Oxford University Press.

Fischer, E. and Reuber, R. (2007) The good, the bad, and the unfamiliar: the challenges of reputation formation facing new firms. *Entrepreneurship Theory and Practice*, 31, pp. 53–75.

Fischer, G., Kotha, S. and Lahiri, A. (2016) Changing with the times: an integrated view of identity, legitimacy, and new venture life cycles. *Academy of Management Review*, 41, pp. 383–409.

Fisher, G. (2020) The complexities of new venture legitimacy. *Organisation Theory*, 1(2), pp. 1–25.

Fisher, G., Kotha, S. and Lahiri, A. (2016) Changing with the times: an integrated view of identity, legitimacy, and new venture life cycles. *Academy of Management Review*, 41(3), pp. 383–409.

Fisher, G., Kuratko, D. F., Bloodgood, J. M. and Hornsby, J. S. (2017) Legitimate to whom? The challenge of audience diversity and new venture legitimacy. *Journal of Business Venturing*, 32, pp. 52–71.

Fisher, G., Neubert, E. and Burnell, D. (2021) Resourcefulness narratives: transforming actions into stories to mobilise support. *Journal of Business Venturing*, 36(4), p. 106122.

Fleck, J. (1994) Learning by trying: the implementation of configurational technology. *Research Policy*, 23(6), pp. 637–652.

Fleck, J., Webster, J. and Williams, R. (1990) Dynamics of information technology implementation: a reassessment of paradigms and trajectories of development. *Futures*, 22(6), pp. 618–640.

Floridi, L. (2024) Why the AI hype is another tech bubble. *Philosophy & Technology*, 37(4), p. 128.

Fombrun, C. and Shanley, M. (1990) What's in a name? Reputation building and corporate strategy. *Academy of Management Journal*, 33(2), pp. 233–258.

Fourcade, M. and Healy, K. (2024) *The ordinal society*. Cambridge, MA: Harvard University Press.

Freeman, C. (1974) *The economics of industrial innovation*. Harmondsworth: Penguin.

(1994) The economics of technical change. *Cambridge Journal of Economics*, 18(5), pp. 463–514.

Freeman, C. and Perez, C. (1988) Structural crises of adjustment: business cycles and investment behaviour. In Dosi, I. G. et al. (eds.) *Technical change and economic theory*. London: Pinter Publishers, pp. 38–61.

Frenzel, F. and Frisch, T. (2020) Tourism valorisation: digitally enhanced tourist value practices and the geographies of inequality. Tourism Geographies.

Friedberg, E. and Crozier, M. (1980) *Actors and systems: the politics of collective action*. Chicago: University of Chicago Press.

Funk, J. (2019) What's behind technological hype? *Issues in Science and Technology*, 36(1), pp. 36–42.

Funk, J. L. (2024) *Unicorns, hype, and bubbles: a guide to spotting, avoiding, and exploiting investment bubbles in tech*. Petersfield: Harriman House.

Furnari, S. (2014) Interstitial spaces: microinteraction settings and the genesis of new practices between institutional fields. *Academy of Management Review*, 39(4), pp. 439–462.

Gardner, J., Samuel, G. and Williams, C. (2015) Sociology of low expectations: recalibration as innovation work in biomedicine. *Science, Technology, and Human Values*, 40(6), pp. 998–1021.

Garfinkel, H. (1967) *Studies in ethnomethodology*. Prentice-Hall.

Gartner. (1988) A compilation of memos, thoughts, letters and stalking horses. *The Gartner Group Research Notebook ('Blue Book')*. Minneapolis: Gartner archive, Charles Babbage Institute, University of Minnesota.

Gartner. (2017) Press Release: Gartner reveals 2017 Cool Vendors that can help keep pace with digital innovation. www.gartner.com/en/newsroom/press-releases/2017-06-15-gartner-reveals-2017-cool-vendors-that-can-help-keep-pace-with-digital-innovation. Accessed 21 July 2025.

Gartner. (2018) *Understanding Gartner's hype cycles*. Gartner Inc. www.gartner.com/doc/3887767. Accessed 19 September 2022.

Gartner, W. B. (2007) Entrepreneurial narrative and a science of the imagination. *Journal of Business Venturing*, 22, pp. 613–627.

Gartner Research. (2018) Understanding Gartner's hype cycles, 20 August 2018. www.gartner.com/en/documents/3887767. Accessed 21 November 2024.

Garud, R. (2008) Conferences as venues for the configuration of emerging organizational fields: the case of cochlear implants. *Journal of Management Studies*, 45(6), pp. 1061–1088.

Garud, R., Gehman, J. and Giuliani, A. P. (2014a) Contextualizing entrepreneurial innovation: a narrative perspective. *Research Policy*, 43(7), pp. 1177–1188.

Garud, R. and Giuliani, A. P. (2013) A narrative perspective on entrepreneurial opportunities. *Academy of Management Review*, 38, pp. 157–160.

Garud, R., Kumaraswamy, A. and Karnøe, P. (2010) Path dependence or path creation? *Journal of Management Studies*, 47(4), pp. 760–774.

Garud, R., Kumaraswamy, A., Roberts, A. and Xu, L. (2022) Liminal movement by digital platform-based sharing economy ventures: the case of Uber Technologies. *Strategic Management Journal*, 43(3), pp. 447–475.

Garud, R., Lant, T. K. and Schildt, H. A. (2019) Generative imitation, strategic distancing and optimal distinctiveness during the growth, decline and stabilisation of silicon alley. *Innovation*, 21(1), pp. 187–213.

(2021) Generative imitation, strategic distancing and optimal distinctiveness during the growth, decline and stabilization of silicon alley. *Culture, Innovation and Entrepreneurship*, 1, pp. 187–213.

Garud, R., Phillips, N., Snihur, Y., Thomas, L. D. and Zietsma, C. (2025) Hype in entrepreneurial settings. *Journal of Business Venturing*, 41, pp. 1–14.

Garud, R., Schildt, H. A. and Lant, T. K. (2014b) Entrepreneurial storytelling, future expectations, and the paradox of legitimacy. *Organization Science*, 25(5), pp. 1479–1492.

Garud, R., Snihur, Y., Thomas, L. D. W. and Phillips, N. (2023) The dark side of entrepreneurial framing: a process model of deception and legitimacy loss. *Academy of Management Review*, in press.

Gawer, A. (ed.). (2011) *Platforms, markets and innovation*. Northampton, MA: Edward Elgar.

Geels, F. W. and Smit, W. A. (2000) Failed technology futures: pitfalls and lessons from a historical survey. *Futures*, 32(9–10), pp. 867–885.

Gegenhuber, T. and Naderer, S. (2019) When the petting zoo spawns into monsters: open dialogue and a venture's legitimacy quest in crowdfunding. *Innovation*, 21, pp. 151–186.

Gehman, J., Grimes, M. G. and Cao, K. (2019) Why we care about certified B corporations: from valuing growth to certifying values practices. *Academy of Management Discoveries*, 5, pp. 97–101.

Gehman, J. and Soublière, J. F. (2017) Cultural entrepreneurship: from making culture to cultural making. *Innovation*, 19, pp. 61–73.

Geiger, S. and Gross, N. (2017) Does hype create irreversibilities? Affective circulation and market investments in digital health. *Marketing Theory*, 17(4), pp. 435–454.

Geiger, S., Mason, K., Pollock, N., Roscoe, P., Ryan, A., *et al.* (2024) *Market studies: mapping, theorizing and impacting market action*. Cambridge: Cambridge University Press.

Ghezzi, A. and Cavallo, A. (2020) Agile business model innovation in digital entrepreneurship: lean start-up approaches. *Journal of Business Research*, 110, pp. 519–537.

Giorgi, S. (2017) The mind and heart of resonance: the role of cognition and emotions in frame effectiveness. *Journal of Management Studies*, 54(5), pp. 711–738.

Giorgi, S. and Weber, K. (2015) Marks of distinction: framing and audience appreciation in the context of investment advice. *Administrative Science Quarterly*, 60, pp. 333–367.

Glode, V., Green, R. C. and Lowery, R. (2012) Financial expertise as an arms race. *The Journal of Finance*, 67(5), pp. 1723–1759.

Godin, B. (2015) *Innovation contested: the idea of innovation over the centuries*. London: Routledge.

Goldfarb, B. and Kirsch, D. A. (2019) *Bubbles and crashes: the boom and bust of technological innovation*. Stanford, CA: Stanford University Press.

Gond, J. and Brès, L. (2020) Designing the tools of the trade: how corporate social responsibility consultants and their tool-based practices created market shifts. *Organization Studies*, 41, pp. 703–726.

Gond, J.-P., Carton, G. and Millo, Y. (2025) Strategy as a performative practice: a self-referential, knowledge-based perspective. In Golsorkhi, D., Rouleau, L., Seidl, D. and Vaara, E. (eds.), *The Cambridge handbook of strategy as practice*. Cambridge: Cambridge University Press, pp. 290–310.

Goodnight, G. T. and Green, S. (2010) Rhetoric, risk, and markets: the dotcom bubble. *Quarterly Journal of Speech*, 96(2), pp. 115–140.

Goodwin, T. (2023) Just a friendly reminder that the Hype Cycle Chart is a complete waste of time. www.linkedin.com/posts/tomfgoodwin_just-a-friendly-reminder-that-the-gartner-activity-7103378626229776385-abm N/?utm_source=shareandutm_medium=member_desktop. Accessed 10 March 2025.

Granqvist, N. and Ritvala, T. (2016) Beyond prototypes: drivers of market categorisation in functional foods and nanotechnology. *Journal of Management Studies*, 53, pp. 210–237.

Granqvist, N. and Siltaoja, M. (2020) Constructions, claims, resonance, reflexivity: language and market categorisation. *Organisation Theory*, 1(1), pp. 1–24.

Gray, B. and Purdy, J. (2018) *Collaborating for our future: multistakeholder partnerships for solving complex problems*. Oxford: Oxford University Press.

Gregory, J. (2000) *Sorcerer's apprentice: creating the electronic health record, reinventing medical records and patient care*. Unpublished doctoral dissertation.

Grimes, M. (2018) The pivot: how founders respond to feedback through idea and identity work. *Academy of Management Journal*, 61, pp. 1692–1717.

Grodal, S. and Granqvist, N. (2014) Great expectations: discourse and affect during field emergence. In Ashkanasy, N. M., Zerbe, W. J. and Härtel, C. E. J. (eds.), *Emotions and the organizational fabric* (Vol. 10). Bingley: Emerald Group, pp. 139–166.

Grodal, S. and Kahl, S. J. (2017) The discursive perspective of market categorisation: interaction, power, and context. *Research in the Sociology of Organisations*, 51, pp. 151–184.

Grodal, S., Krabbe, A. D. and Chang-Zunino, M. (2023) The evolution of technology. *Academy of Management Annals*, 17(1), pp. 141–180.

Gyurko, E. (2009) Managing the Gartner Magic Quadrant: a tool for analyst relations managers (Institute of Industry Analyst Relations (IIAR) White paper series). https://drive.google.com/file/d/0B5n3Psh0yqjkdlg2c2R6ZjNQMDg/view. Accessed 9 October 2019.

Hacking, I. (1990) *The taming of chance.* Cambridge: Cambridge University Press.

Hair, N., Wetsch, L. R., Hull, C. E., Perotti, V. and Hung, Y. C. (2013) Market orientation in digital entrepreneurship: advantages and challenges in a Web 2.0 networked world. *International Journal of Innovation and Technology Management,* 6, p. 1250045.

Hajer, M. A. (1995) *The politics of environmental discourse: ecological modernization and the policy process.* Oxford: Clarendon Press.

Halford, S. and Southerton, D. (2023) What future for the sociology of futures? Visions, concepts and methods. *Sociology,* 57(2), pp. 263–278.

Hampel, C. E. and Dalpiaz, E. (2025) When hype collides with morality: how entrepreneurial framing affects the behaviour and legitimacy of hyped ventures. *Journal of Business Venturing,* 40(4), p. 106506.

Hare, J. (2020) Reconciliation in teacher education: hope or hype. *Reconceptualizing teacher education: a Canadian contribution to a global challenge,* pp. 19–38. Accessed 26 July 2025.

Hashemi, F., Gallay, O. and Hongler, M.-O. (2021) Opinion formation dynamics: swift collective disillusionment triggered by unmet expectations. *Physica A: Statistical Mechanics and Its Applications,* 569, pp. 1–12.

Helgesson, C. F. and Muniesa, F. (2013) For what it's worth: an introduction to valuation studies. *Valuation Studies,* 1(1), pp. 1–10.

Heupel, K., Fonseca, J. A., Rutherford, M. and Edwards, B. (2024) Feeding the hype cycle: entrepreneurial swagger, passion, and inflated expectations. *Journal of Business Venturing,* 39(6), p. 106432.

Heusinkveld, S., van Grinsven, M., Groß, C., Greatbatch, D. and Clark, T. (2021) *The flow of management ideas: rethinking managerial audiences.* Cambridge: Cambridge University Press.

Hewlin, P. F. (2003) And the award for best actor goes to … : facades of conformity in organisational settings. *Academy of Management Review,* 28, pp. 633–642.

Hildebrandt, M. (2008) Defining profiling: a new type of knowledge? In Hildebrandt, M. and Gutwirth, S. (eds.) *Profiling the European citizen: cross-disciplinary perspectives.* Springer, pp. 17–45.

Hirschheim, R., Murungi, D. M. and Peña, S. (2012) Witty invention or dubious fad? Using argument mapping to examine the contours of management fashion. *Information and Organization,* 22, pp. 60–84.

Hirschman, A. O. (1967) *The principle of the hiding hand.* Washington, DC: Brookings Institution.

(2013) *The passions and the interests: political arguments for capitalism before its triumph.* Princeton, NJ: Princeton University Press.

Hjorth, D. and Steyaert, C. (2004) *Narrative and discursive approaches in entrepreneurship: a second movements in entrepreneurship book.* Cheltenham: Elgar.

Ho, J. C. and Lee, C. S. (2015) A typology of technological change: technological paradigm theory with validation and generalization from case studies. *Technological Forecasting and Social Change*, 97, pp. 128–139.

Hochschild, A. (2011) Emotional life on the market frontier. *Annual Review of Sociology*, 37(1), pp. 21–33.

Hogarth, S. (2017) Valley of the unicorns: consumer genomics, venture capital and digital disruption. *New Genetics and Society*, 36(3), pp. 250–272.

Hoppmann, J., Anadon, L. D. and Narayanamurti, V. (2020) Why matter matters: how technology characteristics shape the strategic framing of technologies. *Research Policy*, 49(1), p. 103882.

Hsu, D. H. (2004) What do entrepreneurs pay for venture capital affiliation? *The Journal of Finance*, 59, pp. 1805–1844.

Hsu, G. (2006) Evaluative schemas and the attention of critics in the US film industry. *Industrial and Corporate Change*, 15, pp. 467–496.

Huang, L. and Pearce, J. L. (2015) Managing the unknowable: the effectiveness of early-stage investor gut feel in entrepreneurial investment decisions. *Administrative Science Quarterly*, 60, pp. 634–670.

Hull, C. E., Hung, Y. T. C., Hair, N., Perotti, V. and DeMartino, R. (2007) Taking advantage of digital opportunities: a typology of digital entrepreneurship. *International Journal of Networking and Virtual Organisations*, 4, pp. 290–303.

Hutter, M. and Stark, D. (2015) Pragmatist perspectives on valuation: an introduction. *Moments of Valuation: exploring Sites of Dissonance*, 1, p. 14.

Hyysalo, S. (2006) Representations of use and practice-bound imaginaries in automating the safety of the elderly. *Social Studies of Science*, 36(4), pp. 599–626.

Hyysalo, S., Pollock, N. and Williams, R. (2019) Method matters in the social study of technology: investigating the biographies of artifacts and practices. *Science and Technology Studies*, 32(3), pp. 2–25.

Idoko, O. and MacKay, R. B. (2021) The performativity of strategic foresight tools: horizon scanning as an activation device in strategy formation within a UK financial institution. *Technological Forecasting and Social Change*, 162, p. 120389.

Ikeler, A. (2007) The under-examined public: making sense of industry analysts and analyst relations. *Journal of Promotion Management*, 13, pp. 233–260.

Ingram Bogusz, C., Teigland, R. and Vaast, E. (2018) Designed entrepreneurial legitimacy: the case of a Swedish crowdfunding platform. *European Journal of Information Systems*, 28, pp. 318–335.

Intemann, K. (2022) Understanding the problem of "hype": exaggeration, values, and trust in science. *Canadian Journal of Philosophy*, 52(3), pp. 279–294.

Jackson, S. J. (2017) Speed, time, and infrastructure. In Wajcman, J. and Dodd, N. (eds.) *The sociology of speed: digital, organizational, and social temporalities*. Oxford: Oxford University Press, pp. 169–184.

Jaffri, A. and Khandabattu, H. (2024) Hype cycle for artificial intelligence. www.gartner.com/en/documents/5505695. Accessed 17 March 2025.

Jalonen, H. (2012) The uncertainty of innovation: a systematic review of the literature. *Journal of Management Research*, 4(1), pp. 1–47.

Japp, K. P. (2000) Distinguishing non-knowledge. *Canadian Journal of Sociology/Cahiers Canadiens de Sociologie*, 25, pp. 225–238.

Jarzabkowski, P., Balogun, J. and Seidl, D. (2007) Strategizing: the challenges of a practice perspective. *Human Relations*, 60(1), pp. 5–27.

Jarzabkowski, P. and Kaplan, S. (2015) Strategy tools-in-use: a framework for understanding 'technologies of rationality' in practice. *Strategic Management Journal*, 36, pp. 537–558.

Jasanoff, S. (ed.) (2004) *States of knowledge: the co-production of science and social order*. London: Routledge.

Jasanoff, S. and Kim, S.-H. (2015) *Dreamscapes of modernity: sociotechnical imaginaries and the fabrication of power*. Chicago: University of Chicago Press.

Joly, B. and Le Renard, C. (2021) The past futures of techno-scientific promises. *Science and Public Policy*, 48(6), pp. 900–910.

Joly, P. B. (2010) On the economics of techno-scientific promises. In Akrich, M., Barthe, Y., Muniesa, F. and Mustar, P. (eds.) *Débordements: Mélanges offerts à Michel Callon*. Paris: Presse des Mines, pp. 203–222.

Jordan, T. (2020) *The digital economy*. Cambridge: Polity Press.

Jun, S. P., Yoo, H. S. and Choi, S. (2018) Ten years of research change using Google Trends: from the perspective of big data utilisations and applications. *Technological Forecasting and Social Change*, 130, pp. 69–87.

Justesen, L. and Plesner, U. (2024) Invisible digi-work: compensating, connecting, and cleaning in digitalized organizations. *Organization Theory*, 5(1), 20511558241226840. https://doi.org/10.1177/20511558241226840.

Kalvapalle, S. G., Phillips, N. and Cornelissen, J. (2024) Entrepreneurial pitching: a critical review and integrative framework. *Academy of Management Annals*, 18(2), pp. 550–599.

Karahanna, E., Straub, D. W. and Chervany, N. L. (1999) Information technology adoption across time: A cross-sectional comparison of pre-adoption and post-adoption beliefs. *MIS Quarterly*, pp. 183–213.

Karpik, L. (2010) *Valuing the unique: the economics of singularities*. Princeton, NJ: Princeton University Press.

Kennedy, M. T. (2008) Getting counted: markets, media, and reality. *American Sociological Review*, 73, pp. 270–295.

Kennedy, M. T. and Fiss, P. C. (2013) An ontological turn in categories research: from standards of legitimacy to evidence of actuality. *Journal of Management Studies*, 50, pp. 1138–1154.

Keynes, J. M. (1936) *The general theory of employment, interest and money.* London: Macmillan.

Khaire, M. (2017) The importance of being independent: the role of inter-mediaries in creating market categories. In Durrand, R., Granqvist, N. and Tyllström, A. (eds.) *Categories, categorisation and categorising: category studies in sociology, organisations and strategy at the cross-roads.* Bingley: Emerald, pp. 259–293.

Khaire, M. and Wadhwani, R. D. (2010) Changing landscapes: the construction of meaning and value in a new market category – modern Indian art. *Academy of Management Journal*, 53, pp. 1281–1304.

Khanagha, S., Ramezan Zadeh, M. T., Mihalache, O. R. and Volberda, H. W. (2018) Embracing bewilderment: responding to technological disruption in heterogeneous market environments. *Journal of Management Studies*, 55(7), pp. 1079–1121.

Kiefer, K. (2013) *Predicting and examining links between IPO hype, managerial expectations, and firm outcomes* (Doctoral dissertation, University of Colorado at Boulder).

Kiefer, K. and Hunt, R. A. (2017) Whose hype matters? The battle for value creation in contemporary financial communications. In Laskin, A. V. (ed.) *The handbook of financial communication and investor relations.* Hoboken, NJ: Wiley-Blackwell, pp. 167–177.

Kilduff, G. J. (2019) Interfirm relational rivalry: implications for competitive strategy. *Academy of Management Review*, 44(4), pp. 775–799.

Kindleberger, C. P. and Aliber, R. Z. (2005) Bubble Contagion: Tokyo to Bangkok to New York. In *Manias, panics and crashes: a history of financial crises.* London: Palgrave Macmillan UK, pp. 123–142.

Knight, F. H. (1921) *Risk, uncertainty and profit.* Cambridge: Houghton Mifflin, The Riverside Press.

Knorr Cetina, K. (2010) The epistemics of information: a consumption model. *Journal of Consumer Culture*, 10, pp. 171–191.

Kodeih, F., Bouchikhi, H. and Gauthier, V. (2018) Competing through categorisation: product- and audience-centric strategies in an evolving categorical structure. *Organisation Studies*, 40, pp. 995–1023.

Köhler, J., Geels, F. W., Kern, F., Markard, J., Onsongo, E., Wieczorek, A. ... and Wells, P. (2019) An agenda for sustainability transitions research: state of the art and future directions. *Environmental Innovation and Societal Transitions*, 31, pp. 1–32.

Kohli, R. and Melville, N. P. (2019) Digital innovation: a review and synthesis. *Information Systems Journal*, 29, pp. 200–223.

Komporozos-Athanasiou, A. (2022) *Speculative communities: living with uncertainty in a financialized world*. Chicago: University of Chicago Press.

Konrad, K. (2006) The social dynamics of expectations: the interaction of collective and actor-specific expectations on electronic commerce and interactive television. Technology Analysis & Strategic Management, 18(3–4), pp. 429–444.

Konrad, K. and Alvial-Palavicino, C. A. (2017) Evolving patterns of governance of, and by, expectations: the graphene hype wave. In Konrad, K., Rohracher, H. and von Schomberg, R. (eds.) *Embedding new technologies into society*. Singapore: Jenny Stanford, pp. 187–217.

Konrad, K. and Böhle, K. (2019) Socio-technical futures and the governance of innovation processes – an introduction to the special issue. *Futures*, 44(6), pp. 101–107.

Konrad, K. and Palavicino, C. A. (2017) Evolving patterns of governance of, and by, expectations: the graphene hype wave. In Konrad, K. et al. (eds.), *Embedding new technologies into society: a regulatory, ethical and societal perspective*. Jenny Stanford Publishing, pp. 187–217.

Konrad, K., Van Lente, H., Groves, C. and Selin, C. (2016) Performing and governing the future in science and technology. In Felt, U., Fouché, R., Miller, C. A. and Smith-Doerr, L. (eds.) *The handbook of science and technology studies*. Cambridge, MA: MIT Press, pp. 465–493.

Kornberger, M. (2017) The values of strategy: valuation practices, rivalry and strategic agency. *Organisation Studies*, 38(12), pp. 1753–1773.

Kornberger, M. and Carter, C. (2010) Manufacturing competition: how accounting practices shape strategy making in cities. *Accounting, Auditing and Accountability Journal*, 23(3), pp. 325–349.

Kornberger, M., Justesen, L., Madsen, A. and Mouritsen, J. (2015) *Making things valuable*. Oxford: Oxford University Press.

Kornberger, M. and Vaara, E. (2021) Strategy as engagement: what organization strategy can learn from military strategy. *Long Range Planning*, 54(5), p. 102102.

(2022) Strategy as engagement: What organization strategy can learn from military strategy. *Long Range Planning*, 55(4), p. 102125.

Kriechbaum, M., Posch, A. and Hauswiesner, A. (2021) Hype cycles during socio-technical transitions: the dynamics of collective expectations about renewable energy in Germany. *Research Policy*, 50(9), p. 104262.

Kriechbaum, M., Prol, J. L. and Posch, A. (2018) Looking back at the future: dynamics of collective expectations about photovoltaic technology in Germany and Spain. *Technological Forecasting and Social Change*, 129, pp. 76–87.

Krüger, A. K. and Reinhart, M. (2017) Theories of valuation-building blocks for conceptualizing valuation between practice and structure. *Historical Social Research/Historische Sozialforschung*, pp. 263–285.

Kruse, C. (2015) *The social life of forensic evidence.* Oakland: University of California Press.

Kumaraswamy, A., Garud, R. and Ansari, S. (2018) Perspectives on disruptive innovations. *Journal of Management Studies*, 55(7), pp. 1025–1042.

Latour, B. (1987) *Science in action: how to follow scientists and engineers through society.* Cambridge, MA: Harvard University Press.

    (2004) Why has critique run out of steam? From matters of fact to matters of concern. *Critical Inquiry*, 30(2), pp. 225–248.

    (2012a) *We have never been modern.* Cambridge, MA: Harvard University Press.

    (2012b) The production of public proof. Centre for Research Architecture. *Forensic Architecture*, 5 March. www.forensic-architecture.org/sem inar/production-public-proof/. Accessed 26 July 2024.

Leins, S. (2018) *Stories of capitalism: inside the role of financial analysts.* Chicago; University of Chicago Press.

Levitt, T. (1965) Exploit the product life cycle. *Harvard Business Review*, 43, pp. 81–94.

Liao, T. (2016) Is it augmented reality? Contesting boundary work over the definitions and organising visions for an emerging technology across field-configuring events. *Information and Organization*, 26(3), pp. 45–62.

Lin, Y. K. and Maruping, L. M. (2022) Open source collaboration in digital entrepreneurship. *Organization Science*, 33(1), pp. 212–230.

Lo, J. Y. and Rhee, E. Y. (2022) Too much, too soon: a framework for understanding unintended consequences of cultural entrepreneurship on market emergence. In Lo, J. Y. and Rhee, E. Y. (eds.), *Advances in cultural entrepreneurship.* Bingley: Emerald, pp. 157–178.

Locatelli, R., Schena, C. and Tanda, A. (2021) A historical perspective on disruptive technologies. In King, T., Stentella Lopes, F. S., Srivastav, A. and Williams, J. (eds.) *Disruptive technology in banking and finance: an international perspective on FinTech.* Cham: Palgrave Macmillan / Springer International, pp. 9–45.

Logue, D. and Grimes, M. G. (2022) Living up to the hype: how new ventures manage the resource and liability of future-oriented visions within the nascent market of impact investing. *Academy of Management Journal*, 65, pp. 1055–1082.

Lounsbury, M., Gehman, J. and Glynn, M. A. (2019) Beyond homo entre-preneurs: judgment and the theory of cultural entrepreneurship. *Journal of Management Studies*, 56(6), pp. 1214–1236.

Lounsbury, M. and Glynn, M. A. (2019) *Cultural entrepreneurship: a new agenda for the study of entrepreneurial processes and possibilities*. Cambridge: Cambridge University Press.

(2001) Cultural entrepreneurship: stories, legitimacy, and the acquisition of resources. *Strategic Management Journal*, 22(6–7), pp. 545–564.

Lounsbury, M. and Rao, H. (2004) Sources of durability and change in market classifications: a study of the reconstitution of product categories in the American mutual fund industry, 1944–1985. *Social Forces*, 82, pp. 969–999.

Lundvall, B. A. (1985) Product innovation and user–producer interaction. *The Learning Economy and the Economics of Hope*, 19(2), pp. 19–60.

MacKenzie, D. (2006) Is economics performative? Option theory and the construction of derivatives markets. *Journal of the History of Economic Thought*, 28(1), pp. 29–55.

(2009) *Material markets: how economic agents are constructed*. Oxford: Oxford University Press.

(2011) The credit crisis as a problem in the sociology of knowledge. *American Journal of Sociology*, 116(6), pp. 1778–1841.

(2018) 'Making', 'taking' and the material political economy of algorithmic trading. *Economy and Society*, 47(4), pp. 501–523.

MacKenzie, D. and Caliskan, K. (2025) *Inside digital advertising: platforms, power, and material politics*. John Wiley & Sons.

MacKenzie, D. and Millo, Y. (2003) Constructing a market, performing theory: the historical sociology of a financial derivatives exchange. *American Journal of Sociology*, 109(1), pp. 107–145.

MacKenzie, D., Muniesa, F. and Siu, L. (eds.) (2007) *Do economists make markets? On the performativity of economics*. Princeton, NJ: Princeton University Press.

MacKenzie, D. and Spears, T. (2014) The formula that killed Wall Street: the Gaussian copula and modelling practices in investment banking. *Social Studies of Science*, 44(3), pp. 393–417.

Mackenzie, K. D. (2000) Processes and their frameworks. *Management Science*, 46(1), pp. 110–125.

Macnaghten, P. (2020) Towards an anticipatory public engagement methodology: deliberative experiments in the assembly of possible worlds using focus groups. *Qualitative Research*, 21(4), pp. 446–463.

Magalhães, J. C. and Smit, R. (2025) Less hype, more drama: open-ended technological inevitability in journalistic discourses about AI in the US, the Netherlands, and Brazil. *Digital Journalism*, 18, pp. 1–18.

Malerba, F. (2002) Sectoral systems of innovation and production. *Research Policy*, 31(2), pp. 247–264.

Mallaby, S. (2022) *The power law: venture capital and the art of disruption.* London: Penguin UK.

Mangnus, A. C., Oomen, J., Vervoort, J. M. and Hajer, M. A. (2021) Futures literacy and the diversity of the future. *Futures*, 132, p. 102793.

Mann, J., Drakos, N. and Gotta, M. (2016) *The future of social software in the workplace.* Stamford, CT: Gartner.

Marcus, G. E. (1995) Ethnography in/of the world system: the emergence of multi-sited ethnography. *Annual Review of Anthropology*, 24, pp. 95–117.

Martens, M. L., Jennings, J. and Jennings, P. D. (2007) Do the stories they tell get them the money they need? The role of entrepreneurial narratives in resource acquisition. *Academy of Management Journal*, 50, pp. 1107–1132.

Martin, R. (2015) Rebalancing the spatial economy: the challenge for regional theory. *Territory, Politics, Governance*, 3(3), pp. 235–272.

Martins, L. L. (2005) A model of the effects of reputational rankings on organisational change. *Organisation Science*, 16(6), pp. 701–720.

Master, Z. and Resnik, D. B. (2013) Hype and public trust in science. *Science and Engineering Ethics*, 19(2), pp. 321–335.

Maurer, I. and Ebers, M. (2006) Dynamics of social capital and their performance implications: Lessons from biotechnology start-ups. *Administrative Science Quarterly*, 51(2), pp. 262–292.

Mavadiya, M. (2020) Financial identity as a service (FiDaaS): the prerequisite for financial inclusion. Forbes. www.forbes.com/sites/madhvimava diya/2020/02/21/financial-identity-as-a-service-fidaas-the-prerequisite-for-financial-inclusion/. Accessed 26 July 2024.

Mazzucato, M. (2011) The entrepreneurial state. *Soundings*, 49(49), pp. 131–142.

McBride, R., Packard, M. D. and Clark, B. B. (2024) Rogue entrepreneurship. *Entrepreneurship Theory and Practice*, 48(1), pp. 392–417.

McDonald, R. and Gao, C. (2019) Pivoting isn't enough? Managing strategic reorientation in new ventures. *Organization Science*, 30(6), pp. 1289–1318.

McDowall, W. (2012) Technology roadmaps for transition management: the case of hydrogen energy. *Technological Forecasting and Social Change*, 79(3), pp. 530–542.

McKendrick, D., Jaffee, J., Carroll, G. and Khessina, O. (2003) In the bud? Disk array producers as a (possibly) emergent organisational form. *Administrative Science Quarterly*, 48, pp. 60–93.

Mehrpouya, A. and Samiolo, R. (2016) Performance measurement in global governance: ranking and the politics of variability. *Accounting, Organizations and Society*, 55, pp. 12–31.

Menz, M., Kunisch, S., Birkinshaw, J., Collis, D. J., Foss, N. J., Hoskisson, R. E. and Prescott, J. E. (2021) Corporate strategy and the theory of the firm in the digital age. *Journal of Management Studies*, 58(7), pp. 1695–1720.

Merton, R. C. (1992) Financial innovation and economic performance. *Journal of Applied Corporate Finance*, 4(4), pp. 12–22.

Miller, P. and O'Leary, T. (2007) Mediating instruments and making markets: capital budgeting, science and the economy. *Accounting, Organizations and Society*, 32, pp. 701–734.

Millo, Y., Power, M., Robson, K. and Vollmer, H. (2021) Themed section on accounting and valuation studies. *Accounting, Organizations and Society*, 91, p. 101223.

Min, J. (2024) Near-lies in the era of advanced technology: anticipation and uncertainty. *Technology in Society*, 79, p. 102702.

Minkkinen, M., Zimmer, M. P. and Mäntymäki, M. (2023) Co-shaping an ecosystem for responsible AI: five types of expectation work in response to a technological frame. *Information Systems Frontiers*, 25(1), pp. 103–121.

Mody, C. C. (2016) *The long arm of Moore's law: microelectronics and American science*. Cambridge, MA: MIT Press.

Mokyr, J. (1990) Punctuated equilibria and technological progress. *The American Economic Review*, 80, pp. 350–354.

Molander, O. (2023) Gartner's AI hype cycle is way past its due date. Medium. https://olivermolander.medium.com/gartners-ai-hype-cycle-way-passed-its-due-date-and-are-we-entering-a-classical-ml-winter-7c09041c72c4. Accessed 10 March 2025.

Monteiro, E., Pollock, N. and Williams, R. (2014) Innovation in information infrastructures: Introduction to the special issue. *Journal of the Association for Information Systems*, 15(4), p. 4.

Mouritsen, J. and Kreiner, K. (2016) Accounting, decisions and promises. *Accounting, Organizations and Society*, 49, pp. 21–31.

Muniesa, F., Millo, Y. and Callon, M. (2007) An introduction to market devices. *The Sociological Review*, 55, pp. 1–12.

Mützel, S. (2022) *Making sense: markets from stories in new breast cancer therapeutics*. Stanford, CA: Stanford University Press.

Nambisan, S. (2017) Digital entrepreneurship: toward a digital technology perspective of entrepreneurship. *Entrepreneurship Theory and Practice*, 41, pp. 1029–1055.

Nambisan, S., Wright, M. and Feldman, M. (2019) The digital transformation of innovation and entrepreneurship: progress, challenges and key themes. *Research Policy*, 48, p. 103773.

Narayanan, A. and Kapoor, S. (2025) *AI snake oil: what artificial intelligence can do, what it can't, and how to tell the difference.* Princeton, NJ: Princeton University Press.

Navis, C. and Glynn, M. A. (2010) How new market categories emerge: temporal dynamics of legitimacy, identity, and entrepreneurship in satellite radio, 1990–2005. *Administrative Science Quarterly*, 55, pp. 439–471.

(2011) Legitimate distinctiveness and the entrepreneurial identity: influence on investor judgments of new venture plausibility. *Academy of Management Review*, 36, pp. 479–499.

Negro, G., Koçak, Ö. and Hsu, G. (2010) Research on categories in the sociology of organisations. In *Categories in markets: origins and evolution.* Bingley: Emerald Group, pp. 3–35.

Nelson, R. R. and Winter, S. G. (1982) The Schumpeterian tradeoff revisited. *The American Economic Review*, 72(1), pp. 114–132.

Nerlich, B. (2013) Moderation impossible? On hype, honesty and trust in the context of modern academic life. *The Sociological Review*, 61(2_suppl), pp. 43–57.

Nightingale, P., & Martin, P. (2004) The myth of the biotech revolution. *Trends in Biotechnology*, 22(11), pp. 564–569.

Nordmann, A. (2007) If and then: a critique of speculative nanoethics. *Nanoethics*, 1(1), pp. 31–46.

Nylén, D. and Holmström, J. (2015) Digital innovation strategy: a framework for diagnosing and improving digital product and service innovation. *Business Horizons*, 58(1), pp. 57–67.

O'Connor, E. (2004) Storytelling to be real: narrative, legitimacy building and venturing. In Hjorth, D. and Steyaert, C. (eds.) *Narrative and discursive approaches in entrepreneurship.* Cheltenham: Edward Elgar Publishing, pp. 105–124.

Ometto, M. P., Lounsbury, M. and Gehman, J. (2023) Beyond the hype: cultural entrepreneurship in nanotechnology. In Felin, T., Foss, N. J. and Zenger, T. (eds.) *Organization theory meets strategy.* Bingley: Emerald Publishing Limited, pp. 11–45.

O'Neil, I. and Ucbasaran, D. (2016) Balancing what matters to me with what matters to them: exploring the legitimation process of environmental entrepreneurs. *Journal of Business Venturing*, 31(2), pp. 133–152.

Oomen, J., Hoffman, J. and Hajer, M. A. (2022) Techniques of futuring: on how imagined futures become socially performative. *European Journal of Social Theory*, 25(2), pp. 252–270.

Owen, R., Macnaghten, P. and Stilgoe, J. (2020) Responsible research and innovation: from science in society to science for society, with society. In *Emerging technologies.* London: Routledge, pp. 117–126.

Oxford Economics. (2019) The 'Yes' economy: giving the world financial identity. An independent report for Juvo by Oxford Economics. https://shorturl.at/5XojY. Accessed 24 September 2024.

Palavicino, C. A. A. (2016) Mindful anticipation: a practice approach to the study of expectations in emerging technologies (Doctoral dissertation). University of Twente, Enschede, the Netherlands.

Palmié, M., Wincent, J., Parida, V. and Caglar, U. (2020) The evolution of the financial technology ecosystem: an introduction and agenda for future research on disruptive innovations in ecosystems. *Technological Forecasting and Social Change*, 151, p. 119779.

Park, H. and Grundmann, P. (2025) Institutional work after hype: the case of biogas in Germany. *Energy Research and Social Science*, 119, p. 103820.

Patvardhan, S. and Ramachandran, J. (2020) Shaping the future: strategy making as artificial evolution. *Organization Science*, 31(3), pp. 671–697.

Perez, C. (2015) From long waves to great surges: continuing in the direction of Chris Freeman's 1997 lecture on Schumpeter's business cycles. *European Journal of Economic and Social Systems*, 27(1–2), pp. 69–80.

Petkova, A. (2012) From the ground up: building young firms' reputations. In Barnett, M. L. and Pollock, T. G. (eds.) *The Oxford handbook of corporate reputation*. Oxford: Oxford University Press, pp. 383–401.

Petkova, A. P., Rindova, V. P. and Gupta, A. K. (2008) How can new ventures build reputation? An exploratory study. *Corporate Reputation Review*, 11, pp. 320–334.

(2013) No news is bad news: sensegiving activities, media attention, and venture capital funding of new technology organisations. *Organisation Science*, 24, pp. 865–888.

Pflueger, D. and Mouritsen, J. (2025) Relational work and accounting: what venture capital analysts do with accounting and other information in situations of uncertainty. *European Accounting Review*, 34(4), pp. 1445–1468.

Piazza, A. and Abrahamson, E. (2020) Fads and fashions in management practices: taking stock and looking forward. *International Journal of Management Reviews*, 22, pp. 264–286.

Plante, M., Free, C. and Andon, P. (2020) Making artworks valuable: categorisation and modes of valuation work. *Accounting, Organizations and Society*, 83, p. 101155.

Plummer, L. A., Allison, T. H. and Connelly, B. L. (2016) Better together? Signaling interactions in new venture pursuit of initial external capital. *Academy of Management Journal*, 59, pp. 1585–1604.

Pollner, M. (2002) Inside the bubble: communion, cognition, and deep play at the intersection of Wall Street and cyberspace. In Woolgar, S. (ed.), *Virtual Society? Technology, cyberbole, reality*. Oxford: Oxford University Press, pp. 230–246.

Pollock, N. and Campagnolo, G. M. (2015) Subitizing practices and market decisions: the role of simple graphs in business valuations. In Kornberger, M., Justesen, L., Madsen, A. K. and Mouritsen, J. (eds.) *Making things valuable.* Oxford: Oxford University Press, pp. 89–108.

Pollock, N., Chapple, D., Chen, S. and D'Adderrio, L. (2023) The valorising pitch: how digital start-ups leverage intermediary coverage. *Journal of Management Studies*, 60(2), pp. 346–371.

Pollock, N. and D'Adderio, L. (2012) Give me a two-by-two matrix and I will create the market: rankings, graphic visualisations and sociomateriality. *Accounting, Organizations and Society*, 37(8), pp. 565–586.

Pollock, N., D'Adderio, L., Williams, R. and Leforestier, L. (2018) Conforming or transforming? How organisations respond to multiple rankings. *Accounting, Organizations and Society*, 64, pp. 55–68.

Pollock, N. and Williams, R. (2008) *Software and organisations: The biography of the enterprise-wide system or how SAP conquered the world.* Routledge.

 (2010) The business of expectations: How promissory organizations shape technology and innovation. *Social Studies of Science*, 40(4), pp. 525–548.

 (2011) Who decides the shape of product markets? The knowledge institutions that name and categorise new technologies. *Information and Organization*, 21(4), pp. 194–217.

 (2016) *How industry analysts shape the digital future.* Oxford: Oxford University Press.

Pollock, T. G. and Gulati, R. (2007) Standing out from the crowd: the visibility-enhancing effects of IPO-related signals on alliance formation by entrepreneurial firms. *Strategic Organization*, 5, pp. 339–372.

Polsky, S. (2020a) Podcast 147: Steve Polsky of Juvo [Audio podcast]. Fintech Nexus. www.heyfuturenexus.com/podcast-147-steve-polsky-of-juvo/. Accessed 24 October 2025.

 (2020b) A Q&A with Steve Polsky, founder and CEO of Juvo. Wing.vc. www.wing.vc/content/a-q-a-with-steve-polsky-founder-and-ceo-of-juvo. Accessed 12 October 2025.

Pontikes, E. G. (2018) Category strategy for firm advantage. *Strategy Science*, 3(4), pp. 620–631.

Pontikes, E. G. and Barnett, W. P. (2017) The non-consensus entrepreneur: organizational responses to vital events. *Administrative Science Quarterly*, 62, pp. 140–178.

Pontikes, E. G. and Kim, R. (2017) Strategic categorisation. In Durand, R., Granqvist, N. and Tyllstrom, A. (eds.) *From categories to categorisation: studies in sociology, organisations and strategy at the crossroads.* Bingley: Emerald, pp. 71–111.

Porac, J. F., Thomas, H., Wilson, F., Paton, D. and Kanfer, A. (1995) Rivalry and the industry model of Scottish knitwear producers. *Administrative Science Quarterly*, 40, pp. 203–227.

Porter, T. M. (2004) The culture of quantification and the history of public reason. *Journal of the History of Economic Thought*, 26(2), pp. 165–177.

Potts, J. (2017) Hype as a public good for innovation. In Potts, J. (ed.) *Innovation commons: the origin of economic growth*. Cambridge, MA: MIT Press, pp. 55–74.

Power, M. (2015) How accounting begins: object formation and the accretion of infrastructure. *Accounting, Organizations and Society*, 47, pp. 43–55.

(2021) Modelling the micro-foundations of the audit society: organisations and the logic of the audit trail. *Academy of Management Review*, 46, pp. 6–32.

(2022) Theorizing the economy of traces: from audit society to surveillance capitalism. *Organization Theory*, 3(3).

Powers, D. (2012) Notes on hype. *International Journal of Communication*, 6, p. 17.

(2019) *On trend: the business of forecasting the future*. Urbana: University of Illinois Press.

Preda, A. (2019) *Noise: living and trading in electronic finance*. Chicago: University of Chicago Press.

(2020) Financial noise. In Borch, C. and Wosnitzer, R. (eds.) *The Routledge handbook of critical finance studies*. London: Routledge, pp. 96–114.

Protess, D. and McCombs, M. E. (2016) *Agenda setting: readings on media, public opinion, and policymaking*. London: Routledge.

Puyou, F. R. and Quattrone, P. (2018) The visual and material dimensions of legitimacy: accounting and the search for societies. *Organisation Studies*, 39, pp. 721–746.

Quattrone, P. (2015) Governing social orders, unfolding rationality, and Jesuit accounting practices: a procedural approach to institutional logics. *Administrative Science Quarterly*, 60(3), pp. 411–445.

(2017) Embracing ambiguity in management controls and decision-making processes: on how to design data visualisations to prompt wise judgement. *Accounting and Business Research*, 47(5), pp. 588–612.

Quinn, W., & Turner, J. D. (2023) Bubbles in history. *Business History*, 65(4), pp. 636–655.

Rady, J., Townsend, D., Hunt, R. and Simpson, J. (2025) The expectations game: the contingent value of hype as a rhetorical strategy in resource mobilization processes among AI start-ups. *Journal of Business Venturing*, 40(4), p. 106499.

Ram, H., Giacomin, V. and Wakslak, C. (2024) Entrepreneurial imagination: insights from construal level theory for historical entrepreneurship. *Business History*, 66(2), pp. 364–385.

Ramel, D. (2024) Cloud AI services slide back to rock bottom in Hype Cycle Chart. Campus Technology. https://campustechnology.com/articles/2024/07/08/cloud-ai-services-slide-back-to-rock-bottom-in-gartner-hype-cycle.aspx. Accessed 17 March 2025.

Ramiller, N. C. and Swanson, E. B. (2003) Organising visions for information technology and the information systems executive response. *Journal of Management Information Systems*, 20(1), pp. 13–50.

Recker, J. and Von Briel, F. (2019) The future of digital entrepreneurship research: existing and emerging opportunities. In *Proceedings of the 40th International Conference on Information Systems*, Munich, Germany.

Rindova, V. P. and Fombrun, C. J. (1999) Constructing competitive advantage: the role of firm–constituent interactions. *Strategic Management Journal*, 20(8), pp. 691–710.

Rindova, V. P. and Martins, L. L. (2022) Futurescapes: imagination and temporal reorganization in the design of strategic narratives. *Strategic Organization*, 20, pp. 200–224.

Rindova, V. P., Martins, L. L., Srinivas, S. B. and Chandler, D. (2018) The good, the bad, and the ugly of organisational rankings: a multidisciplinary review of the literature and directions for future research. *Journal of Management*, 44(6), pp. 2175–2208.

Rindova, V. P., Petkova, A. P. and Kotha, S. (2007) Standing out: how new firms in emerging markets build reputation. *Strategic Organization*, 5, pp. 31–70.

Ringel, L., Espeland, W. N., Sauder, M. and Werron, T. (2021) Worlds of rankings. *Research in the Sociology of Organisations*, 74, pp. 1–23.

Rip, A. (2000) Fashions, lock-ins and the heterogeneity of knowledge production. In *The future of knowledge production in the academy*. Society for Research into Higher Education and Open University, pp. 28–39.

(2006) The tension between fiction and precaution in nanotechnology. In Fisher, E., Jones, J. and von Schomberg, R. (eds.) *Implementing the precautionary principle: perspectives and prospects*. Cheltenham: Edward Elgar, pp. 423–448.

(2018) Aggregation machines – a political science of science approach to the future of the peer review system. In Hisschemöller, M., Hoppe, R., Dunn, W. N. and Ravetz, J. R. (eds.) *Knowledge, power, and participation in environmental policy analysis*. Abingdon: Routledge, pp. 391–413.

(2019) *Nanotechnology and its governance*. London: Routledge.

Rip, A. and Voß, J. P. (2013) Umbrella terms as mediators in the governance of emerging science and technology. *Science, Technology and Innovation Studies*, 9(2), pp. 39–59.

Roberson, T. M. (2020) Can hype be a force for good? Inviting unexpected engagement with science and technology futures. *Public Understanding of Science*, 29(5), pp. 544–552.

Robinson, D. K., Le Masson, P. and Weil, B. (2012) Waiting games: innovation impasses in situations of high uncertainty. *Technology Analysis & Strategic Management*, 24(6), pp. 543–547.

Rona-Tas, A. and Hiss, S. (2010) The role of ratings in the subprime mortgage crisis: the art of corporate and the science of consumer credit rating. In Lounsbury, M. and Hirsch, P. (eds.) *Markets on trial: the economic sociology of the U.S. financial crisis*. Bingley: Emerald, pp. 115–155.

Rosa, J. A., Judson, K. M. and Porac, J. F. (2005) On the sociocognitive dynamics between categories and product models in mature markets. *Journal of Business Research*, 58, pp. 62–69.

Rosa, J. A., Porac, J. F., Runser-Spanjol, J. and Saxon, M. S. (1999) Sociocognitive dynamics in a product market. *Journal of Marketing*, 63(4_suppl1), pp. 64–77.

Rosenberg, N. (1976) On technological expectations. *The Economic Journal*, 86(343), pp. 523–535.

(2009) Uncertainty and technological change. In Foray, D. and van Ark, B. (eds.) *The economic impact of knowledge*. London: Routledge, pp. 17–34.

Rotolo, D., Hicks, D. and Martin, B. R. (2015) What is an emerging technology? *Research Policy*, 44(10), pp. 1827–1843.

Roussel, P. A. (1984) Technological maturity proves a valid and important concept. *Research Management*, 27(1), pp. 29–34.

Ruef, A. and Markard, J. (2010) What happens after a hype? How changing expectations affected innovation activities in the case of stationary fuel cells. *Technology Analysis & Strategic Management*, 22, pp. 317–338.

Rutherford, M. W., Buller, P. and Stebbins, J. M. (2009) Ethical considerations of the legitimacy lie. *Entrepreneurship Theory and Practice*, 33, pp. 949–964.

Samiolo, R. and Mehrpouya, A. (2021) Between stakeholders and third parties: Regulatory rankings and the organization of competition. In Ringel, L., Espeland, W. N., Sauder, M. and Werron, T. (eds.) *Worlds of rankings*. Bingley: Emerald, pp. 77–100.

Santos, F. M. and Eisenhardt, K. M. (2009) Constructing markets and shaping boundaries: entrepreneurial power in nascent fields. *Academy of Management Journal*, 52(4), pp. 643–671.

Sauder, M. (2008) Interlopers and field change: the entry of US news into the field of legal education. *Administrative Science Quarterly*, 53(2), pp. 209–234.

Sauder, M. and Espeland, W. N. (2009) The discipline of rankings: tight coupling and organisational change. *American Sociological Review*, 74(1), pp. 63–82.

Sauder, M. and Fine, G. A. (2008) Arbiters, entrepreneurs, and the shaping of business school reputations. *Sociological Forum*, 23(4), pp. 699–723.

Schiebinger, L. and Proctor, R. (2008) *Agnotology: the making and unmaking of ignorance*. Stanford, CA: Stanford University Press.

Schindler, J., Kallmuenzer, A. and Valeri, M. (2024) Entrepreneurial culture and disruptive innovation in established firms – how to handle ambidexterity. *Business Process Management Journal*, 30(2), pp. 366–387.

Schot, J. and Geels, F. W. (2008) Strategic niche management and sustainable innovation journeys: theory, findings, research agenda, and policy. *Technology Analysis & Strategic Management*, 20(5), pp. 537–554.

Schumpeter, J. (1912) *The theory of economic development*. Cambridge, MA: Harvard University Press.

Schumpeter, J. A. (1942) *Capitalism, socialism and democracy*. London: Routledge.

  (1947) The creative response in economic history. *The Journal of Economic History*, 7(2), pp. 149–159.

Selin, C. (2008) The sociology of the future: tracing stories of technology and time. *Sociology Compass*, 2(6), pp. 1878–1895.

Sharma, S. K. and Meyer, K. E. (2019) Bringing water to innovation deserts. In *Industrializing innovation-the next revolution*. Cham: Springer International, pp. 149–154.

Shestakofsky, B. (2024) *Behind the start-up: how venture capital shapes work, innovation, and inequality*. Oakland: University of California Press.

Shi, Y. and Herniman, J. (2023) The role of expectation in innovation evolution: exploring hype cycles. *Technovation*, 119, p. 102459.

Shiller, R. J. (2015) *Irrational exuberance*. Princeton, NJ: Princeton University Press.

  (2019) *Narrative economics: how stories go viral and drive major economic events*. Princeton, NJ: Princeton University Press.

Shimel, A. (2013, May 30) What makes a Cool Vendor so cool? Network World. www.networkworld.com/article/745252/what-makes-a-cool-vendor-so-cool.html.

Silberstein-Loeb, J. (2011) Puff pieces and circulation scams: middlemen and the making of the newspaper advertising market, 1881–1901. *Business Archives*, 103, pp. 77–92.

Simakova, E. and Coenen, C. (2013) Visions, hype, and expectations: a place for responsibility. In Owen, R., Bessant, J. and Heintz, M. (eds.) *Responsible innovation*. Chichester: Wiley, pp. 241–256.

Simmel, G. (2008) Sociology of competition. *Canadian Journal of Sociology*, 33(4), pp. 957–978.

Slavich, B. and Castellucci, F. (2016) Wishing upon a star: how apprentice-master similarity, status and career stage affect critics' evaluations of former apprentices in the haute cuisine industry. *Organisation Studies*, 37, pp. 823–843.

Smets, M., Morris, T. I. M. and Greenwood, R. (2012) From practice to field: a multilevel model of practice-driven institutional change. *Academy of Management Journal*, 55(4), pp. 877–904.

Smith, A. and Raven, R. (2012) What is protective space? Reconsidering niches in transitions to sustainability. *Research Policy*, 41(6), pp. 1025–1036.

Smith III, F. L. (2020) Quantum technology hype and national security. *Security Dialogue*, 51(5), pp. 499–516.

Smith, W. (2009) Theatre of use: a frame analysis of information technology demonstrations. *Social Studies of Science*, 39(3), pp. 449–480.

Sørensen, K. H. (1996) *Learning technology, constructing culture: socio-technical change as social learning*. Trondheim: Norwegian University of Science and Technology.

Soublière, J. F. and Gehman, J. (2020) The legitimacy threshold revisited: how prior successes and failures spill over to other endeavors on Kickstarter. *Academy of Management Journal*, 63(2), pp. 472–502.

Spieth, P., Röth, T., Clauss, T. and Klos, C. (2021) Technological frames in the digital age: theory, measurement instrument, and future research areas. *Journal of Management Studies*, 58(7), pp. 1962–1993.

Spivack, A. J., Lahti, T., Burström, T. and Wincent, J. (2025) Legitimacy perceptions amid institutional pluralism: how hype over decoupled practices influences entrepreneurial ventures. *Journal of Business Venturing*, 40(4), p. 106391. https://doi.org/10.1016/j.jbusvent.2024.106391.

Srinivasan, A. and Venkatraman, N. (2017) Entrepreneurship in digital platforms: a network-centric view. *Strategic Entrepreneurship Journal*, 12, pp. 54–71.

Stark, D. (2009) *The sense of dissonance: accounts of worth in economic life*. Princeton, NJ: Princeton University Press.

Stark, D. (ed.) (2020) *The performance complex: competition and competitions in social life*. Oxford: Oxford University Press.

Steinert, M. and Leifer, L. (2010) Scrutinising Gartner's hype cycle approach. In Kocaoglu, D. F., Anderson, T. R., Daim, T. U. and Bayus, A. M. (eds.) *PICMET 2010 Technology management for global economic growth*. Piscataway, NJ: IEEE, pp. 1–13.

Stephens, N., King, E. and Lyall, C. (2018) Blood, meat, and upscaling tissue engineering: Promises, anticipated markets, and performativity in the biomedical and agri-food sectors. *BioSocieties*, 13, p. 368.

Stiennon, R. (2012) *Up and to the right: strategy and tactics of analyst influence*. Scottsdale, AZ: IT-Harvest Press.

Stinchcombe, A. L. (1965) Social structure and organizations. In March, J. G. (ed.) *Handbook of organizations*. Chicago: Rand McNally, pp. 142–193.

Stirling, A. (2020) Engineering and sustainability: control and care in unfoldings of modernity. In *The Routledge handbook of the philosophy of engineering*. London: Routledge, pp. 461–481.

Suddaby, R., & Greenwood, R. (2001) Colonizing knowledge: Commodification as a dynamic of jurisdictional expansion in professional service firms. *Human Relations*, 54(7), pp. 933–953.

Swanson, E. B. (2020) How information systems came to rule the world: reflections on the information systems field. *The Information Society*, 36(2), pp. 109–123.

Swanson, E. B. and Ramiller, N. C. (1997) The organising vision in information systems innovation. *Organisation Science*, 8, pp. 458–474.

Swanson, E. B., Ramiller, N. and Wang, P. (2025) Organizing vision revisited and reimagined for a changing world. *Journal of Information Technology*, 40, Advance online publication.

Swedberg, R. (2014) *The art of social theory*. Princeton, NJ: Princeton University Press.

  (2018) Folk economics and its role in Trump's presidential campaign: an exploratory study. *Theory and Society*, 47(1), pp. 1–36.

Taleb, N. N. (2010) *The Black Swan: the impact of the highly improbable*. New York: Random House Trade Paperbacks.

Teague, B., Gorton, M. D. and Liu, Y. (2020) Different pitches for different stages of entrepreneurial development: the practice of pitching to business angels. *Entrepreneurship and Regional Development*, 32, pp. 334–352.

Thévenot, L. (1984) Rules and implements: investment in forms. *Social Science Information*, 23(1), pp. 1–45.

Thompson, N. A. and Byrne, O. (2022) Imagining futures: theorizing the practical knowledge of future-making. *Organization Studies*, 43(2), pp. 247–268.

Thompson, N., Verduijn, K. and Gartner, W. (2020) Entrepreneurship-as-practice: grounding contemporary theories of practice into entrepreneurship studies. *Entrepreneurship and Regional Development*, 32(3–4), pp. 247–256. doi:10.1080/08985626.2019.1641978

Tihanyi, L., Howard-Grenville, J. and DeCelles, K. A. (2022) From the editors – joining societal conversations on management and organisations. *Academy of Management Journal*, 65(3), pp. 711–719.

Tracey, P. and Stott, N. (2017) Social innovation: a window on alternative ways of organizing and innovating. *Innovation*, 19(1), pp. 51–60.

Tutton, R. (2017) Wicked futures: meaning, matter and the sociology of the future. *The Sociological Review*, 65(3), pp. 478–492.

Tvede, L. (2013) *Business cycles*. London: Routledge.

Überbacher, F. (2014) Legitimation of new ventures: a review and research programme. *Journal of Management Studies*, 51, pp. 667–698.

Überbacher, F., Jacobs, C. D. and Cornelissen, J. P. (2015) How entrepreneurs become skilled cultural operators. *Organisation Studies*, 36(7), pp. 925–951.

Urry, J. (2016) *What is the future?* Cambridge: John Wiley and Sons.

Vaara, E. and Whittington, R. (2012) Strategy-as-practice: taking social practices seriously. *The Academy of Management Annals*, 6(1), pp. 285–336.

Valliere, D. and Peterson, R. (2004) Inflating the bubble: examining dot-com investor behaviour. *Venture Capital*, 6i, pp. 1–22.

Van de Ven, A. H. (1992) Suggestions for studying strategy process: a research note. *Strategic Management Journal*, 13(Special Issue), pp. 169–188.

Van Lente, H. (1993) *Promising technology: the dynamics of expectations in technological developments*. Enschede.

 (2012) Navigating foresight in a sea of expectations: lessons from the sociology of expectations. *Technology Analysis & Strategic Management*, 24(8), pp. 769–782.

Van Lente, H. and Bakker, S. (2010) Competing expectations: the case of hydrogen storage technologies. *Technology Analysis & Strategic Management*, 22(6), pp. 693–709.

Van Lente, H. and Rip, A. (1998) Expectations in technological developments: an example of prospective structures to be filled in by agency. In Disco, C. and van der Meulen, B. (eds.) *Getting new technologies together: Studies in making sociotechnical order* (De Gruyter Studies in Organization, Vol. 27). Berlin: De Gruyter, pp. 203–230.

Van Lente, H., Spitters, C. and Peine, A. (2013) Comparing technological hype cycles: towards a theory. *Technological Forecasting and Social Change*, 80(8), pp. 1615–1628.

Vasterman, P. L. (2005) Media-hype: self-reinforcing news waves, journalistic standards and the construction of social problems. *European Journal of Communication*, 20(4), pp. 508–530.

Vatin, F. (2013) Valuation as evaluating and valorising. *Valuation Studies*, 1, pp. 31–50.

Veneziano, M. and Gerli, C. (2025) Mapping the use of emerging technologies within the public sector across the EU: the case of Public Sector Tech Watch. *Futures*, 167, p. 103564.

Vergne, J. P. and Wry, T. (2014) Categorising categorisation research: review, integration, and future directions. *Journal of Management Studies*, 51, pp. 56–94.

Vinsel, L. and Russell, A. L. (2020) *The innovation delusion: how our obsession with the new has disrupted the work that matters most.* New York: Crown Currency.

Volberda, H. W., Khanagha, S., Baden-Fuller, C., Mihalache, O. R. and Birkinshaw, J. (2021) Strategizing in a digital world: overcoming cognitive barriers, reconfiguring routines and introducing new organizational forms. *Long Range Planning*, 54(5), p. 102110.

Von Briel, F., Recker, J. and Davidsson, P. (2018) Not all digital venture ideas are created equal: implications for venture creation processes. *The Journal of Strategic Information Systems*, 27, pp. 278–295.

Von Briel, F., Selander, L., Hukal, P., Lehmann, J., Rothe, H., Fürstenau, D. and Wurm, B. (2021) Researching digital entrepreneurship: current issues and suggestions for future directions. *Communications of the Association for Information Systems*, 48, pp. 284–304.

Wadhwani, R. D. and Lubinski, C. (2025) Hype: marker and maker of entrepreneurial culture. *Journal of Business Venturing*, 40(2), p. 106455.

Wagner, E. L., Newell, S., Ramiller, N. and Enders, J. (2018) From public ideology to sociomaterial reproduction of agile principles: the case of Pivotal Labs. *Information and Organization*, 28, pp. 192–210.

Wagner, K. and Som, O. (2021) Digital entrepreneurship. In Fayolle, A. (ed.) *World encyclopaedia of entrepreneurship*. Northampton, MA: Edward Elgar.

Wang, P. (2010) Chasing the hottest IT: effects of information technology fashion on organisations. *MIS Quarterly*, 34, pp. 63–85.

(2015) Whatever happened to business process reengineering? The rise, fall, and possible revival of business process reengineering from the organising vision perspective. In Grover, V. and Markus, M. L. (eds.) *Business process transformation*. London: Routledge, pp. 23–45.

(2021) Connecting the parts with the whole: towards an information ecology theory of digital innovation ecosystems. *MIS Quarterly*, 45, pp. 397–422.

Wang, X., Reger, R. K. and Pfarrer, M. D. (2021) Faster, hotter, and more linked in: managing social disapproval in the social media era. *Academy of Management Review*, 46(2), pp. 275–298.

Ward, J. M. (1987) Integrating information systems into business strategies. *Long Range Planning*, 20(3), pp. 19–29.

Weber, R. (2016) Performing property cycles. *Journal of Cultural Economy*, 9(6), pp. 587–603.

(2019) *From boom to bubble: how finance built the new Chicago.* Chicago: University of Chicago Press.

Webster, A. and Gardner, J. (2019) Aligning technology and institutional readiness: the adoption of innovation. *Technology Analysis & Strategic Management*, 31(10), pp. 1229–1241.

Wedlin, L. (2006) *Ranking business schools: forming fields, identities and boundaries in international management education.* Northampton, MA: Edward Elgar.

(2011) Going global: rankings as rhetorical devices to construct an international field of management education. *Management Learning*, 42(2), pp. 199–218.

Weiss-Blatt, N. (2021) *The techlash and tech crisis communication.* Bingley: Emerald.

Wenzel, M., Cabantous, L. and Koch, J. (2025) Future making: towards a practice perspective. *Journal of Management Studies*, Advance online publication.

Wenzel, M., Krämer, H., Koch, J. and Reckwitz, A. (2020) Future and organisation studies: on the rediscovery of a problematic temporal category in organisations. *Organisation Studies*, 41(10), pp. 1441–1455.

Williams, R., Stewart, J. and Slack, R. (2005) *Social learning and technological innovation: experimenting with ICTs.* Aldershot: Edward Elgar.

Williamson, O. E. (1975) *Markets and hierarchies: analysis and antitrust implications.* New York: Free Press.

Wood, M. S., Dwyer, S. M. and Scheaf, D. J. (2024) Navigating the temporal commitments of entrepreneurial hype: insights from entrepreneur and backer interactions in crowdfunded ventures. *Journal of Business Venturing*, 39(6), p. 106437.

Woodie, A. (2014) Most hyped tech: big data out, IoT in. Big DataWire, www.bigdatawire.com/2014/08/20/hyped-tech-big-data-iot/. Accessed 10 March 2025.

Woolgar, S. (ed.) (2002) *Virtual society?: Technology, cyberbole, reality.* Oxford: Oxford University Press.

Wry, T., Lounsbury, M. and Glynn, M. A. (2011) Legitimating nascent collective identities: coordinating cultural entrepreneurship. *Organisation Science*, 22, pp. 449–463.

Wüstenhagen, R., Wuebker, R., Bürer, M. J. and Goddard, D. (2009) Financing fuel cell market development: exploring the role of expectation dynamics in venture capital investment. In Truffer, B., Markard, J., Wüstenhagen, R. and Wiek, A. (eds.) *Innovation, markets and sustainable energy.* Cheltenham: Edward Elgar. pp. 227–256.

Yoo, Y., Boland Jr, R. J., Lyytinen, K. and Majchrzak, A. (2012) Organizing for innovation in the digitized world. *Organization Science*, 23(5), pp. 1398–1408.

Zaloom, C. (2009) How to read the future: the yield curve, affect, and financial prediction. *Public Culture*, 21, pp. 245–268.

Zankl, J. and Grimes, M. (2024) Taming unicorns: toward a new normal of responsible entrepreneurship. *Academy of Management Review*, Advance online publication.

Zilber, T. B. (2007) Stories and the discursive dynamics of institutional entrepreneurship: the case of Israeli high-tech after the bubble. *Organisation Studies*, 28, pp. 1035–1054.

Zuckerman, E. W. (1999) The categorical imperative: securities analysts and the illegitimacy discount. *American Journal of Sociology*, 104, pp. 1398–1438.

Index

Note: Page numbers in italics refer to figures; those followed by 'n' to footnotes.

For EU product safety concerns, contact us at Calle de José Abascal, 56–1°, 28003 Madrid, Spain or eugpsr@cambridge.org.

www.ingramcontent.com/pod-product-compliance
Ingram Content Group UK Ltd.
Pitfield, Milton Keynes, MK11 3LW, UK
UKHW022135120526
471007UK00012B/1054